Blacks, F

Blacks, Reds, and Russians

SOJOURNERS IN SEARCH OF THE SOVIET PROMISE

ଓଠ

JOY GLEASON CAREW

Rutgers University Press
New Brunswick, New Jersey, and London

First paperback printing, 2010

Library of Congress Cataloging-in-Publication Data

Carew, Joy Gleason.
  Blacks, Reds, and Russians : sojourners in search of the Soviet promise / Joy Gleason
Carew.
      p. cm.
  Includes bibliographical references and index.
  ISBN 978-0-8135-4306-2 (hardcover : alk. paper)
  ISBN 978-0-8135-4985-9 (pbk. : alk. paper)
  1. African Americans—Soviet Union—History.   2. African Americans—Soviet Union—
Biography.   3. African American intellectuals—Soviet Union—Biography.   4. African
American scientists—Soviet Union—Biography.   5. Visitors, Foreign—Soviet Union—
History.   6. Intercultural communication—Soviet Union.   7. Soviet Union—Race
relations.   8. Soviet Union—Intellectual life—1917–1970.   9. Soviet Union—Relations—
United States.   10. United States—Relations—Soviet Union.   I. Title.
  DK34.B53C37 2008
  947.084'2092396073—dc22   2007044896

A British Cataloging-in-Publication record for this book is available from the British Library.

Visit our Web site: http://rutgerspress.rutgers.edu

Manufactured in the United States of America

For Jan, Shantoba, Eliza, and Maurice

CONTENTS

PREFACE

*A*s I have gone about the research for this book, I have been struck by the close parallels of my and my relatives' experiences in the Soviet Union in the 1950s, 1960s, and 1970s with the experiences of the early black sojourners, who went in the 1920s and 1930s. Although I crossed paths with only a few of their descendants or those who knew them, I later found that I had spent time in many of the same places and experienced some of the same reactions. These experiences were sometimes perplexing, sometimes frustrating, but were more often an intriguing surprise. Yet, when I returned to the country, now known as Russia, twenty-five years later, I found myself wrestling with two impulses. I was excited at the prospect of returning to familiar regions and seeing new ones. At the same time, I felt some trepidation about what I had read about the country since the collapse of the Soviet Union and its command economy. It worried me to see an increasing number of stories about social and economic strife, not to speak of the rise in xenophobia and racism. Would the new market-driven Russia be as hospitable? I could not help but think about Fyodor Dostoyevsky's *Brothers Karamazov* and the Grand Inquisitor, who kept asking whether human beings could handle the pressures and responsibilities of free will: "You made man decide about good and evil for himself, with no guidance than Your example. But did it not occur to you that man would disregard Your example, even question it[,] . . . when he was subjected to so fearful a burden as freedom of choice?"[1]

During the 2004 trip, I crossed the wide expanse of European Russia from Moscow to the Urals by train and spent time in Perm, one of the formerly closed cities. Few realize that these cities were closed not only to foreigners but also to people within the Soviet Union, as they were strategic sites for the Soviet military. This unusual entrée allowed me to sample the effects of the now-decentralized post-Soviet Russia through the present-day life of provincial people. In former times, these cities would have been on the periphery of social change, and contact with the West would have been narrowly filtered through the central government in Moscow. Yet the Perm I experienced was clearly marketing itself to a larger world with programs, festivals, and other events. It was striking not only to see well-stocked stores and SUVs in the streets but also to ponder the significance of gated communities, Western-style houses with guard dogs, and university campuses that were now fenced off from the communities around them.

My first sojourn in the Soviet Union occurred in the spring and early summer of 1967 with my Russian class from Ohio State University. Like Harry Haywood, a political activist of the 1920s, who made his first crossing in the spring of 1926, my classmates and I also experienced the rough Atlantic seas and were relieved to finally land in Leningrad. Still, I was delighted to have made the crossing on the *MS Pushkin*, named after the "father" of Russian literature, a descendant of an African.

During the many months of my first Russian visit, my fellow students and I zigzagged across twenty-one hundred miles as we made our way south through the European section of the Soviet Union. From Leningrad in the northwest, we traveled southeast to the historic city of Novgorod, and then on to the capital, Moscow. From there, we veered southwest into Kiev before shifting toward the southeast again to visit the sobering Volgograd (the former Stalingrad of World War II fame).[2] Our final stop before returning to Moscow was Yalta on the Black Sea, southwest of Volgograd. Yalta, with its Mediterranean climate, was a favored resort area for legions of tired factory workers and others from northern cities.

That long journey brought home the challenges that have historically confronted the Soviet Union—and, indeed, still concern the Russia of today—namely, how best to manage a vast country while meeting the needs of its diverse regions, cultures, and nationalities. The most superficial of observations demonstrated the country's complexities. In the course of our long journey, the climate had gone from the gray, dreary days of the northern spring to the glorious sun of the Black Sea region. The cuisine had changed from the heavy, greasy dishes of the north to an almost overwhelming abundance of fresh fruits and vegetables in the south. The architecture had changed from the lyrical Italianate styles of Leningrad to the rather stolid and utilitarian structures of Moscow and then to the whitewashed facades of the resorts and guesthouses in the south.

That journey brought another revelation. I was continuously struck by the realization that the reaction toward me, traveling, like my parents a decade earlier, as the sole black person in a group, was not one of distaste or disinterest but one of intense curiosity. Invariably, I would have to answer the questions—What are you? Are you a Negro (the common Russian term for an African American at the time)? How could you (as a member of an oppressed minority) afford to come all the way to the Soviet Union?

Soviet propaganda traditionally represented blacks as universally poor, dark, and downtrodden. The U.S. civil rights struggles and a focus on the problems of the inner cities and their predominantly black populations reinforced these notions. Thus, it was difficult to conceive of blacks as coming in a range of colors or from different social classes and to understand that African America contained not only workers but also intellectuals. In my later research, it became evident that some of the black sojourners of the 1920s and 1930s proved equally confusing to their Soviet hosts. Despite this confusion, I could understand why the sojourners nevertheless sensed an overwhelming spirit of solidarity and goodwill: the Soviet experiment allowed them relief from the stresses of second-class citizenship at home. Also, like them, I determined that my role was not only to learn about the Soviet Union and its people but also to teach the Soviets about blacks.

I first became interested in the links between the Soviet Union and peoples of African descent when I began my studies of Russian and Russian culture in the early 1960s under the tutelage of Stepha Gerrassi at the Putney School in Vermont. I would continue my study under others at college and privately, but Stepha had left me with a particular curiosity because of my love and respect for her. Later in that decade, when I had my first opportunity to visit the Soviet Union as a college student, I happily grasped the opportunity to test my Russian and to see and experience some of the places I had read or heard about. A special curiosity was the log of stories of my parents' warm reception there in 1957.

Because of a general fascination with other cultures of the world, my parents traveled frequently; thus, they were delighted when they found they could join a group of educators for a unique three-month 'round-the-world tour. Although my father was a physician and my mother a university professor, taking such a trip was not all that common for African Americans in the 1950s. A special feature was that their group would be among the first to visit the Soviet Union in the Nikita Khrushchev era. My father knew Paul Robeson through the fraternity they shared and was well aware of his struggles with the U.S. government over his support of the Soviet Union. He was curious to test Robeson's contention that Soviet relations with blacks were quite different from those between whites and blacks in the United States. And, during the next year, he helped host a fundraiser for Robeson.

My parents' group traversed the country from east to west, starting in the Russian Far East and then traveling west across the Urals and on into European Russia. They arrived in Moscow a year after Khrushchev made his landmark acknowledgement of Stalin's crimes and two years before the United States and the Soviet Union signed cultural-exchange agreements. They readily shared their stories with others and suspected that they might have inspired fellow Chicago resident and publisher John H. Johnson to join the delegation that accompanied Vice President Richard Nixon and the 1959 American National Exhibit team.

My parents were impressed with the friendliness and generosity of the Russian people toward them, compared with the more brusque and disinterested behavior directed toward many of the other Americans. No doubt they stood out as two of the three blacks in this group of thirty-one, but they found this distinction to be an asset in the Soviet Union. The Russians frequently escorted them to the front of long lines or let them into special clubs when others were turned away. In the end, they came away with the realization that they had been treated with far greater civility in the Soviet Union than they had ever been in the United States. But, in fact, their experiences were not unique. Langston Hughes wrote of similar experiences when he went there in the 1930s. Even as late as the latter part of the 1970s—over forty years after the period of which Hughes was writing and some twenty after my parents' first visit there—I had witnessed similar preferential treatment.

Typical of a Russian-language student of my generation, I was steeped in the literature—particularly nineteenth-century and early Soviet-era texts. And I initially looked at the country and its people through the prism of the romantic history portrayed in the stories and novels I had read. Once there, I found my favorite writers' vistas laid out before me—I was in the land of Mikhail Bulgakov, Ilya Ilf, Evgeny Petrov, and Maksim Gorky. I walked down the streets of Leningrad and Moscow and peered into corners of dimly lit rooms as I tried to imagine where Nikolay Gogol's characters might have lurked or Dostoyevsky's "brothers" might have resided. I felt a special delight in crossing bridges referenced in works and looking into the dark recesses of onion-domed churches and cathedrals. I marveled at the wooden cottages and stands of birch trees flying by my train window and tried to connect these images with the writings of Leo Tolstoy and Ivan Turgenev. I saw the desk where Aleksandr Pushkin composed his poetry and stared up at his contemplative face on village-square statues. I was intrigued that this same Pushkin, whose great-grandfather, Hannibal, was an African, could have made it possible for the Russian people to appreciate their own language and culture. Pushkin helped them free themselves from a long-standing inferiority complex based on the elites' valuing of France, French language, and other European cultures over theirs.

My knowledge of the contemporary Russian citizen was much more limited than my knowledge of Russian literature. I was looking at Russia and its people as described by my beloved Russian teachers, who were long past their prime and had lived an expatriate life longer than I had lived on this earth. I had imagined my future Russian hosts as replicas of Khrushchev or Leonid Brezhnev, who led the country from 1958 to 1964 and from 1964 to 1982, respectively— dumpy and stern-faced figures who barked orders at everyone. At the time, their images were omnipresent on U.S. television and in the press. Instead, however, I found a much more diverse people, physically as well as in demeanor.

In the 1970s, I returned to the Soviet Union three more times, as a teacher of Russian and later as a guide working for a New York-based international people-to-people exchange organization. I had met the directors when I first wanted to take my Russian-language students to the Soviet Union in the early 1970s, and subsequently I was asked to serve as one of the leaders for a number of other groups. The last of these tours was in 1979, when my husband and I were part of the leadership team for a group of fifty black physicians and their wives. No doubt, I was sought out for the position because I was Russian-speaking and because, as a black person, I was seen as someone who could serve as a bridge to the Soviet Union and Russian culture for these novice black travelers to the country. Like my parents some twenty years earlier, they looked at the Soviet Union not only from the perspective of being Americans but also through the particular prism of being blacks. From the perspective of U.S. physicians, their expectations of the "backwardness" of Soviet medicine were confirmed by the equipment and facilities they observed. Yet, at the same time, from the perspective of blacks, they were struck by the willingness of strangers to offer them help. The fact that two of the spouses, lost on a shopping trip, were escorted back to their hotel by helpful Russians astounded them. Many mused that it was a shock to find people—black or white—who would be so generous with their time. Would they or people they knew back in the United States have been so accommodating? Happily, the memories that many of them took back home were broadened beyond the images of headlines and stereotypical typecasting.

A special delight on that trip was to be able to see the country through my husband's, Jan Carew's, eyes. He had been invited to the Soviet Union as a guest of the Soviet Writers' Union in the 1960s, and he eventually took two journeys there. Jan's first novel, *Black Midas*, which depicted the trials and triumphs of wildcat gold and diamond miners in his home country of Guyana, had been translated into Russian and several of the minority languages of the Soviet Union. The first edition had come out in thousands of copies and had generated a considerable amount of interest and royalties. At that time, these royalties could be spent only in the Soviet Union, and Jan was curious to meet the people who were so interested in his work. His experiences were quite different from mine as a student and a leader of educational groups. Jan regaled me with stories of the wonderful hospitality he had received, the special lodging and meals, holidays on the Black Sea, and trips to Soviet Asia. During this 1979 trip, he took me to the Soviet Writers' Union to renew old acquaintances, and we were greeted by a younger generation of writers.

Jan also helped me appreciate the dynamics of Cold War race relations, as the Soviets and their allies made special overtures to attract visitors from newly independent states. In the early 1950s, he had been offered an unlimited scholarship to study at the famed Charles University in Prague, Czechoslovakia.

I got another perspective on the personal relationships that could develop between the Russians and the larger African diaspora when I took a group of my Russian-language students there for a winter visit in the 1970s. My predominantly black group of students from Malcolm X College, a small community college on the west side of Chicago, was filled with curiosity seekers, eager to travel to foreign countries. Many had not even been outside Chicago, and most had not been on an airplane. Their study of Russian had opened a floodgate of new experiences, and along with them had come new expectations about adventures beyond the boundaries of Chicago. Surprisingly, two of my students had traveled to the Soviet Union before with the previous Russian-language teacher, and during that visit they had met some African students who were studying at

Patrice Lumumba University. They were amazed to meet these students, who had been given full scholarships to pursue multiyear technical or professional training programs. Now, on this trip, these two students were eager to show their fellow students how the wondrous Soviet Union welcomed not only them but also other peoples of color into its midst. My students learned many lessons in cultural accommodation during that trip, one of which was based on the simplest act. One of the young women in the group was proudly wearing a large Afro hairstyle, typical of that period. She was a constant source of stares and discussion—particularly among the older women we met at the hotel. She was rather disturbed by this attention, taking it as some kind of implied threat. One day, before she could prevent it, one of these older women managed to pat her hair and immediately broke out into an excited description of the result. "Why, it's so soft. It feels like lamb's wool! How beautiful she is!" Thereafter, whenever this woman saw my student, she would present her with small gifts of cookies or offer to bring her tea, which my student started to look forward to in view of the frigid temperatures of the Russian winter. My student went from her inner-city-Chicago fear of white people to the realization that here she could form friendships with people who, on the surface, had seemed very much like those who worried her back home. For the duration of her stay, these women smiled broadly whenever they saw her and were more than eager to engage her in a conversation about her various activities. These conversations improved not only her Russian but also, most important, her sense of the possibilities of cross-racial relations. We had traveled many thousands of miles to cross this cultural bridge.

Each time I returned to the Soviet Union later in that decade, I was usually in the company of other educators or professionals. In all but two of these cases, I was the only black in the group. I continued to excite the curiosity of those with whom I came into contact. Both the Russians and the Americans would get around to asking the same questions—How come you know Russian? How it that you are leading/accompanying this group of Americans (that is, white people from the United States) to the Soviet Union? Not only was it difficult for Russians to "place" a black person in a position of authority but doing so was of concern to the Americans also. The fact that I was Russian-speaking only added to their puzzlement.

I discovered other connections between blacks and Russians when I learned about Afro-Russian descendants Lily Golden, Yelena Khanga, Slava Tynes, James Patterson, and Eslanda Goode. Their parents, and grandparent in the case of Yelena, had been part of the wave of blacks who moved to the Soviet Union in the 1920s and 1930s. Lily and Slava were children of agricultural specialists. James was the son of one of the *Black and White* film artists. Eslanda was a niece of Paul Robeson's; her father, Frank, Robeson's brother in-law, had moved to the Soviet Union in the early 1930s. My husband had met Eslanda during one of his trips to the Soviet Union in the 1980s and was instrumental in helping her find a job teaching Russian at a historically black university in the United States. I had met Yelena Khanga (Lily Golden's daughter) in Chicago when we were both on a panel about blacks and Russia in the early 1990s. Her book, *Soul to Soul: A Black Russian American Family, 1865–1992*, had just come out, and she was on an extended book tour of the United States. Patterson, Eslanda, and I were on the same panel in the latter part of 1990s at the U.S. State Department's Foreign Service Institute, where we discussed the black sojourners to the Soviet Union and their descendants.

Although I could draw on my own experiences to imagine some of the adjustments and challenges the black sojourners faced, several differences remained. I was familiar with a post-Sputnik Soviet Union, whereas those who had gone in the 1920s and 1930s had to deal with the demands of living in a country still reeling from the effects of World War I, the Russian Revolution, and the subsequent civil war. I was traveling to the Soviet Union from a post–civil rights, black-powered United States, while those of the 1920s and 1930s were wrestling with the physical and psychological burdens of a Jim-Crowed United States. Those early pioneers experienced new levels of freedom in the Soviet Union that allowed for a kind of spiritual rebirth, which itself led to great intellectual development and productivity.

When Jan received his scholarship to study in Czechoslovakia in the early 1950s, he was the first Guyanese recipient of an Eastern Bloc scholarship. During his later visits to the Soviet Union in the 1960s, he met a number of other scholarship recipients and subsequently interviewed many of them when they went to England for their holidays. His documentary novel *Moscow Is Not My Mecca* (U.S. edition, *Green Winter*) presaged concerns about examples of racial intolerance that surfaced in the 1970s and 1980s. The legacy of ignoring these early warnings is that, even today, students of color studying in post-Soviet Russia are facing the challenges of racism.

In the early 1990s, I took the position of director of the Center for the Study of Critical Languages at Lincoln University in Lincoln University, Pennsylvania. There I got to know Eslanda, who was Afro-Russian. Her recollections stretched across her life and those of her parents and offered insights into the lives of other black sojourners and their children as well. Black sojourners constituted a relatively small community in the second half of the twentieth century, and most were clustered around Moscow. Additionally, Eslanda's stories of Robeson's visits to the country and of the effect of Robeson's presence on the Russian people, her family, and the other black expatriates were equally enlightening.

Interestingly, Eslanda's fair complexion was a constant source of confusion for the black students and faculty at the historically black college where we worked. Had she not pointed out that Robeson was her uncle no one would have guessed that she had black blood. Also, many of her students had great difficulty making sense of the fact there could be a black Russian. Thus, while the Russians were perplexed by light-skinned blacks (as experienced in the 1920s by Otto Huiswood, in the 1930s by some of the *Black and White* film group, and by me in the 1960s and 1970s), the blacks at Lincoln found it difficult to conceive of Russians with African American or African parentage.

Over the next several years, Eslanda and I collaborated on a number of projects, including workshops and seminars, in which we discussed the subject of blacks in Russia. Eslanda also taught a course on this subject. Besides our investigation of the early years, we spent considerable time piecing together a picture of life in early post-Soviet Russia.

Valentina Soboleva, who came to Lincoln University later, brought the interesting perspective of having been one of the Russians who married an African student and later accompanied him to his country. Soboleva lived in the Sudan for over twenty years but eventually left that marriage and took her Afro-Russian children back to the Soviet Union. Like the Afro-Russian descendants of the black sojourners who married African or other Third World students, Soboleva worried about the limited opportunities for her children in the Sudan, not to speak of problems with racism. She was certain that they would have better chances in the Soviet Union.

In the 1990s, I had also come to know William "Bill" Davis. This large, ebullient man was full of intriguing stories of his years working with some of the black expatriates in the Soviet Union and their descendants. A retired career Foreign Service officer, Davis had served at various posts around the world until his retirement in 1988. But it was Davis's role at the 1959 American National Exhibit that helped reconnect many of the expatriates with relatives and friends back in the United States. Over the subsequent thirty years, Davis kept in touch with many of them and made use of his position in the Foreign Service to help a number visit the United States in the late 1980s.

In more recent years, I have had the opportunity to interview some of the other descendants of the black sojourners and expatriates to learn about their parents' and their lives in the Soviet Union. I have also been able to get a sense of the challenges they faced as they tried to adjust to U.S.-style race relations during their visits to the United States. The United States had historically held a certain mystery and dread for them because it was the country their parents or grandparents had fled for the opportunity to live under the Soviet experiment. At the same time, as was true for many young people growing up in the Soviet Union during the Cold War, the very thing that was prohibited (capitalism and the United States) became fascinating. Thus, in the final years of the Soviet Union and with the approach of Mikhail Gorbachev's *glasnost*, some of these descendants were happy to make their first sojourns in the United States.

Since the mid-1980s, others have come to the United States for visits of varying length. Some of them have attended universities; others have settled in the United States. But all have discovered some uncomfortable aspects of being black in the United States. Most of the first-generation Afro-Russian descendants were raised by their Russian or white American mothers in Russia—their fathers having died or left the country earlier in their lives. Thus, their Russian cultural ties are stronger than their sense of blackness. For many, therefore, the compromise has been to make periodic visits to the United States but also to maintain close connections with family and friends in Russia.

This work explores these and other relationships as a means for gaining some insight into the role of the Soviet experiment in fostering new kinds of relationships and into the particular connections formed between blacks from the United States and people in the Soviet Union.

Blacks, Reds, and Russians

Introduction

ℚ☯ꙅ

*H*ow could a country that turned a brutal
and despotic face to its own people offer a hopeful visage to blacks suffering
from generations of oppression and Jim Crow? How could a country whose
Stalinist leadership eliminated thousands of people from all walks of life, sti-
fling human potential and intellectual creativity, shelter and encourage growth
among blacks who journeyed to its shores?

Much has been written about Joseph Stalin's purges and draconic mea-
sures to compel his nation's growth and development. Little known are the
special international race relations in the 1920s and 1930s that brought Soviets
and blacks together. Frustrated with the limitations of a racist United States and
escaping from their own arenas of terror, a number of blacks went to Russia in
search of the Soviet promise of a better society. These sojourners were intellectuals, writers, and outstanding figures in the arts and entertainment; they were
also farmers and engineers and people with other technical skills. In the Soviet
Union, they discovered a country that welcomed them and their talents when
the United States did not. And, having taken this bold chance to reshape their
destinies, they ultimately not only found personal fulfillment but also played
important roles in moving a backward Soviet society forward.

The Soviets also had their own ambitions in this enterprise. The political
leadership intended to train fresh cadres in the struggle against colonialism and
imperial domination. The fact that these recruits were blacks from the United
States, who were considered more advanced in their revolutionary sympathies
than those from colonial countries, added a special twist. Not only were these
people whose discontents might be channeled into productive action in helping organize other disaffected blacks and workers in the United States, but they
might help the Soviets reach other populations of color elsewhere. No less important, from the ordinary Russians came the desire to welcome people who had
arisen from a seemingly endemic backwardness and thrown off their shackles
and who were looking to help the Russians build their new society.

The 1930s brought additional challenges to the Soviets' intensions to develop their country. The nation was now increasingly confronted with the contradictory pressures of meeting the objectives of Stalin's ambitious five-year plans, while being seriously hampered by the effects of the purges of the country's own scientific and technical specialists. This dearth of expertise and technical know-how forced the Soviets to look outside their borders. Thus arose the campaigns to attract foreign specialists to replace the indigenous ones who had been eliminated. During this period blacks in the United States with technical and professional skills and sympathies for the Soviet experiment were actively recruited along with the thousands of whites who were also attracted to these opportunities. The Soviets also discovered an additional advantage: the black specialists could serve as bridges between the country's non-Russian people of color and the plans of a modernizing Soviet state.

Ultimately, the majority of the black sojourners of the 1920s and 1930s returned to the United States shortly after their study or contract periods. The final push was in 1937, when the Stalinist government began to pressure those still in the country to take up Soviet citizenship. But a smaller group decided to remain, as the prospects of life under the Soviet experiment seemed far brighter than the certainty of returning to the Great Depression and a life under the crippling Jim Crow in the United States.

Claude McKay and Otto Huiswood were the first to go, in the 1920s, leading a black-Soviet story that lasted over seventy-five years. Stretching beyond the 1920s through the 1930s, the Stalinist purges, and War World II, these early relationships helped shape the racial dynamics of the Cold War era. W.E.B. Du Bois's 1926 experience was equally profound. It amazed him to compare the legacy of slavery, which he so eloquently labeled "the veil," in the United States of the 1920s and 1930s with his observations of the former serfs of Russia who were actively engaged in reshaping their society. Du Bois's support of the Soviet experiment remained intact as he found ways to make decennial trips up to his last days, in the 1960s.

Like other blacks of the 1920s, these men had celebrated the victory of the Allied Powers in World War I, hoping that it would lead to improved race relations in the United States. Yet, despite the service of many thousands of blacks, instead of taking part in victory parades, the returnees found themselves thrown back into the old pattern: a segregated society bent on denying them their basic civil and human rights. Paradoxically, these largely Christian sojourners were drawn to a Communist state because they could see parallels between the Christian ethic that all men were equal in the sight of God and the Communist credo of equality and opportunity for all. Although few seemed to have contemplated moving there permanently, all were determined to at least have the chance to sample this new social experiment.

This historiography draws heavily on the personal accounts found in the writings of select black sojourners and interviews with their descendants or others who knew them. Thus, primary perspectives come from autobiographies, such as those by Harry Haywood, William L. Patterson, Robert Robinson, and Homer Smith; family histories done by Yelena Khanga and Lily Golden; and shorter autobiographical writings of McKay, Du Bois, Langston Hughes, Paul Robeson, and others. Interviews with Frank Goode's daughter, Eslanda, and with William Davis and Jan Carew, who knew some of the sojourners, were conducted over a period of years. Other interviews, such as those done with George Tyne's daughter and granddaughter, Amelia and Anastasia, were shorter in term. Finally, the sociocultural context through which to interpret these works and interviews comes from biographies, histories, and other analyses of individuals, events, and contemporaneous programs.

Dignity and Opportunity

This book reconsiders aspects of the Soviet experiment in the sociopolitical context of the time. New lines of human relations were emerging on global levels, and the blacks who left the United States in the 1920s and 1930s found unusual opportunities in the Soviet Union. Within this hospitable environment, many made seminal contributions to the building of the Soviet economy, and a number chose to raise their families there and became integrated into Russian society.

Some of the sojourners, like McKay and Du Bois in the 1920s, and Hughes and Robeson in the 1930s, were well known. The stories are yet to be told of many others who went in the 1920s and 1930s. We know about McKay, Du Bois, Hughes, and Robeson because of their repute and access to the press, but the fact that so many others were also drawn to the Soviet Union indicates a broad response. They all had this in common: they were willing to leave the United States, in which their forebears had deep roots, for the chance—no matter how briefly—to construct new lives in the Soviet Union.

The quest for dignity and opportunity not only attracted black intellectuals but also lured fellow travelers, technical and industrial specialists, agricultural specialists, and others. They came from the industrial centers in the North and the agricultural regions of the South; they were artists and recent college graduates. Although a certain segment went for political reasons, particularly in the 1920s, most went in the 1930s for economic opportunities and a chance for personal and professional fulfillment. In the process, many lent their talents to the development of Soviet industrial and agricultural innovations.

Sojourners in search of the Soviet promise, they stayed for different lengths of time, depending on their relationship with the Soviet government and the Russian people. Nonetheless, the effects of their tenure in the country reached beyond their immediate objectives. Some ultimately played key roles in shaping Soviet policies toward blacks not only in the United States but also in the global context. The black sojourner presence in the Soviet training programs of the 1920s also served as the foundation for the later development of Soviet alliances with Africans and other peoples of color keen to develop their backward societies. The Cold War–era scholarships, which attracted many other peoples of color to the Soviet Union and Eastern Bloc countries, were modeled in part after the black-Russian successes of the early years.

Even in this first decade of the twenty-first century, the imprint of these early black-Soviet ties continues. Post-Soviet Russia may have been in the U.S. superpower shadow in the years immediately following the collapse of the Soviet Union, but now, Russia, under Vladimir Putin, using its vast reservoir of raw materials, is increasingly inserting itself into global affairs. Most troubling to U.S. interests has been the Russian approach to African and other Third World nations as an alternative resource to the United States.

In Search of the Soviet Promise

For the majority of the black sojourners, the move toward the Soviet experiment was not a messianic quest. Those going for political training had an ultimate goal of using those organizing skills to mobilize black communities of resistance back home. Those who signed the one- to three-year contracts for technical or artistic jobs were going because they were glad to have well-paid jobs during the Great Depression and happy to escape the pressures of Jim Crow. That many of them renewed those contracts rather than return to the United States immediately afterward is a clear indication of their general satisfaction with this choice.

As the black sojourners of the 1920s and 1930s returned from the Soviet Union, the mystique of their experience thrilled others. Word spread about the different treatment they received under the Soviet experiment and of the multiple Russian expressions of solidarity with their travails in the United States. McKay and Du Bois published their assessments in *The Crisis*, while others held meetings to spread the news.

Risking their professional and personal lives, Du Bois and Robeson made several journeys to the Soviet Union. Hughes went only once but found a way to extend his stay a full year, from June 1932 to June 1933, and memories of that experience provided him with material for years afterward.

The McCarthy period and the fear of Communism in the late 1940s and early 1950s split Hughes from Du Bois and Robeson when Hughes recanted his support of the Soviet experiment in order to save his career. However, while Du Bois's and Robeson's steadfast support of the Soviet Union brought them no small amount of ostracism, it also excited the interest of younger generations of people of color in other countries. Even for Hughes, despite his later attempts to hide or destroy previous pro-Soviet work, it was not easy to erase the encouragement that his earlier writings had given blacks in search of a better life.

Cross-Racial Partnerships

Although the subject of the black sojourners who went to the Soviet Union has not surfaced often, it still provokes questions. People ask what Russia could offer blacks and, conversely, what could blacks could offer the Russians. It is also perplexing to many why people would leave the United States for a Communist state and risk being tainted for it. Indeed, the story of the black sojourner experience opens a new vista on the black experience and offers insights into the geopolitical stratagems that often underlay relationships between different peoples willing to cross the color line. This is not just a story of the earlier part of the twentieth century. It enters into the post-World War II–Cold War contests between the West (especially the United States) and the East (as the Soviet Union and allied nations became known) and offers insights into the new kinds of alliances and opportunities that arose for people of color around the globe. Through this story, one sees the broad dimensions of the African diaspora, which reaches beyond the paradigm of slavery and the triangular trade. Traditional models focus on the connections between peoples of Africa and the Americas due to the slave trade, but few consider the impact of later movements of people of African descent. People voluntarily moved from Africa to other parts of the world, particularly in the 1900s. Their descendants in the Americas also moved north from the Caribbean and South America to the United States and Canada, and some of them later moved east across the Atlantic Ocean to Europe. People moved from place to place and country to country in search of increased opportunity, and all left their imprint on new societies. The story of the connections between blacks and the Soviets in the twentieth century is part of this larger diasporic story.

The blacks who chose to go to the Soviet Union followed the same impulses that inspired the Pilgrims, as well as the generations of immigrants who followed in their wake, to cross the Atlantic for a new life. For some, the quest was to go back to an African homeland. This rationale appeared in the Garveyite and other African nationalist impulses that attracted thousands of blacks after World War I. For others, it was simply a search for a country without discrimination or racial prejudice. This longing to find a better place went beyond ideology. The economic difficulties of the Great Depression in the United States encouraged many to act with urgency. But the desire to locate a place where one was not judged by race or skin color and where one could earn a decent living inspired a bold minority to trespass across oceans and continents.

The U.S. public and governmental reactions to blacks' emigration to the Soviet Union depended on the nature of the traveler's relationship with the Soviet Union or the Communist Party or both and on the growing intensity of anti-Communist propaganda. In some instances, the scrutiny of the Federal Bureau of Investigation (FBI) and other agencies of surveillance was intense; in other cases, these security bodies seemed indifferent. Otherwise, the public commentary that surfaced was not compelling enough to prevent their journey. Furthermore, during the Great Depression, Soviet recruitment programs often served as a useful pressure valve, siphoning off the most discontented workers while affording U.S. industrialists entrée into an economic sphere not suffering the effects of a depressed market. The Harlem riots, while alarming, were relatively small and contained, but what would happen if legions of white American workers in major industrial centers across the country rose up? Instead, hundreds of American specialists with a range of skills accepted contracts to go to the Soviet Union for one-, two-, or three-year periods, and many readily renewed them. Most were white, but some were black.

Coming Out from Robeson's Shadow

Robeson's connections to the Soviet Union and his apocryphal story have overshadowed those of the others. Held up as the archetypal experience of the black link to the Soviet Union, his story has served as an example of the "consequences" of such alliances. Robeson was a modern-day Icarus, who, flying too close to the sun, was struck down for his trespass. Like the carcasses of blacks left hanging in the trees to warn others, Robeson's example was hung up for others to see, a warning to not go down that path if they did not want to suffer a similar fate. Yet, for Robeson, who did suffer at the hands of the McCarthyite tribunal, the political was personal. He was convinced that he had a role to play, and he was willing to serve as a lightning rod not only drawing the ire of the United States but also channeling black attention to events in the Soviet Union. Admired by some and vilified by others in the United States for his stance, Robeson was, on a global scale, wildly popular. The international campaign to free him during the years of internal exile never abated, and his steadfast campaign to couple the anticolonial struggle to the Soviet experiment was watched by blacks the world over.

But, the specter of Robeson's experiences in the anti-Communist climate of the United States did inhibit the flow of information about others who had connections to the Soviet experiment. Most of their stories have been left largely untold because of self-censorship or for lack of a publisher. Regrettably, few of these early sojourners left extensive accounts, although references to them appear in a number of other sources. The challenge, therefore, has been to glean information from the letters, the occasional autobiographical work, articles, books, and other research material. Additionally, biographies and other works, as well as interviews with descendants and others who knew these sojourners, serve as corroborating and contemporaneous sources. There is also the advantage of doing this research in the post-Soviet era, for previously inaccessible official documents in both the Soviet Union and the United States have now become available to researchers. These materials provide substantiation and background for the actions of black sojourners, expatriates, and others.

Other Sojourners

McKay, Huiswood, Du Bois, Hughes, and Robeson were, in fact, part of a large cohort of blacks, both male and female, who were drawn to the Soviet experiment. Fellow traveler Haywood mentioned forty-six other blacks in his autobiography. Woodford McClellan noted ninety or more in a 1990s article on the black presence in the Comintern schools. Other sources indicate that several hundred blacks went for a range of reasons and stayed for varying lengths of time. But many more, particularly those who went as fellow travelers or were posted outside of Moscow, did not necessarily appear in these lists. Additionally, some made more than one trip; and others went and never returned to the United States. Regrettably, their numbers are unknown. Many were forced to use fictitious names or to hold their stories in abeyance for fear of being labeled "black and red" during the Cold War.

Some traveled with their spouses or female companions. The Soviets understood that recruiting people who could bring their families would help them adjust to life in a strange land. This model would be replicated years later, when Oliver Golden recruited a group of sixteen agricultural specialists with the help of George Washington Carver.

Besides Golden's group in 1931, another group of twenty-two, composed of artists, intellectuals, and college students, including Hughes, went to work on the *Black and White* film in 1932. These were not the first artists attracted there. They followed poet McKay, who went in 1922, and a number of jazz groups, including blacks, that toured the country in the mid-1920s. Black artists, like Ira Aldridge, had been welcomed there in tsarist times as well.

Most of the black sojourners stayed in the Soviet Union for several weeks to a few years before returning to the United States. However, two from the agricultural group, Golden and George Tynes; two from the film group, Lloyd Patterson and Wayland Rudd; and Frank Goode married, took up Soviet citizenship, and remained in the Soviet Union for the rest of their lives. Others established relationships with Russian women, and some left children behind. Besides those described above, there were still others who went individually or in small groups under different auspices, and some of these sojourners also decided to make the Soviet Union their home.

Although this work begins with the 1920s-era sojourners, it stretches through the first half of the twentieth century to observe the black expatriates and their families in the later years. The aspirations of the black sojourners who were attracted to the Soviet experiment were largely met by an appreciative people and the Soviet government. Despite the rise of Stalinist terror, they, as black expatriates, and their Afro-Russian descendants continued to occupy a special place in Soviet history and society. Theirs was not always an easy life, but, because of their special skills or political expediency, they and their descendants have survived into the present day. Only one, Lovett Fort-Whiteman, is known to have died in the purges of the 1930s.

The black sojourner story is told largely through the personal experiences of fourteen men and their families and a select number of other individuals. (The family lines of these fourteen men are charted in the Appendix.) The welcoming but challenging environment of the Soviet experiment offered them opportunities to work and to contribute in ways they could not have in the United States. In brief, the story of the black sojourners to the Soviet Union offers an opportunity for enlightenment, particularly for those who live in countries, such as the United States, where racism has long called into question the ability of blacks to make significant contributions to society. Their story stands as a prime example of a people's willingness to challenge the status quo and forge their own destinies.

CHAPTER 1

A Journey Begins

ℰℵℷ

I have proposed to organize a group of Negro specialists who have had a theoretical and practical training in the production of cotton, to be sent to the Soviet Union. This group is to be indorsed [sic] by you. . . . I shall also arrange a tour for you to the Soviet Union to demonstrate your findings in the field of agriculture.[1]
—Oliver Golden to George Washington Carver (December 1930)

Thank you for your splendid letter which has reached me. . . . I shall be interested in knowing the further plans . . . [and] endeavor to do the best I can in this important matter.[2]
—Carver to Golden (January 1931)

*E*ighteen years before writing this letter, Oliver Golden, Tuskegee student-turned-dropout, had been spirited out of town with the compliance of university officials because he had been in a fight with a local white.[3] But now he was back with the proposal of a lifetime. He wanted George Washington Carver to nominate talented Tuskegee students for projects in the Soviet Union.

Golden's earlier, abrupt exit had been not only for his safety but for the safety of the school he had looked forward to attending. Southern black schools depended on the patronage of the white community, and their administrations did everything they could to avoid raising the ire of local whites. But Golden, who was not a young, compliant person when he arrived, had come from a family of some means. He was already twenty-five and a skilled tailor, and he had done a stint at Alcorn College in Mississippi. Tracing the footsteps of his mentor, who had originally taught at Alcorn, he saw Tuskegee not as a beginning but as a bridge to even greater opportunity.

Golden's story, along with that of his descendants, was unique in that one can get a sense of the broad sweep of the black-Soviet relationship over time in one family. It also offers a rich insight into many of the factors that encouraged so many other black sojourners to look to the Soviet experiment and into the challenges they faced once they made that decision. The Golden family experienced the Soviet experiment from the mid-1920s, when Golden was one of the earliest black students in the Soviet Union; through his and his family's experiences as part of the agricultural specialist team in Uzbekistan in the 1930s and 1940s, on through his daughter's years in Moscow from the 1950s into the

1980s, and on into the post-Soviet era with his granddaughter's bridging of Russian and American cultures.

Golden's service in a segregated U.S. army unit during World War I had primed him to seek out alternatives. Even in the midst of a war, blacks were not trusted to be among the fighting soldiers. Instead, like Golden, they were relegated to the service sectors. Only if they were seconded to the French army were they treated as equals and able to fight side-by-side with whites. But despite his government's attempts to curtail his contributions during the war, Golden found aspects of his stay in France liberating. He discovered French *fraternité* and a new political solidarity. The French saw the black American soldiers as their liberators and welcomed their presence among them. Also, these segregated units threw vastly different blacks together, and the more politicized gave their brethren new ways of analyzing their struggles. James Ford, who would become one of the most influential members of the newly formed Communist Party in the United States in the 1920s and 1930s, was one of Golden's political mentors.

Two years later, a demobilized Golden was thrown back into the Jim Crow pool and working jobs as he could find them when a happenstance encounter with Lovett Fort-Whiteman changed his life forever. Fort-Whiteman was recruiting blacks to study in the Soviet Union and to take part in the revolutionary Soviet experiment. Golden was ready to go. "I would have done anything to get off those dining cars."[4] He was sent in 1926 to Moscow, where he was among the first black American students to do political studies at the University of the Toilers of the East. But his exposure to the Soviet experiment went beyond the political as he began imagining new ways to rewrite the social compact between white and black. Having survived the trauma of losing his wife Jane, who had accompanied him to Moscow but then died unexpectedly, he was now deeply grateful to a society that could encourage the outpouring of support he had received.

Out of this crucible of political, social, and personal turmoil came Golden's idea to bring in a group of agricultural specialists like himself. Their skills could be put to building the Soviet experiment and helping its benefits reach into the lesser-developed regions of the country. Thus, with the blessing of the Stalinist regime and Carver's assistance, Golden gathered some of the most skilled black agronomists, research chemists, and specialists in animal husbandry and cotton growing to join him in taking up contracts with the Soviets. The group arrived in 1931 and was sent to Uzbekistan. By the late 1930s, in the face of pressure from the Stalinist government to renounce their U.S. citizenship, most of the members chose to return to the United States, leaving Golden and a fellow specialist, George Tynes, behind. The two had started families, and painful memories of life for blacks in the United States encouraged them to tie their futures to the Soviet experiment. Shifting from being sojourners to being expatriates, they then joined the many peoples of the growing Soviet Union, surviving each new challenge as it arose.

Golden died in 1940, but his legacy was carried on by his second wife, Bertha, a Jewish American who had accompanied him to the Soviet Union in 1931, and their young child, Lily. Bertha and Lily had struggles and successes much like the ordinary people among whom they lived, their relationship to Golden and the other black specialists both shielding them and occasionally intruding.

A door opened in the early 1950s, when college-age Lily was allowed to enter the prestigious Moscow State University with the help of the black expatriate community and other influential friends in Moscow. Not only did she gain entrance, but through their help she found housing and the illusive "free diploma," which allowed her to stay to do graduate work.

Lily was at Moscow State University in the late 1950s and early 1960s, when the Cold War battles over the hearts and minds of African and other Third World people brought new people of color into the Soviet Union. This generation of sojourners was attracted to new social and political models and welcomed the offers of scholarships for advanced education and professional training that could help them build their newly independent nations.

The black expatriate community also welcomed the new social dynamics of having these communities of color in their midst, and many nursed the romantic notion of contributing their skills to helping these countries develop—much like the contributions made by their fathers in the 1920s and 1930s to the Soviet Union. Some even aspired to find husbands. But, as Lily discovered, her generation of Afro-Russian daughters did not have happy marriages. The clash of cultures and expectations, while not so apparent in the Soviet Union, became sharp once they moved to their husband's countries. Frustrated by the unanticipated limitations placed on them and their children, many of these women overcame enormous odds to return to the Soviet Union.

The Golden family story continues into the post-Soviet era through Yelena Khanga, who was born in 1962, the granddaughter of Oliver Golden and the daughter of Lily and Abdullah Hanga (Khanga). Khanga's parents' union did not last, and she was raised by her Afro-Russian mother and American Jewish grandmother. And, like many first-generation and second-generation descendants growing up in the Soviet Union, she had Russian as her principal cultural identity while her features showed her connections to the larger African diaspora.

With the collapse of the Soviet Union at the end of the 1980s, Khanga found herself bridging Russian and African American cultures in new ways. Ambitious and fluent in English, she accepted an invitation to participate in a journalist exchange program in the United States. A short while later, she was pulled into President Mikhail Gorbachev's entourage when he first visited Washington, D.C. Afro-Russian Khanga suddenly found herself both representing the Soviet Union and introducing the notion of a "black" Russian to Americans. She generated considerable media attention in the United States and back in the Soviet Union, as her family's story reopened the discussions of comparative

human relations in the two societies. Khanga represented a blend of the generation of black sojourners who had left the United States because of racism in the
1920s and 1930s and the post-World War II sojourners from newly independent
nations, who looked to the Soviet Union and the Soviet experiment for help.

Khanga's notoriety as an Afro-Russian member of Gorbachev's 1987 delegation also provoked some adjustments in U.S. behaviors. No black woman
could have been said to hold a comparable position in the United States at the
time. However, partly in response to Gorbachev's decision to select Khanga for
his group and with an eye to the African and other nations, the U.S. government
did draw two blacks, General Colin Powell and Dr. Condoleezza Rice, into its
circles of power shortly thereafter. Two years later, when Gorbachev returned
to the United States, President George Herbert Walker Bush was quick to point
out that he, too, had a black woman working within his administration: the So-
vietologist Rice. Within two years, Rice was named to the position of national
security adviser, the first black woman, following the first black man, to hold
this position.

Post-Soviet Russia has brought new kinds of opportunities to the descendants of the black sojourners of the 1920s and 1930. Some, like Khanga, and her
mother, Lily, have been able to cross U.S. and Russian cultures, traveling back
and forth between the United States and the Soviet Union/Russia. Khanga's
book, *Soul to Soul: A Black Russian American Family, 1863–1992*, brought her
additional notoriety, which not only drew audiences to her in the United States
but led to her playing various roles in Russian media. Because of these U.S. connections and her "exotic" mix of Russian, African, and African American, the
Russians, have, in turn, found her unique and fascinating.

Besides the Golden family, at least thirteen other family lines can be traced
from the 1920s–1930s sojourners to the present time (see the Appendix); these
lines include one hundred people. The Soviet experiment offered the original
sojourners political and personal outlets that could not be found in the United
States. They, in turn, lent their skills to building the Soviet economy, and their
children and grandchildren have become a part of the Soviet-Russian fabric.

PART I

❧

The Fellow Travelers

CHAPTER 2

Early Sojourners Claude McKay and Otto Huiswood

SHAPING THE "NEGRO QUESTION"

ଛ୨୦

The label of propaganda will be affixed to what I say here. I
shall not mind; propaganda has now come into its respectable
rights and I am proud of being a propagandist. . . . Those
Russian days remain the most memorable of my life.[1]
—Claude McKay (1923)

*T*he Bolshevik Revolution was cata-
clysmic. Russia was completely remaking itself, and the ripples of this social
change were exciting millions of other frustrated and neglected people. As news
of the revolution spread, poet Claude McKay, like so many other blacks who had
looked to the Soviet energy with envy, began to wonder—Why not me, too?

A pained McKay, responding to the riots of the "Red Summer" of 1919 in
Chicago, Washington, D.C., and Elaine, Arkansas, wrote, "If we must die, let it
not be like hogs/ . . . If we must die, O let us nobly die/ . . . Like men we'll face
the murderous, cowardly pack/ Pressed to the wall, dying, but fighting back!"[2]
He, too, chaffed at the limitations of being black in the United States. Seven
years earlier, filled with anticipation and expectation, he had moved north in
search of increased opportunities. He had been attracted by the work of Booker
T. Washington and went to study agriculture at the Tuskegee Institute. The
United States for him was "a new land to which all people who had youth and
a youthful mind turned," and he thought, "Surely there would be opportunity in
this land, even for a Negro."[3]

But McKay could not tolerate the stultifying existence under the state-
sponsored terrorism of Jim Crow. Comfortably middle class in Jamaica, he was
suddenly plunged into the detritus of society. His stay at Tuskegee was short,
and after a few years at Kansas State College he found his way to New York.
McKay finally located his milieu. There were outlets for his poetry and a progressive community that sympathized with his discontents. Most important, he
met John Reed, and because of Reed he was able to make his "magical pilgrimage" to Soviet Russia.[4]

McKay's Political Growth

McKay was a dapper, dark-skinned, middle-class Jamaican in 1912, when he joined hundreds of ambitious young people migrating north from the Caribbean in hopes of moving beyond the limitations of their small colonial societies. But, like the many other aspirants of color from abroad, he soon discovered that the mirage of the greener pastures belied the numbing effects of racial segregation. Indeed, for McKay, Jim Crow in the United States was even more painful than the class-bound divisions common to colonial societies. "I had heard of prejudice in America but never dreamed of it being so intensely bitter; for at home there is also prejudice of the English sort, subtle and dignified, rooted in class distinction—color and race being hardly taken into account."[5] What little social cushion his middle-class status had afforded him in Jamaica was completed wiped out by the all-in-one stamp of racism in the United States.

McKay's view shifted from decrying the conditions of the poor under English colonial rule to a more romanticized view of his homeland. As George Hutchinson noted, "Jamaica became the rural, even pastoral, 'motherland,' and all the evils previously found in Kingston were now projected onto the (cold, hard, male) land of the 'The White House.'"[6] McKay also began to align himself with others who contended that the best way to fight discrimination was to confront it openly. But this aggressive stance put him at odds with the cautious stewardship of Tuskegee and what he saw as Tuskegee's "semi-military, machine-like existence."[7]

It troubled him that Tuskegee was not training its students to challenge the status quo but rather was adjuring them to be politically quiescent and to hone themselves into efficient workers at the level to which white society had relegated them. "The school emphasized vocational training and the development of character and habits presumably acceptable to the great American [white] middle class . . . [in order to make] model citizens through a combination of hard work, discipline, [and] moral training."[8] There was a constant worry that Tuskegee might suffer because of the actions of some of its errant students, and the institution was quick to react to those who might draw in the ire of the white community. Oliver Golden, also a student at Tuskegee in that 1912 period, was one of those troublesome students. Almost twenty years later, an equally cautious Tuskegee administration would frustrate Langston Hughes in its refusal to take a stand on the 1930s Scottsboro Boys case.[9]

McKay lasted less than a year at Tuskegee before he decided to move to Kansas State College to continue his studies in agriculture.[10] In contrast to the hushed posture of black Tuskegee, the white radical politics in Manhattan, Kansas, attracted McKay. Observed Wayne Cooper, "Progressive reform was at the moment triumphant in America. . . . On the Left, the Socialist Party of America had . . . reached a peak of influence, [and] the Industrial Workers of the World (IWW) [was insisting] on absolute racial equality in all its organizing campaigns."[11] The combination of sympathetic teachers, relief from Jim Crow, and access to the popular socialist newspaper *Appeal to Reason*, allowed McKay to envision a new kind of life for himself and his aspirations broadened.[12] Thus, when given the opportunity to move to New York in 1914, he did not hesitate.

The move to New York brought McKay to the nexus of three major roads in his life: access to money, marriage, and introduction into a new activist community. The donation from a benefactor made the move possible and relieved him of his immediate economic worries. He also thought it was a good time to marry his long-time love from Jamaica and bring her to New York to live with him, but his wife was not happy and the marriage fell apart. Instead, McKay was drawn toward another kind of family in New York. As he put it, New York presented "my first positive reaction to American life[;] . . . it was like entering a paradise of my own people." Importantly, this new "family" included black socialists and a widening circle of leftist activists.[13]

One of these activists was Max Eastman, whom McKay met after Eastman's publication, *The Liberator*, printed some of his work. Eastman was a major figure in the New York left community, and through his publications *The Masses* and, later, *The Liberator* he was a staunch supporter of the Bolshevik revolution in Russia. Eastman liked McKay's work and arranged for McKay's clarion call to blacks, "If We Must Die," to appear in a special two-page spread of the *Liberator* in July 1919.[14] He knew McKay was speaking for the returning black World War I veterans and many thousands of blacks who had dared to take jobs in northern factories when white workers were sent off to the European front.[15] These were people who had come to believe that opportunities were opening to blacks. But, now, after the war, they were being attacked and pushed back into unemployment. Calling on his fellow black citizens, McKay was demanding that they fight back, "Though far outnumbered let us show us brave/ And for their thousand blows deal one deathblow!"[16]

Over the next four years, from 1919 to 1923, the *Liberator* published over forty poems, eleven articles, and a number of book reviews of McKay's.[17] Noted Tyrone Tillery, "[McKay's] work's appearance in *The Liberator* [was] the culmination of a five-year struggle to find a milieu compatible with his intellectual temperament." But, as McKay also discovered, publishing in the progressive press had its hazards. Continued Tillery, "Publication also brought less-welcome attention from the Justice Department's committee investigating African-American radicalism and sedition[;] . . . the government was convinced that McKay was attempting to induce blacks to see 'red.'"[18] The Justice Department's assessment of McKay's political sensibilities was correct. Besides his work with the *Liberator*, which he later coedited, McKay had joined the highly secretive African Blood Brotherhood (ABB), to which a number of black Communists belonged.[19] An incubator of progressive thought and action, the ABB included people such as Cyril Briggs, Richard B. Moore, W. A. Domingo, Otto Huiswood, Edward Doty, Grace Campbell, H. Phillips, Gordon Owens, Alonzo Isabel, and Lovett Fort-Whiteman.[20]

McKay's friendship with Reed represented another branch of his political leanings. Reed had worked with Eastman on the *Masses* and was one of the founders of the Communist Labor Party of America, one of the progenitors of the Communist Party of the United States of America (CPUSA).[21] Reed wanted McKay to come to the Second Communist International congress in Moscow in 1920 because he thought McKay would be a prime person to address the gathering on matters pertaining to the blacks in the United States.[22] A comrade of Vladimir Ilich Lenin's since the earliest days of the Bolshevik revolution, Reed knew Lenin was interested in the revolutionary potential of American Negroes.[23] In a prerevolutionary thesis, Lenin had commented that "[the] similarity of the economic position of the Negroes with that of the former serfs in the agrarian centers of Russia is remarkable."[24] And, in preparation for the Second Communist International, Lenin had again raised the issue as part of the role of the newly structured Comintern: "[It should] render direct aid to the revolutionary movements among the dependent and underprivileged nations (for example, Ireland, the American Negroes, etc.) and in the colonies."[25] These were the early seeds of what would later be known as the "Negro Question." At the congress itself, although McKay did not go, Reed and Lenin were still determined to not let the subject drop. In a series of small notes, they conferred with each other. Reed wrote, "Comrad [sic] Lenin, Do you want me to say something about the American Negroes? . . . —Reed." Lenin responded on the same paper, "Yes, absolutely necessary. I do inscript [sic] you in the list of speakers.—Lenin."[26] Lenin also instructed Reed to prepare two reports for Comintern deliberations.

McKay was worried that his political sophistication was not great enough for him to address the Comintern, and he found an offer to travel to England less intimidating.[27] There, he frequented the International Socialist Club and met Sylvia Pankhurst, a member of the British Workers' Socialist Federation, who encouraged him to do a serious study of Marxism. Pankhurst also invited McKay to write for her paper, *The Workers' Dreadnought*, and from July to November 1920 he contributed a large number of articles, poems, and reviews. He later served as an editor.

The experience with Pankhurst was a bittersweet one, though. McKay enjoyed the exposure through the publications but was distressed when she fell from grace. Although she had maintained a "hands off Russia" posture toward the new Soviet Russia, she later suffered terribly when the Comintern forced the British Communist Party to remove her from its ranks. McKay was confused by her removal. On the one hand, he was strongly attracted to the Soviet experiment's egalitarianism and solidarity with the black struggle. On the other, he wondered why the Comintern, led by the Soviets, allowed for so little initiative at the local level.[28]

In the spring of 1921, McKay returned to the United States triumphant from his experiences in England and ready to take a more central role than he had in the past in the international progressive community. Now, he was calling for blacks to "seize the opportunities presented by the death of the old order in

Europe and the birth of the new in Russia." In fact, as Cooper observed, McKay was "among the first to signal the beginning of a black colonial revolt against that British imperialism that would peak after World War II."[29] McKay was predicting not only the tide of anticolonial uprisings but also the fact that the Soviets would have a role to play in pushing this agenda.

McKay the Sojourner

McKay finally decided he was ready to make his sojourn to Soviet Russia two years after Reed's invitation; in the meantime, Reed had died. McKay no longer thought about having a formal role, but he was eager to see the Soviet experiment in action, to "see into the new revolutionary life of the people and report on it."[30] McKay, the artist, was also intrigued with the idea that the Soviet experiment might encourage new kinds of creative collaborations: "[The] promise of Soviet internationalism as by definition a multiracial, multilingual project . . . lay as much in the ability to create a new kind of art . . . as it did in the ability to create new kinds of social and political affiliations."[31]

Undeterred by having neither Reed's formal invitation nor financial support from the Soviets, he planned to use his own sweat equity and draw on his growing network of progressive friends to help him make his way.[32] Noted Allison Blakely, "[McKay] raised the fare . . . by selling copies of his works with autographed photos. He then signed on as a stoker on a freighter bound for Liverpool, England. From there, he went on to Moscow by way of London and Berlin."[33] En route, he expected to get help from the International Socialist Club and Pankhurst in England, but Pankhurst had fallen out of favor with the British Communist Party, and, as a former associate of hers, he, too, could not expect its aid. Luckily, an acquaintance from that earlier era, Edgar Whitehead, was willing to provide that much-needed support. Whitehead had been the executive secretary of Pankhurst's group and was now working for the Comintern in Berlin. With Whitehead as his escort and bearing a letter from Crystal Eastman, who was close to the Comintern leadership, McKay was able to meet with the Russian officials and get permission to go to Russia. Having originally set out in September, he finally began his much-anticipated sojourn in Soviet Russia in November 1922, one week before the Comintern congress was to begin.[34]

Still, McKay's arrival in Moscow in 1922 caused some consternation. Although he had obtained his visa in Berlin, the Comintern leadership in Moscow did not expect him. Furthermore, the carefully assembled U.S. delegation was not pleased to have anyone else represent the United States. Attempting to discredit him, the Americans raised an objection, noting that McKay had come via England and, thus, represented the English Communists rather than the Americans.[35] Members of the delegation also tried to intimidate him by physically ejecting him from the hotel.[36]

Little did they know that McKay had a powerful ally in Moscow: the Japanese Communist and Comintern founder Sen Katayama. Katayama had spent many years in the United States and was intimately familiar with Jim Crow and the other humiliations faced by blacks and other peoples of color. He was also well aware of the potential of blacks in the rising progressive movements of the United States and an ardent supporter of the Comintern's developing interest in the Negro Question.[37] An irate Katayama issued a long statement accusing the Americans of trying to infect the Comintern with U.S.-style racism: "The subsequent conduct of the American delegation proves so. . . . To cite an instance. A pure or full-blooded Negro representative of the ABB, Comrade McKay, was kicked out of the Hotel Lux [and] brutal treatments [were] meted out [to him] by the same American delegation."[38]

With Katayama's support, there was no question of McKay's being allowed to stay. Noted Cooper, "[Katayama's word] carried more weight than the ill will of the American delegation."[39] The Comintern leadership named McKay a "fraternal delegate" and invited him to speak to the gathering on the Negro Question. Katayama would prove to be a champion not only for McKay in 1922 but also for other black sojourners through the 1920s and into the early 1930s. Before he died in 1933, Katayama was actively engaged in virtually every program relating to black people. As Harry Haywood, a student in the 1920s, noted, "We often came to him with our problems."[40]

With the imprimatur of Katayama and the Comintern Executive Committee, the attendees greeted McKay as "a great poet and representative of his oppressed race."[41] He gave his speech in English, but the Comintern quickly published a Russian-language version the next day in *Pravda*, the party paper. Subsequently, the Comintern published an English-language version in the January 1923 *International Press Correspondence*, and copies were sent to other parts of the world.[42]

McKay was ecstatic. "Stepping upon Russian soil I forthwith became a notorious character. And strangely enough there was nothing unpleasant about my being swept into the surge of revolutionary Russia."[43] In a two-part piece that appeared in the December 1922 and January 1923 issues of the *Crisis*, he wrote, "I was received as though the people had been apprised of, and were prepared for, my coming. . . . I was caught, tossed up into the air, and passed along by dozens of stalwart youths. . . . I was welcomed thus as a symbol, as a member of the great American Negro group."[44]

Huiswood and West Indian Activism

Ottto Huiswood's case is interesting for a number of reasons. Born in Dutch Guiana, he was working as a printer in New York when he joined the socialists and then later, the communists. His light skin color had been to his advantage back in Dutch Guiana, where, as true in many colonial societies, the lighter-skinned frequently enjoyed a higher social status. Yet, the privilege he enjoyed in his home country by virtue of his light color and social status also led to his discontents in the United States. After experiencing some modicum of increased opportunity at home, he aspired to have more, and his move to the United States was fueled by this desire. He could not have anticipated that when he arrived in the United States, his former social status would be canceled out by his being reclassified as a black man. Like McKay, Huiswood was also drawn to the progressives because they were calling for changes in these intractable social conventions.

A Cobbled-Together Delegation

Huiswood and the others in the U.S. delegation represented a new party, the Workers Party of America, the precursor of the CPUSA. This new party had been formed in response to pressure from the Comintern, just as Huiswood's presence in the delegation was. The 1920 and 1921 Comintern congresses had been confronted with two warring Communist parties from the United States: the Communist Party of America and the Communist Labor Party. Reed was a founding member and one of the leaders of the Communist Labor Party. Charles Ruthenberg led the Communist Party of America.[45] At the time, the Communist Party of America had about twenty-four thousand members while the Communist Labor Party had about ten thousand. The Comintern demanded that the two merge, informing Reed's Communist Labor Party that if it wanted to be officially recognized, it had to join together with the larger Communist Party of America. Because they were originally formed in opposition to each other, their ultimate paper merger continued to belie serious internal strain. These differences occurred despite the fact that they shared a common origin in the Socialist Party and common demographics in their memberships. The majority of their members were relatively recent European immigrants, including people from the former tsarist Russia. The proportion of foreign-born to U.S.-born members of the CPUSA itself did not shift significantly until the 1930s. Still another striking difference between the two was that Reed, the former head of the Communist Labor Party, was the one who pushed the Negro Question in the Comintern, yet Ruthenberg's Communist Party of America had the larger number of black members in the early 1920s.[46]

The Soviet-led Comintern was able to exert such pressure on Communist parties elsewhere, as in England and the United States, because the Soviet revolutionary movement was the only such movement that had successfully overthrown a previous government. The Soviets had also established a totally new socialist regime. As Robinson noted, "[The] Third International [was] dominated by Lenin and the policies of his Bolshevik cadre [and] it became necessary for member national parties to pledge their loyalties to the Comintern, the Soviet Union, and in practical terms, to the Bolshevik Party."[47] Thus, Huiswood, as a representative of the mismatched Workers Party of America, had gone to Soviet Russia under the doubly difficult conditions of being a last-minute addition to a delegation of a malformed organization that itself was not fully clear about its own identity or purpose. The Comintern could see that this new party's leaders were so busy fighting among themselves that actively seeking out blacks was of

secondary interest. Thus, Huiswood was pulled out for special tasks to crystal-
lize the Negro Question.

A Role for Huiswood

Despite the friction between the U.S. delegation and McKay, delegate
Huiswood, like McKay, found his stay in Moscow most propitious. McKay
might have been lionized, but Huiswood was also recognized, although differently. Ultimately, Huiswood's role in Comintern work proved even greater than
that imagined by the U.S. Communist Party, with which he had traveled.[48]

Huiswood's presence in the U.S. delegation was both fortuitous for him
and a necessary compromise for the party. Under the name of J. Billings, he
was listed as a charter member and one of the party's ninety-four founders.[49]
Yet the leaders had not originally selected him for the prestigious position of
representing the party at the Comintern congress. However, realizing that they
would be under extra scrutiny, they determined that Huiswood's inclusion might
be a way to assuage some of the concerns. Also, as Robinson observed, "Lenin
had indicated disappointment in the directions and organizational priorities established by the American Communist Party. He suggested further that Blacks
should play a critical role in the party."[50] Katayama still questioned whether
skin color might have favored Huiswood over other blacks. Noted Kate Baldwin, "Katayama writes that Huiswood was chosen to ameliorate the agitation
for some sign of action on the negro [sic] question; while at the same time,
Huiswood was chosen precisely because of his light (less obtrusive) skin color."
McKay himself pointed out that "[Huiswood] was . . . yellow," while he [Mc-
Kay] possessed "unmistakable Negroidness."[51]

Nonetheless, Huiswood welcomed the opportunity to make his own sojourn in Soviet Russia. There was no question that he had the appropriate credentials to be a delegate. Not only was he a founding member but he had been
the "national organizer" of the ABB in the early 1920s, an organization that had
been key to bringing blacks into the Communist Party.[52] He was also ready to
get down to work. The Comintern, too, was keen to find someone who could
help shape its Negro Question. McKay might be a good "salesperson" and could
rally the crowds, but Huiswood was good at the behind-the-scenes work that
was needed, including work on later written debates over the Negro Question. In
the end, Katayama noted with satisfaction, "the Negro delegates Billings [Huis-
wood] and McKay were received by the Congress and made a profound impression on the Congress and the Congress treated the Negro problems with a due
respect and consideration."[53]

Selling the Negro Question

Huiswood's light skin might have eased the U.S. Communist Party's
fears of demonstrably showing they had blacks in their midst, but it proved

problematical for the Soviets. In this sense, McKay's arrival could not have come at a better time, for his dark visage became the public face of the Soviets' alliance with people of color. "The Soviet leaders apparently had a specific objective in mind; for McKay soon found himself being photographed with [Grigory Yevseyevich] Zinoviev, [Nikolay Ivanovich] Bukharin, [Karl] Radek, Katayama, and other Party luminaries. At the opening of the Congress, McKay, not Huiswood, was seated on the platform as representing the symbolic presence of the black American worker."[54] McKay's darker skin stood in greater contrast to the white faces of the Russians around him, and, therefore, his propaganda value as a symbol in photos and publications was also greater. Furthermore, McKay's darker color also fit in with the Soviets' preconceived notions of blacks in the United States as having some kind of "African-ness." As Baldwin noted, Huiswood was "simply too *American* to be sufficiently African. He was too light-skinned to afford the crucial racial distinctions."[55] The Soviets even questioned whether someone so light-skinned could suffer from black oppression and, hence, represent the Negro Question effectively.

McKay was clearly having fun with this distinction. "When the Negro delegate was invited to attend meetings and my mulatto colleague went, the people asked, 'but where is the chorny (the black [man])?'"[56] Continuing the point, he noted, "And so always the conversation revolved around me until my face flamed. The Moscow press printed long articles about the Negroes in America, a poet was inspired to rhyme about the Africans looking to Socialist Russia and soon I was in demand everywhere[,] . . . at the lectures of poets, journalists, the meetings of soldiers and factory workers."[57]

McKay was so familiar to the Soviet public that he was held in high esteem for years afterward. His speeches were readily published, and the Soviets commissioned him to do a long piece on the situation of blacks in the United States. McKay produced a series of essays that were published under the title *Negroes in America* while he was still in the country. He also wrote a collection of short stories alongside the essays, and these were later put into a single work entitled *Trial by Lynching: Stories about Negro Life in North America*.[58] He traveled around the country, addressing various groups, and Leon Trotsky, with whom he became friends, honored him with an extended tour of the military. At each stop, he was roundly toasted and celebrated.[59] In each case, the Soviets made good use of the press photos. One familiar photo showed McKay on a Red Army airplane after a brief wintertime flight.[60]

In addition to the goodwill and solidarity building, McKay looked forward to attracting other blacks to the Soviet experiment once he returned to the United States. "McKay left Moscow feeling that a new day was at hand[;] . . . he confidently predicted that more blacks would travel to the Soviet Union and would be impressed with a land apparently free of racism."[61] His *Crisis* article stated, "Besides brandishing the Rooseveltian stick in the face of the lesser new world natives, America holds an economic club over the heads of all the great European nations, excepting Russia. . . . As American influence increases in the

world . . . the more necessary it becomes for all struggling minorities to organize extensively for the worldwide propagation of their grievances."[62]

McKay's visit lasted only six months, and the record is vague as to why he
left when he did. He may have recognized his limitations and his preference for
following an independent line, and he may have suspected that, sooner or later,
the Soviets would expect more from him.

The Negro Commission and
Development of the Negro Question

Although the topic of working with U.S. blacks had surfaced in the 1920
congress, the formal establishment of the Negro Commission did not occur until
1922, after McKay's and Huiswood's visits. The Soviets were particularly interested in gaining the attention of blacks in the United States because of their
swelling numbers in the industrial centers to the north and growing proletarian
sensibilities.[63] And, as noted by Cedric Robinson, Lenin surmised that they were
"clearly to be expected to be the most angry element."[64]

The Soviets appreciated the potential of these urban blacks but expected
less from those in colonial societies, which they saw as being still mired in plantation and traditional agrarian systems. If anything, they contended, the more
advanced, U.S. black proletariat could take the lead and help direct the lesser-
developed colonial blacks toward socialism. The Negro Commission raised this
possibility under the heading of the "Negro Question." As Haywood noted, it
"characterized the position of U.S. Blacks as an aspect of the colonial question [and] stressed the special role of American Blacks in support of liberation
struggles of Africa, Central and South America and the Caribbean."[65]

McKay Realigns, Huiswood Stays the Course

When they first met in 1922, Huiswood observed of McKay, "You're all
right for propaganda. It's a pity you'll never make a disciplined party member."[66] But as much as he tried to remain aloof and to separate himself from Mc-
Kay, he came to realize that he had to stay close to McKay if he wanted anyone
to listen to his opinions on the Negro Question. Still, Huiswood's assessment
of McKay proved accurate. McKay never liked the mundane requirements of
party development, preferring to take an independent path. Later, he converted
to Catholicism and began to repudiate his earlier contacts with the Communists.
His autobiographical text, *A Long Way from Home*, chronicles his change of
heart.[67] Huiswood, however, was not bothered by party work and continued to
work for both the U.S. party and the Soviets well after that first journey. In fact,
Huiswood was happy to do another, longer sojourn in the Soviet Union in 1927,
when he was selected for further political training at the Comintern's Lenin
School.[68]

Ultimately, the contrast between McKay and Huiswood can be seen in other aspects of their experiences there. The Soviets were responding to their bifurcated political objectives: the expediency of propaganda and the demands of party work. McKay's usefulness to them was to look the part of an "American" black and to appeal to the emotions of people. Huiswood's talents were in the crafting of discussion papers and other background materials to support the Comintern's campaigns.[69] In fact, years later, as further testament to Huiswood's value to the inner sanctum of the party leadership, Huiswood was the first black person elected to the Executive Committee of the Communist International.[70] He was also selected to lead the Comintern's International Trade Union Committee in the 1930s;[71] and he was appointed editor of the committee's publication, *The Negro Worker*, after George Padmore's departure.[72]

When it came to meeting the top luminaries of the Comintern and the Soviet government, it was Huiswood who was taken to see the ailing Lenin. As Haywood noted proudly, Huiswood was "the first Black man to greet the great Bolshevik."[73] McKay was taken to see Lenin's wife, Nadezhda Krupskaya and Trotsky.[74] But both McKay and Huiswood were made honorary members of the Moscow Soviet (city council).[75]

Interestingly, these two men, so integral to the early development of the Comintern's position on the Negro Question, which focused on U.S. blacks, were themselves not African American. Also, in contrast to blacks reared in the United States, they brought worldviews shaped by their experiences of growing into manhood as former colonials. Their progressive sensibilities were later sharpened by the shock of their exposure to racism in the United States. Having these dual perspectives may have put them in a position to appreciate the role of international collaboration in the fight for self-determination. As Cooper noted, "McKay and Huiswood together represented the general perspective of several West Indian radicals in the United States. . . . [They were] simultaneously more nationalistic, class conscious, and international-minded than were American-born blacks."[76] In fact, most members of the ABB, to which both McKay and Huiswood belonged, many of whom would later join the CPUSA, were from the West Indies.[77]

McKay, Shining the Beacon for Others

As a writer and public figure, McKay was clearly the better known and more influential of the two in the early period. Through his publications and speeches, he was able to spread the word of the Soviet experiment quite effectively. After he left the Soviet Union, he chose to stay in Europe and North Africa and did not return to the United States for another twelve years, but his work reached far beyond the confines of progressive encampments and captured the imaginations of blacks of many political persuasions. McKay announced, "The Negro, as the most suppressed and persecuted minority, should use this period of ferment in international affairs to lift his cause out of his national obscurity and force it forwards as a prime international issue." Then, presaging later collaborations between blacks and Russians, he called out, "Russia is prepared and waiting to receive couriers and heralds of good will and interracial understanding for the Negro race."[78] Within two years, fellow travelers would begin to arrive; within three years, W.E.B. Du Bois would go and later join the chorus of supporters; and by the early 1930s groups of specialists and others would also take up this call.

CHAPTER 3

Harry Haywood, KUTVA, and Training Black Cadres

ℰ𝒳ℴ

In the manner of the old Underground Railroad, I was
passed on from one set of comrades to the next. . . . Upon
landing, I presented my visa and passport to the authorities.
Addressing me in English, a man in civilian dress said, "Oh,
you're going to the Comintern school in Moscow?" "Yes,"
I replied. He immediately took me in [his] charge.[1]
—Harry Haywood (1978)

"Several weeks after I received my passport, I heard the FBI had been making inquiries about me. . . . [As] my departure time drew near, I hid out at the home of comrades on Chicago's Westside [while my] political credentials, typed on silk, were sewn into the lining of my coat sleeve."[2] Spirited out of Chicago and passing through Canada and Germany, Harry Haywood embarked on his own search for the promised land, finally landing in Leningrad in April 1926.

This was a mere year after Haywood (né Haywood Hall) had formally joined the Communist Party, although several years after his political credentials had been tested in other progressive arenas.[3] Like many other black World War I veterans, Haywood had not been content to return to a life under Jim Crow and spent years looking for "an organization with which to make revolution." His Soviet experience changed him from simply being "a disgruntled Black ex-soldier" to being what he termed "a self-conscious revolutionary."[4] As he learned, the battles were far broader than his fight against Jim Crow. "This was my first experience with Irish revolutionaries and their experiences excited me[;] . . . we had a lot in common. . . . [I admired] their sense of national pride [and awareness] of the international importance of their independence struggle."[5]

Early Education

Born in Omaha, Haywood was still young when his family moved to Minneapolis. His early life in these less cosmopolitan and predominantly white environments shielded him from the full brunt of Jim Crow. There were times, though, when "the ugly reality of race would intrude upon the dream world of my childhood." A substitute teacher came to his school one day. "[She] was a Southerner from Arkansas. During history class she started talking about the Civil War [and how] the slaves . . . did not really want freedom because they were happy. . . . Her villain was General Grant, whom she contrasted unfavorably with General Robert E. Lee." Haywood challenged her comments, and his classmates seemed to generally agree with him. But he discovered a mixed response back home. "When I told my Mother she supported me. . . . But Father was not so sure. 'You might have gotten into trouble.'"[6] To Haywood's mind, confronting this woman's racism was a good thing. It was especially satisfying when we saw that he had the support of his white classmates and mother. But his father's cautionary statement stung him, and he feared that as long as he was black in the United States and living under Jim Crow, he, too, would have to bow to the pressures of white society. In these circumstances, his older brother, Otto, stood out as his hero: Otto was waging a protracted campaign to frustrate his parents' efforts to have him accept the status quo.

As he got older and moved away from his parents' supervision, Haywood's personal and political trajectories often mirrored his brother's. Although brilliant in school, Otto had refused to continue his studies, even when offered a special scholarship to a Jesuit college. "Father was an ardent follower of Booker T. Washington. His ambitions for his sons were very modest. . . . He thought of jobs a notch or two above his own station, like a postal employee, a skilled tradesman, or a clerk in the civil service. . . . Otto came to the conclusion that there was no use in continuing his education. That it was irrelevant. Opportunities for educated Blacks were few." Later, when Otto joined the Communist Party, Haywood aspired to follow in his footsteps. "Otto [joined] in succession, the Wobblies, or Industrial Workers of the World (IWW), the African Blood Brotherhood and finally the Communist Party."[7]

Haywood was seventeen when he set out on his own for Chicago in 1915. He found a job at the Tip Top Inn that led to other good positions, "I got a job as a busboy at the Tip Top Inn, then considered the finest restaurant in town[;] . . . if you had been a waiter at the Tip Top Inn you could work anywhere in the country. After a few months I was promoted to waiter and felt that I had perfected my skills. During the next three years I worked at a number of places."[8]

Although these jobs gave him a certain amount of financial stability, Haywood was not satisfied. He had made friends with a group of men at the Eighth Illinois Black National Guard Regiment, and through their stories he had begun to envision a life of adventure in the army. "Intrigued by their experiences, I joined the Eighth Regiment in the winter of 1917. I was nineteen." Haywood delighted in the fact that the regiment was headed by a black man and that it "emphasized racial solidarity." World War I was on, and Haywood was certain to be called up, but he thought that the Eighth Regiment would bring "romance, adventure, travel," and, most important, "escape from the inequities and oppression that was the lot of Blacks in the U.S."[9]

Lessons from the Military

But Haywood's romantic notions were quickly dashed, as he realized that the fighting between whites and blacks in civilian life had parallels in the service. Riots broke out near areas where black soldiers were stationed, and in the aftermath of the 1917 Houston riot eighteen soldiers had been hanged.[10] Many of the black soldiers stationed there were not from the South and, hence, familiar with the segregated policies of this southern town. Thus, the clashes with the police were exacerbated by attacks by white soldiers from the base as well as white townspeople.

But there was more to these tensions than conforming to the rules of Jim Crow. His brother's experience at Camp Stewart in Virginia was not atypical. The black soldiers were regularly taunted, bullied, and were given poorer rations and housed in worse conditions than white soldiers, and the blacks were frequently commanded by malicious officers who did little to improve their lot. "Otto told us his worst experience was . . . during the terrible cold winter of 1917–1918." Despite the cold weather, the black troops were living in tents without wooden floors or heat; some had blankets, but others did not. Like the other new arrivals, Otto was "forced to stand around fires outside all night or sleep under trees for partial protection from the weather. For months there were no bathing facilities nor clothing for the men."[11] Eventually, after persistent complaints from the men and an investigation, the conditions were changed, but the painful memories could not be erased.

Racism also took strange twists when these black regiments were sent abroad. The majority, like Oliver Golden, were assigned to service positions behind the lines. Haywood was among those attached to the French army. The U.S. authorities claimed this reassignment was necessary in order to prevent "friction" between the U.S. white and black soldiers. Even then, in an attempt to maintain U.S.-style discriminatory practices abroad, they cautioned the French commanders that they might have problems with the blacks. "Not satisfied just to separate us; they tried to extend the long arm of Jim Crow to the French . . . [pointing to] a menace of degeneracy . . . [and] want of intelligence. . . . [They warned that the French should not] commend too highly the black American troops, particularly in the presence of [white] Americans [and should make] a point of keeping the native cantonment population from 'spoiling' the Negroes."[12]

Indeed, the problem of " 'spoiling' the Negroes" did occur. The French had no qualms about fraternization with those who were laying their lives on the line to save them, and they readily recognized valorous actions of the blacks. "Our regiment was not sorry to be incorporated into the French military. In fact, most of us thought it was the best thing that could have happened. The French treated Blacks well—that is, as human beings. There was no Jim Crow. At the time, I thought the French seemed to be free of the virulent U.S. brand of racism." Black soldiers received tumultuous welcomes by the newly freed French villagers, and, by the end of the war, Haywood's regiment had "won twenty-one Distinguished Service Crosses, sixty-eight Croix de Guerre, and one Distinguished Service Medal."[13]

Haywood's memories of life outside the United States were further enriched by another chance encounter. He and his fellow soldiers came across a regiment of Russian Cossacks in August 1918. "When we asked them who they were, one of them replied in halting English that they were Russian Cossacks[;] . . . their division, which had been fighting on the western front, had been withdrawn from the lines, disarmed and placed in quarantine. They were considered unreliable, he said, because of the revolution in Russia." Haywood found this story intriguing. "I was not even sure of the meaning of the word *revolution*—some kind of civil disorder I conjectured. . . . [When I] returned from France . . . I began reading about the Russian Revolution . . . and the significance slowly dawned on me. . . . Here, I felt, was a tangible accomplishment and real power."[14]

Early Political Training

The postwar climate also fostered new kinds of alliances in the large industrial centers, like Chicago, Detroit, and New York. These cities had the greatest concentration of heavy industry and industrial workers, and thousands of immigrants from Europe had brought new ideas and attitudes into the mix. "Chicago in the early twenties was an ideal place and time for the education of a Black radical. . . . It was a major point of contact for these masses with the white labor movement and its advanced, radical sector. In the thirties it was to become a main testing ground for Black and white labor unity."[15]

Chicago and the events of 1919 proved a milestone in Haywood's political life, "On July 28, 1919, I literally stepped into a battle that was to last the rest of my life. Exactly three months after mustering out of the Army, I found myself in the midst of one of the bloodiest race riots in U.S. history. . . . It came to me then that I had been fighting the wrong war. . . ." Starting with a fight on a beach where a black boy accidentally crossed the invisible demarcation between the white and black swimming areas, this six-day riot left over thirty people dead, more than 500 people injured, and 1,000 burned out of their homes. And, for Haywood, it was "the great turning point in my life."[16]

But, while his heart was clearly left-leaning, Haywood feared that his lack of an advanced education in general and, of political training in particular, put him at a disadvantage. "At the time the racist deluge simply revealed great gaps in my own education and knowledge."[17] Thus, he set up a systematic program of self-education, expanded his reading, and joined political discussion groups.

In 1922, Haywood felt he was ready to follow his brother into the Communist Party. But Otto, knowing about the internal problems of the party, convinced him to put this request off until later. "A number of Black recruits had dropped out. They resented the paternalistic attitude displayed to them by some of the white comrades who . . . treated Blacks like children and seemed to think that the whites had all the answers."[18] Instead, Otto directed Haywood to join the African Blood Brotherhood (ABB).[19] Many of ABB's members were Communists as well, and, in fact, this was the first time that Haywood met black Communists other than his brother and sister Eppa.[20] Cedric Robinson noted, "The largest membership was in the New York home office, but there were sizeable contingents in Chicago, Baltimore, Omaha, and West Virginia."[21]

Haywood was not immediately thrilled with the idea of joining the ABB but acknowledged that "it was stimulating and rewarding" and that it was through the ABB that he was able to forge "his first active association with Black industrial workers [who were] literate, articulate and class conscious, a proud and defiant group which had been radicalized by the struggles against discriminatory practices."[22]

Also in the ABB Haywood originally came across the idea of establishing a self-governing state for blacks. Cyril Briggs, the ABB founder and editor of the *Amsterdam News*, had published a number of editorials discussing the idea as early as 1917. Little did Haywood know that by the end of the 1920s the Comintern would also adopt this idea as part of its "Negro Question," and Haywood would be assigned the task of developing support for it. But although the Comintern would continue to push for the separate U.S. state well into the 1930s, the ABB would later shift its attention to the development of a black-led state in Africa.[23] The ABB itself began to dissolve in the 1920s, as many of its members took on central roles in the CPUSA. As Haywood commented, "Its eventual demise coincided with the growing participation of its leadership in the . . . Communist Party."[24]

Continuing to press his brother to help him join the Communist Party after a stint in the ABB, Haywood's efforts were again diverted when the party leadership directed him to join the Young Communist League (YCL) first. Dutifully joining the YCL in 1923, Haywood was by then twenty-five, and as he recalled, "I expressed doubt that I could be considered a youth at the age of twenty-five. They replied that there were a number of members of my age. . . . All that was needed . . . was for one to have the 'youth angle' . . . the ability to understand youth and their problems and to be able to communicate with them."[25]

Again, Haywood grudgingly admitted that this period of tutelage was useful. He and H. V. Phillips were the only blacks in the organization, and he agreed with Phillips that "more of us Blacks [were] needed in the League."[26] More important, though, through the YCL he met Bob Mazut, a Russian representative from the YCL International. "[Mazut] took particular interest in me. I believe Phillips and I were the first Blacks he had ever really known and for us he was the first real Soviet communist we had ever met. . . . I told him I wanted to go there [the Soviet Union] and see it for myself. 'You undoubtedly will,' he said in a matter-of-fact tone, as if the matter were settled."[27]

Lovett Fort-Whiteman and the Recruitment of Blacks

Haywood was finally allowed to join the Communist Party in 1925, three years after his first attempts. This same year fellow ABB member Lovett Fort-Whiteman returned from Moscow and began serving as the head of the Comintern-backed American Negro Labor Congress (ANLC).[28] Fort-Whiteman was planning to send Haywood's brother, Otto, along with Golden, William L. Patterson, and Roy Mahoney to do political studies in Moscow.[29] Haywood was tapped for the second cohort, to be sent in 1926.

Haywood was originally suspicious of Fort-Whiteman. "My feelings about him were rather mixed. I was both repelled and fascinated by the excessive flamboyance of the man."[30] Although he was a political operative when Haywood first met him, Fort-Whiteman had set out to be a Shakespearean actor when he first arrived in New York in 1916. Not long after his arrival, though, his attentions were increasingly drawn to the fiery rhetoric of the black protest in Harlem. He enrolled in the socialist Rand School, then joined the Workers Party, and later the ABB.[31] But Fort-Whitman also found ways to blend his theatrical talents with his role as a recruiter for the Soviets. "[Fort-Whiteman] had affected a Russian style of dress, sporting a *robochka* (a man's long belted shirt) which almost came to the knees, ornamental belt, high boots and a fur hat. Here was a veritable Black Cossack who could be seen sauntering along the streets of Southside Chicago."[32]

Sent to the Soviet Union for political studies in 1924, Fort-Whiteman was immediately swept up in the discussions of the Negro Question at the Fifth Comintern congress. He was enthusiastic about the potential of socialism but was worried that the leadership was not reaching out to blacks properly. There was no question that black people were ready for revolutionary action, but Garvey was tapping into this sentiment, not the Communists. Pushing his way to the podium, he told the assembled, "The ideas of Marx have spread slowly among Negroes because Communists have not realized that the problem must be dealt with in a specialized way."[33] The Comintern leadership agreed and named him to head the new recruitment arm for the United States.

Observing Fort-Whiteman's strategies, Haywood noted, "[Fort-Whiteman] held a number of press conferences in which he delineated plans for the American Negro Labor Congress, and as a Black communist fresh from Russia, he made good news copy."[34] The *New York Times* reported that Fort-Whiteman had announced he had ten black candidates "training for the 'Russian diplomatic services [in the Soviet Union]' "[35] and that they "will work for the Communist movement among backward colored races in various parts of the world, and will return to the United States for work among their own people."[36] As Earl Ofari Hutchinson added, these were, in fact, some of the earliest students enrolled "at the School of the Toilers East [KUTVA], a Party-run training school for African and Asian Communist recruits in Moscow."[37]

Fort-Whiteman made arrangements for a number of blacks to go to the Soviet Union for training, but the U.S. party was not as committed to incorporating them or any other blacks in its work. Once Fort-Whiteman left, as he frequently moved between U.S. cities and the Soviet Union, the ANCL work and recruitment of blacks fell off dramatically. Noted Haywood, "Despite our efforts and work, the ANLC never got off the ground. Few local units were formed, resolutions and plans were never carried into action." Eventually, the Comintern stopped funding it, and the ANCL was discontinued. The only tangible sign of its existence was its newspaper, the *Negro Champion*, which the party continued to publish for a number of years afterward.[38]

Making the Move to the Soviet Union

Because of his work with the ANLC and Fort-Whiteman, Haywood had begun to draw the attention of the FBI. Thus, in contrast to Otto's departure for the Soviet Union the year before, which had been heavily publicized, Haywood's departure was clandestine. "I was passed from one set of comrades to the next: from Detroit, Rudy Baker, the district organizer, forwarded me on to the Canadian Party headquarters in Toronto. . . . They sent me to Montreal where comrades housed me and booked passage for me to Hamburg."[39]

Finally arriving in Moscow, Haywood was relieved to see his brother again. "I was overjoyed at the sight of him and his friend, who turned out to be a fellow student. . . . We embraced Russian style, and I began to feel more at home in this strange land." As much as he was glad to see his brother, though, he was even more amazed at the overall welcome blacks received in Moscow. A dramatic example was the response to the illness of Jane Golden, Golden's first wife. "An expression of sadness crossed his face, however, when I asked him about the rest of the Black students. He then informed me of Jane Golden's illness. . . . [She] was not expected to live. The situation had saddened the whole Black student body, and, for that matter the whole school."[40]

This was Haywood's first awareness that he had entered a new kind of society, one that fostered a humane relationship among people. Within the short span of a year, these students from around the globe and their teachers had knit themselves into a community. Jane was not a student, but she had accompanied her husband, Oliver, when he went to do his studies in the Soviet Union. She had "become very popular . . . a real morale booster, whose spirit had helped all of them through the period of initial adjustment. . . . Here was a Black woman, not a member of the Communist Party, who had so easily become accustomed to the new Soviet socialist society." Haywood was moved to see so many people affected by her sudden death. "Jane Golden's funeral and the school collective's response to her death made a profound impression on me. Through these events, crammed into the first three days of my stay in the Soviet Union, I came to know something about my fellow students and the new socialist society into which I had entered."[41]

Blacks and KUTVA

Haywood had been sent to study at the University of the Toilers of the East in the Name of Stalin, which had been founded in 1921.[42] KUTVA was designed "to [train] cadre [Communist leaders] from many national and ethnic groups within the Soviet Union . . . [and later] cadres from colonies and subject nations outside of the Soviet Union."[43] KUTVA-trained students were then sent back to their respective communities to carry on Communist programs, thus, helping to consolidate the Bolshevik gains.

This was an extremely ambitious undertaking, as could be seen by the sheer number and diversity of the students. "[The] student body represented more than seventy nationalities and ethnic groups. . . . [It was] divided into two sections—inner and outer." The inner section came largely from the Soviet East and included "Turkmenians, Uzbeks, Tajiks, Bashkirs, Yahuts, Chuvashes, Kazaks. . . . From the Caucuses there were Azerbaidzhanis, Armenians, Georgians, Abkhazians. . . . There were Tartars from the Crimea and the Volga region." Blacks from the United States were included in the outer section, which incorporated other non-Soviet students such as "Indians, Indonesians, Koreans, Filipinos, Persians, Egyptians, Arabs and Palestinian Jews from the Middle East, Arabs from North Africa."[44] Haywood's classmates from the United States were Harold Williams, a West Indian; Kweku Bankole (aka Bankole Awooner-Renner), an Ashanti (from Ghana); and Roy Mahoney (aka Farmer), an African American from Ohio.[45] Most, like Haywood, traveled under a pseudonym, having changed their names to protect family members back home and to elude the U.S. security services. Describing his decision, Haywood noted, "At the time, we all felt that any Black applying for a passport would be subjected to scrutiny. Therefore, when I applied . . . [I used the] first names of my Mother (Harriet) and Father (Haywood). This name was to stick with me the rest of my life."[46]

When Haywood arrived in 1926, he was one of only ten or eleven black people in Moscow, a city of over four million. Six or seven students were attending KUTVA, and there were two other women, Emma Harris and Coretta Arli-Titz, who had settled in the city prior to the Russian Revolution.[47] Both women had already had illustrious careers as entertainers and had married Russians, but by the time Haywood and other Soviet-era sojourners arrived, they were widowed and living less comfortable lives. Still, despite the political changes, they had decided to stay on under the new Soviet experiment, rather than return to the United States and Jim Crow.[48]

In his autobiography, Haywood mentioned forty-six blacks that he met or personally knew of, the majority of whom were African American.[49] Some blacks had come from other countries, but many of these seemed to have gone to the Soviet Union through England or the United States. Most of those who went in the 1920s were fellow travelers, like Haywood and Otto. They were doing political studies or had gone to attend Communist Party congresses. Among the others he mentioned were members of larger groups that went on specific contracts in the early 1930s: the agricultural and technical specialist groups and the *Black and White* film group.[50] Other sources have estimated that there were "ninety American blacks" in the Soviet Union between 1925 and 1938.[51]

For those blacks who were not originally from the United States, political training at the Comintern schools usually came as a result of their having gone to the United States, England, or one of the other European countries.[52] McKay, Huiswood, and George Padmore were recruited through the United States, although they originally came from Jamaica, Dutch Guiana, and Trinidad, respectively. Haywood's classmate Bankole (aka Bankole Awoonor-Renner), from Ghana, had studied journalism in England but then had gone to the United States to attend Tuskegee Institute. He later enrolled at the Carnegie Technical Institute in Pittsburgh, and there he joined the YCL. The YCL sent him to Moscow in 1926.[53] Williams was originally from the West Indies but was recruited in Chicago when he was serving in the U.S. merchant marine.[54]

Many Routes to and from KUTVA

Most of those who did formal political studies were involved in some kind of progressive activity prior to going to the Soviet Union; however, not all were members of the Communist Party like Haywood. Nonetheless, their Soviet sponsors hoped that they could be drawn in later through their political studies and other exposure to the Soviet experiment. Haywood and his brother, who went in the mid-1920s, were among the first to attend the full, formal, three-year course of study in the Comintern schools. Some, like Fort-Whiteman, who went earlier, underwent short, intensive courses of study. The students of the 1920s and 1930s were predominantly men, although there were some women, like fellow travelers Maude White (aka Katz) and Marie Houston, who went in 1927 and the early 1930s, respectively.[55]

It was common practice for a pair of black KUTVA students to meet the newcomers when they arrived at the train station in Moscow. Haywood and his brother were assigned to meet White when she first arrived in 1927. Recalling that first encounter, Haywood wrote, "We rented a drosky [horse-drawn wagon] and proceeded to the station. It was a cold winter night, the temperature was somewhere around thirty-five below zero." Haywood's first impressions of White were not particularly favorable. "When we got there, we saw the young Black woman. . . . She had on a seal skin coat, silk stockings and pumps, and by the time we got there she was practically hysterical with the cold. . . . 'Get me out of here,' she shouted. Otto and I looked at each other, both thinking . . . we're going to have a rough time with this one. We couldn't have been more wrong. Maude got right into the swing of things . . . and stayed in Moscow for three years."[56]

William L. Patterson, another KUTVA student from the 1920s, was in the same class as White. His political turning point had been the Nicola Sacco and

Bartolomeo Vanzetti case. "I returned from Boston profoundly shaken [by the failure of the campaign to save the men]. . . . I wanted and needed . . . a complete change in my way of living."[57] Patterson came under the tutelage of Briggs and the ABB, and Briggs encouraged him to start reading certain texts, beginning with the *Communist Manifesto*. Later, he brought Patterson into reading and discussion groups so that he could deepen his understanding of these texts. Patterson was then formally enrolled in the party's Workers School. A few months later, in 1927, he received notice that he would be sent to the Soviet Union. "I was informed that I was being considered for a trip to the Soviet Union. I was amazed—and pleased. I could not help comparing my coming departure with the trip I had taken in 1919 under my own initiative. At the time I was in flight from my country's pervasive racism; I had been driven from home. . . . Now I was going [to] learn from those who had defeated their oppressors. That I was invited at all was living proof of the universality of that struggle."[58]

But Patterson's selection did not have the unanimous support of all senior CPUSA members. Still suffering from internecine racism, Jay Lovestone, for one, was totally against allowing Patterson to go. As Patterson recalled, "Lovestone . . . condescended to visit me in Harlem. In the course of our conversation, he notified me not to expect to return [from the Soviet Union] as one of the leaders of the Party."[59] But Lovestone's warning only steeled Patterson's resolve to go and learn what he could from the Soviets. "What I learned would be tested in the crucible of struggle when I returned."[60]

After his return in 1931, Patterson took on various jobs for the CPUSA, actively looking for opportunities to share his experiences with others. "The Soviet Union was a new world in the making. This called for the making of a new man, a new people. There was in the treatment accorded me a wholesomeness born of the new freedom they were experiencing and wanted for others. . . . I tried to bring the message of hope I had found. . . . The people over there were proving every day that workers were far more capable of ruling the land than the upper classes. I told them how discrimination on the basis of color, class, sex, religion or nationality could be eliminated; that socialism was the answer to the depression as well as to other problems plaguing our land."[61] But Patterson's most famous contribution was the work he did for the International Labor Defense (ILD) and the fight to free the Scottsboro Boys.[62] The combination of his U.S. and Soviet political studies armed him in such a way that he was able to prevail against the mighty U.S. juggernaut. "It took seventeen years! It took all kinds of maneuvers [and] tremendous sacrifices of time and energy by thousands of good people around the world—many of them Communists, and many of them not Communists. . . . But at the end, not one boy was lynched. All were freed."[63]

Other students were returning home and putting their training to work too. When Herbert Newton, who spent four and a half years in the Soviet Union in the first half of the 1930s, returned to the United States, he "was the only Black member of the 'Atlanta Six,' a group of Communist organizers charged under Georgia's Insurrection Act and facing possible electrocution. They had been arrested at an anti-lynching and unemployed demonstration in Atlanta . . . [then] were released on bail as a result of protest all over the country."[64] White worked as an organizer for the Needle Trades Workers Industrial Union and remained an active member of the party in Harlem.[65]

The KUTVA Program

KUTVA's program of study combined theoretical and practical Marxist training with Russian-language courses. The Marxist training was the key to preparing these students for future political work, but the Russian-language training was the key to helping them integrate into Russian society. However, of the two, the political training clearly held the highest priority. The international students had classes in one of three languages to help them get into their studies quickly. "We students from outside the Soviet Union were subdivided into three main language groups: English, French, and Chinese. English and French were the dominant languages of the many colonial areas represented at the university. Spanish was later added when Latin American students began to arrive."[66] Padmore was asked to lecture at KUTVA in the early 1930s; he listed some of KUTVA's courses as "history, foreign languages, economic[s], political science, philosophy, sociology, party and trade union organization, techniques of propaganda and agitation, public speaking and journalism."[67] Otherwise, the greatest challenge was to learn Russian. As Haywood commented, "On first hearing it, the language had sounded most strange to me. I could hardly understand a word and wondered if I would ever master it. . . . I applied myself seriously to it [and] in six months I was able to read *Pravda* with the help of a dictionary."[68]

The theoretical studies were supplemented by a broad base of practical experiences in order to provide an experiential understanding of the Soviet experiment. "We used to attend workers' cultural clubs and do volunteer work, like working Saturdays to help build the Moscow subways. Education for us was not an ivory tower, but a true integration into the Soviet society, where we received firsthand knowledge from our experiences."[69] Much of this practical work took the students out of the city and often provided valuable object lessons on the role of socialism among the rural and less cosmopolitan people. These projects also served as cultural bridges, as the Soviet authorities used these opportunities to teach other people in the Soviet Union about people from other parts of the world. Thus, blacks from the United States found themselves in the curious position not only of teaching people about U.S. culture or sharing their technical expertise but also of teaching them about African America.

One of Haywood's projects sent him to a region sixty-six miles away from Moscow. Although it was relatively close to Moscow, most of the inhabitants had never been in the capital, nor had they come across black people. For Haywood's part, this was the first time he was traveling to this region, and he was equally unfamiliar with his surroundings. "I had my first close-up observation of the peasant question in the USSR. I visited a peasant village in an agricultural district to talk with the people and make observations. . . . I was let down in the middle of the village square and looked around to get my bearings[;] . . . in no time at all, a crowd had gathered to stare at me." Already comfortable with speaking Russian, Haywood overhead various comments, " 'Who is he?' 'Why is he so Black.' 'What nice teeth.'" Deciding to take charge, Haywood turned to a young man standing nearby. " 'Zdravstvuute [Hello],' I said. 'Could you direct me to the town committee?' He seemed to be surprised that I could speak Russian, but getting himself together, he directed me to a building across the square." The young man could not suppress his shock. " 'Who are you? Where did you come from,' the young man asked. 'I'm an American Negro from the United States,' I replied. . . . Someone else spoke up. " 'I thought all people in the United States were white.'"[70] As with Huiswood and McKay in 1922, the average Russian thought only African people were black, or, as Haywood overheard someone explain to the others, "He's probably from Africa. There the sun is so hot that people who have lived there for thousands of years become black."[71] Haywood took these reactions with equanimity, realizing that these were not instances of racism but of naivety.

For the duration of his stay in the Soviet Union, he noted that on only one occasion was he negatively singled out because he was black. A drunken man on a Moscow streetcar muttered, "Black devils in our country." Instead of taking offense, Haywood was intrigued by the reaction of the other passengers. "What then occurred was an impromptu, on-the-spot meeting, where they [the other passengers] debated what to do with the man. I was to see many of this kind of 'meeting' during my stay in Russia."[72] Here were ordinary people accepting responsibility for maintaining the goals of a nondiscriminatory society and deliberating over their options for correcting racist behavior in others.

Just before he left, in 1930, he heard of another example that underscored his assessment of "the contrast between the socialist world which I was leaving and the racist world which I was about to re-enter. [A black man was] insulted, beaten up and thrown out of the restaurant by two of his white American fellow workers. This attempt to transplant American racism to Soviet soil was met by outrage[;] . . . the culprits were arrested immediately, not for assault and battery but for white chauvinism, a social crime and therefore far more serious."[73] The black man was Robert Robinson, who had chosen to do a sojourn in the Soviet Union not for political reasons but because the Soviets offered him a good job with good pay. The incident happened in a city far to the south of Moscow, yet, Haywood noted, the Muscovites seemed to make an extra effort to show their solidarity to blacks in their midst. "Our [the black students'] very presence reminded [ordinary Russians] of the incident. People were very sympathetic to us."[74]

The Lenin School

In 1926, the Soviets established a second institute for political training—the Lenin School. Students with special promise and or from the industrialized and sophisticated environs of the United States or Western Europe were to attend classes there. Haywood, who was the first black person to attend, noted, "Formally called the International Lenin course . . . the school was to train sixty to seventy qualified students both in theoretical and practical subjects, which included observations of Soviet trade unions and collective farm work. . . . It was a school of great prestige and influence within the international communist movement."[75] Subsequently, Huiswood, Phillips, Leonard Patterson, and Albert Nzula, a Zulu from South Africa, were sent there.[76]

Adjusting to Study and Life in the Soviet Union

The Soviet political-training programs were completely subsidized by the Soviet government, affording the international students experiences unlike any they might have had before. "The students had the rights of citizens, voting and participating in local elections. . . . [We also] received full room and board."[77] Woodford McClellan added that all students, both white and black, "received preferential treatment on all fronts . . . board, room, and education at prestigious institutions, clothing and travel allowances, special tutors, paid vacations in the Soviet Union and at home, and fairly easy access to high officials. . . . The privileges set the foreigners aside from the mass of Soviet citizens."[78]

In return for these benefits, the Soviet expectations were high. The choice to use English, French, Chinese, and later Spanish, helped introduce the students into this milieu and their studies, but they had come with varying levels of literacy, academic experience, and cultural background. The pressures on both the students to comprehend fully their lessons and on the teachers to convey the often complex political theories were daunting. Haywood observed some of the frustrations of working with highly motivated but poorly prepared students. "Harold Williams [Dessalines] of Chicago was a West Indian. . . . Williams had little formal education and some difficulty in grasping theory, but was instinctively a class-conscious guy."[79] However, those who had the most difficulty often were working-class whites and blacks who had not completed secondary education prior to going to the Soviet Union, and significant numbers failed to complete the three-year program of study. By the early 1930s, the Lenin School course of study was adjusted to accommodate different levels of preparedness, including one new program, a "fourteen-month course [involving] ten months plus ten days in classroom work ('theoretical study'), two months of practical work including three days on a collective farm, and fifteen days in party organizational work. Five days were set aside for revolutionary holidays, and assignments came in the fifteenth month."[80]

Settling into the daily life in the 1920s–1930s Soviet Union was challenging from various perspectives. The students had to contend with the weather and antiquated heating systems. They also had to accommodate Russian reactions to their presence. Haywood's autobiography, like the printed accounts of the many other black sojourners, seldom mentioned incidents of Russian-initiated racism, more often pointing to those instances in which foreigners were involved. Furthermore, the sojourners were far more interested in describing how the Russians and Soviet authorities would immediately chastise the perpetrators than in identifying the perpetrators as Russian. For many, the Robinson case stood as a prime example of the authorities' actions.[81]

But this was not always the case, as seen in a report from another black student. "When I was going around the country as a MOPR [International Organization for Aid to the Fighters for Revolution] delegate, in the cafeteria at the Vyshinii-Volochek station, the secretary of the . . . [regional] branch of MOPR came up to me and said, 'What's this? A monkey?'"[82] Not only was the insult hurtful, but the delegate was disappointed that his status in MOPR did not seem to shield him. In other instances, students discovered that people had strange notions of both what a Negro should look like and the language he spoke. "[A] mulatto [student] found greater acceptance in Russia because of his color. Kalmek [a student from a French African colony] said a woman in the KUTV[A] cafeteria had pointed at him and said with a laugh, 'Now that's a Negro.'" Another student was confronted by "people in the street, ignorant even of the existence of African languages, [who jeered] at blacks and asked them to say a few words in 'Negro.'"[83]

It would appear, however, that the demonstrations of racism among the Russians were limited more to verbal insults than to physical action. Blacks such as Robinson were physically assaulted, invariably at the hands of whites from the United States, England, or Canada. Unfortunately, most of the blacks attending KUTVA were also placed in the same section with these students: Section 9, the Anglo-American sector.[84]

Occasionally, students had to prompt the Soviet authorities to act. As a result of student protest, the Executive Committee of the Comintern (ECCI) appointed special commissions to investigate some of these allegations. Padmore, who was a member of the Red International Labor Union (the Profintern) in the late 1920s, was named to one of those ECCI commissions. As McClellan reported, one such investigation "uncovered 'white chauvinism' (i.e. racism) and 'political hooliganism' in the Anglo-American Sector and blamed faculty, staff and the party cell. Mindless prejudice, complicated in some instances by sexual tensions and often fueled by vodka, lay at the root of the hostility." Some of these commissions, balking at the notion that there could be racism in the Soviet Union, admonished the selection committees to do a better job choosing future candidates: "Comintern authorities believed the discipline, education, and more careful selection of students by the American and Canadian Communist parties would extinguish it."[85]

At the conclusion of this particular investigation, several students—both white and black—were expelled from their studies in Moscow, and others were formally censured. Two African Americans, Robert Ross (né Gary Johnson) of Minneapolis and Henry Scott of New York, were among those expelled for "hooliganism." Robert Robinson, who came to know the men while he was a technical specialist in the country, contended that the issue was less a lack of previous political training and more a lack of regular exposure to advanced academic studies. "[When blacks] first came to the Soviet Union searching for social equality and political enlightenment, they were enrolled at . . . KUTVA. [But this] initial experience was difficult for them [Ross and Scott], for reasons having nothing to do with racism in Russia. Neither of them had finished high school in the United States and neither had academic exposure to political theory." They were also "competing [with] graduates of Oxford and Cambridge . . . and American whites who were college-educated. . . . A clique that excluded blacks developed . . . [and] there was an implicit understanding . . . that . . . blacks were genetically inferior."[86]

African students were also occasionally expelled, and most of them returned home. Ross and Scott decided to remain in the Soviet Union however. Continued Robinson, "[They] were unable to return as a failure and face the people in America who had sponsored their trip." Yet, he pointed out, "for the Kremlin propagandists, it was no waste of rubles . . . regardless of how they [African Americans and Africans] were treated or performed. The important thing was the pictures [of blacks]. They could spread the image around the world of Soviet society as a place where blacks and whites studied Marxist-Leninist doctrine together in harmony."[87]

In fact, both men found ways to function in the Soviet Union, despite their lack of success at the political training. Ross, who had no particular skills before he went to the Soviet Union, found a niche as a formal state-paid propagandist. He was employed by the Soviet government to give lectures on U.S. racism and eventually went into acting.[88] Scott, who was a trained dancer, managed to find employment with the Jewish pianist and jazz band leader Alexander Tsfasman. Billed as a lead dancer for the group, Scott stayed in the Soviet Union until 1938.[89]

Pushing for a Sovereign State in the United States

Haywood's Soviet studies and other work in the Soviet Union clearly affected his later nomination to the CPUSA's Politburo, the central policy-making section. Internal Comintern documents stated, "Andre Marty, a French Communist member of the ECCI[,] evaluated the American slate for his Comintern colleagues. . . . [He suggested] that the CPUSA be allowed to substitute a more experienced black leader for [Abner A. V.] Berry. This was done: Harry Haywood became the new candidate member. Haywood, who had lived in Moscow from 1926 to 1930, attended both Moscow's University for the Toilers of the East and the International Lenin School, and become a member of the Soviet Communist party, stood well with the Comintern."[90] Haywood had also been charged with two major campaigns while still in Moscow: to make the case for the Negro Question and to develop support for the idea of setting up a sovereign state for blacks in the United States.[91]

Haywood was initially skeptical of a sovereign state for blacks. "To me, the idea of a Black nation within the U.S. boundaries seemed far-fetched and not consonant with American reality." He remembered that the ABB leadership itself could not agree where it might be located. "Briggs . . . had no definite idea for the location of the future 'colored autonomous state,' suggesting at various times Washington [state], Oregon, Idaho, California or Nevada." Notably, none of these states were in the South, where most blacks lived. Haywood wanted a program of unity with whites. "I saw the solution through the incorporation of Blacks into U.S. society on the basis of complete equality, and only socialism could bring this to pass. . . . [To set up a separate state] was to create new and unnecessary roadblocks to the already difficult path to Black and white unity."[92]

The work on the Negro Question and the CPUSA had its own complications. The Comintern's efforts to elevate the Negro Question had had some success. By 1929, five blacks held high positions in the CPUSA: "Otto Huiswood, Otto Hall, Cyril Briggs, Edward Welsh and John Henry were elected to the new Central Committee [of the Comintern (ECCI)]." Unfortunately, this CPUSA delegation, which was posted to meetings in Moscow and elsewhere abroad, did not necessarily reflect any fundamental change in race relations partywide in the United States. "The line up . . . represented an alliance of convenience and had little to do with ideology. Up to that time there had been no serious discussion in the Party of the Sixth Congress resolution on the Negro Question."[93]

The Negro Question and the Idea of Self-Determination

Toward the end of the 1920s, after encountering several educated and articulate Africans, particularly a cohort from South Africa, segments of the Comintern leadership began to consider taking a direct route to organizing these other people of color. Blakely noted that "by the time of [the] Comintern's Hamburg Conference of Negro Workers in 1930 [the Soviets knew] that they must rely upon African Negroes to lead their own revolution in Africa."[94] The Comintern launched the International Trade Union Committee of Negro Workers (ITUCNW) with Padmore as its secretary. This was "the first attempt to bring together black workers on a world scale. . . . [Its founding conference] was the first time Black workers from Africa and the Americans had gotten together."[95]

This program worried Haywood. First, he saw the ITUCNW drawing Comintern attention away from the struggles of blacks in the United States, and, second, he did not trust Padmore. "At the time I sized him up as a pragmatist with only a superficial grasp of Marxist theory. Politically, he appeared to be a staunch supporter of the fight for independence in Africa and the West Indies, but was adamantly opposed to the right of self-determination for U.S. Blacks."[96] For his part, Padmore, as a former colonial subject, was clearly impatient with the Comintern's two-tier program of training a special cadre of U.S. blacks to be sent to organize colonial peoples elsewhere. "Africans feel that they are quite capable of leading themselves. . . . Africans are quite willing to accept advice and support. . . . But they want to make their way under their own steam."[97] Additionally, he considered the idea of self-determination for U.S. Negroes theoretically and logistically impossible.

Huiswood and Haywood Do Battle

By the latter part of the 1920s, the Negro Question had taken on a certain momentum, and no small part of this development was having Haywood and Huiswood in Moscow to lead the debate. Like Padmore, Huiswood was against the idea of a sovereign state. He contended that it was "absurd to compare the condition of blacks in America to that of blacks in Africa and the West Indies. In those countries, blacks were a majority. They had defined national boundaries and were ruled by an outside European power . . . [while] American blacks were 'racially persecuted,' . . . they were not 'colonially exploited.'"[98] Haywood accused Huiswood of "creating non-existent differences between the position of Negroes in Africa and the West Indies on the one hand and of those in the U.S.A. on the other. . . . The Negroes in the United States are . . . an 'internal colony' of American imperialism." He further contended that American blacks experienced exploitation like colonials. "The fact that the exploitation varies in degree—e.g. the Negroes in the U.S. are not as intensely exploited as for instance the Negroes in the Congo—is due mainly to differences in cultural and economic development between the Negro populations in the two countries and not in the character of their exploitation."[99] Additionally, Haywood warned, "Comrade Huiswoud [sic] in. . . . his article written one year and a half after the Fourth Congress . . . not only revives the opportunist formula 'race' question, but attempts to give it a theoretical basis . . . [placing] himself in direct opposition to the CI [Communist International]."[100] This was a dangerous allegation because any wandering into a discussion of race was politically inflammatory. The search for ways to distinguish issues as they related to black people kept the apologists busy. Race could encompass physical distinctions as far as the color of the skin or type of hair or facial, body shape. It could not be used in the question of nationality or self-determination, which were tied to the historical and political links of a nation-state. Despite this distinction, the Comintern leadership knew that keeping the Negro Question in the discussion was a way to attract blacks to the Soviet experiment.[101]

But many of the planners were caught off guard was just how visceral and divisive the fight over the Negro Question could be. As they came to see, many corresponding Communist groups, such as those in the United States and Britain, did not share the same confidence in blacks. So, while the call for a discussion of the Negro Question attracted progressive blacks, the chauvinist behavior of local parties was not so welcoming. Noted Padmore, "It is a pity that white Communists in Britain and America are not entirely free from racial prejudice. . . . They have done more harm than good to the Soviet cause."[102]

Padmore Does His Sojourn

Padmore was a major figure in the Comintern's efforts to develop support for its Negro Question. Born Malcolm Nurse, Padmore was originally from Trinidad. The son of a schoolmaster, he was highly educated, and, like McKay and Huiswood, he had moved to the United States to further his education.[103] Arriving in 1926, he did undergraduate studies in sociology at Columbia University in New York City and then enrolled in pre-law studies at Fisk, a historically black college in Tennessee. But Padmore, chaffing at the treatment of blacks in the U.S. South, also got into trouble with local whites and was forced to leave Fisk early.[104]

Returning to New York City, he immediately joined the Communist Party and took the pseudonym George Padmore.[105] The party then sent him to Washington, D.C., where he could resume his legal studies at Howard University while continuing his party work.[106] After he was attached to the William Z. Foster campaign, he was selected to join Foster on his 1929 trip to the Soviet Union.

As was the case with Haywood and Huiswood, Padmore's relationship with the Soviets proved greater than the CPUSA or he might have expected. Blakely noted, "Padmore's was a career pattern the Soviet leaders would surely have liked to duplicate many times over."[107] For one, Padmore was more than ready to go to the Soviet Union. Even after discovering that the party had bought only one-way tickets for him and his wife, Padmore was not willing to miss this opportunity to do his sojourn. Furthermore, his wife was not particularly sympathetic to his political goals, and leaving her behind was, apparently, one way to solve that domestic problem.

Once in the Soviet Union, he found himself lauded by the Soviets, virtually overshadowing Foster. Padmore quickly rose in the estimation of the inner circles of the Comintern leadership. Blakely noted that he was also appointed to the Moscow Soviet (the city council) and had an office in the Kremlin. Given the ultimate honor of a place on the reviewing stand in Red Square for May Day 1930, Padmore was happy to indicate to a group of British visitors that such recognition would have been impossible for a black man in Trinidad.[108]

Padmore was added to the executive of the Profintern and sent to Hamburg to serve as the secretary of the ITUCNW's outreach to Negro workers.[109] Padmore's prestige grew as he published a number of articles in the *Moscow Daily* and served as an editor of the ITUCNW's publication the *Negro Worker*. Observed Blakely, "[Padmore was a] pivotal figure for the Soviet policy [in Africa] for what he symbolized as well as for what he did. . . . He and James Ford played guiding roles in the formation of the [ITUCNW] which . . . [promoted] revolution among Negro populations around the world."[110]

Padmore and the Pan-Africanist View

Over time, though, Padmore became impatient with what he saw as Communist paternalism. "What I want is that Marxism and Communism be harnessed into the service of coloured peoples and not coloured peoples into the service of Marxism and Communism."[111] For its part, the Comintern accused him of the cardinal sin of putting advocacy for Negroes above working-class unity.

Despite his disagreements with the Comintern policy, though, Padmore never repudiated Marxism and continued to extol the Soviet experiment's nonracist model. Even as late as the mid-1950s, he still held that "the Russian people are undoubtedly the least colour-conscious white folk in the world. The coloured Soviet Citizens of Central Asia . . . enjoy absolute racial equality with those of Slav descent. . . . The Soviet leaders, whatever may be said against them, treat any manifestation of racial chauvinism with great severity."[112] Padmore's ultimate dissatisfaction—like that which would ultimately sour Haywood and even Huiswood—was that the solidarity they experienced among the Russians while in the Soviet Union was not so evident once they expanded their political activities in the larger global arena. Forced out of Comintern and ITUCNW work in 1934, Padmore's bitter assessment was that "the Russians like the British ruling class have no permanent friends, nor permanent enemies but only permanent interests—namely, the survival of the Soviet Union."[113]

Padmore never returned to the United States. At first he relocated to England. Then, in 1957, at the invitation of Kwame Nkrumah, he moved to Africa to help develop the newly independent Ghana.

Haywood and Ekaterina

As Haywood prepared to leave the Soviet Union in the winter of 1930, he was sobered by the realization that he was leaving his wife of three years behind. He had met Ekaterina (Ina) in 1926 and they married that following spring. But Ina, a ballerina, and Haywood, a student, both with demanding schedules and few options for places to live, did not live together for much of their married life. Ina continued to live with her mother, and Haywood stayed in the university dormitory. Their only time as a couple was on the weekends, which they spent together at Ina's mother's apartment.

Ina brought fresh perspectives to Haywood's life, as he began to experience other aspects of the Soviet experiment with her. "[Ina] introduced me to the cultural life of the Soviet capital. Together we attended theaters, movies, concerts at the Conservatory of Music, and Moscow ballets and operas at the Bolshoi theater."[114] As they planned their future, they knew there might be some difficulties, but Haywood was optimistic. "We had agreed that [our marriage] should not be terminated with my departure. Our idea was that we would eventually get Ina to the States. . . . Of course there would be some difficulties, but to my mind they were not insurmountable. Ina . . . would have little trouble adjusting to a new environment and would be accepted by the black community in any of the urban centers of the north."[115]

Haywood was right in that the Soviet bureaucracy impeded her departure with him in 1930. But when he returned two years later, in 1932, it was not the

Soviets but representatives of the U.S. government who stood in their way. The U.S. authorities were not accommodating, and Haywood was convinced that racism lay behind the objections. Pressing his case with the U.S. officials, "[I was] assisted by my friend William Patterson, then national secretary of the International Labor Defense [in the United States]. We felt the best result was to threaten the immigration authorities with public exposure—it was a clear case of discrimination against a Black man! We enlisted the support of several liberals . . . demanding to know the reasons for the delay. . . . 'Is it because she is white and Mr. Hall is a Negro' they asked."[116] The U.S. authorities claimed they would not allow any Communist into the country, but Haywood was not convinced that the notion of a mixed-race marriage was not even more distasteful. Haywood was never able to bring Ina to the United States, and, eventually, he lost touch with her.[117]

Male-female relations were not always so amicable, though, and, on one occasion, the tensions between male and female almost landed Haywood in severe trouble. He had been sent on a rest trip to the Crimea where he encountered one of the staff persons from the school. "A Russian woman who had worked in the chancellor's office at KUTVA . . . returned from the Crimea and was spreading malicious slander about me. . . . I remember having seen [her] and had greeted her, but paid her no more attention. Perhaps that was the trouble." Although he tried to ignore the rumors and his friends did not seem to mind, his wife began to get nervous. "Ina was afraid the rumors would cause me harm in other quarters." Her instincts were correct as one of the newer black female students was particularly upset. "A few days after the incident, I ran into Marie Houston, a Black KUTVA student from the U.S. Marie had a grudge against me for taking sides against her in her personal disputes with other students. . . . As I was about to pass on she lashed out, 'Hey man, I've been hearing all about your carryings on. . . . What you trying to do, scandalize our name? . . . By the way when you gonna be cleansed? I sure gonna be there!'" "Cleansing" was a communal tribunal in which everyone who studied and worked at KUTVA participated. This process of self-criticism was to "purge from our ranks all noxious elements, factional trouble makers and self-seeking careerists. . . . In other words it was to be a scrutiny of both conduct and conviction." Haywood was called up before the assembled, but he was not censured, as Houston had predicted. "Eventually my turn came. . . . I took the stand and sketched my background and Party experiences, what I got out of study at the school, what I intended to do when I returned home. No one rose to criticize me [and] Marie didn't even show up."[118]

Strengthening the Black Presence in CPUSA

The return to the United States in November 1930 was painful for Haywood. A Russian colleague, Nasanov, had been worried that the difficulties would be mainly within the CPUSA leadership, but it was the Great Depression that truly unnerved Haywood.[119] For the past four and a half years, he had been living in a society that, although it did not have luxury items, offered a life relatively free of drastic disparities. He had safe housing, food, health care, and paid vacations, and all expenses for his studies were covered by the Soviet government. "Everything seemed quite strange. . . . Out in the street I caught a taxi to the national office of the Party, which was then located on East 125th Street in Harlem. I looked at the people along the way. Despair seemed written on their faces; I don't believe I saw a smile all the way uptown. What a contrast to the gay and laughing crowds in Moscow and Leningrad. I had arrived in the first year of the Great Depression; my own depression deepened."[120] At the same time, though, this was an extremely active time for recruiting blacks. Noted Haywood, "Unemployed Councils were built, uniting Blacks and whites. . . . There were marches on city hall and movements against evictions. . . . Harlem was soon to become a powerful center of the Black liberation movement."[121] As Hutchinson added, "The bread and butter issues that directly hit blacks in their pocketbooks were the issues that won over the community and brought [in] fresh recruits."[122]

Dissention in the Ranks

But the unity that had attracted Haywood to the party and that had kept him active through the 1930s, did not last long after World War II.[123] Within four years after his return to the United States, Haywood had risen to the pinnacle of the CPUSA. "I was now a member of the Politburo and head of the National Negro Department."[124] Despite this prominence, it had worried him that his leadership positions were taking him further and further from the masses. One solution was to seek reassignments to outlying districts. But, by 1937, still restless and looking for ways to serve those less fortunate, he requested the party's permission to join the hundred black volunteers in the famous Lincoln Brigades in Spain.[125] He was forty-four at the time. "Why did I go? For me, a communist, Spain was the next logical step. As a black man, I was acutely aware of the threat of fascism. Blacks have always faced the most brutal, racist oppression in the United States, but fascism would mean a heightening of the terror. . . . Finally, I felt the presence of Black communists in Spain would help emphasize the solidarity between the Afro-American and Spanish people in the struggle."[126] The party was not pleased but finally agreed to accommodate him.

For his general livelihood, Haywood chose to work in the merchant marine. This job not only kept him close to ordinary workers but made it possible for him to travel and meet with progressives in other parts of the world. "I knew the history of struggles of the National Maritime Union. . . . The NMU was the largest of all seamen's unions, reaching a membership of about 100,000 during the war. . . . NMU seamen were known as worldwide emissaries of labor . . . [and wherever they docked, they offered] assistance and support."[127]

By the late 1950s, Haywood and the CPUSA leadership had parted ways. "Those of us who had defended the revolutionary position on Black Liberation had been driven from the CP—either expelled or forced to resign."[128] Haywood disagreed with the contention that blacks were being successfully assimilated into the mainstream of the party. "The Party's leaders insisted that Blacks were well on the way to being assimilated into the old reliable American 'melting pot.' This . . . underscored the treacherous depths of the revisionist betrayal. The CPUSA did not even attempt to mobilize labor support for the Black struggle, and the labor aristocracy maintained hegemony over the workers' movement. . . . The melting pot suddenly exploded in their faces." By the 1960s, the slow response to the civil rights efforts, plus the assassinations of John F. Kennedy, Martin Luther King Jr., and Malcolm X, brought blacks to a new boiling point. Again, Haywood accused the CPUSA of being clueless. "The Black Revolt surged up from the Deep South and quickly spread its fury across the entire country. Advancing wave upon wave—with sit-ins, freedom marches, wildcat strikes, and, finally, hundreds of spontaneous insurrections—the Black masses announced to their capitalist masters and the entire world that they would never rest until their chains of bondage were completely smashed."[129]

The party, with which he had worked for so many years and which offered such promise in the 1920s and 1930s, seriously miscalculated how best to keep blacks involved. The CPUSA lost not only Haywood but large segments of black support during the civil rights movement in the 1950s. By the 1960s, the black struggle was swept up in the Black Power movement instead. In summation, a bitter Haywood wrote, "Thus abandoned to the leadership of the chauvinist bureaucracies, sharp divisions were sown between Black and white workers. This was in clear contrast to the unity built by communists in the thirties when the Party and the working class had played a leading role in fighting for the special demands of Blacks, making the Scottsboro Boys a household word from the tenements of New York to the ghettos of Watts."[130]

CHAPTER 4

W.E.B. Du Bois and the Soviet Experiment

ℰℐℐ

[I stood] in astonishment and wonder at the revelation of Russia.[1]
—W.E.B. Du Bois (1926)

"*I*n pregnant language reminiscent of a Protestant Reformation divine," David Levering Lewis recounted, "Du Bois told of standing 'in astonishment and wonder at the revelation of Russia' that had come to him. He might be 'partially deceived and half-informed,' but if what he had seen and heard with his eyes and ears in Russia was Bolshevism, [Du Bois wrote] 'I am a Bolshevik.'"[2] In 1928, two years later, Du Bois reminisced, "I have seen a bit of Russia; just a two month's glimpse of this tremendous land. But what I saw convinced me of certain things: that Russia is earnest." Putting the world on notice, he continued, "[whether] the present Russian Government succeeds or not, the thing that it is trying to do must and will be done sometime if the world continues to progress."[3] In the 1950s, thirty years later, a prescient and still supportive Du Bois wrote, "Without the looming power of the Soviet Union, China would still be under the paws of Britain, France and America. Only the support of the Soviet Union gave Egypt and the Near East, the courage to stand up and defy Western imperialism. And if in the near future, freedom and independence come to Egypt, Tunis, Algeria, Morocco, and British West Africa, it will be principally because one of the greatest nations on earth, having accomplished socialism today, exists and prospers."[4]

Du Bois's initial 1926 sojourn was a revelation. He had never felt more "comfortable and inconspicuous."[5] He was no longer Ralph Ellison's "invisible man" but found himself welcomed as any other human being, despite being a Negro and a minority.[6] In the Soviet Union, he felt he was a part of humanity rather than separate from it, and repeated examples of this new egalitarianism were exhilarating.

In contrast to the perceptions of those who stayed a block of years or who went frequently, Du Bois's view of the Soviet Union was punctuated by his decennial sojourns. Thus, he saw a country shaped by enormous fluctuations in its evolution. His visits placed him in the Soviet Union at the height of Lenin's

NEP prosperity in 1926;[7] in the early stages of the Stalinist purges and prewar climate of 1936; in a country still recuperating from the devastation of World War II in 1949; and at a time of relative ease under Khrushchev's "peaceful co-existence" policy in 1958 and 1959. Each time, despite having to adjust to new realities, Du Bois continued to find much to admire. As he commented after his 1949 visit, "I spent ten days in Moscow and sensed the substance and reality of what we call the Soviet Republics beginning to take definite form. I do not yet know this land in any scientific sense of the word. But in the three visits in 23 years I have a sort of spectroscopic roundness of conception and sense of time which replaced figures."[8]

Prior to his first trip in 1926, Du Bois had heard from progressives, both white and black, that the Soviet experiment was worth studying. Such figures as Bertrand Russell, H. G. Wells, Lincoln Steffens, and Max Eastman were calling attention to it. Briggs and McKay had made visits there and were encouraging others to do so as well. Du Bois read the accounts in the *Crusader*, the *Masses*, and the *Liberator* and had accepted McKay's proposal to submit pieces for the *Crisis*.[9] Also, as would happen to Robeson in England, Du Bois came across African delegates at the Pan-African congresses there, who also pointed to the developments in the new Soviet Russia.[10]

Initially skeptical, he found it hard to believe that a program that had come about through a violent revolution could bring positive change for blacks. He published a series of cautionary pieces in the *Crisis* in the early 1920s: "Negro and Radical Thought" (July 1921), "The Spread of Socialism" (September 1921), and "Socialism and the Negro" (October 1921.)[11] He also questioned the Soviets' ability to move beyond their racial animosities. "Russia is incredibly vast, and the happenings there in the last five years had been intricate to a degree that must make any student pause. . . . [But] how far can the colored people of the world, and particularly the Negroes of the United States, trust the [white] working classes?"[12] Yet Du Bois could not continue to ignore the fervor of others he admired, nor get the best of his own curiosity. One such tempting testimonial came from James C. Jackson in 1924.[13]

> This letter comes from a village deep in the heart of Russia. I am an American Negro, a native of the South, here in Russia making a study of social conditions. The above named village is the seat of the summer colony of the University of the Toilers of the East [KUTVA], located at Moscow. I have been invited from Moscow to this colony as a guest. One must visit Russia to understand and appreciate the many beautiful social developments. . . . There is a perfect spirit of internationalism here. . . . Here in Russia the desire for information concerning the Negro is fervent. There is no race of which knowledge is sought with such eagerness as of the Negro. I am kept busy writing articles for newspapers and magazines both in Russia and Ukrainia [the Ukraine] and giving lectures. . . . I have been much pleased to know that your little book,

"The Negro," and Rene Maran's novel, "Batoula" have been much read
in student circles here.[14]

Although leaning toward the idea of a sojourn, the pragmatic Du Bois did not
rush to make his first visit. Like McKay, he felt he needed additional preparation
and, in particular, an increased understanding of Marxism. He began a serious
study of Karl Marx's and Friedrich Engels's writings, and the more he read, the
more he wanted to see how Marxism was being applied in the new Soviet Russia. His attitude began to change, and by the end of 1925, Du Bois himself countered criticism of the Soviet experiment by noting that the Soviets were "trying
to do a great and wonderful thing for the economic organization of industry."[15]

There was also the question of his role as a progressive leader. He was
now fifty-eight, and the stature he had attained from spending decades in the
fight for the rights of blacks was beginning to wane by the middle of the 1920s.
Younger blacks, such as Briggs, McKay, and Asa Phillip Randolph, were attracting increased attention. The *Liberator*, an openly partisan publication, portrayed Du Bois as having "sneered" at the Russian revolution, further tarnishing
his image.[16]

As luck would have it, Du Bois acquired an anonymous benefactor, whom
he described only as someone at whose feet he sat when learning about the
Soviet experiment. Du Bois was already making plans to visit Switzerland and
Germany, but with this extra encouragement he agreed to extend his journey to
include a visit to the Soviet Union. He no doubt looked forward to his return to
Germany because he retained fond memories from his days as a student in the
1890s. But this experience would stand in stark contrast to that which he would
witness in the Soviet Union. Germany was also shockingly different from the
Germany of his student days, thirty years before, in 1892 and 1893, when he had
done advanced studies at the Kaiser Fredrick Wilhelm (later Humboldt) University in Berlin.[17] Now, he saw the German people "struggling on the ruins of the
empire" as they wrestled with the economic devastation of the 1923–1924 period.[18] Presaging the effects of the Great Depression in the United States, which
would strike five years later, the people seemed to have no hope.

Conversely, this was the third year of strong economic growth in the Soviet Union, and the peasants on through a rising middle class seemed to be ben-
efiting from the contacts with foreign businesses and new industries. Du Bois
was swept up by the energy around him. "Russia is at work. . . . God how these
officials work! . . . Here was a people seeking a new way of life through learning and truth."[19] Du Bois spent a month in Moscow and a second month split
among the provincial cities of Nizhny Novgorod, Kiev, and Odessa. Returning
to his desk at the *Crisis*, he published the first of his laudatory pieces, "Russia
in 1926."[20]

Plunged back into life in the United States, Du Bois was not able to visit
the Soviet Union for another ten years. This was a difficult time for him. Not
only had he returned to Jim Crow, but, with the rise of the Great Depression, he

felt pressed to show how Marxist analysis could provide logical explanations for the failure of capitalism. He was equally frustrated with the apparent inability of the NAACP (National Association for the Advancement of Colored People) to provide people a with "positive program of construction and inspiration." Having resigned from his editorship of the *Crisis* and from the board of directors, he turned his energies to giving courses at Atlanta University. Teaching one of these courses, Karl Marx and the Negro, was decidedly more satisfying than working with the NAACP.[21] Although he maintained his faith in Marxism and the Soviet experiment over these years, thanks to periodic accounts from other blacks who traveled there, he did not have as much confidence in the U.S. Communist Party. As he wrote in a letter to George Streator, "I am . . . bitterly opposed to the American brand of communism which simply aims to stir up trouble and to make Negroes shock troops in a fight whose triumph may easily involve the annihilation of the American Negro . . . while at the same time, I regard Russia as the most promising modern country."[22]

The Scottsboro Test

That the CPUSA won the contest for the hearts and minds of the black community over the Scottsboro case was particularly painful for Du Bois to bear.[23] To his mind, this was a prime example of CPUSA opportunism, despite the fact that an African American, William L. Patterson, played a central role in pressing the case.[24] A 1931 piece, "The Negro and Communism," detailed his opinions:

> The Scottsboro, Alabama, cases have brought squarely before the American Negro the question of his attitude toward Communism. The importance of the Russian Revolution can not be gainsaid. It is easily the greatest event in the world. . . . Russia occupies the center of the world's attention today and as a state it is recognized by every civilized nation, except the United States, Spain, Portugal and some countries of South America . . . [but] the ultimate object of the [U.S.] Communists, was naturally not merely nor chiefly to save the boys[;] . . . it was to make this case a center of agitation to expose the helpless condition of Negroes and to provide that anything less than the radical Communist program could not emancipate them.[25]

A large part of the problem was the role of agency. It rankled Du Bois, as it did Haywood, that the imbedded racism among the CPUSA leaders prevented them from recognizing the true abilities of blacks. Du Bois was certain that the leadership and energy for social change could come from within black ranks.

Still, as Lewis pointed out, the NAACP and the CPUSA response to the Scottsboro accusations could not have been more different, a fact that also troubled Du Bois. The NAACP suffered from bureaucratic lethargy and political elitism, and its leadership had equivocated on whether and how best it should

represent the boys. "Defending nine unlettered black males, whose questionable character seemed self-evident, against a charge of gang-raping two white
women in the Deep south was hardly an inviting prospect. . . . [NAACP Director
Walter] White, officially appointed as James Weldon Johnson's successor only
two weeks before the trials, regarded the Scottsboro Boys as more of a risk than
an opportunity."[26] The CPUSA leadership, however, through the ILD, immediately plunged in with its considerable resources.

William Pickens, despite his position as NAACP field secretary, was impressed as well. Noted Lewis, "Pickens praised the Communists for 'moving
[more] speedily and effectively than all other agencies put together,' and went on
to urge 'every Negro who has intelligence' to send contributions to the *Worker*
and the ILD."[27] Although Pickens was forced to recant and the NAACP engaged
in a massive smear campaign to cast doubt on the ILD and its leaders' intentions, grassroots support for the ILD flowed in.[28] Solidarity parades of whites
and blacks were held in major industrial centers, and editorials were published
in major black papers.[29] People were no less powerfully swayed by hearing from
the mother of Eugene Williams, one of the Scottsboro Boys, that "we are not too
ignorant to know a bunch of liars and fakers when we meet up with them and we
are not too ignorant to know that if we let the NAACP look after our boys, that
they will die."[30]

Du Bois himself was disappointed that the NAACP was spending so much
time fighting the CPUSA and ILD and was not devoting enough to the Scottsboro case. He had to admit as well that the CPUSA was the only national party
that was making efforts to include Negroes. Neither of the two mainstream political parties, Democrats or Republicans, were doing so.[31]

The Quest Stretches across Europe and into Asia

Du Bois's second sojourn to Soviet Russia, in 1936, was financed in part
by a grant from the Oberlander Trust of Philadelphia. The trust had been set
up four years earlier to promote cultural exchanges between the United States
and German-speaking nations. Ostensibly, Du Bois was to study industrial educational models in Europe and to compare them with Booker T. Washington's
philosophy. But he had more ambitious plans.

Du Bois's previous cautiousness was replaced by a general impatience,
and his pieces in the *Crisis* had become increasingly strident. The board of the
publication moved to censor his work. White complained that a January 1934
editorial by Du Bois "was contrary to NAACP policy, [and] highly embarrassing
to the association in its efforts to persuade the Roosevelt administration toward
positive action in regard to the Black people of the nation." In July 1934, Du Bois
responded, "It seems to me a good deal better to do my talking unattached."[32]

Freed from the restrictions of NAACP policies, Du Bois approached his
next trip to Europe and Asia with fresh expectations. Besides Germany and
Austria, he looked forward to seeing "the Towers of the Kremlin and the black

waters of the Volga, the plains of Genghis Khan, the great Wall of China."[33] He planned to visit additional parts of the Soviet Union and to see China and Japan, and he thought he should do a comparative analysis of fascism, communism, and democracy. As he wrote publisher Alfred Harcourt, on his return, "I want . . . to compare . . . the means and methods by which governments today are trying to face new problems of work and wage, income and wealth . . . and draw into the picture the colored peoples of the world; the people of China, Japan, and India, and the peoples of Africa."[34] The book was never written, but some of Du Bois's observations appeared in the popular press, such as in his weekly column "A Forum of Fact and Opinion" in the *Pittsburgh Courier* and in the *Negro Digest*. Other observations appeared in scholarly publications, such as the *Journal of Negro Education* and the *American Journal of Sociology*.[35]

Again, the stop in Germany proved problematic. Du Bois had expected to procure his visa for the Soviet Union in Berlin as before, but relations between the Soviets and Hitler had become strained. Having discovered that no visa was forthcoming, he fretted that he was not going to have the time to do research in the Soviet Union. As Lewis noted, "The sole concession [made by the Soviets] was a brief stop in Moscow and permission to transit the Soviet Union."[36] Du Bois did not know that his Soviet contact, Karl Radek, to whom he had been directed by the black expatriate columnist William Burroughs, then living in Moscow, had been caught in the first wave of Stalin's purges.[37] Radek, who was now under suspicion and soon to be discredited, was not in a position to serve as Du Bois's intermediary.

Several groups of blacks had gone to the Soviet Union by now, from technicians and agricultural specialists to artists and intellectuals.[38] Du Bois had looked forward to seeing the country from both his and their perspectives. Instead, Moscow was just a brief way-station for him, as the authorities quickly passed him through the country in first-class accommodations on a Trans-Siberian train to Asia.

Lewis noted that this brief stay also shielded Du Bois from some of the less pleasant signs of changes in the country, such as the purges. "Permitted a short sojourn . . . Du Bois would have seen nothing to prevent his sharing Hughes' impatience with the critics of the Russian experiment." Instead, writing of his brief visit, Du Bois "applauded the Soviet program, which had made of the working people of the world 'a sort of religion,' a form of scientific idealism he posited as being indispensable to progress."[39] Du Bois formed this positive assessment despite the fact that he was not able to meet with those he hoped to see in Moscow or elsewhere and despite the fact that throughout the long, six-thousand-mile journey to the east his experiences were enclosed by train windows. As he described the lengthy journey, he saw views that were "endlessly varied images of the startling, the bleak, the dull, and the awe-inspiring" and had conversations with his traveling companions in which they "communed over drinks and discussed life and politics as the November gales howled and the lights of the diner reflected against streaming snows."[40] The brief pass-through journey of 1936 ended with a quiet crossing of the Mongolian border and a continuation onto elaborate programs in China and Japan.[41]

Reflecting on that journey almost ten years later, Du Bois still waxed poetic, however. In a 1949 article published in *Soviet Russia Today*, he wrote, "We came to Irkutsk in the black mist of early morning. . . . Baikal is a jewel hung in space at that fateful spot where Europe becomes Asia and where the waters part to make Pacific and Atlantic. Behind is Russia and Europe; before is Russia and China. Here meet the Past, the Present, and What Will Be."[42]

Pan-Africanism and Peace in a Postwar World

Du Bois's 1949 visit to the Soviet Union came about under quite different circumstances. He had been enticed back into the NAACP to head the Department of Special Research, which had been specifically set up for him. Du Bois considered his new duties to be "to collect facts and documents, and arrange statements, articles and booklets, concerning the people of Africa and their descendants, and concerning other colored races, so as gradually to form a body of knowledge and literature, designed to educate the world in matter[s] of race and cultural relations." He was also actively engaged in the peace movement, which, to his mind was a logical venue in which to continue the fight for the rights of blacks. With the victory over fascism came a resurgence of nationalist impulses in the colonial nations and a heightened civil rights activism against Jim Crow in the United States. As he noted, his "initial work in this direction will be the preparation of material to be presented to the Peace Conference or Conferences after the close of this war in behalf of the peoples of Africa and other colored groups so as to demand for them an assured status of security and progress in the post-war world."[43]

Long an internationalist, Du Bois had been the convener of a series of Pan-African congresses from 1919 to 1927, which drew people from various parts of the world. He was approached again in 1944 to call for a new Pan-African congress. "I am writing to . . . Mr. Max Yergan and Mrs. [Amy Jacques] Garvey [widow of the late Marcus Garvey] asking each if they would join me as conveners of a Fifth Pan-African Congress to meet in London. . . . I do not insist upon "Pan African" but suggested it merely to indicate a certain continuity in our efforts since the First World War."[44] This 1945 gathering in Manchester, England, attracted representatives from Nigeria, the Gold Coast, Sierra Leone, Gambia, Jamaica, Trinidad, Barbados, British Guiana, and other colonies, as well as from the United States and Europe. Padmore was actively engaged in the conference logistics, as was Kwame Nkrumah, who would become the president of Ghana in 1957.[45]

Du Bois's Pan-Africanism and peace efforts were coming together. He was invited to join the National Council of Arts, Sciences, and Professions (ASP) in their peace campaign in early 1948. In March 1949, he spoke at their Cultural and Scientific Conference for World Peace in New York.[46] The ASP leadership also asked him to represent the organization at the World Congress of Peace that was to be held in Paris in the next month. Speaking in the Paris stadium in April, Du Bois stated, "Let us not be misled. . . . Leading this new colonial imperialism comes my own native land, built by my father's toil and blood, the United States. . . . Drunk with power, we are leading the world to hell in a new colonialism with the same old human slavery which ruined us; and to a Third World War which will ruin the world."[47]

The denouncement of U.S. policy would eventually come at high cost to Du Bois, as it would to Robeson, who also addressed that international gathering. Further damage occurred a short time later when Du Bois, called before the U.S. House Committee on Foreign Affairs, steadfastly insisted that "the real enemy was not Russia and communism but 'soulless and utterly selfish corporate wealth.'"[48]

While the ASP and Du Bois were under suspicion by the U.S. government, the ASP attracted interest on the other side of the Cold War divide. Invited to send a representative to Moscow for the all-Soviet conference on peace in August of that same year, Du Bois quickly volunteered to go on its behalf. "I did not hesitate. It seemed the opportunity of a lifetime."[49]

The only American in attendance, Du Bois reiterated his views before a crowd of six thousand. He warned that the United States was playing a damaging role in world affairs. Conversely, it thrilled him to see the many, diverse people who had gathered in support of these efforts in the Soviet Union. "The crowd was a sight to make one bend forward and stare. Not that it was bizarre or especially strange, but it represented a nation, a new nation, a new world."[50] A more sobering contrast was drawn out later in a piece entitled "Russia: An Interpretation," which Du Bois published in *Soviet Russia Today*. "There in Moscow [I met] 1,000 representatives from all ends and every race in Russia, to say that peace for Russia was not a theory but a grim necessity. Fourteen nations joined them in this demand, but only one American represented our 140 million people. It is a distinction which neither I nor the rest of America enjoyed." And, striking directly at the heart of the anti-Communist smears, Du Bois pointedly noted, "The Soviets started a generation ago, with a population too ignorant and inexperienced to run a state, much less a state capable of conducting modern industry. It started with a dictatorship, but a dictatorship of the proletariat, under the leadership of the Communist Party, which can in no way be equated with the dictatorship of Hitler, . . . to defend this state against an organized and powerful Europe determined to overthrow it by any and all means. . . . That it succeeded so far as it has gives one renewed faith in mankind."[51]

Treasonable Acts

These and similar acts were deemed treasonable by the U.S. government. Du Bois and the new Peace Information Committee (PIC) he chaired were notified that they must register as agents "of a foreign principal in the United States" under the Foreign Agents Registration Section. Initially sent notices on August

11, 1949, they managed to delay the action through a series of maneuvers in the fall. However, it was only a matter of time before the authorities would act forthrightly. U.S. officials were furious at Du Bois's international prominence and equally furious at the positive responses to a PIC petition drive. Although thousands of signatures had been collected, Secretary of State Dean Acheson called the drive "a propaganda trick in the spurious 'peace offensive' of the Soviet Union."[52] In February 1950, the Justice Department indicted Du Bois and the other officers of PIC as foreign agents, and, from February to November, Du Bois was locked in a new battle.

The campaign to bring Du Bois and the PIC down underscored another difference between the United States and the Soviet Union when dealing with the color line. Du Bois, who was treated with the greatest civility and housed in the most comfortable accommodations in the Soviet Union and Europe, was now fighting the case of his life in a segregated Washington, D.C. As Lewis noted, the Dunbar Hotel was the "single habitable hostelry available to people of color." None of the other better hotels would accept blacks. But the legal team from New York, not to speak of Du Bois's codefendants from the PIC, included a number of whites. Du Bois had also engaged two local black attorneys because he recognized the importance of having them on the defense team and because the New York attorneys were not registered to practice in D.C. As Du Bois could not stay in the other hotels, he and his white legal team had to stay at the Dunbar. "The New York attorneys and three of the defendants had arrived at the Dunbar not yet realizing the full Jim Crow implications of an extended stay in Washington. To continue the battle for peace and justice from two separate and unequal locations would have amounted to a preposterous mockery of principles. In violation of local ordinances, then, the Dunbar management agreed to house the interracial defendants."[53]

The *United States v. Peace Information Center* defendants were acquitted in November 1949. "The [foreign agents registration] act was attacked under the due process clause on the ground that its provisions are not sufficiently definite to establish and formulate an ascertainable standard of guilt."[54] But this was only a temporary victory, as the subsequent McCarthy trials wreaked havoc on Du Bois's livelihood. Support for the Soviet experiment and the calls for world peace and racial equality all seemed to be an abomination to U.S. officialdom.

Du Bois published *In Battle for Peace* in 1952 for the same reasons that Robeson issued *Here I Stand* in 1958: both were determined to set the record straight. Pilloried for their support of the Soviet experiment, they had their passports revoked from 1951 to 1958, and they were prevented from traveling to other countries. Domestically, the U.S. government's slander campaign included terror and intimidation to keep people away from them. This campaign affected not only their ability to support themselves but their access to others. This was a major concern for both, particularly as it threatened their ties to the black community.

Black conservatives and institutions canceled Du Bois's lecture tours, and no institution wished to be associated with a possible enemy of the government.

Observed Lewis, "[Du Bois's] own Talented Tenth hesitated, cogitated, and then decided in the main to keep a safe distance—notwithstanding notable exceptions." Expressions of solidarity did not totally evaporate. Du Bois found support from the progressive white community and growing numbers of blacks who were not generally included among the traditional elites. They willingly lent their names to protest documents and arranged alternative lecture tours. Lewis continued, "If representative Negroes were in short supply for the Du Bois cause, those who did not fit the classic Talented Tenth profile began to show their support. . . . Joining with the left, blacks and whites, labor, students, and church people united in their support."[55]

Heartened and unrepentant, Du Bois published a piece in the *New World Review* entitled "Colonialism and the Russian Revolution," reminding his readers of the important role the Soviet experiment had played in the freeing of many former colonial nations. "The Russian Revolution was the greatest event in the first half of the twentieth century. . . . We could wish that all men who in blood and tears have helped raise mankind out of the gutter had been scholars and gentlemen. But usually they have not been. . . . Even if their effort to raise the many has been sustained by the oppression of the few, we thank God that . . . they accomplished as much as they did."[56]

In June 1958, the U.S. Supreme Court handed down the landmark ruling in the *Kent, Rockwell v. Dulles* and *Briehl, Walter v. Dulles* cases. Both men had sued when their passports were withheld, alleging that doing so infringed on their Bill of Rights freedoms.[57] The lower courts had supported the Justice Department's requirement; however, the Supreme Court did not. In a 5–4 decision, the highest court decreed that the withholding of passports of any U.S. citizen because of his or her political beliefs was unconstitutional.[58] Furthermore, the "Red Scare" had already lost its ferocity with Senator Joseph McCarthy's own political censure in 1954, and, by the mid-1950s, Cold War tensions had also abated considerably. Thus, the court's decision came at a time when national sentiments had already changed.

There were other signs that change was in the air. Hundreds of tributes flooded into Du Bois's ninetieth birthday celebration at the Roosevelt Hotel in New York in March 1958. A short year before, people had been avoiding him, and yet this event attracted over a thousand celebrants. A month later, when he was invited to address students and faculty at the historically black Howard University, they heard the ninety-one-year-old Du Bois say, "Today, the United States is fighting world progress, . . . progress which must be towards socialism and against colonialism."[59]

Du Bois Returns to the Global Community

Within two months after the Supreme Court decision in June 1958, Du Bois applied for and received his new passport, and he immediately set off on a fresh global tour to Europe, the Soviet Union, and China. He was eager to visit China, which had undergone its own political revolution in the intervening years. First, he liked the idea that the Chinese were also people of color who suffered discrimination and thought they would feel solidarity with other oppressed people of color. Second, the Chinese experiment, like the Soviet experiment, might provide models that newly independent African nations could implement in their own societies. "Today . . . one Socialist state [the Soviet Union] is in many respects the most powerful member of the United Nations and cannot be ignored. A second Socialist state [the People's Republic of China] is only temporarily excluded. . . . Socialism is growing in other parts of the world at an irresistible rate. With such Socialist states and the education they promote, the peace which is their goal and the morality toward which economic justice opens the way, a world state would gradually be realized."[60]

The Soviets were particularly pleased to have Du Bois's support and had regularly published articles by and about him. He was awarded the prestigious International Lenin Prize in 1958. They had also published Russian translations of many of his works, some of which, as Kate Baldwin noted, were published in the Soviet Union before they came out in the West.[61] Thus, when Du Bois arrived in the Soviet Union in 1958, he returned as a familiar guest.

This visit included an invitation to the week-long African and Asian Writers Conference in Tashkent. Du Bois was finally able to see the Soviet experiment at work in Soviet Asia. He also met two other key people there: Robeson and Lily Golden. Robeson was there for the opening ceremonies of the concurrent event, the International Festival of African and Asian films. Lily was the daughter of the black expatriate Oliver Golden, part of the agricultural specialist team that had been sent to Uzbekistan to help rebuild the Soviet cotton industry. In fact, the location of these festivals in Uzbekistan was no accident. This was a region where, as Hughes put it, "the colored citizens lived";[62] the Soviets understood the importance of having blacks and other peoples of color see the improvements made in this formerly backward region.

Returning to Moscow, Du Bois was swept up in official activities for the next several months. He and his wife, Shirley, were given places of honor as they sat next to Khrushchev for the November 7th ceremonies celebrating the Russian revolution. Du Bois began work on a Russian edition of his John Brown biography and other publications.

Du Bois's private meetings with Khrushchev were also fruitful. His interpreter noted that their second session "went splendidly, just the four of them in the premier's private office in the Kremlin with talk of novels and Russian geography."[63] The two-hour discussion was so cordial that Du Bois managed to persuade Khrushchev to set up an Africa Institute in the prestigious Soviet Academy of Sciences. Continued the interpreter, "Du Bois explained the need for the creation of an institute for African studies in the Soviet Academy of

Sciences with a learned clarity that was equally impressive. At the end of the two hours, Khrushchev announced that the African institute would be authorized immediately." [64] This was a key step in Du Bois's continuing efforts to unite the Soviet experiment with African freedom. As Gerald Horne noted, Du Bois "was a friend of the Soviet Union because he saw it alone among the big powers as rendering concrete aid, military and otherwise, to the colonized and semicolonized world."[65] In a 1959 article in *New Times*, Du Bois wrote, "The problem of education in Africa is beset with quite a few difficulties. It is not that the Africans are not eager for knowledge or lack ability. . . . Providing opportunities for higher education to young Africans is of major importance. . . . I am often asked what road Africa will follow. My belief is that [it must] inevitably move towards socialism."[66]

The Soviet scholarship program bringing in large groups of African students was clearly one response. Another was the establishment of the Africa Institute in 1959. Baldwin noted, "[Du Bois] suggested that the academy 'establish a course of cooperative international and interracial study' and aim 'at the promotion of scientific research into all the activities, past and present of the peoples of Africa, in cultural, political and economic organizations; together with a simultaneous study of their physical, psychological and biological environment; their work in literature and art and in all human accomplishment.'" The Soviets placed the well-known Africanist Ivan Potekhin at the head and Du Bois and Potekhin began a series of collaborations. In a May 1960 letter, Potekhin reiterated the Soviet commitment to supporting Du Bois's work, noting, "the Encyclopedia [Africana] should become an enterprise of international scale, and the center of the whole work should be in Africa, preferably Ghana, and the control and coordination of the efforts should be placed in the hands of Africans."[67]

This same Africa Institute also tied Du Bois to the Afro-Russian expatriate community in Moscow. Khanga suggested that her mother's presence in Tashkent and later, in Moscow, may have influenced Du Bois's decision to press for the Africa Institute at that particular time. "Dr. Du Bois was a friend of my grandfather [Oliver Golden] and he was talking with twenty-two-year-old Lily about her future on the day before he was scheduled to drop by the Kremlin for a chat with Premier Nikita Khrushchev."[68] After spending some time with Lily and the Robesons in Tashkent, all of them returned to Moscow. Later, when Du Bois fell ill trying to keep up with the hectic pace, Lily was happy to take her new boss, Professor Ivan Potekhin, to meet him while he was recuperating. "Dr. Du Bois was hospitalized in Barvicha Government Sanatorium, outside Moscow. He was weak, but they [Potekhin and Du Bois] were able to maintain a conversation. . . . So freely did they relate to each other that it seemed as if they were old friends renewing a long conversation."[69]

But perhaps the culmination of that momentous year was Du Bois's recovery and ability to join in the festivities at Khrushchev's New Year's celebration at the Kremlin along with Robeson and his wife.[70] It had been an arduous, but fruitful journey for both.

Du Bois and the Chinese Experiment

Du Bois's interest in the Soviet experiment carried over into a curiosity about the work the Chinese were doing, and he was looking forward to his February 1959 visit. He knew that this would be a different country from the one he saw in 1936. During that earlier trip, he had met Generalissimo Chiang Kai-shek, who was leading the Nationalist fight against the Communist forces. Now, so many decades later, he would be the guest of Chou En-lai, the premier and foreign minister in Chairman Mao Tse-Tung's (Zedong's) Communist People's Republic of China.

In the China of 1936, he was treated with great hospitality, but "[never] had he experienced such extremes of wealth and poverty, of refinement and degradation—all of it based on an inexhaustible supply of cheap labor. 'Three things attract white Europe to China. . . . Cheap women; cheap child labor; cheap men.'" China's subordinate status had angered him. Speaking to a carefully selected group formed at his request, he described his past and provided an outline of U.S. race relations. He also "plunged in recklessly," asking, "What did these distinguished men of affairs and arbiters of culture and information intend to do about European hegemony. . . . 'But how do you propose to escape from the domination of European capital? How are your working classes progressing?'"[71] To his mind, the China of 1936 faced a troubled future.

The China of 1959 was dramatically different. Although his visit was as carefully scripted as his first, Du Bois saw "a fable of disciplined bees working in revolutionary unison. Cataloging the public places, restaurants, homes of officials, factories, and schools visited," he saw only "happy people with faith that needs no church or priest." Du Bois called it the "the vast miracle of China today," which had been transformed under Mao's leadership.[72] He shared this enthusiasm in a piece of the same name in the June 1959 issue of the *National Guardian*.[73]

The Chinese overwhelmed him with their graciousness during his two months there. Chou En-lai celebrated Du Bois's February 23rd birthday by hosting a private party at his home. He also declared February 23rd a national holiday and invited Du Bois to address the students at famed Pekin (Beijing) University. Du Bois loved such platforms. Taking the podium, he said, "By courtesy of the government of the 680 million people of the Chinese Republic, I am permitted on my 91st birthday to speak to the people of China and Africa and through them to the world. . . . Hail humankind!"[74]

Du Bois knew that his remarks were being broadcast to Africa and overheard by the Western spy networks. Thus, he took full advantage of the opportunity to point to the new social models being constructed in China. Acknowledging that the Chinese were also people of color and had been discriminated against, Du Bois continued, "One thing alone I own and that is my soul. Ownership of that I have even while in my own country for near a century I have been nothing but a 'nigger.' On this basis alone . . . Speak, China, and tell your truth to Africa and to the world. What people have been [as] despised as you have? Who more than you have been rejected of men?. . . Tell this to Africa, for today African stands on new feet, with new eyesight, with new brains and asks: 'where am I and why.'"[75]

During that 1959 tour, Du Bois was also given the special honor of a visit with Chairman Mao. These two old warriors debated the future of blacks in the United States and "the primacy of economics and psychology among evolving groups." As Lewis continued, "When the Chairman presumed to explain at some length the 'diseased psychology' affecting the American Negro, Du Bois interjected to say that Negroes and the working people of his country were not afflicted by a psychological condition but by their lack of income." Mao continued by asking numerous questions, and, after responding to them, Du Bois said that he regretted having failed at some of his projects on behalf of African America. But Mao disagreed, "Shaking his head, [he] told Du Bois that a man's only mistake is to lie down and let the enemy walk over him. 'This, I gather, you have never done. You have continued the struggle for your people, for all the decent people of America.'"[76]

In the early 1960s, Du Bois decided it was time to use his remaining energies to help with African independence. He accepted Nkrumah's invitation to come to Ghana and looked forward to pursuing his *Encyclopedia Africana* project.[77] He also formally joined the Communist Party on the eve of his departure for Africa in 1961. He did begin his prodigious project, but he died two years later, in 1963, at age ninety-five.

Throughout his latter years, Du Bois continued to press for alliances with socialist nations. At the same time, though, he cautioned that these relationships were partnerships in nation building and required mutual respect:

> Africa does not ask alms from China nor from the Soviet Union. . . .
> It asks friendship and sympathy and no nation better than China can offer this to the Dark Continent. Let it be given freely and generously. Let Chinese visit Africa, send their scientists there and their artists and writers. Let Africa send its students to China and its seekers after knowledge. It will not find on earth a richer goal, a more promising mine of information. . . . Visit the Soviet Union and visit China. Let your youth learn the Russian and Chinese languages. Stand together in this new world and let the old world perish. . . . Listen to the Hebrew prophet of communism.[78]

In the final analysis, for Du Bois, the Soviet and later the Chinese experiments contained laudable examples for new societies. As he told his readers in *In Battle for Peace*, "I also respect and admire the Union of Socialist Republics.

I regard that land as today the most hopeful nation on earth, not because of its theory, but because of what it has accomplished. It has in a generation raised hundreds of millions of debased serfs out of illiteracy, superstition and poverty to self-respecting, hard working manhood. . . . If American Negroes had had half the chance of the Russians to learn to read, write and count, there would be no Negro question today."[79]

PART II

❧

The Technical and Agricultural Specialists

CHAPTER 5

Robert Robinson and the Technical Specialists

୧୪୬

The shop was my laboratory. . . . I enjoyed our
accomplishments, and the respect of my peers.[1]
—Robert Robinson (1988)

"*I*n 1930 I was twenty-three years old and I had been working at Ford for three years. . . . Then in April 1930, it happened. The Russians arrived. . . . They stopped near my machine [and] a young man approached and began speaking to me in very thickly accented English. . . . I did not know why they were speaking to me, and felt uncomfortable. I wished they would go away and leave me to my work. When the young man asked me if I was willing to go to Russia to teach young apprentices the toolmaking trade, I said, 'Sure,' thinking they . . . would stop bothering me." A few months later, after having decided to take up the offer, Robinson found himself steaming into Leningrad's harbor. "It was a gorgeous spring day. . . . The sun was shining brightly. . . . My spirits were high, and I felt like the weather was a good omen, telling me that my hasty decision [had] been a good one."[2]

Robinson had joined thousands of U.S. specialists, white and black, who accepted Soviet contracts. Part of a massive Soviet program to import the expertise to reconstruct its industrial base, these economic sojourners were happy to leave the Great Depression behind for the prospect of good pay and a "workers' paradise." Homer Smith, another black sojourner of the 1930s, observed that "one of the great paradoxes of this achievement was that Capitalism was providing enormous amounts of machinery and a large number of engineers and technicians. . . . Ships arriving at Leningrad, Odessa and Vladivostok were loaded to capacity with the finest and most modern capitalist machinery. Foreign engineers and technicians were pouring in from America, Germany, England, France, and Italy to lend their knowledge and skills to strengthening the foundations of Communism."[3] Robinson was in the tool-and-die industry, but there were other kinds of black specialists, such as broadcast specialist Williana Burroughs and civil engineers like Bernard Powers, and there was Smith, who was at one point a postal-systems specialist.[4] For the black sojourners, the Soviet promise held out an additional inducement: finding a place where Jim Crow would not rule their lives. Like Robinson, all were looking for a chance to feel "comfortable . . . less pressured . . . more accepted for what I was, a human being whose skin happened to be dark."[5]

Welcoming International Technical Support

As early as 1918, Lenin set the stage for inviting specialists to help build the new Soviet Russian economy. Calling on his political compatriots, he stated that the country still needed these highly trained people, whom he termed "bourgeois specialists." "Do not fear using 'bourgeois specialists.' . . . Without the guidance of experts in various fields of knowledge, technology, and experience, the transition to socialism will be impossible, because socialism calls for a conscious mass advance to greater production of labor compared with capitalism and on the basis achieved by capitalism." He was even willing to go so far as to break some of the basic tenets of socialism, acknowledging that the state might have to pay these specialists at higher rates than it paid ordinary workers.[6] Initially successful, this highly controversial plan attracted a number of "bourgeois specialists," and their skills were used to get Soviet factories and plants running again. By the end of the 1920s, a number of improvements had been made, but Stalin imagined even greater possibilities. His was a program not only to catch up to other nations but to bypass them, and industrialization moved from being a goal to becoming a national mantra. "We are advancing full steam ahead along the path of industrialization—to socialism . . . leaving behind the age-old 'Russian' backwardness. We are becoming a country of metal, an automobilized country, a tractorized country."[7]

Stalin's draconic plans achieved prodigious feats. According to Roy Medvedev, from 1928 to 1933, the Soviets built "1,500 big enterprises [including] machine-tool production, automobile and tractor manufacturing, chemical works, and airplane factories, the production of powerful turbines and generators, of high-grade steel, of ferrous alloys, of synthetic rubber, artificial fibers."[8] But the effect was not on Russia alone. Stalin's planned economy also attracted the attention of major industrialists in the United States and other Western nations wrestling with the vagaries of the capitalist market system. Many were eager to find safer locations for their investments than the West, and the newly formed Soviet Russia, which lay outside these networks, was relatively unscathed.[9] Du Pont, RCA, Ford, Stuart, James & Cook, and General Electric all set up business there.[10] Hughes, who, like Smith, went as part of the 1932 *Black and White* film group, discovered tractors from Chicago in Soviet Central Asia.[11]

Although the U.S. government did not overtly encourage contacts with the Soviets, it did allow Amtorg (the Soviet trade mission based in New York) and other agencies representing the Soviet Union to set up offices in the United States in the 1920s and into the early 1930s.[12] In many cases, Amtorg became a stand-in for a Soviet embassy. This situation changed only in 1933, when Roosevelt formally recognized the Soviet Union.[13] U.S. businesses were happy

because the Soviet contracts were lucrative, and the U.S. government was satisfied because these employment outlets could help diffuse some of the social
tensions among U.S. workers.

The Soviets particularly admired the work of industrialists Frederick Taylor and Henry Ford. "Taylor had become famous for regulating the actions of
workers to improve their efficiency. . . . His system is still known as "Taylorism." . . . [And] Henry Ford, whose plants the Soviets saw as the embodiment
of Taylorism, was revered in the Soviet Union."[14] The Soviets' fascination with
Ford's River Rouge plant led to the 1929 contract to establish a similar factory
in Nizhny Novgorod (Gorky).[15] The contract covered not only sales of auto-
mobiles but also provision of the equipment and technical know-how to build
a comparable all-in-one facility. As Vincent Baker contended, with economics
leading the way, "it didn't matter what the politics were, it only mattered where
the marketplace was."[16]

The Soviets also wanted skilled workers who "would inspire Soviet workers and help raise Soviet factories to American levels of productivity."[17] In some
cases, workers laid off from their jobs in the United States were now working in
plants abroad that were joint U.S.-U.S.S.R. ventures. Smith pointed out that "the
two greatest tractor plants—one at Stalingrad, the other at Kharkov—were designed, built and put into operation by American engineers and technicians. . . .
In 1938, I visited the Rostov Agricultural Machinery Plant at Rostov-on-
Don. . . . Had it not been for the Russian workers around me, I could have been
in an American agricultural machinery plant."[18]

The U.S. workers could not resist the opportunity to take on these contracts.
The applicant pool grew so large that the Soviets began to be more selective and
were able to offer fewer upfront inducements than at the beginning. Nonetheless
U.S. workers signed up. Noted Baker, "[The Soviets received] 100,000 appeals
for immigration [from the U.S. to the Soviet Union] in eight months [and] virtually any American was signed up. Now the Soviets could afford to pick and
choose from the ready supply of skilled workers and specialists. No longer did
Amtorg have to provide transportation or make other guarantees."[19] An August
1930 *New York Times* piece observed, "Americans have shown great enthusiasm
for the work. . . . Many have . . . have applied for membership in the Russian
unions and declared that they will stay [in the Soviet Union]."[20] Most were given
one- to three-year contracts, which could be renewed, and some, like Robinson
and Smith, spent not only one or three years there but decades.

Not all the black technicians went to the Soviet Union for jobs; some went
to labor congresses and for political training. A 1931 *Amsterdam News* article
entitled "Reds Send Three to Russia" stated, "Three colored and 11 white workers have been elected members of the American Workers' Delegation to Soviet
Russia . . . to attend the 14th anniversary celebration of the Russian Revolution. . . . They will be in Russia five weeks."[21]

Over time, though, Soviet suspicions of the specialists' loyalties revived,
and hundreds were fired or suffered from other actions by the government.

According to Robinson, "Until 1935 all of the engineers in the Soviet Union were either from the czarist intelligentsia or foreigners . . . [and] had experienced the benefits of a market-driven economy in the pre-Soviet era. [But, because of their rising discontents,] a network of saboteurs in many industrial provinces [arose]. . . . Stalin set in motion a countermeasure—the purge. . . . Many from my factory were sent away."[22]

Robert Robinson, Tool-and-Die Specialist

Originally from Jamaica, Robinson had studied toolmaking for four years before he arrived in the United States. By the age of twenty, he had set his sights on Ford in Detroit, despite the accounts of discrimination and his own experiences. "After I got settled in the [United States], I sent out a batch of resumes . . . [but] when I reported to each company . . . [they] explained to me lamely why the job was no longer available. I went to Detroit knowing there were obstacles to being hired in a skilled position, even though I was qualified. But I went determined to try."[23] Ford plants drew not only white workers but also blacks, as these plants were among the few places that would hire them. As LeRoi Jones noted, "[By 1920] the proportion of Negroes in the North had increased to 14.1 percent; five-sixths of those in the North were in large cities. . . . The mills of Bessemer and Gary called. . . . Ford was one of the first companies to hire many Negroes and the name *Ford* became synonymous with Northern opportunity."[24] Robinson was hired in 1927 after repeated attempts, but it was years before Ford allowed him to join the technical crew in the tool-and-die section.

The Promise of a Soviet Contract

At the time of the Soviets' visit in 1930, Ford had 270,000 people working around the clock in three shifts. Ford jobs were considered good jobs, but this image belied the true promise of a job at Ford. Blacks were seldom put into skilled-worker crews or recognized as technicians. "I . . . weighed the risks. I was no fool. I knew that the Ford Motor Company belonged to the white man's world. It would be tough for any black man to land a skilled job there," Robinson recalled.[25]

Robinson was the sole black person in a division of seven hundred tool-and-die technicians at the time. But the Soviet recruiters were offering contracts that would give them double their wages and provide a range of other free services. "That whites were competing for the same job made it easier for me to sign the contract. To get something they wanted was appealing; it also helped to ease my doubts about actually going to the Soviet Union, because I was aware of media accounts criticizing the Soviet system."[26]

Robinson had had a rough time being accepted by his co-workers in Detroit. But, thanks to a stubborn streak, a basic suspicion of others, and a willingness to persevere, he had managed to rise from a floor sweeper to a trained machinist. Furthermore, his meticulousness served him well. It had not only helped him avoid the attempts to sabotage his work at Ford but made him particularly attractive to the Soviets. "[The recruiter] said, 'During the past week, I have noticed your work, background and character.' . . . Then he told me that he was so confident of my ability that he had decided to wave my taking the mathematical and mechanical drawing tests that applicants were required to take. He was willing to sign a one-year contract right away."[27]

Robinson, like so many who were drawn by these offers, understood the precariousness of life for blacks in the United States and the great lure of trying out a new system. Most professed no particular political bent, and the financial benefits clearly overrode concerns about any stigma attached to the Soviet Union. "I was making $140 month, which I figured was hard to beat anywhere. [The recruiter] offered me $250 a month, rent free living quarters, a maid, thirty days paid vacation a year, a car, free passage to and from Russia, and they would deposit $150 out of each month's paycheck in an American bank. . . . I thought to myself, 'America is in the grip of a serious depression and I could be laid off any day at Ford. . . . White Americans are lining up for this chance. Why not me too?'"[28]

But as much as he was impressed with the potential contractual arrangements, Robinson did not consider how different life could be once he left Jim Crow behind. A number of dramatic incidents made him seriously aware of the possibilities. Robinson had arrived late for the preliminary testing for applicants for Soviet contracts, which was being done by American adjudicators. The impatient adjudicator shouted at him, "You black monkey, you were supposed to be here a half hour ago. Couldn't you get your face here any quicker than that?" Then, for the full period of the exam, the man kept cussing at him. But, later, when he went to meet with the Soviet recruiters, he was received quite differently. "I must say I was bewildered [when the Russian] man asked me to sit down. . . . He asked me if I wanted to go to Russia, and he continued talking without letting me answer his question. Then he began to flatter me, which sounded awfully good, especially after my morning ordeal."[29]

Another incident occurred just before he left the country when he went to see his mother in Cuba. Although he was born in Jamaica, he grew up in Cuba. Taking the bus south, he inadvertently broke some Jim Crow rules. "I hopped on a Greyhound bus in Detroit. . . . In Atlanta . . . I chose the worst seats in the bus . . . because I figured they would be the safest. White folks would not want to sit here. But in Macon [Georgia] a number of passengers got on. . . . A young white couple sat down next to me. . . . I stiffened a little and scrunched up closer to the window. . . . I was very tired [and] . . . needed to sleep. . . . Suddenly I was wide awake! My head was spinning; it had crashed against the bus wall. The man . . . was standing over me . . . his fists clenched."[30] Robinson had crossed the social barrier by not giving his seat to the whites, and he knew they were out to kill him. "What could I do? . . . [They] could turn into an angry mob. . . . Suddenly, strangely. . . . I did something I never would have done. . . . I stood up and [cried] out, '. . . Yo soy Cubano! [I'm a Cuban!] Yo soy Cubano!'" Robinson had found the only loophole available to him in this climate of racist rage—being a foreigner. Once the white people understood that he was not a home-grown black, he could be forgiven for not knowing the rules. Robinson was saved temporarily as the other passengers prevailed, and he was allowed to stay on the bus until his stop at Key West.[31] These memories were still fresh when he set out for the Soviet Union a few weeks later.

After receiving his money and tickets from Amtorg, Robinson joined forty-four other technical specialists—all white—for the first leg of their journey. Once they got to England, Robinson discovered that not only was he not allowed to stay in the same hotel as the others, but he was never included in any of the group activities for the four and a half days they were there.[32] His experiences on the Soviet steamship *Rykov*—the next leg of his journey—were quite different. "I gained my first fascinating insight into the workings of the Soviet system." Robinson, the machinist, was struck by the extremely efficient manner in which the ship was run, "the cleanliness and orderliness . . . even the engine room, which is usually the dirtiest place."[33]

On their first day aboard the *Rykov*, when Robinson went for his meals and sat down at a table, the white Americans got up in a huff. Based on his experiences in the United States, Robinson did not see these actions as extraordinary; he simply considered them a continuation of U.S. patterns. The next day, however, after this behavior was repeated, the ship's captain stood up and said, "Comrade specialists, you are all invited to work in the Soviet Union. Under the Soviet system there is no discrimination based on nationality or the color of a man's skin. Everyone in Soviet Russia is equal. I am not authorized to segregate anyone on this ship. I am asking that everybody—all of the passengers—obey Soviet law."[34] Robinson, the black man fleeing Jim Crow, was amazed to find the Russians defending him. There were no further racist incidents for the remainder of the journey.

Still, vestiges of U.S. racism continued to follow him after he landed in the Soviet Union. When the hotel desk clerk in Leningrad assigned him the same room as three white Americans, the white men insisted on being placed elsewhere. But the Soviets would not allow them to move. "The hotel clerk told me that the three white men had waited all day to try and get a separate room. They had taken their appeal all the way to the hotel manager. But none of the guests had checked out by midnight, so they reluctantly returned to me. There they remained for the next four days, never saying a word to me."[35]

Over the next week, though, he began to relax. "[Leningrad] was unlike any city I had ever seen. . . . We were . . . given a tour of the city and I was included. Here in Russia, they were not running a 'white's only' tour. I was not being left behind."[36]

Stalingrad Incident

However, the incident that would illustrate the clearest distinction between systems—and that would ultimately catapult Robinson to fame in the Soviet

Union and infamy in the United States—occurred in mid-July 1930. Robinson, along with a team of one hundred white American specialists, was assigned to the Stalingrad tractor plant. "Everything went fairly smoothly, unlike the trauma of my breaking-in period at Ford. . . . My third day of work was a good one." Robinson found himself getting into "a comfortable routine" and his "productivity was increasing."[37]

> However, my feelings of satisfaction were short-lived. [Following my tenth day of work,] . . . [on] my way home . . ., a strapping American . . . said, "Robinson, be careful when you go to the Volga. On the night you arrived all the Americans got together and decided to drown you." . . . On the tenth day after my arrival in Stalingrad . . . Louis leapt in front of me and began beating me with his fists. Brown was able to pin down my arms to prevent me from hitting back, but I broke loose and struck back at Louis. . . . Then something inside me exploded—the rage that had been building for years. . . . My teeth caught his neck. I dug them deeper.[38]

Robinson did not back down. Although his fighting back did not dampen the white Americans' intent to injure him, the ferocious response from so small a man was totally unexpected. Robinson, too, was startled at his actions. Despite the many insults and injustices he had endured in the West, he had managed to swallow the bile. But his brief period under the Soviet experiment allowed him to discover strengths he did not know he had. Swept away by rage, he was not going to let white Americans terrorize him. "I . . . felt like someone who had just achieved some marvelous physical feat. . . . Never again, I vowed, would I run away from racist attackers. I fell on my bed exhausted, but overcome by the sweet sensation of liberation, which I was feeling for the first time in my life."[39]

After the fight broke up, and the wounded limped away, the investigation started. Robinson expected the authorities to take the side of the white Americans, so he was pleasantly surprised when the magistrate insisted on hearing his account of the incident. Initially, the men were sentenced to five years in prison, but after an appeal the sentences were reduced. Still, one was summarily expelled from the country, and the other was limited to serving out the remainder of his one-year contract before being forced to leave. "The Stalingrad newspaper ran an editorial denouncing American racial prejudice and warned the American specialists not to export their 'social poison' to Russia. Our nation's laws forbid racism, declared the newspaper. . . . They all deplored the attack on me. Many viewed me as a hero. . . . I was dazzled by the adulation and attention showered upon me."[40]

Harry Haywood, who was in Moscow at the time, noted that this incident had broad implications:

> The location was Tractorstroi, a basic unit of the Five-Year Plan with a capacity of 50,000 tractors a year. The plant stretched fifteen miles

along the Volga River. They had brought over about three hundred and fifty highly skilled white mechanics from the United States, who—together with their families—formed a small American colony. They had their own restaurants supplied with the best food, tobacco and wines that the Soviets could furnish. Into this situation stepped a lone Black toolmaker, Robert Robinson, a native of Jamaica and a naturalized US citizen. . . . This attempt to transplant American racism to Soviet soil was met with outrage. It was made a political issue of high order by the Soviet trade unions and Party organizations. Factory meetings were called throughout the Soviet Union. . . . They adopted resolutions which were sent to Tractorstroi. The slogan of the day became, "American technique yes! American race prejudice no!"[41]

Although the Soviet government had granted the foreign specialists a wide range of special dispensations, the authorities were not willing to tolerate racist behavior. Much to the amazement of these specialists, when signs of American race prejudice surfaced, the response was quick and resolute.

The story traveled into the larger global community. Several articles appeared in the *New York Times* in August 1930, "Americans Essay Color Bar in Soviet," "Attack on Negro Red Still Stirs Moscow," and "Apologizes to Russians."[42] Noted Robinson ruefully, "The bad publicity had branded me a 'Red,' a 'Bolshevik,' and 'coal-black protégé of Joseph Stalin.'"[43]

New Rewards

When Hughes met Robinson in Moscow in 1932, two years after the event, Robinson was still enjoying some of the fruits of his notoriety. "The pictures of Negro workers are often displayed in the windows of shops on the main Moscow streets. During the recent May holidays there was a huge picture of Robinson, the colored udarnik [worker] at the Ball Bearing Plant."[44] By now, Robinson had been transferred to a new plant just outside Moscow. He had also been elected to the Moscow Soviet. Hughes, who liked profiting from Robinson's access to special events, noted, "Robinson was well liked and was elected by his fellow factory workers to the Moscow City Soviet. Robinson invited me to a performance of Eugene Onegin at the Bolshoi Opera House, to which tickets were very hard to get. Being a worker in heavy industry, he could secure priority seats, so as his guest I sat in the orchestra of one of the great theaters of the world."[45] Unlike governments in the West, the Soviets held that access to art—be it theater, opera, or the ballet—should not be limited to the elites of a society. Thus, from those early years and up to the end of the Soviet period, tickets remained accessible to the ordinary person.

Prior to his transfer, Robinson was undecided about whether he would stay. "For two days I struggled over the question of whether to remain, or leave. . . . Should I stay . . . or should I head home and face the uncertain prospect of finding a job." Still, he did understand that a posting in the capital could bring even greater opportunities. "At the VATO,[46] I sat across from a man who studied my file for a few minutes and then told me that the First State Ball Bearing Plant had opened in Moscow . . . and there was an urgent need for a person with my qualifications. He recommended that I . . . see the director. . . . [The director] received me warmly, saying that . . . he was impressed by what he had learned about my qualifications in the gauge grinding field. He said he needed such a man there, and offered me a one-year contract. I accepted this offer on the spot." The new position was everything Robinson could hope for. "I was free to design and construct devices that turned our department into one of the most efficient at the plant. . . . My greatest joy was simply having the freedom to detect a problem and create a mechanical solution."[47]

At Ford, Robinson had swept the factory floor for eight hours a day for four months before he was allowed to enroll in the plant's technical program. It took another fourteen months before he graduated and then almost two years before he could work his way up to being recognized as a toolmaker. Now, in the Soviet Union, his skills were immediately put to use. Some six years later, in 1937, he would also be recommended by his shop party secretary for entry into a formal program at the Evening Institute of Mechanical Engineering and could get the advanced training he had always hoped for. Best of all, the Soviet government would pay for it.[48]

Robinson's stellar work record and his being an example of the Soviet fight against racism helped him in other ways. "Because of my record, the factory's administration approved my request to visit my mother in the United States during the summer of 1933. Before leaving, they urged me to sign another one-year contract. They imagined correctly that I would find depression-ridden America an undesirable place to be." Indeed, Robinson's decision to remain in the Soviet Union was fueled not only by his desire to put his talents to work but also by the realization that a part of his paycheck was supporting his mother. He had moved his mother from Cuba to an apartment in Harlem, and the $150 dollars of his salary being deposited in his New York bank account was for her.[49]

Harlem in 1933 was sobering. "I was glad to be home, but strolling down 125th Street in Harlem left me with a chill. . . . Here was the face of the depression. I had lived in Harlem before, and it was nothing new to see its residents struggle to make ends meet. But the level of poverty and suffering I was seeing now was so much greater."[50]

But Robinson was something of a novelty, and his mother's apartment became a gathering place for blacks looking for improvements in their lives. "[I was] drawing old friends from the neighborhood and even from Detroit. They bombarded me with questions about life in the Soviet Union. . . . I told everyone about the Soviet system of employment, under which workers do not receive a fixed salary but rather are paid by the piecework system, earning according to their output. When some heard of the absence of Jim Crow and unemployment, they were eager to journey to the U.S.S.R. as I had." Even when he described the Spartan living conditions and "not counting on having running water or indoor plumbing," they remained enthusiastic. "One young doctor . . . pressed me about how he could get a job in a Soviet hospital. I gave him the name of an organization that recruited professionals in a variety of fields to work in Russia."[51] Although Robinson always contended that he was apolitical, he, along with others who returned from the Soviet Union for these brief visits in the 1930s, played important roles in attracting other blacks to the Soviet experiment.[52] Not only were they doing well compared with blacks in the United States, but their intentions to return to the Soviet Union intrigued others.

When Robinson's fellow workers nominated him for the Moscow Soviet, it was not an honorary position. He was still well-known because of the incident at Stalingrad, but this was also the first time any black technician had been officially elected. It was Robinson's job to inspect factories and report on their progress. "These reports were due on the fifteenth of each month, and I would often be asked to read my findings to the Soviet. Members of the city legislature would then vote on whether my recommendations should be adopted, which they always were." The Soviets placed a lot of faith in their industrial sector, and the choice of Robinson was a testament to the fact that the authorities believed he would take his job seriously. "No one in the plants, not even the director or chief engineer, had the power to appeal my findings. . . . My work for the Moscow Soviet was considered so important that I was excused from my regular job whenever I went on an inspection mission." With one word from Robinson, directors of plants or divisions could be severely reprimanded for not meeting the goals of the five-year plans. Both jobs and positions could be lost. [53]

Robinson's example was also useful for propaganda. He frequently appeared in the press and was given a number of awards and other citations for his inventions. Few blacks could have hoped for this kind of authority or recognition in the United States. From the Stalingrad incident in 1930 to the move to the First State Ball Bearing Plant in Moscow in 1932 to his election to the Moscow Soviet in 1934, Robinson found himself a national symbol whose story would be repeated for years to come, both inside the country and abroad. In one instance, he was invited for a private meeting with Paul Robeson. He was pleased to see that Robeson had heard about him. "Robinson, we are happy you came over to see us, so that we could learn that you, a black man, are taking part in the development of this great new social order. Keep in touch."[54]

Attempting to Leave

In fact, their paths did cross again in 1949, but their interests and impressions of the Soviet experiment had diverged. By this point, Robinson had lost many friends and acquaintances in the purges, and he feared for his life as a foreigner. The war years had also been difficult for him, as they had for all others. And although he had already made several unsuccessful appeals to leave, he hoped that Robeson could help. But Robinson's change of heart was a disappointment and a potential liability for Robeson. As Eslanda Robeson later told him, "Robinson, you asked Paul to help you go to Ethiopia. We have thought about your request, and he has decided that he cannot help you. You see, we do not really know you well enough, to know what is in your mind. Suppose he were to help you leave, and then when you arrive in Ethiopia, you decided to turn anti-Soviet."[55]

Robinson's and Robeson's paths crossed one more time, eleven years later, in 1961. Discovering that Robinson was still in the country and still highly respected by his fellow workers, Robeson accepted his invitation to sing at his factory in Moscow. Standing before the assembled at the First State Ball Bearing plant, Robeson said, "Comrades, my dear friend Robert Robinson, who has worked with you for decades, invited me to your factory. I am very happy to meet you face-to-face. I want to sing a few songs for you, which I hope you will like."[56] For the moment, at least, Robinson was happy to accept the recognition given him by Robeson.

But Robinson was never completely comfortable with all the recognition for his various accomplishments given him over the years. To his mind, the accolades came with a double edge, especially as he always intended to return to the United States. He clearly welcomed the pay, the opportunity to do his work, and the special access to cultural programs and to important people. But he knew that there would be consequences. "I had also been blacklisted in my professional field. My brother had written me that I should not expect to get my job back with the Ford Motor Company, or with anyone else for that matter."[57]

Additionally, shortly after the larger world discovered he was a member of the Moscow Soviet in 1934, the U.S. State Department decided to put an end to his Soviet sojourn. Contacting him through the U.S. embassy in Moscow, they insisted that he return to the United States or forfeit his privileges to live there in the future. He was accused of having exceeded the maximum five-year limit for naturalized citizens to live outside of the country. The officials purposefully ignored the fact that Robinson had spent six weeks in New York the summer before. "By now I had decided that I would probably renew my contract when it expired in six months, despite the political dangers of being on the Moscow Soviet. I kept returning to the thought that going back to the United States at the time would be like committing suicide. There was the difficulty of a black man getting a job based on experience and ability during a crippling depression. I had an elderly mother to support."[58]

He tried to enlist Smith's help, as Smith was now working full time as a foreign correspondent. "I asked a black American journalist, Homer Smith, to come with me and help plead my case. Smith was bright, distinguished looking . . . and had spent considerable time in Russia. . . . The ambassador had once been a journalist, and I thought that Smith would be a useful ally."[59] But their efforts were to no avail. And to complicate his quest, the Soviets had given Robinson yet another award for his work.

A few weeks later it got even worse. . . . I was honored by the Soviet government for inventing a mechanical device that would save 15,500 rubles annually in production costs at my factory. I accepted the award gratefully. I had earned it by doing something worthwhile, and I enjoyed the gesture of appreciation. I was given a medallion engraved with Stalin's profile, with a gold, green and red ribbon flowing from it. Russian newspapers carried articles about me and unfortunately, so did American ones. . . . Powerful people in the US . . . saw me as a traitor, as one who was submitting himself willingly to Soviet propaganda. I do not suppose [that they] considered that I actually might have earned the award.[60]

Only in the Soviet Union could Robinson achieve the technical output and recognition he desired. And the country to which he wanted to return eventually saw him only as a black man and a dupe of Soviet propaganda. The 1934 *Time* magazine article that had described him as "a coal-black protégé of Joseph Stalin" quoted him as stating that he was not a Communist, but, he complained, the article still "implied that I was lying, and that in my heart I was a Marxist and a traitor." As time was running out, Robinson decided to approach the Soviets with an unusual proposal. "I asked the Soviet authorities if I could become a Soviet citizen for now, but then return to the United States when I wanted to and to have the Soviets consider me an American."[61] Robinson naively interpreted their acquiescence as an agreement to what he considered provisional arrangements. He found out later, though, when he was ready to leave after World War II, that switching from Soviet to U.S. citizenship was not so easy.

Because he was persona non grata as far as the U.S. government was concerned, his appeals could be directed only to the Soviet authorities. This time, though, despite a continually strong work record, his attempts to gain permission to go to the United States to visit his dying mother fell on deaf ears in the Soviet bureaucracy.[62] "In July 1945, I filed for permission to visit my mother. She was getting older, and I longed to see her and my brother. I had to wait a year for a response from the Department of Visas and Registration of the Ministry of Foreign Affairs. At the end of that time, they rejected my request without explanation."[63]

He finally found the means to leave in 1974. In this case, it was the Soviet interest in Africa that helped. Robinson had made friends with several members of various African delegations to Moscow. Initially trying with the Ethiopians, he later turned to his friendship with the Ugandan delegation to Moscow. Finally, in response to the Ugandan invitation that Robinson help train machinists in Kampala, the Soviets agreed to allow him a forty-five-day leave. It was an interesting turn of events, for Robinson was fulfilling a plan proposed by the Soviets fifty years earlier: that blacks from the United States could help train blacks in the lesser-developed parts of the world. Prototypes of this model had been tested with the black agricultural specialists and the people in Uzbekistan and other Soviet provinces in the 1930s.[64]

After his departure for Uganda, Robinson vowed that he would find a way to return to the United States. Four years later, in 1978, he finally managed to do so with the help of William Davis, an African American Foreign Service officer whom he had originally met in Moscow years earlier.

Homer Smith, Member of the *Black and White* Film Group, Postal-Systems Specialist, and Journalist

Robinson originally met Smith when Smith arrived in Moscow with the *Black and White* film group in the summer of 1932. They did not meet again until late 1933. By this time, Smith was working full-time in the Moscow post office and part-time as a journalist sending articles to the black press in the United States. Originally from Minnesota, Smith was excited by the "reports of the Soviet experiment, the Five-Year Plan, and the classless society that was abuilding in Russia. The Daily Worker wrote glowingly that Soviet Russia was the one political state which stood for social justice for all oppressed peoples. Who, I thought, was more oppressed than the Negro? Who else was being lynched with hideous regularity?"[65]

In 1931, Smith wrote to the Moscow post office offering his postal-service skills. At the time, he was working at the U.S. postal service as a fall-back arrangement because he could not find work in his chosen profession of journalism. Many educated blacks found the post office a respectable, economic sanctuary. As Haywood observed, "It was almost the only clerical job open to Blacks. . . . The Post Office became a refuge for poor Black students and unemployed university graduates. For some of the latter it was a sort of way-station on the road to their professional careers."[66] Way-station or not, Smith correctly anticipated that his postal-services training would be more interesting to the Soviets than his fledgling skills as a journalist. "I began getting my dollars and clothes together. Being somewhat conservative, though toying with radical ideas, I had no desire to starve in the streets of Moscow. . . . [I stated] my qualifications, and was thrilled to receive a reply almost immediately offering me a position as consultant to the Moscow Post Office at a higher salary than I was then receiving."[67]

Smith had studied journalism at the University of Minnesota. White schoolmates of his, such as Harrison Salisbury, whom he would come across during the later stages of World War II in Moscow, could get jobs as junior reporters in the major press outlets. But no U.S. news outlet of any significance would give Smith a chance. "Newspapers weren't hiring Negroes in those days and though I might have gotten a job on one of the Negro papers elsewhere represented on campus, it was something less than I aspired to."[68] But when Smith and Salisbury met again in 1944, even Salisbury was struck by how their paths—one white man and one black man—now converged. As he wrote in the preface to Smith's memoir, "I was standing at the window of a Russian railroad car. . . . In this strange and unexpected milieu we were not only fellow Minnesotans—we were fellow students at the University of Minnesota, had studied in some of the same classes and had even worked together on the student newspaper."[69]

Thus, while Smith proposed to help the Soviets in the postal service, he also hoped that he would be in the unique position of being a black journalist living in the Soviet Union. "The Negro Press had no correspondent in Russia and the editors of the several papers . . . were agreeable that I represent them under my pen-name of Chatwood Hall."[70]

Smith and the Black and White *Group*

Smith provided few details on his journey to the Soviet Union, and here his memoirs diverged from those of Hughes and others familiar with the *Black and White* film group. Other sources pointed to his having been a part of that group, although his accounts were written as if he were not.[71] One chapter of Smith's memoirs on the *Black and White* project, entitled "The Black and White Film Fiasco," was written as though he was a spectator to their travails rather than one who participated in them. It is possible—although he did not corroborate this conjecture—that even if he had proposed to the Soviets that he provide training in postal services in 1931, he might have been informed that he had to travel to the Soviet Union with an officially sanctioned group. As he was a black man, he might also have been directed to join the group that Louise Thompson was trying to assemble for the *Black and White* project at about that same time. Thompson was having trouble assembling the fifteen persons she needed for her group, and she was willing to include people who did not have previous experience in the theater. Perhaps Smith joined them as a kind of lark or as a means to get to the Soviet Union.[72] Or maybe he left out his association with the Soviet propaganda film in his memoirs to maintain an image of the impartial journalist he had become.

Nonetheless, he was among the twenty-one blacks who went to the Soviet Union for the *Black and White* project, arriving in Leningrad in late June 1932. Hughes wrote of him:

> When our contracts with Meschrabpom Films were terminated . . . [in the fall of 1932,] three of the members of our group remained in Russia permanently—the actor, Wayland Rudd; the artist Lloyd Patterson; and the former postal clerk from Minneapolis, Homer Smith. All three, so I was informed, eventually learned to speak Russian well and took an active part in the life of the Soviet capital. . . . Homer Smith supervised the installation of the first special-delivery service in the Russian post offices and helped modernize their postal-money-order system along American lines. At the same time he acted as Moscow correspondent for various American Negro newspapers.[73]

Adjusting to Working for the Post Office in Moscow

When Smith reported for work at the Moscow post office, he was a bit taken aback at the Soviets' enthusiastic response to his presence. His office and other accommodations were far more commodious than he had anticipated.

> My first task in Moscow was to report for work in the post office. A spacious office was assigned to me on the ground floor of the three-story graystone building which was formerly the old Czarist Post Office. My staff was to consist of three persons—Madame X, my personal interpreter; Boris Novikov, a veteran postal employee, who was to be my personal assistant; and Ludmilla Gneditch, my translator-typist. They all knew English surprisingly well. . . . I drew up a list of needed appurtenances—desks, chairs, typewriters (one with an English keyboard, the other with Russian characters), a supply of paper, ink pencils. . . . Surprisingly, within one week he [Boris] had obtained everything.[74]

These arrangements were remarkable from two perspectives. First, Smith's previous positions at the post office in Minneapolis had warranted neither a staff of three nor a large office. Second, his Soviet hosts were willing to obtain the items he requested despite severe shortages. The typewriter with the English keyboard they found was, in fact, an Underwood made in the United States.

Over the next few weeks, Smith did an assessment of the Moscow postal services. "I then began examining . . . a bureaucratic, red-tape-ridden postal service. I found duplication of effort, lost motion, unnecessary paper work, over-staffing, and downright inefficiency on all sides. We roamed the post office, as I made detailed and voluminous notes."[75] Developing a series of reports, he suggested ways to implement some U.S.-style techniques. Soon, he was given increased responsibility: he was to inspect and make recommendations for up-grading other postal locations and services. He wrote, "My scope of operations was not to be limited to Moscow, nor would I be tied down to my desk. . . . Field trips to study the operational problems of other Soviet post offices [were arranged]. . . . The postmaster received these initial recommendations eagerly and with expressions of appreciation, and promised that as many of my suggestions as possible would be 'put into life.'"[76]

Although Smith professed faith in the Soviet promise of a new society, he was clearly struck by the fact that his earliest imaginings of the country did not match the reality. The stock-market crash and the tough years of the Great Depression had hardened life for the ordinary people in the United States, yet he imagined life in the Soviet Union would be better. Much to Smith's dismay, he found "a depressive aura prevailed everywhere. Poverty and hunger gripped [Russia]. The people were shabbily dressed, obviously haggard, with tired, woebegone faces. . . . In my walks around the city I found long lines of hungry men and women standing at grocery and butcher shops in the hope of getting something to eat."[77] Still, as one of the foreign specialists, Smith also learned that although ordinary Russians may have been suffering, foreign guests were not. For the duration of his fourteen-year stay, he was given adequate accommodations, and because he had foreign currency and authorization, he could do his shopping in stores that catered to foreigners and high Russian officials. These perquisites also made him popular. "The most popular and sought after persons in Moscow were members of the sizable foreign community, consisting of American, German, and English. It was reasoned by the Russians, and rightly, that these foreigners would possess foreign currency and/or passes to Insab, a special well-stocked food shop to which only foreigners employed by the Soviet Government had access."[78]

Smith had to admit that ordinary people seemed to be extremely tolerant of their privations and were inordinately courteous and hospitable toward him.[79] Although he was glad to be treated well, he was uncomfortable.

> If I had been looking for racial equality in Russia, I found it so abundant that it proved, in my opinion, to amount almost to racial inequality. . . . Negroes would always be given precedence. If a Negro was standing in line at a shop, some Russian was sure to tug him by the arm and lead him to the front of the line. If it was a matter of a dance with a Russian girl, a Russian man would always give way. . . . In a barber shop or restaurant, although a Russian might have been waiting his turn, he would always be willing to relinquish it to a Negro. . . . Most of us had become very fond of the likable, open-hearted and hospitable Russian people, some of us had even married Russian girls.[80]

Like Robinson, Smith's only encounters with racial prejudice in the Soviet Union happened with white Americans. One white American woman was so perturbed to find that she had been booked into the same train compartment as Smith that she ended up sitting on her bags in the passageway.[81] It was common practice to sell tickets for single seats; thus, men and women could find themselves sharing a single train compartment. The Russians, male and female, seemed to handle this arrangement with no difficulty, but this woman was clearly not ready to share space with a person who was both black and male. "The woman persisted in making a fool of herself, and demanded that something be done or she would see the stationmaster. The conductor informed her that the stationmaster had nothing to do with issuing tickets. 'You have your correct ticket, Madam.' . . . She [was] far from home in a country whose morés were far different from those she was accustomed to. Then, too, perhaps my brown color was responsible for her perturbed reaction."[82] Smith thought that incident ended there, but after relating the account to a Russian traveling companion later, he discovered that his story was worthy of major press coverage. "I related to her the somewhat amusing story of the woman who refused to occupy the compartment with me. 'The decadent bourgeois swine! That's the kind of misanthrope that capitalism spawns,' my companion exclaimed." Much to Smith's amusement, a journalist from *Trud*, a trade-union newspaper, contacted him as well and before long, an article appeared "with Marxist overtones."[83]

Another instance of racism occurred when Smith went with Robinson to meet the U.S. ambassador, William Bullitt, and they were summarily rebuffed. As Robinson described the event, "I was taken back by his [the American ambassador's] abrupt, absolute statement. I could not think of what next to say. But Smith came right to my defense. 'Comrade Bullitt,' he said, 'must this man go back to the States where both he and his mother would have to stand on a soup line while . . .' The ambassador cut Smith off in mid-sentence. 'I am no comrade of yours or anyone else. Do not address me as "comrade,"' said an outraged Bullitt. Smith quickly shot back, 'you must know by now that in this country there is no "mister." . . . There is only comrade in this country.'"[84] Both men were summarily "escorted" out of the ambassador's office. Bullitt was caught in the position of having to represent the United States in an environment where he was forced to use "comrade" with the Soviets. At the same time, as a white American on his own turf in the embassy, he was clearly not willing to allow this black upstart to bring him down to this common ground. For Smith's and Robinson's parts, though, "comrade" represented a new kind of relationship between men, and they welcomed the opportunity to throw aside the racist and class-ridden customs of the United States they had left behind.

Smith remained with the postal services for almost three years before he shifted to being a full-time foreign correspondent. "I had been sending news dispatches to the Negro Press in America. During the next three years, my pieces began to appear with some regularity is such papers as the Chicago Defender and the Afro-American, as well as in Crisis Magazine, the organ of the N.A.A.C.P."[85] But fear of the purges encouraged him to move swiftly. Some of the high officials whom he knew personally had begun to disappear. "It really hit home . . . when my boss . . . was liquidated along with several other postal officials I knew personally. . . . This jungle terror was not for me, I decided, so when my contract expired in 1935 I did not renew it. Instead I cast my lot with news reporting."[86]

Foreign Correspondent

Shifting from being a postal-systems specialist to working as a foreign correspondent protected Smith from many of the strictures that were later imposed on the other expatriates. Others still resident in the country toward the latter half of the 1930s were pressed into assuming Soviet citizenship or leaving. By 1935, Smith had already been published numerous times in the United States, and, as a "friend" of the Soviet experiment, he was considered a useful conduit of information about the country. Luckily for Smith as well, he was in the right place at the right time, and a new opportunity presented itself. "It happened that I was the only Negro journalist ever stationed in Russia. I was also the only Negro war correspondent on the Russian-German front, and to carry this a bit further, I was the first Negro to be accredited a war correspondent."[87] Smith's increasing prominence in the Western media helped even during the difficult years of the late 1930s and early 1940s, as he was not prevented from communicating with persons outside the country or from receiving items from abroad.[88]

However, marriage to Marie Petrovna, a Russian, in 1938 presented new challenges and a new role. Before, he was an adviser to the Soviets on postal systems. Now, he was a black man advising a white Russian woman on the elitist morés of the diplomatic corps. Smith might have come from a provincial section of the United States, but he quickly learned the skills necessary to live and work among the international diplomatic elites. His wife, however, had a proletarian background in the Soviet Union and had not learned the Western etiquette common to these environments. "The teaching of western etiquette to children was considered unpardonable kowtowing to trivial and decadent bourgeois deportment and customs." Now the wife of a foreign correspondent, Marie Petrovna was being invited to state dinners and other formal functions. "Our marriage was later to give Marie Petrovna her first opportunity for moving in high bourgeois society. The names of the foreign correspondents were in the invitation lists of all the foreign diplomatic missions in Moscow. There were continual rounds of cocktail parties and receptions marking the national days of different countries. The gracious manners of foreign society were detested by the regime [Soviets]. . . . Being a guest at bourgeois affairs was new and strange for Marie Petrovna. . . . I had to coach her in the practices and manners."[89] Despite the fact that these diplomats were now operating in the Soviet Union, the land of social equality, within their elite circles, there remained certain cultural patterns. Smith, as a black man fighting his way into the profession, was particularly mindful of how important it was to conform to these norms if he were to remain on their lists.

At the same time, Marie Petrovna's knowledge of Moscow and Russian culture in general was key to the day-to-day business of life. Particularly after the war broke out, she negotiated some of the other necessary connections that helped them get through.

Smith's view of the Soviet experiment moved from outright enthusiasm to pessimism to a kind of ambivalence over his fourteen-year tenure in the country. He hoped that the society, having made it through the war, could return to his early 1930s expectations, and he contemplated staying. "When the War ended victoriously for Russia and her Western Allies, I found myself faced with the decision. Should I remain in Russia?. . . . The Ethiopian Minister in Moscow . . . told me that an Ethiopian visa would be issued whenever I wanted it. Any desire of remaining was predicated upon the hope that the regime might not return to its pre-war civilian repressions. . . . At one time I had entertained the idea that if the Kremlin showed any indication of turning Russia into a really democratic country, I would not mind remaining. But I was soon disappointed."[90]

It appeared that the Soviet government was determined to be even more vigilant than before to prevent Western "decadence" from filtering into the country, and Smith knew that foreigners were sure to be part of that feared decadence.

At the same time, the Soviets' growing ties with Africans in the postwar era opened a new avenue, and Smith had friends in the Ethiopian embassy. "In the summer of 1946, my decision was reached. I accepted a position working in the Editorial Department of the English section of the Ethiopian Government's Press and Information Office. I could continue to write for AP [Associated Press] and the Negro Press from Ethiopia. . . . As a foreign correspondent, the Russians could not very well place any obstacles in the way."[91]

Smith still faced a dilemma: how to bring his wife out with him. He was not willing to end his marriage as many other blacks had done. "Exit visas just were not given Russians to go abroad, not even wives of foreign correspondents."[92] Smith left in October 1946 and, with the help of the Ethiopians, was able to arrange to have his wife join him a year later. They stayed in Ethiopia until 1962, when Smith, his wife, and their two children moved to the United States.

Williana Burroughs, Fellow Traveler and Broadcast Media Specialist

Williana Burroughs was a sojourner of a different sort. She looked to the Soviet experiment not only for her personal ambitions but also to shield her two youngest children from the pain of Jim Crow.[93]

Her personal history with the Soviets stretched from an initial visit to the country in 1927 on through World War II. A Hunter College graduate and schoolteacher, she had been active in the U.S. Communist movement in the 1920s. Toward the end of that decade, she was sent to the Moscow meetings as a CPUSA delegate. Her husband, Charles, and two youngest sons accompanied her, and there is every indication that they had already decided to find a way to leave the two boys behind in the Soviet Union. Following a 1987 interview with Charles Jr. in Chicago, Jack Houston wrote, "Burroughs, who was born in Brooklyn, was taken to the Soviet Union by his mother, Williana, in the summer of 1927. . . . After spending the summer in Moscow, his mother left him and his brother at a boarding school and returned to New York, where she taught public school."[94] At the time, Charles was nine, and his younger brother, Neal, five.

The boys stayed in the Soviet Union until well past their teenaged years. The schools they attended were unique in that although they were state schools and were funded by the Soviet government, they were open only to senior Soviet officials and select foreigners. Robeson would later follow the Burroughses' example when, he, too, decided that his nine-year-old son, Paul Jr., would do better growing up under the nonracist Soviet experiment than in the United States.

In a 1931 letter to a close friend, Mrs. Charles Young, Charles Burroughs Sr. wrote, "Williana has been twice to Russia the second time for a period of ten months. Our two smaller boys have been there during the past three years. They are in the state schools and are given every attention. They were in excellent health when we last heard from them."[95] Charles Sr. devoted much of the rest of his letter encouraging Young to support her son's interest in joining the agricultural specialist group being formed by Golden. Burroughs herself moved to Moscow a few years later and remained there through the war.[96]

Prior to her extended sojourn, Burroughs had been the CPUSA's candidate for lieutenant governor of New York. Although she did not win, her candidacy served as a strong example of the party's commitment to bringing in blacks and women.[97] When she requested the party's support for her intensions to go to the Soviet Union, they were happy to back her. A May 4, 1937, letter from the CPUSA to the Comintern leadership stated, "Please communicate to the Radio Centre . . . our recommendation for the post of editor of Comrade Mary Adams (Wilhemina [Williana] Burroughs). Comrade Burroughs is an old member of the CPUSA and had been active in a leading capacity in the New York District for many years. She is one of the leading members of our Teachers' fraction [sic]."[98]

The Soviets placed her at Radio Moscow, where she worked for the next seven years. She joined a select cadre of Communists from the United States, Canada, and England who served as linguistic bridges for the Soviet Union before and during the war. Like the U.S. Voice of America, these short-wave broadcasts covered a wide range of topics and were key to maintaining support from outside communities.

In 1940, Burroughs requested permission to return to the United States. However, with the war tensions to the west of its borders, the Soviet Union could not afford to lose any of its English-language specialists, and she was asked to stay on. Within a year, Russia entered the war, and her services were all the more crucial. However, the last two years of her stay, from 1943 to 1945, were extremely difficult for her. Her living and working conditions deteriorated, and her health began to fail. By 1945, when she was finally given permission to leave with her younger son, Neal, she was deathly ill. Burroughs died shortly after her return to the United States.

Bernard Powers, Civil Engineer

Bernard Powers, a civil engineer and Howard University Engineering School graduate, went to the Soviet Union in 1931 with the agricultural specialist group. When he and Hughes met in 1932, he had already been in the country for a year. As Hughes wrote of the unexpected encounter, "We gradually emerged from the desert one afternoon to speed through a fertile oasis of water and greenery, cotton growing, trees in fruit, then crowds of yellow-brown Uzbeks in brightly flowered robes, waving from stations. As we pulled into the depot, there stood a young Negro."[99]

Powers had been assigned to an engineering crew upgrading roads in the Soviet Union's far-off republics.[100] Most of the rest of the agricultural specialist group, with which he traveled to the Soviet Union, had been posted to a collective farm in Yangiyul, a small village outside Tashkent. Powers lived in Tashkent.

Like Robinson and Smith, Powers had opted to take his chances with a Soviet contract rather than stay home and accept jobs for nonskilled workers in the United States. As a trained engineer, he found the Soviets were willing to attach him to the engineers' crew and immediately induct him into the Soviet Engineers Club. Thus, he was enjoying the same privileges as the other engineers, including access to the same housing, and he could shop at the select foreigners' shops.[101]

By the time Hughes met him, he had already settled in and was conversant in both Russian and Uzbek. Hughes spoke some Russian and virtually no Uzbek and was without his translator at the time. Happily, Powers was available to serve as his linguistic and cultural intermediary. "I told him of my experiences of the night before. He laughed fit to kill, as did the various Uzbeks and Tadjiks gathered. . . . When Powers, via a two- or three-way translation, later that evening, had made Hajir understand my lack of success with the Tartar lass, . . . Hajir asked a Tadjik-Uzbek speaking friend in the room to explain to an Uzbek-Russian speaking friend to explain in Russian to Powers to explain to me . . ."[102]

Powers also introduced Hughes to the team of agricultural specialists in the area, and the two of them ended up spending the Christmas holiday with Golden later on. Hughes wrote, "One of the Negroes at the Soviet collective forty miles from Tashkent where the seed-selection station and cotton experimental laboratories were located, came into Tashkent to invite Bernard Powers and me to spend Christmas with them. . . . I would be passing the holidays with my own people."[103] When Hughes first arrived in the region, he described green fields and trees with fruit on them. But by the time he and Powers were making their way on to Yangiyul, the weather had turned for the worst. The snow, mud, cold, and uncomfortable train ride made Hughes wonder why anyone in his right mind would chose to live and work there. "The trip was physically worse than any Jim Crow train trip I ever made in the U.S. . . . I said to myself, 'If I ever get back to Tashkent after this, I will go right straight—by plane, if possible—home to the U.S.A. Never another foot of travel in the USSR!'"[104]

Powers had used his foreign worker's card to obtained tickets at the stationmaster's office in order to bypass the long lines, but, in the end, they had no better riding conditions than anyone else on the train. By the time the two got to their stop, Hughes was ready to run back home. Finally settling into the warm houses of the agricultural specialists, though, Hughes grudgingly admitted he could see how they were able adjust to the challenges of living in Uzbekistan, even if he could not. "Powers, who had come through that chilling ride with me, thawed out before supper and was grinning like a Cheshire cat, joking with the other men's wives."[105] It took several drinks by the fire and a good night's sleep before Hughes could observe his surroundings more charitably.

The black specialists, like Powers, Burroughs, and Smith, brought more to their sojourns in the Soviet Union than their skills. As blacks, they represented new lines of human relations, and, together with their Soviet hosts, these sojourners were collaborating on a new kind of society. Hughes's and Powers's sojourns to Soviet Asia were so important that the famed sculptress Nina Zaratelli insisted on memorializing them in special projects. She did a bust of Powers's head and a bas relief of Hughes's. Hughes also noted with satisfaction that Zaratelli had chosen his newfound Uzbek friend, Nichan, as a model for a major work to symbolize the new Uzbek youth.[106] "Ten years ago Nichan himself had been a homeless orphan, an Oriental bespizorni [elsewhere, Hughes refers to this term as indicating a kind of wandering juvenile delinquent], . . . wandering the caravan trails of Central Asia. The Soviet government had corralled him into one of their schools and had found him eager and alert, with qualities of leadership. Now, Nichan was in charge of the athletic activities of thousands of boys and girls, who, like himself, until recently had never had a chance."[107]

Hughes and Powers parted company in January 1933, and Hughes returned to Moscow. Powers stayed on for a number of years, evidently returning to the United States in the latter part of the 1930s with the majority of the agricultural and technical specialists. A later mention of Powers appeared in one of Hughes's letters to Arna Bontemps. In 1962 Hughes wrote, "Found in the mail on my return today that another old friend died in Montana—Bernard Powers whom I write about in "I Wonder" [*I Wonder as I Wander*] of Howard [University] and Tashkent."[108]

Other Industrial and Technical Specialists

Smith identified two other black technical specialists of the 1930s: Richard Williams of New York, an electrical engineer, who was posted to the Ministry of Heavy Industry in Moscow in 1934; and Dick Williams, a maintenance engineer, who studied at Columbia University and who was posted to the famed Magnitogorsk Metallurgical Works in the Urals mountains.[109]

Smith's account of Williams's experiences underscored the dilemmas of the cross-racial coupling that could occur. Dick had arrived in 1933 and had married a Russian doctor, by whom he later had a child. But Dick, who was often away on his postings, worried that the child looked Asian. Ignoring the reasonable explanation that Russians, whose country was two-thirds Asian and many of whose people had Asian antecedents, Dick could not square the child's appearance with his own. Noted Smith, "Despite my urgings . . . that he had a fine and intelligent wife who was a respected member of the learned profession, Dick could not reconcile himself to his child's Oriental appearance. They separated, she remaining in Moscow, and he fulfilling his commitment as an electrical engineer in the Cossack Country of the Ukraine."[110]

Robinson specifically mentioned only a few other blacks in his memoir; this strategy was, no doubt, part of the cautious style he had developed as part of his survival tactics behind the Iron Curtain, and it was intended to protect both him and the others. Furthermore, his book was written late in his life and over a decade after he left the Soviet Union. Some of his generalizations were correct. "There were a few other Blacks in Russia when I was there, but they arrived as pilgrims reaching paradise. I understood how they felt, because what they left behind in the United States . . . was nothing to grieve over. . . . The handful of blacks who emigrated to the Soviet Union were serious, independent minded, sensitive, and usually well-educated. They all viewed Lenin as their Moses." However, other statements were not so accurate. "Every single black I knew in the early 1930s who became a Soviet citizen disappeared from Moscow within seven years. The fortunate ones were exiled to Siberian labor camps. Those less fortunate were shot."[111] Contrary to Robinson's summary statement, most of those who stayed on married, raised families, and led productive lives, largely blending into the mainstream population. Only one, Lovett Fort-Whiteman, was known to have been sent to a labor camp and to have died as a result of the purges.

Still, Robinson offered an observation that could well have applied to many who decided to become expatriates. "So deep was their belief—and their need to believe—that they refused to notice the Bolshevik's shortcomings."[112] For many, the choice to go to the Soviet Union, as well as to stay on after the 1930s, Robinson included, represented an enormous investment in a faith that the society they were joining could accomplish at least some of its noble goals. To countenance that it was not able to live up to its promise would be far too painful to bear.

CHAPTER 6

George Washington Carver, Oliver Golden, and the Soviet Experiment

ତ୍ୟତ

*Russia is the only country in the world today, that gives
equall [sic] chances to black and white alike.*[1]
—Oliver Golden (1930)

"*I* wonder if you would consider the following proposition: I have proposed to organize a group of Negro specialists who have had a theoretical and practical training in the production of cotton, to be sent to the Soviet Union," wrote Oliver Golden to his former teacher, George Washington Carver. "This group is to be indorsed [sic] by you [and if] it meets with your approval, I shall also arrange a tour for you to the Soviet Union to demonstrate your findings in the field of agriculture. The expenses of this tour will be taken care of."[2]

Carver was intrigued; he liked challenges. He answered, "Thank you for your splendid letter which has reached me, and I have looked it over quite carefully.... I shall be interested in knowing the further plans ... [and] shall endeavor to do the best I can in this important matter."[3] Thus, on December 12, 1930, began a unique partnership: an aging scientist and a prescient former student, pooling their resources to send skilled blacks to help modernize the Soviet economy.

Golden was part of a vast network of people working on behalf of the Comintern to recruit technically skilled workers for the Soviet Union. Stalin's five-year plan called for speeding up the country's economic recovery, and no expense was being spared. Now, the attention was being directed to the expansion of the country's cotton industry in Soviet Central Asia.

Golden, who had done political studies in the Soviet Union in the 1920s, wanted Carver to serve as a senior technical adviser to the Soviet Ministry of Agriculture and to bring some his most talented students with him. "It is absolutely necessary that you go on a tour of Russia. ... Your going to the U.S.S.R., and the successes of these men will give Tuskegee an international character."[4] Carver and Tuskegee had already achieved that international character with projects in Africa, Japan, and India, but both men knew the Soviet program could be another coup for this historically black institution.

The Agricultural versus the Industrial Sector

Two currents of opinion were shaping the Soviet five-year plans toward the end of the 1920s. One held that, as a traditionally agrarian country, the expansion of the agricultural sector was of primary importance. The other held that the agrarian sector was, in fact, the weaker link to the country's future—if it was to compete with industrialized nations. Instead, special attention should be directed to shoring up the industrial base first. Nicholay Bukharin, close confidant and heir-apparent to Lenin, championed agriculture. But, Stalin, who displaced Bukharin after Lenin's death, opted to emphasize industry.[5]

Bukharin's writing had shaped much of the party line from 1925 through 1927, but, by late 1928 and early 1929, he and his supporters (the Bukharists) had lost much of their popular and political support. Bukharin was not averse to the idea of rapid industrialization, but he was adamant that it would fail without the development of the agricultural sector.[6] To his thinking, by helping the peasants rebuild their base, the whole country—not just the urban areas—would benefit.

Stalin, however, fascinated with the developments in Europe and the United States, wanted to push industrialization, and his policies were the ones implemented. Thus, the government focused on industrialization in the beginning and only later turned to building the agricultural base. Even then, the quest was not for simple agricultural improvements but for an industrial template for the redevelopment. In other words, agricultural development was to proceed with centralized planning and forced collectivization. But the industrial model did not prove so effective for the agricultural sector, as the Soviets were frequently confronted by recalcitrant peasants and slow-downs. As Roy Medvedev noted, "Collectivization was supposedly designed to achieve a rapid increase in total agricultural output [but the] gross agricultural output declined through the first five-year plan."[7]

Golden reasoned that because the Soviets were willing to import expertise for their industrial development, they would be equally interested in having agricultural specialists. Thus, he proposed that teams of black specialists be assembled and that, as a bonus, he might be able to attract the famous Carver to lead them. He also correctly surmised that when given the option of taking up a Soviet contract and living in a nonracist society, highly motivated blacks would choose it. Like the technical specialists, the participants were not restricted to membership in the Communist Party or other organizations. But their personnel records were vetted by the Soviets' representatives before contracts were issued. Basically, though, if these candidates were willing to go, the Soviets were willing to take them. Golden, however, mindful of the important example they would be setting as black specialists, insisted on character references from well-regarded persons, such as Carver, in the hopes of identifying the most qualified candidates.

Foreign Specialists and the "Negro Question"

After the Sixth Congress of the Comintern in 1928, the CPUSA was under increased pressure to find ways to engage the black community. This campaign was somewhat easier in the northern urban centers, to which blacks had moved in search of work, than in the South, but the largely rural South was where most blacks lived. The exception was the party's work with the Alabama Sharecroppers' Union and the Scottsboro campaign.[8] Thus, Golden's proposed black agricultural specialist group was a particularly useful model.

Black-Soviet collaborations had evolved since the days when the focus was on fellow travelers, political education, and expansion of the political base. Now, blacks were to be included in the building of the country's economic base—not as laborers but as skilled persons. But Golden also understood the necessity to move swiftly. "Fifty of America's largest industrial concerns have sent 2,000 of their representatives to Soviet Russia to help develop the Russian industry. Yet so far we have not on record any Negro specialists in Russia. . . . It is necessary to get these men stationed in leading positions, so when other groups come, whether white or black, they will work under the supervision of these specialists."[9]

Another benefit was to have people of color sharing their skills and teaching other people of color. As Bertha Golden recalled of her husband's commitment, "It meant something special to him for a black to help other people of color. . . . It would mean more to an Uzbek . . . to see an educated, skilled black American than to see only white specialists. It would show what was possible when people pulled themselves out of oppression."[10] That the Soviets could envision these "advanced" blacks from the United States as role models for others was an inspiration for Africans and blacks who were fighting for their dignity back home.

As a result, their collaborations had a dramatic impact on Soviet cotton production. Noted Khanga, "In Yangiyul, the Americans strove to develop a new breed of cotton, one capable of maturing in the relatively short Uzbek growing season. For nearly three years, the men painstakingly crossed Uzbek seeds with American seeds, which they brought over on [the ship] the Deutschland. . . . By 1935, Uzbek collective farms were producing a new strain of cotton that took 25 percent less time to mature than cotton in the American South."[11]

Adviser to World Leaders

The Soviet offer was only the latest in a long line of requests made of Carver. No stranger to appeals from afar, Carver found his advice constantly sought as his discoveries, improvements, and innovations attracted worldwide attention. By the late 1920s, his research generated interest both nationally and internationally. Although known primarily for his work with peanuts, Carver also developed new products from the sweet potato and clay.[12] An article that appeared in the Harrisonburg, Virginia, *Daily News Record* noted, "Dr. Carver has won . . . recognition in constructive chemistry from the largest scientific fraternities and societies in the world. He was elected a member of the Royal Society of Arts, in London [England], in 1917."[13] Correspondence in the Carver archives includes many references to his being recommended for the Nobel Prize, and he was constantly sought for lecture tours, during which he would share some of his research. Among his many admirers was U.S. President Franklin Roosevelt, who was known to make use of Carver's peanut oil.[14] In 1939, Roosevelt presented Carver with the Roosevelt Medal (named after former President Theodore Roosevelt) in honor of his contributions to society.[15]

Carver regularly investigated new objects and shared his findings. In March 1929, when responding to a problem raised by people at Libby's Pine Apple Products, he wrote, "I am greatly interested in your recent communication and appreciate very keenly your situation. . . . I am quite positive that your problem can be controlled."[16] He was also involved in a project to help the Indian leader Mahatma (Mohandas) Gandhi meet his nutritional needs. As he wrote to a mutual friend, "A new day is dawning for India. I believe Mr. Ghandy's [sic] physical strength can be greatly improved, by following out the ideas we discussed in the matter of foods. With the whole wheat flour, grits, hominy, graham flour, etc. etc., which can be made on the little mill shown you, and with the splendid native fruits and vegetables you have, properly compounded, will give you a splendid nourishing and palatable food stuff." Always looking for opportunities to spread information to the widest possible public, he added, "You can use it in your school, they will in turn carry the message into the various communities from whence they came, bringing to my mind greater health, strength and economic independence to India."[17]

Carver regularly corresponded with friends and colleagues, as well as with prominent businesspeople and public officials. Among these were automaker Henry Ford and two U.S. Secretaries of Agriculture: James Wilson and Henry A. Wallace. Carver's relationship with Wallace was particularly noteworthy. A farmer himself, Wallace was interested in Carver's work. Their correspondence included invitations for Wallace to visit Tuskegee in 1933 and continued into the time when Wallace became vice president under Franklin Delano Roosevelt in 1941.[18]

Carver also understood the importance of maintaining a network of international contacts and made a point of keeping Tuskegee Institute's president, Dr. Robert Russa Moton, informed about new projects and proposals. "Libby [and] McNeil of Libby Honolulu, Limited, Libby's Pine Apple Products . . . [have] written a long letter here explaining their troubles. . . . They say we now turn to or want the best man in America or Europe to come over for a year and study the problem."[19]

Carver's fame had not come easily, nor was the road he trod without some dangers. There were severe prohibitions against whites and blacks sharing entrances and water fountains, meeting in the same facilities, and working on common projects as equals. The so-called offences could be created on the spot, including infractions such as " 'window peeping,' 'unpopularity,' 'insulting [white] women,' 'being disreputable,' 'self defense,' 'giving evidence,' and sometimes 'cause known.' "[20] Lynching was of particular concern. Nonetheless, he maintained his schedule as best he could, addressing predominantly white audiences in the North, Midwest, and South. Over time, though, the combination of his age and health and the challenges of the less than commodious arrangements under Jim Crow laws caused him to begin to decline invitations.[21]

Carver's primary focus was to serve the southern black community and work on common, readily available items. In fact, he patented only three out of hundreds of innovations and developments so that others would not be prevented from using or improving on them. It was also vital that he continue his work at Tuskegee, where he could have direct contact with young blacks. He had absolute faith in the ability of those he was training. Writing to the Lion's Club in June 1929, he stated, "It is all too clear that unless farming partakes of the intellectual as well as the muscular it will fail. There must be vision or the people will perish. The vision today is in the young men of the South who will lead along creative paths in the laboratories and in the fields. Their knowledge combined with their love for and their loyalty to the South will not only save it but give it leadership."[22] His commitment to Tuskegee and his students was such that he turned down Thomas Edison's offer of a lucrative salary of $50,000 if he would agree to move his research to the Edison labs in the North.[23] But Carver's credo held that the true aspirations of the research scientist should be to develop products that were socially oriented rather than commercially driven. Furthermore, he believed that the South, especially the blacks of the South, must be prepared to set the example for the rest of the country.

Negotiations with Carver

Responding to Golden, Carver wrote, "I am grateful to learn of your proposition. I am very confident that such a group as you designate can be found, and personally, I think it is a fine thing. Now as to going myself, I am not so sure whether my strength will permit it or not. It depends on just how strenuous the work will be. It may be necessary to select a person who is much younger than myself."[24] Passing the offer on to one of his protégés, John Sutton, he wrote, "At times you have expressed a desire to go abroad. The Soviet Russian government has asked me to select 25 to 30 colored specialists in cotton growing to go over there and stay two years to help develop the cotton industry in their new territory. I have told them that I am not sure that I can go myself. He [Golden] says he is coming down from New York for a conference with me to complete further arrangements. I do not know, of course, all the details with reference to remuneration, etc., but provided the remuneration is sufficient I am wondering if such a trip would interest you."[25]

Although pleased with the overall proposal, Carver still needed to verify the project's—and Golden's—bona fides. In a January 24, 1931, letter, he noted, "As soon as you hear from the Commissar of Agriculture of the U.S.S.R., I shall be interested in knowing the further plans. I shall endeavor to select the 25 or 30 men you wish, although the number is rather large and I am not sure about them. The remuneration, naturally, would have much to do with their decision to go. As to myself I can give you no definite promise until I talk the matter over with you, as it will mean much for me to go away from the Institute for six months, or naturally, any length of time, but I shall endeavor to do the best I can."[26] Without Carver's help, Golden's attempts to assemble this group of black agricultural specialists would have likely come to naught. Carver had prestige and a vast network of students, former students, and colleagues, all of whom would act with little hesitation if he supported a project.

On April 18, 1931, Golden expanded the offer. Those taking up these contracts not only would receive their transportation to and from the Soviet Union but would have all-expense paid vacations on the Black Sea, full health benefits, housing, and the possibility of taking their families with them. Most important, they were being sought by a young nation that officially outlawed racial inequality and promised to put them to work immediately. And again, he warned, time was of the essence.

> At last we have an answer from Moscow. The reason for its delay was due to the thousands of applications coming from various countries. . . . Now for our proposition. Instead of 25 or 30 cotton specialists, we want specialists of all branches of agriculture. Such as cotton, live stock, gardeners, poultry, rice raisers, etc., numbering 50 or more if possible. This does not mean only men, women specialists are accepted on the same basis as men. As I stated in my previous letter, the passage to and from the U.S.S.R., for the men and their families, will be paid by our office. The minimum salary will be between three and four hundred rubles a month. (Equivalent to one hundred fifty to two hundred dollars). This is the minimum. The maximum will be much more, but this will be determined according to your recommendation and their ability. But no one will receive less than the above figure.[27]

These working conditions were incredibly different from anything Carver and his students knew of in the United States, and, Golden had stated that women specialists would be paid the same as men. That the number was increased, though, made both realize that Tuskegee could not be the sole source for recruiting black specialists. Nonetheless, Golden was certain that with Carver's backing, the best graduates from other institutions could be attracted to the project too. In fact, when the group was assembled in the fall of 1931, students and graduates from Tuskegee, Hampton Institute, Wilberforce, and Howard were among those looking to work in the Soviet Union.

The greatest achievement would have been to have the famed Carver head the group. As he closed his April 18, 1931, letter, Golden reiterated the importance of the project and of Carver's role in it.

1. Russia is inviting you to see her country, the largest agricultural country in the world, and to get your views.
2. It would be a pleasure, we think, for you to accompany your men into a new field of work. . . .
3. You owe it to your race. Russia is the only country in the world today that gives equall [sic] chance to black and white alike.[28]

A Cautious Approach

Besides being a result of his age and health, Carver's hesitation to personally commit himself may have been a response to Tuskegee's delicate position as a small black institution in the southern United States. Like most historically black institutions at the time, Tuskegee was heavily dependent on white philanthropic and local support. Under the conservative stewardship of Moton, who took over following the death of the equally careful Booker T. Washington in 1915, Tuskegee maintained a low-key posture. Hughes alluded to this problem when he published his essay "Cowards from the Colleges," in the *Crisis* in 1934. "Two years ago, on a lecture tour, I visited more than fifty colored schools and colleges. . . . I had been aware of the lack of personal freedom that exists on most Negro campuses. . . . Can it be that these endowments, incomes, gifts—and therefore salaries—springing from missionary and philanthropic sources and from big Northern boards and foundations—have such strings tied to them that those accepting them can do little else?"[29] This was certainly not the first international project for Carver, but his projects with the Japanese, Koreans, and in Africa had not presented the same thorny political issues.[30] At the same time, he knew the U.S. government scrutinized connections Americans might make with the Soviets. So, although Carver could support the ambitions of his former students and encourage them to take up Soviet contracts, he himself had to be careful as to how he—and, by implication, Tuskegee—negotiated these contacts.[31]

Facing External Scrutiny

Even in the early stages of the negotiations, word had gotten out that the Russians had approached Carver. Carver was used to receiving letters on many topics and even those proposing to counsel him on various matters. He must also have been intrigued by the opposing positions surfacing in the commentary. An editorial in the *East Tennessee News* stated, "If it is worth while for the Russians to take Carver and his associates all the way to northeastern Europe to learn from him . . . it ought to be worth while for southern cotton interests to make use of his knowledge in this country. . . . It may be that Russia's recognition of Carver may lead to his acceptance in the United States as a genius of the laboratory."[32] A similar wily observation appeared in the *Christian Index* of the Baptist Convention of the State of Georgia under the heading "Russia Calls Carver." "The article in question states that Dr. George W. Carver . . . has been invited by Soviet Russia to . . . demonstrate the best method of agricultural production and exploitation. Though Carver is a Negro, his fame as an agriculturist is well known among the leaders of the Soviet states. He is a man of becoming modesty and has not had the publicity that one of his ability and achievement deserves. He has many Southern white friends who appreciate him. . . . The outcome of the Soviet's invitation will be watched with interest."[33]

Ultimately, Carver did not go to the Soviet Union; however, he made sure to stay in touch with some of the agricultural specialists. This correspondence not only satisfied his intellectual curiosity as he counseled them on their work but also his personal interest to see how they fared under the Soviet experiment.

The Agricultural Specialist Group Forms

In a June 1931 letter to Carver written shortly before the group was due to leave, Golden stated, "I am very successful in the organization of the group. Each day brings many new enthusiastic applicants."[34] In addition to his and Carver's efforts, others were also helping. As Charles Burroughs Sr. wrote to encourage Charles Young's mother, "[Tomtom] should be able to go very far in his field. . . . The promise [of] unlimited possibilities and the absence of all restrictions to his advancement make the Russian experience all the more preferable. . . . And above it all there would be the satisfaction of helping to build a new world, one that belongs to and serves its builders and workers."[35]

The agricultural specialist team represented a wide array of institutions and skills. Golden and Sutton were from Tuskegee, George Tynes was from Wilberforce, Joseph Roane attended Virginia Normal, Bernard Powers went to Howard, and others had gone to Hampton.[36] Frank Gorden and Charles Young had finished Ohio State University.[37] Their specialties went beyond cotton culture; they included agronomy, civil engineering, animal husbandry, irrigation technology, and research chemistry.

The group's departure was delayed for two months, and during this interlude Golden decided to ask Carver for a favor—a letter of recommendation for himself. "A letter of recommendation from you naturally adds . . . prestige. . . . It may be necessary. I was born and reared on a cotton farm in Mississippi, as you know. I had many years of practical experience in agriculture and two years of theoretical training at Tuskegee Institute."[38]

In early October 1931, Golden, together with a group of fourteen, boarded the *Deutschland*.[39] It was ten months after Golden had first entered into negotiations with Carver.[40] The team was made up primarily of black men but included Roane, who was Native American and Irish, and several wives.[41] They landed in the Soviet Union on November 7, 1931.

CHAPTER 7

The Agricultural Specialists
Journey to the Soviet Union

ℰℋℐ

They are giving me the opportunity here and I shall
do my best to justify their belief in me.[1]
—John Sutton (1932)

"*T*he last time you heard from me I was simply a physiologist working in the cotton fields of Central Asia. Now I am a research chemist following in the footsteps of my illustrious teacher, Professor G. W. Carver. . . . As my example and guide in this pioneer experimental work, I have you. From nothing at all, as a beginning you made undying history thru your application to the 'study of things.' I firmly believe that I can and will make world famous discoveries in the field in which I am working. Life shapes itself into queer and unexpected patterns. To think that I owe all this to you," wrote John Sutton to his mentor.[2]

Sutton was one of fifteen black sojourners who left New York in October 1931 to take up Soviet contracts as agricultural specialists.[3] Led by Oliver Golden, these highly trained specialists looked forward to relief from Jim Crow, a chance to do something meaningful, and good pay. Like the technical specialists, they were willing to put their intellectual and "sweat" equity behind projects in the Soviet Union because their home country had little use for them as skilled professionals.

The Goldens and Forming a Group

When Golden contacted Carver in 1930, he was working as a short-order cook to pay his bills and was attempting to recruit workers for Soviet contracts. After two years in the Soviet Union, he was trying to find the best way to put his political studies to good use. Lily Golden noted that her father was not particularly comfortable with the regular party work, but he found his niche when he came upon the idea to merge black agricultural expertise with the needs of the peoples in the Soviet republics. "There were . . . plenty of white Americans . . . [and] people from Europe mirrored the flow from America. . . . My father . . . felt that Blacks also had a role to play in the success of the socialist experiment.

99

Oliver Golden was also persuaded that help needed to be given to the non-European peoples of the Soviet Union—the Uzbeks, Turkmen, Chukcha—who had been colonized and who in American terms were 'colored.' . . . He believed that Black people could help their own kind."[4]

His partner in putting this project together was a young woman, Bertha Bialek, whom he met in New York. The two of them had been arrested following a protest. She was different from the first two women in his life. She was not black like his first wife, Jane, nor a national minority, like Anya, with whom he later fell in love in the Soviet Union. Yet, in her own way, Bertha, too, was a social outsider. She was a Polish Jew whose family had moved to New York in the first wave of post-World War I immigrants. Despite having been middle-class in Poland, the family's fortunes plummeted with their immigration to the United States, and at eighteen Bertha had joined her brother Jack in a garment factory. In this highly charged milieu, she became politically active, and, within a year, she followed her brother into the Communist Party. It was her party work that brought her into contact with Golden. As one of her oldest friends told her granddaughter, "How else for your grandmother? I know she wasn't especially looking for a husband—black, yellow or white. This was around 1927, and your grandmother was earning enough money for her own apartment. Bertha and your grandfather had a shared belief in equal justice for all, regardless of race, color, or creed. She didn't fall in love with Golden *because* he was a black man. It's just that Bertha wouldn't have let his color stop her from seeing the person inside."[5]

Continuing her grandmother's story, Khanga observed, "The bitter [struggles of the International Ladies Garment Workers' Union] fueled my grandmother's political activism throughout the 1920s. She clearly relished her memories of . . . rising at dawn to walk the picket lines [and] of occasionally landing in jail."[6] Lily continued, "My mother was again in prison, where she met Oliver Golden, who had also been arrested for participating in a demonstration. The family legend has it that it was love at first sight—in a New York prison cell."[7]

Bertha helped Golden with a number of projects, including typing the letters to Carver. As their common political views brought them into contact on a regular basis, they also developed an emotional attachment. But the final question, of crossing the color line, was difficult.[8] Continued Lily, "It took time till [sic] she was ready to marry Oliver Golden. Even in the 1920s, marrying a Black man required from a white woman considerable courage. . . . Bertha was approaching a nervous breakdown. . . . [But] no white doctor would come to Harlem [where she was living with Golden], and no Black doctor would risk lynching in order to touch a white woman. A doctor friend of hers told her that the solution was to make up her mind, then her nerves would calm. She decided to marry. From that day till [sic] her death, she never had a moment of sickness or regret."[9] Still, as Khanga noted, life for this mixed-race couple was not easy. "Harlem was really the only place where an interracial couple of modest means and no celebrity could hope to live with safety and tolerance. Even there, Oliver and Bertha had to pay twice as much for a room as they would have had to pay in another neighborhood."[10]

When the agricultural specialist group left in October 1931, Golden and his wife Bertha were the only two who had a clear political purpose. For the others in the group, the purpose was more one of self-fulfillment. "For several of the men sailing on the Deutschland, the Soviet offer meant their first, and only, chance to work as professionals rather than waiters."[11] Observing the photos that appeared in the New York *Amsterdam News* just before the group left, Lily commented, "The photos show a group of young blacks, among whom my father—at 44—was the oldest. My mother was 18 years younger. . . . The others were between 25 and 35. Their faces radiated happiness and expectation, mingled with some uncertainty about the future. These were the faces of romantics and idealists, all of them looking so beautiful because [of] their aim of helping others."[12]

The eleven agricultural specialists were Oliver Golden, Bernard Powers, John Sutton, George Tynes, C. T. Hopkins, Frank Faison, Frank Gordon, Welton Curry, A. M. Overton, Joseph Roane, and Charles Young. Also, Golden, Faison, and Roane took their wives.[13] A *Baltimore Afro-American* article provided further details on the project and its members. Under the dual headings of "Eleven Cotton Specialists to Develop Industry in Russia" and "Son of Colonel Charles Young Off to Russia," the article identified Young as a graduate of Ohio State University and a teacher at Prairie View College in Texas. "[Young was] the son of the late Col. Charles Young, [highest] ranking colored officer in the U.S. Army. . . . Young believes that his father would approve of his course in working for the New Russians."[14] As to the others, the article continued:

> Welton C. Curry, 24, former football player at Virginia State College from which he graduated . . . with a B.S. in Agriculture degree; John W. Sutton, 34, formerly an instructor in agriculture at Tuskegee Institute and Prairie View College . . . and recently a graduate student at Iowa State College. Also Ames G. W. Tynes, 25, former star half back at Wilberforce University where he completed his course in Agriculture last June; B. L. Hopkins, 30, Norfolk, VA, a teacher of vocational agriculture in the Tidewater district . . . and a graduate of . . . Virginia State College. . . . A. M. Overton, 24, Hartford, NC, teacher . . . and graduate in agriculture from the Agricultural and Technical College, Greensboro, NC. . . . Honeymooners J. J. Rane [Roane], 23[,] . . . from Virginia State College [and his new wife,] Miss Sadie Russell; O. J. Golden, former Tuskegee student and dirt farmer in Mississippi, W. C. Avant of Omaha, Neb.; Frank Faison, Jr. Greensboro, NC; and Frank Gordon, M.S. in Agriculture, Ohio State University [, as well as the] engineer B. Conrad Powers, of Huntsville, Alabama.[15]

The article noted that four other blacks accompanying the group were not agricultural specialists but were slated for other roles. They were seaman

Morris Wickman, steelworkers Sam Langford and A. J. Lewis, and coalminer J. W. Jones. Ten white workers departed with them as well. Then, to underscore the uniqueness of this interracial team, the point was made that "the party was given a farewell demonstration on Monday night at Cooper Union. Workers of both races joined in the celebration."[16]

The Group Heads Out

When this group of black sojourners embarked on their four-week journey to the Soviet Union, most knew little more about the physical challenges than they did about the political ones. Golden was the only one who had been to the Soviet Union. Observed Khanga, "My grandfather was probably the only card-carrying Communist . . . in the group. A few of the men certainly sympathized with Marxism (what they knew of it), while others had no particular interest in communism and no knowledge whatsoever about the Soviet Union."[17] Even Golden, who had done some practical training projects during his student years, is unlikely to have gone as far east as Soviet Asia. What he did know about those far-off regions would have come from his friendship with Anya, who was from Siberia, and other provincial students.

Roane told Khanga in an early-1980s interview, "I hardly knew where the Soviet Union was when Golden came to my college to speak. No one called me a Communist for going, because no one in my circle knew exactly what a Communist was. . . . I signed on for two reasons. In the first place, Amtorg [the official Soviet agency that hired foreign workers] was offering better pay for a month than a lot of people would make in a year in the Depression. Secondly, I was young and I wanted to see the world. I thought this might be the only chance I'd ever get."[18]

Two members of the group also had bold and adventuresome wives. Like Jane Golden in 1925, these nonpolitical women, Sadie Roane and Faison's wife, were unusual in that they were willing to take this long journey. This spoke to a combination of spousal love, the responsibilities of marriage, and the personal need to free themselves from the restrictions facing blacks. As Khanga reported, they welcomed the new freedoms. "The four-week voyage . . . was a vacation. . . . They [Roane and Sadie] toasted one another with vodka, an unfamiliar drink lavishly provided by their Soviet hosts. They also took Russian lessons—the Soviets had supplied a tutor. . . . But . . . he and his wife didn't learn much Russian."[19] This was also the first time that most of the group had been outside the United States. As Roane recalled, "We could do whatever we wanted, go wherever we wanted. There was no back of the bus, you could just get on and ride. . . . I'd never in my life . . . been able to walk into a restaurant and know I would be served food, and treated like any other customer."[20]

But the journey was not always so pleasant for all of them. Bertha, the sole white woman traveling with this group of blacks, was seriously threatened in Germany. As Lily recounted the incident, "They stepped ashore at Hamburg, where the boat docked overnight. Of course 1931 was not yet 1933 in Germany. . . . Fascism was just beginning. . . . But my mother told me later that she hadn't felt comfortable walking on Hamburg streets in the company of 15 [sic] Black men. German rowdies screaming insults and brandishing fists followed them."[21]

Conversely, for many coming out of the shadow of Jim Crow, it was even harder to envision a life without such affronts. Noted Roane, "When Golden spoke at my college, I didn't believe him when he said there was no segregation in the Soviet Union. Why should I?" But as the days passed in the Soviet Union and no incidents arose, these novice visitors began to understand that they were operating under a different system. Noted Khanga, this "deeply [affected] each member of the group, including those who had a scant interest in communism." The only discriminatory event Roane could recall of his time in the Soviet Union occurred when two white Americans tried to throw him and a friend out of a barbershop. But, as he reportedly happily, the Russian barbers "threw the whites out of the shop with lather still on their faces."[22]

Encountering the Soviet Union

The arrival in Leningrad in November 1931 brought the agricultural specialists their first taste of Russian winter and Soviet bureaucracy. It was cold and damp, and they faced assorted delays while the authorities sorted out their papers. Their arrival had not gone without some fanfare, though, and the local hospitality helped the time pass. As Lily noted, "It was the 14th anniversary of the October Revolution.[23] They were met at the port by delegations of workers from factories, representatives of the Communist Party and of the State. For a few days in Leningrad, they were in euphoria." Enthusiastic guides ushered them around the city and fed them. And when the arrangements had been made, their hosts installed them in a special train carriage reserved for foreigners. It was to be a long, ten-day journey across the country to Soviet Asia, covering nearly two thousand miles.[24]

This lengthy train ride, with the enormously varied countryside and many different peoples getting on and off the train, introduced the specialists to the country's great physical and human diversity. At each stop, local vendors from the surrounding farms, speaking languages they could not understand, offered items for sale, most of which were new to this group. Hughes, who took a similar trip a year later, wrote, "First, the rich farm lands of the Black Earth region slid by our windows with stations where buxom peasant women from the kolhozes sold chickens and eggs; then the Volga at sunset, famous old river of song and story; later, Orenburg where Asia begins and where we saw camels in the streets; then the vast reaches of the Kirghiz steppes and the bright tip of the Ural Sea like silver in the sun."[25]

Arriving in Uzbekistan, it was immediately clear why this region was targeted for their cotton project. This region had a history of producing cotton that went much further back than the tsarist presence in European Russia.[26] Continued Hughes, "In the autumn, if you step off any train almost anywhere in the fertile parts of Central Asia, you step into a cotton field, or into a city or town whose streets are filled with evidence of cotton nearby. The natives call it 'white gold.' On all the dusty roads, camels, carts and trucks, loaded with the soft fiber, head towards the gins and warehouses. Outside the towns, ofttimes as far as the eye can see, the white bolls lift their precious heads." The landscape was thousands and thousands of miles away from the southern United States, yet it resembled the country they had left behind. "The same thing is true of the southern part of the United States . . . except that on our roads there are no camels. Mules and wagons bear the burdens. And Negroes do most of the work."[27]

Not yet at the end of their journey across space, time, and culture, the agricultural specialists were met by "drivers in *arby*, traditional open-air Uzbek carts pulled by donkeys," and an open-air cart ride in that November climate was quite sobering. Roane's adventure the next day confirmed that there were many new experiences to be had in Soviet Central Asia. Observed Khanga, "On his second day in Tashkent, Joe Roane pondered whether he had wandered onto a movie set when he got lost in a snowstorm and was suddenly confronted by an Uzbek riding a camel and brandishing a saber. This romantic apparition spoke neither Russian nor English, and Roane spoke no Uzbek, so he was unable to ask for directions back to his hotel. On the streets of Tashkent in 1931, a driver in a car was a more remarkable sight than a driver on a camel."[28]

Leningrad and Moscow had cars, trucks, and streetcars. Tashkent had streetcars too, but it also had camels, donkeys, horses, and open-air carts as major means of transportation. Tashkent combined the many cultures of the people who had come to inhabit it. It had historically been a major transshipment point and a crossroads of the famed Silk Road.[29] Hughes was most impressed when he made his first entry. "It was dark when I reached this largest and most important town in Soviet Central Asia, the regional capital of all that section of the world, where there are streetcars, bright lights, European shops, theatres and even night clubs."[30]

Hughes's initial encounter with Powers at the train station in Tashkent had not been coincidental. As when the technical specialist Robert Robinson met Paul Robeson in Moscow in 1934 and when Otto Hall met his brother, Harry Haywood, in 1926, the Soviets ensured that blacks were part of the welcoming committees for new blacks coming through the region. This practice increased the possibility of spreading positive news about the Soviet experiment and helped build a friendly community of supporters among people of color in the global arena. The black sojourners were also happy to see other blacks, who brought in a spiritual connection to the global black community and, sometimes, artifacts, such as magazines or records. Eslanda Goode, Robeson's niece, noted that they looked forward to these visits because he and his wife often brought items from black America.[31] Khanga remembered such items as well. "Momma's room housed our most prized possession: a Japanese-made phonograph given to us by an American friend. . . . [And we had records by] Sarah Vaughan, Ella Fitzgerald and Ray Charles."[32]

Hughes was also looking forward to seeing how the black agricultural specialists were participating in the Soviet experiment when he agreed to join them for Christmas. He could not help but be amused at watching Powers negotiate the local bureaucracy. He had been in the country long enough to know that the black specialists enjoyed certain social levers that blacks in the United States lacked and that Powers could bypass certain Soviet regulations and practices. He even liked the fact that Powers had access to private clubs in Tashkent. "Powers had been there a few times with some of his engineer friends, so he had told me, 'It's the kind of place where I can wear a tuxedo.'"[33] Now, watching Powers get the tickets, Hughes observed, "The lines at the ticket windows contained hundreds of persons in each queue. . . . As our train was scheduled to leave shortly, Powers decided to use his foreign worker's card and go directly to the stationmaster's office for tickets rather than wait in line. This worked. The stationmaster purchased our tickets for us quickly and we passed onto the train platform."[34]

Life in Uzbekistan

Powers and a few others were stationed in Tashkent. But the majority of the agricultural specialist group continued on another forty miles to the Machine-Tractor Station and the Seed Selection Station of the State Cotton Trust in Yangiyul. Boarding another, more rudimentary regional train, they also discovered that Yangiyul had no formal train station. Yangiyul was a whistle stop, and people were simply let off in the middle of the countryside, where they would be met by someone who would take them to the farm. As Hughes observed from his trip a year later, "At dusk, the train finally slowed down at the place where we were to spend Christmas—it did not even stop. It just whistled so that those who intended to descend there might jump off into the blizzard. This collective had no village attached, I learned later, so trains did not really stop there. As a convenience, they did slow down."[35] Unlike Hughes, though, who had made separate travel arrangements with Powers, Golden's group went there under official auspices. It is likely, therefore, that the authorities would have seen to it that the train actually stopped so that all of the agricultural specialists could get off safely with their bags and other bundles.

People treated these local trains like buses. They crammed themselves and their possessions into every space. "The coaches were antiques, with each having open platforms at both ends. Even these platforms were already filled with people. Powers and I went from coach to coach until we found a platform where we could at least mount the steps to stand in the cold outside the coach. . . . After one or two more rural stops, I managed to push, half-frozen, into the car, which was without heat but steamy with human breath and vile with the stench of camel drivers, peasants and bazaar merchants, with all the sacks, bundles and baskets of onions and melons they had piled beneath the seats, in the aisles and on the shelves overhead."[36]

When the two were met by Golden, Roane, and Young at the Yangiyul stop, they were miserable. Hughes was in a foul mood. "I jumped off [the train] into the snow and immediately . . . sunk into a mixture of slush and mud almost to [my] ankles." Even in the warmth of Golden's quarters, his demeanor did not change significantly. "Nothing cheered me up, or thawed me out for hours. . . . I just sat glumly by the fire, nursed my cognac. . . . Every so often someone poured me another drink and left me in the corner with my thoughts." It took some solid food of "stewed rabbit, hot bread and buttered squash" to help him feel better. Then, he was able to see that "they were delightfully amiable hosts, these cotton-collective Negroes from America in the middle of a mud-cake oasis frosted with snow."[37]

Hughes's initial assessment was critical. "Conditions on the Soviet collective, while a great change for the Uzbeks, were for Negroes from America more primitive than most of them had known at home. . . . The houses were comfortable, but there were no fireplaces, no gas stoves, no radio programs, and no juke boxes." But, after spending time with them, he began to reconsider. "They were largely dependent upon themselves for social life in that far-off oasis. But despite their problems they were not a gloomy group, and Christmas with them was a very jolly period for me."[38]

Golden's daughter, Lily, who grew up in Uzbekistan, provided another perspective. "Creature comforts were totally lacking. Yangi-Yul in those days was a small kishlak—Uzbek village—consisting of yards fenced in by walls made of dried manure and mud.[39] Inside the courtyards, the huts were made of the same materials. . . . There was no means of heating, no indoor cooking stoves." At the same time, Lily noted, "Everything was spotlessly clean since the yards were washed down with water at least twice a day because of the desert heat." Also, the agricultural specialists did not live in these traditional huts but in a large European-style house, divided up into apartments. Continued Lily, "They were not unhappy. My father had prepared them for the material hardships. And, spiritually, they felt free and independent, warmed by the knowledge that they were helping others."[40]

Bertha Golden and Sadie Roane

Regrettably little is known about most of the women who went in the agricultural specialists group. All the men had certain skills and were assigned to various projects, but the wives did not have clearly defined roles.[41] Some sources provide a modicum of details on Sadie Roane. Much more is known about Bertha Golden because of the books written by her daughter, Lily, and granddaughter, Yelena Khanga. Nothing is known about Frank Faison's wife.

Khanga noted that at each stage of her grandmother's life, moving from Poland to New York, then from girlhood into womanhood, and then into her relationship with Golden, her grandmother accepted each challenge as it came. In an interview, Bertha's friend Pearl noted, "Equal rights: Think what that meant to people who had grown up afraid to go out at night because they were Jews. And that is what the immigrant Jews had in common with the blacks, who had also known fear in America."[42] Pearl continued, "She was always working for a cause; that was her idea of fun."[43]

Sadie's response to the Soviet experiment provided a striking contrast to that of Bertha. Bertha had been involved with the Communists and progressive campaigns for years prior to moving to the Soviet Union. The sojourn was to be another step in her political life. Newlywed Sadie was following her new husband, Joe, on an adventure, what he termed the "most exciting periods of their lives."[44] Although neither was looking to move abroad permanently, the prospect of a going abroad was far more attractive than staying in Virginia.

When the agricultural specialists got to Yangiyul, Bertha was initially uncomfortable with the special arrangements made for the foreigners. Conversely, Sadie was happy with them. Although living conditions were more Spartan than in the United States, having a good salary and help around the house and the general prestige of being part of the specialists group were welcomed. Observed Blakely, "The Soviet authorities were determined to provide them with the type of lifestyle they believed scientists enjoyed in the United States. Sadie Roane and the other wives did not work outside the home and were given Russian servants. In addition, housing, food, child care, and medical care were all free; plus Roane received a salary equivalent to six hundred dollars per month. . . . Contrasted with the opportunities available to a 'colored scientist' in the United States, and with conditions during the existing Great Depression, it is understandable that the Roanes renewed their contracts until 1937."[45]

Some returned to the United States after their first two years because of the living and working conditions and concerns over the "high incidence of malaria."[46] Others were glad not to return to the meaningless, low-paying jobs left to Negroes, especially as their salaries were helping support family back home. Also, as was true for the technical specialists, many had arranged to have their salaries paid partly in the United States.[47] Importantly, some of them had started families, and this circumstance factored into their decision making. The Roanes were the first to have a child when their son Joseph was born in 1932. The Goldens were next with a daughter born in 1934. George Tynes married a Ukrainian woman, and John Sutton married a Russian, and their first children were born in 1934 and around 1936, respectively.

Still, in 1937, when confronted with the Soviet ultimatum to relinquish their U.S. citizenship, most decided to return to the United States. But, noted Roane, they had forgotten what life was like for blacks in the United States. "In just a few years—you'd be surprised—you could forget what segregation was like."[48] Now, not only were they blacks, but they were viewed as "red and black." Roane had trouble finding work, and his income plummeted from the equivalent of six hundred dollars a month in the Soviet Union to ninety dollars a month when he finally found a teaching job.[49] They might have returned to an advanced society with the gas stoves, radio programs, and juke boxes missed by Hughes, but their cost of living had increased dramatically. And they no longer had the other social cushions they had enjoyed in the Soviet Union.

They had also returned with more than simple memories of their lives in the Soviet Union; they had a son named Joseph Stalin Roane. Although his name unnerved Khanga when she met him in the 1980s, it was the source of amusement for them. "The younger Roane [Joseph Stalin Roane] considers this a good joke on every new, unsuspecting acquaintance. (For a Russian of my generation, the joke is to say the least, unsettling.) . . . They had decided to name their son Joseph when he was born in 1932. The Soviet interpreter (the Roanes' Russian was still shaky) added the middle name 'Stalin' on the birth certificate."[50] Allison Blakely, who also interviewed the Roanes in the late 1970s, noted that naming a baby Joseph Stalin was a common practice in the Soviet Union in the early 1930s.[51] But the fact that the Roanes never changed the name suggests that they retained a certain fondness for their Soviet sojourn. Observed Blakely, "Although the Roanes left the Soviet Union during Stalin's purges, their leaving had no direct connection with these events. They had spent two years in Central Asia and their remaining years in the northern Caucasus and the Ukraine. . . . They left with an overall positive impression of Soviet society, having been especially impressed by the prevailing spirit of collective effort. Like Tynes, they also noted the apparent absence of any racial bias directed toward them."[52]

Bertha and Oliver Golden also welcomed the Soviet experiment, but, in contrast to Sadie's response to the special social supports, Khanga noted that "my grandmother . . . was extremely uncomfortable whenever she was exposed to any special privileges."[53] She envisioned living simply alongside those with whom she was working, and as they made their way from Leningrad to Moscow, she probably thought she would live in one of the typical log houses she had seen from her train window. However, the wood of the European part of the Soviet Union would not have been so plentiful in the Uzbek deserts. Typical Uzbek houses were made of mud and dung and sat low and close to the ground.[54] However, the Soviets wanted to make the foreigners happy and made other arrangements for them:

> The food and physical comforts of my grandparents' apartment attested to the fact that contract workers from abroad were not expected to live like ordinary Soviet [or Uzbek] citizens. The Americans had a large house, divided into separate apartments. They were able to supplement food supplies with purchases from special, well-stocked stores open only to foreigners. This was important, because forced collectivization of the land created famines in Uzbekistan and many other areas during the thirties. . . . [But these] kinds of privileges, taken for granted by

both foreigners and Party leaders . . . were obviously at odds with my grandparents' commitment to egalitarianism.[55]

Before she left the United States, Bertha was aware that the Russian people (and by extension non-Russians, like the Uzbeks, in the distant parts) did not have the kind of creature comforts enjoyed in the United States. As an immigrant to the United States from Poland, Bertha had already learned to reduce her life to essential items. Thus, she took only two conveniences with her: her sewing machine and typewriter. She was later forced to sell the sewing machine but held on to the typewriter because of her duties in handling the correspondence and, later, working as a translator. "[Grandmother] traveled light precisely because she was bound for a poor country. She said she had no desire to flaunt the kind of material well-being enjoyed by most Americans, even during the Depression, in comparison to most Soviet citizens."[56]

Although the wives did not have assigned jobs, Bertha took it upon herself to work with the young Uzbek women and to find ways to help them move beyond the age-old Muslim restrictions. She encouraged them to become educated and to take off their veils. Khanga wrote, "In the countryside, many aspects of life had not changed for centuries. Polygamy was common and a great many women wore veils over their faces (though both practices had been abolished by Soviet law). My grandmother took on the task of persuading women to shed their veils; she encountered resistance from older women and men of all ages, but young women liked the novelty of the sun and wind on their bare faces."[57] The project was not simply to have the women mimic Western modes of living. Bertha's goals matched those of Soviets, who considered the liberation of women a vital step in modernizing the region.[58] But the Soviets, too, were confronted by Uzbek traditionalists.[59] Continued Khanga, "The Soviet government's attempts to improve the status of women, through compulsory elementary schooling for both sexes and laws prohibiting the sale of girls into marriage, generated fierce opposition among religious and tribal leaders. Gradually, however, the status of women did change for the better—and I consider this a genuine achievement of the revolution. Even before *glasnost*, I would rather have been born a woman in Uzbekistan than, say, in Pakistan or Afghanistan."[60]

Dispersal to Other Projects

For the first two-year posting to the collective farm in Yangiyul, the agricultural specialists worked primarily on cotton, sugar beets, and peanuts. Their tenure in Yangiyul was well worth the time. They were "responsible for introducing at least one important new strain of cotton to the area and to the Soviet economy."[61] This work had not been easy, but they had the tireless energy of the Uzbeks to help them complete the project. As Roane told Khanga, "It was backbreaking for the people who actually tilled the soil. . . . The Uzbeks were tireless workers. They could almost make water run uphill. I'd seen something like this in the South, but irrigation didn't pose the same kind of problem."[62]

In 1934, the agricultural specialists were reassigned to other parts of Soviet Asia and the Caucasus region to help train others. "Roane . . . was sent to help the Georgians operate a tomato-canning plant. George Tynes went off to breed poultry on numerous farms. John Sutton continued working on a process for making a new kind of rope."[63] Golden was reassigned to a teaching post at the Institute of Irrigation and Mechanization in Tashkent.

The Special Contributions of Sutton and Tynes

John Sutton was a research chemist who had initially studied at Tuskegee under Carver. He then went to Drake and the University of Massachusetts in Amherst (then the Massachusetts Agricultural College). Carver had thought of him almost immediately when he received Golden's proposal to put together a group of experts and wrote him about it on January 26, 1931. But, for some reason, it took Sutton almost seven months to return his completed application and other documentation to Golden. Luckily for him, though, the group's departure had been delayed, and Golden could still accept him. As Golden wrote Carver in August, "Today, I received a letter from Mr. Sutton of Texas. He has filled out and returned his questionnaire and a recommendation from you." Sutton himself was pleased to signal his mentor that he had embarked on his new life when he sent a quick message on October 15, 1931: "I'm taking ship for Russia tonight."[64]

Like Tynes and Golden, Sutton also happily renewed his Soviet contract in 1934. He was on the edge of a new discovery: developing a new kind of rope made out of rice fiber. He had also married and was expecting his first child. In a letter to Carver, dated July 1, 1932, he wrote, "I have been lately appointed manager of a newly organized laboratory of Technology in the Soviet Rice Institute. My main function is to discover some methods of utilizing to better advantage the rice plant. . . . Of course, new and inexperienced in this sort of creative work I am very much in need of your advice and support. . . . I suppose you have heard that I am married to a Russian girl. . . . I speak the Russian language quite freely, read the newspapers and even write letters. My wife of course is of great aid to me in this."[65]

This was one of many letters between the two men as Sutton was keen to bring Carver's expertise into their work. He also anticipated problems with his reassignment. "I have written you 3 letters since I heard from you last June but just after that I moved away from Tashkent and my mail has never quite caught up with me since."[66] Now, Sutton's new return address was "Kapacuogap, Ceb-Kab," which appeared to be written in English, but was, in fact Russian lettering. He was then in the northern Caucasus (Ceb-Kab or Sevr Kavkaz) region.[67]

Sutton's work with rice fiber was groundbreaking. Robinson, who also knew Sutton, observed, "Before Sutton's invention, Soviet rope was weak and often broke apart. But because of his work, Russia could stop importing jute and hemp and became a major exporter of string twine."[68] However, Sutton later complained that production of the rope was thwarted by corrupt bureaucrats following his departure in 1937.[69] As Robinson reported from their conversation, "One day, after Sutton returned temporarily to Moscow from the Uzbek Republic in Central Asia, I asked him what life was like for him, professionally. 'To tell you the truth . . .' he replied, 'life in Uzbekia is far from simple, I meet resistance every step of the way when I try to introduce new methods of technology. People are so accustomed to doing things the old way, they really do not want to change. Our efforts also suffer from a great shortage of equipment. . . . I receive promises from everywhere that the situation will be looked into, but nothing has changed. I just give in and do the job the way the people want it done and keep my innovations to myself. But then I feel guilty, because the result is just the opposite of what I was brought here to do.'"[70]

Despite these complaints, though, racism was never the issue. For Sutton, the frustration was fighting people over replacing the old with the new. Technical specialist Robinson, who had arrived in the Soviet Union the year before the agricultural specialist group, had also learned ways to work within the system. He counseled Sutton, "Resistance to change is not as great, or as direct, as it was when I first arrived. . . . My proposals are rejected, ignored or accepted, but then I am not allowed to implement them. I solve the problem by working after hours, and then inviting the superintendent, the chief engineer, the department foreman, and party secretary to a demonstration of how the job can be done more efficiently and in less time. At that point, and with all of them there, they cannot very well sabotage that already-completed project."[71] However, Sutton's situation was more complex than Robinson's. Robinson was posted to industrial centers in Stalingrad and Moscow. Sutton, along with the other agricultural specialists, was posted to rural locations in the far eastern and southern sectors of the country. These were places in the early stages of modernization, and the agricultural specialists often had to contend with cultural traditions that were decidedly not European.[72]

Sutton left the country in 1937. As Khanga noted, these departures could be quite sudden. "Every non-Soviet citizen was ordered to leave the country, sometimes on forty-eight hours notice, unless he was willing to give up his American citizenship. . . . Sutton, like many of those forced to leave abruptly, left behind a Russian wife and son."[73] Two years later, in 1939, Sutton tried to bring his son, Juan, to the United States, but it was on the eve of World War II. After that, he lost contact with the boy and his mother. They were located only in the 1970s, and by then Sutton had died.[74]

Although Sutton left and his work virtually ceased, Tynes remained in the country for the rest of his life. A specialist in the breeding of fowl, he shared skills in various parts of the country as he was sent to different posts.[75] After the farm in Yangiyul, the Soviets posted Tynes and his growing family to Georgia, the Crimea, the Volga region, and, finally, Moscow. His last assignment was at a large duck research farm outside of Moscow, where he remained until he retired in 1974.

Unlike Sutton, Tynes accepted Soviet citizenship. From the first, Golden's speeches had excited him about the Soviet experiment. Recounted Lily, "Tynes later told me that he met my father on the streets of Harlem, where he listened to Oliver speaking about the situation in the Soviet Union and its problems. On the spot he asked to join the group. That started a friendship that lasted as long as they lived."[76]

A Legacy of Collaborations

Khanga observed, "I've occasionally heard patronizing suggestions about the propaganda value of these black American agronomists. There's no doubt that certain Party hacks did want to display blacks as propaganda trophies . . . but any well-informed Soviet agricultural official certainly understood how well-trained these men were by any standard and how rare their skills would be in a primitive agricultural economy. The Soviets needed cotton breeders and irrigation experts, of whatever color, as badly as they needed engineers and auto workers in other parts of the country. That's why they were willing to pay foreigners in precious hard currency."[77] A secondary, although no less important, effect of their presence was the solidarity and goodwill that resulted from their throwing themselves into the daily lives of ordinary people in far-off regions of the country. They were particularly keen to help those who, like themselves, had suffered from racism and, in the process, came to levels of satisfaction they had not known before. As Hughes noted, "I shall always remember what the natives themselves told me: 'Before, there were no schools for Uzbek children—now there are. Before, we lived in debt and fear—now we are free. Before, women were bought and sold—now no more. Before, the land and the water belonged to the beys [ruling elites]—today they are ours—and we share the cotton.'"[78]

PART III

❧

The Artists and Intellectuals

CHAPTER 8

Langston Hughes and the Black and White *Film Group*

ᘐᘐ

*They left the train to touch their hands to Soviet soil,
lift the new earth in their palms, and kiss it.*[1]
—Langston Hughes (1956)

*I*n June 1932, Langston Hughes joined a group of twenty-one people to make a film in the Soviet Union. "This unexpected chance to work in films in Russia seemed to open a new door to me."[2] Homer Smith was equally excited. "I yearned to stand taller than I had ever stood to breathe total freedom in great exhilarating gulps, to avoid all the hurts that were increasingly becoming the lot of men (and women) of color in the United States. . . . Moscow seemed the answer."[3] For Henry Lee Moon, it was a bridge to his future. "It meant the end of my frustration in trying to penetrate the color bar at the *New York Times* where my efforts were repeatedly rebuffed with the Times' standard response, 'No, not yet.'"[4]

Black and White was to be a major Soviet propaganda film that would show the American Negro "in his true character" and expose the evils of racism. The story, situated at a steel mill in the American South, would demonstrate the solidarity between white and black workers overcoming the most draconian of situations. It was to "be a departure from the traditional pattern [and trace] the development of the Negro people in America, their work, their play, their progress, their difficulties—devoid of sentimentality as well as of buffoonery." The film was sure to be welcomed "by discriminating patrons of the cinema and those people sincerely interested in the Negro."[5]

All the official *Black and White* film members were black, save one, Allen McKenzie. Six of them, Hughes, Wayland Rudd, Juanita Lewis, Thurston McNairy Lewis, Dorothy West, and Estelle Winwood, had previous experience in the theater. Most, save Hughes, Smith, Louise Thompson, and one or two others, had no formal political agenda. Most were temporary sojourners, glad to be going for their contracted time; and some were secretly hoping to find ways to stay on. Noted Hughes, "[The] two professionals [Rudd and Winwood] were also the only real mature people in our group, everyone else being well under thirty and some hardly out of their teens . . . an art student just out of Hampton, teacher, a girl elocutionist from Seattle, three would-be writers other than myself, a very pretty divorcee who traveled on alimony, a female swimming instructor, and various clerks and stenographers." Smith noted, "They came from such distances as California, Minnesota and even Montego Bay, Jamaica. . . . Wayland Rudd, who had worked in 'Porgy'; Taylor Gordon, writer and concert singer; Loren Miller, now a prominent Los Angeles attorney; Ted R. Poston, New York newsman; and Henry Lee Moon, prominent publicist and author, were amongst the twenty-two." Faith Berry's list was the most comprehensive: Lawrence O. Alberga, an agricultural worker; Matthew Crawford, an insurance clerk; Sylvia Garner, a singer and actress; social workers Constance White, Katherine Jenkins, and Leonard Hill; George Sample, a law student and Jenkins's fiancé; Mildred Jones, an art student; Juanita Lewis, a singer; Mollie Lewis, a graduate student; Thurston McNairy Lewis, an actor; Allen McKenzie, a salesman; Frank C. Montero, a student; Henry Lee Moon, a reporter; Lloyd Patterson, a paperhanger and artist; Theodore R. Poston, a reporter; Wayland Rudd, an actor; Neil Homer Smith, a postal clerk and journalist; and Dorothy West, a writer and actress. Although several of the participants had the last name Lewis, Berry did not indicate whether any of them were relatives.[6] Two of them, McKenzie and Rudd, were also known to have white female traveling companions.[7]

No matter their personal reasons, the journey was important enough that they were willing to pay their own passage. Organizer Thompson had assured them that they would be reimbursed once they got to the Soviet Union, but they still had to put forth their money first. Hughes wrote, "Very few professional theatre people were willing to pay their own fares to travel all the way to Russia to sign contracts they had never seen. Only a band of eager, adventurous young [people] were willing to do that."[8]

A week before they left, *Amsterdam News* columnist and project public-relations representative Moon issued a press release. He stated that the twenty-two-member group represented a "fair cross section of Negro life" and noted that they were to be guests of the Soviet Meschrabpom production company in Bremen, Germany, before they arrived in Leningrad on June 25th. The film project itself was to start in Moscow on July 1.[9]

The Journey Across

From the moment the film group boarded the ship, they knew they were embarking on a new adventure. They were traveling third class but enjoyed an ease of life that many had not experienced before.[10] Hughes had fun. "I practiced German, studied Russian, played deck games, and danced."[11] Roane, one of the agricultural specialist group, who had made a similar crossing the year before, had recounted a similar liberating experience. "The four-week voyage . . . was a vacation."[12]

Interestingly, the members of the *Black and White* film group were not the only blacks on board the S.S. *Europa*. Ironically, Alain Locke and Ralph

Bunche had booked passage on the same boat. These two were traveling first class and would not normally have come across the *Black and White* film group; however, once they knew about the others, they were determined to see them. Despite strained relations with Hughes, Locke took it upon himself to "spy" on the group for his benefactor, Charlotte Mason. He was, in fact, on his way to a European cure, thanks to Mason. Reported Locke, "Yesterday morning was up earlier than usual . . . asking for the passenger list. . . . The Russian Negro party is in third class. . . . [I] finally got permission to go over. . . . [Langston] looked surprised for a moment, then suddenly glum." Mason had also been Hughes's and Thompson's benefactor, but their relationship had broken off over the Scottsboro case. Locke knew, though, that Mason was still curious to know what her past protégés were doing. Bunche, also fascinated with the group and their impending project in the Soviet Union, prevailed on Locke to make an introduction. Noted Berry, "Every day [Locke] went down to third class and associated with the Hughes-Thompson group. . . . [But] for all his curious interest . . . [he] had no desire to associate with them publicly on the ship. When Ralph Bunche . . . asked for an introduction . . . Locke obliged . . . [and then] hurried off."[13]

Besides encountering basic civility on the ship, the group discovered other unexpected freedoms. They were scheduled to have a two-day layover in Berlin while they gathered their Soviet visas. However, the Soviet consulate had not been alerted about their impending arrival, and there was some question about whether they would get their visas. The uncertainty was frustrating, but Berlin brought new and unexpectedly pleasant experiences for many. Hughes observed, "Negroes were received at hotels without question [and we] ate in any restaurant we could afford. . . . I could not help but remember my recent experiences in the [U.S.] South with restaurants that served whites only, and auto camps all across America that refused to rent me a cabin in which to sleep."[14]

Later, continuing across the Baltic Sea on a Swedish ship, Hughes mused, "I have never seen such a white boat. And all other people were white, too. We were the only dark passengers. But voyagers and crew were so cordial and friendly to us that we might well have been royal guests."[15] Helsinki was also welcoming. "The people were friendly there, too. They did not seem to look upon Negroes as curiosities . . . though some Finns had never seen so many."[16]

Setting out from Helsinki by train, they were finally on the last leg of their journey. Wrote Hughes, "[The] next day we took the train headed for . . . the land where race prejudice was reported taboo. At the border were young soldiers with a red star on their caps. Spread high in the air across the railroad tracks, there was a banner: "Workers of the World Unite." When the train stopped beneath this banner for passports to be checked, a few of the young men and women left the train to touch their hands to Soviet soil, lift the new earth in their palms, and kiss it."[17]

Whether the full group participated in this grand gesture is beside the point. All were keenly aware of the enormity of their decision to make this sojourn. They had to reflect on the long crossing of over four weeks and worry how they might be treated in each new setting. Thus, this gesture was an expression of relief and hope. It was relief that the journey was almost over and hope that the Soviet experiment would live up to its promises of a welcoming, nonracist society.

A Soviet Welcome

Leningrad was their first major Russian city, and the Soviet response was more than they could have expected. The U.S. War Department in the U.S. Legation in Riga reported that *Komsomolskaya Pravda* had made the following announcement: "Leningrad. Twenty-two American Negroes have arrived from America on their way to Moscow to the motion picture factory MEZHABPOM-FILM to act as consultants in the production of the new film entitled 'Blacks and Whites' and for participation therein as actors.[18] The Negro delegation is a 'Large Motion Film Committee' which was created in America at the initiative of the American Communist Party."[19] The film was to be "made by the MEZ-HABPOMFILM, the Film-producing company owned by the International Labor Relief. . . . MEZHABPOMFILM-RUS operated since 1923. . . . Its annual production amounts to 25–30 artistic films and from 10–15 cultural films." According to the report, the film would depict "the class struggle in America, the exploitation of the Negro people through the days of slavery to the present, and the growing recognition of the necessity for solidarity between the Negro and White worker."[20]

It is doubtful that any member of the *Black and White* group was fluent in Russian. Still, no one needed to read the local press to get a sense of their importance. Wrote Hughes, "Moscow met us at Leningrad—in the persons of some of the officials of the Meschrabpom for whom we were to work. And among them was a Negro! . . . Comrade Whiteman."[21] Lovett Fort-Whiteman's presence was an important gesture. A political studies student in the 1920s, he had been a major recruiter of blacks to study and work in the Soviet Union. Now settled in the country, he had contributed to the scenario for *Black and White*;[22] he had a vested interest in making this new group feel welcome.

Installed in Leningrad's October Hotel, the group's first meal was "all the way from soup on through roast chicken . . . right down to ice cream."[23] Again, they were taken aback because all had been warned about the food shortages in the country. Berry noted that they were told, "If you can't carry [it] from New York, then buy it in Berlin. Everything: Canned goods, sugar, soap, toilet paper. . . . Otherwise you will go hungry."[24]

After a few days' rest, they were put on the train to Moscow, where again they were greeted enthusiastically. Hughes wrote, "We emerged from the train to the clicking of a battery of newspaper cameras. . . . Our hands were shaken. We were hugged and kissed. We were carried along in the crowd to the bright sunshine of the street outside . . . [and passed] through streets full of cheering Muscovites."[25] The June 28, 1932, *Moscow Daily News* reported, "Twenty-two

American Negroes arrived here on June 26 especially to take part in the film. One of them is Langdon [sic] Hughes, Negro novelist, poet and playwright. There are actors, actresses, students, newspapermen and other workers among them."[26]

Solidarity with Blacks

Hughes correctly surmised that their presence represented more than the simple arrival of a group to make a film about racism in the United States. First, the Russians held positive memories of other blacks who had gone there in tsarist times and in the early Soviet era. "The professional artists in our group were by no means the first. . . . Ida Forsyne had danced the cake walk in Moscow at the turn of the century, and Abbie Mitchell and Georgette Harvey had had great popularity in St. Petersburg in Tzarist days. As far back as 1858, as the Moor in Shakespear's [sic] *Othello*, the New York Negro actor, Ira Aldridge, had created a sensation."[27]

Second, the Russians were fond of the late-eighteenth-century Afro-Russian poet Aleksandr Pushkin and continued to celebrate his contributions to Russian language and culture. Noted Hughes, "[I saw] a lavish production based on Pushkin's famous poem. Pushkin, a descendant of the 'the Negro of Peter the Great,' is adored in Russia and his mulatto heritage was constantly played up in the press when I was there. His *Onegin* and *Boris Goudunov* [sic] are standard in all Soviet schools."[28]

Third, there was the campaign to free the Scottsboro Boys. "At that time, with the Scottsboro Case on world-wide trial in the papers everywhere, and especially in Russia, folks went out of their way to show us courtesy."[29] This same case had inspired Hughes to write some of his overtly political poems. Frustrated by the inactivity of the black leadership, he published "Red Flag on Tuskegee" in the Baltimore *Afro American* along with an article stating, "If the Communists don't awaken the Negroes of the South, who will? Certainly not the race leaders whose schools and jobs depend on white philanthropy and preach 'be nice and keep quiet.'"[30]

The Scottsboro case was so well known that virtually every Russian the group met seemed to know about it. As Hughes observed, "The children in the Moscow streets, wise little city children, will ofttimes gather around you if you are waiting for a streetcar, or looking into [a] shop window. They will take your hand and ask you about the Scottsboro boys."[31] Hughes was so impressed that he wrote the play *Scottsboro Limited* while in the Soviet Union and asked that any proceeds from the translation and sales of his booklet be given to the Soviet Scottsboro Defense Fund.[32] He also sent some poems and the play to New York and directed that the proceeds go to the U.S. Scottsboro Defense Fund.[33]

The impending *Black and White* film production and the Scottsboro publicity campaign were part of a longstanding Soviet program to discredit capitalism. Smith noted that the film "would be exhibited around the world, especially in the colored countries of Asia and Africa, as 'documentary' proof of the manner in which capitalist America discriminated against and oppressed its colored citizens."[34] Thus, the Soviets hoped that the film would set the Soviet experiment apart from the common social models of the time and, like the political-training programs of the 1920s, help spread Communist influence into other countries.

Hughes and Thompson, delighted to see these expressions of solidarity with the Scottsboro Boys, happily joined in. But some members of the *Black and White* group were uncomfortable with these expressions of support. They even avoided participating in the mass solidarity demonstrations in Moscow, claiming that they "had not come to Moscow to act like Communists."[35]

In fact, evidence of this reluctance had shown itself during the crossing. Hughes, Thompson, and Miller had decided to send a solidarity message in support of a CPUSA- and Comintern-sponsored lecture tour by Ms. Ada Wright, the mother of one of the Scottsboro Boys. "The group had not reached the middle of the Atlantic before the members began to argue and split into opposing political camps. . . . Only a minority would vote with Langston, Louise Thompson and Loren Miller to send a cable."[36]

This response disappointed Thompson deeply. It was she who had pulled the group together, and, indeed, without her tireless work, the project might not have existed. On the journey of a lifetime, she was excited at the prospect of being able to do her own sojourn in the Soviet Union. "Wherever we go we are surrounded by workers, greeted and cheered. . . . For all of us who experienced discrimination based on color in our own land . . . it was strange to find our color a badge of honor."[37] It seemed a perfect partnership; not only could she, and the group, experience the Soviet experiment, but these talented blacks, who were often overlooked, could put their talents to good use.

Thompson and the Co-operating Committee

Receiving Soviet authorization, Thompson formed in the early 1930s what came to be known as the Co-operating Committee for Production of a Soviet Film on Negro Life. Hughes was to be tapped as the scriptwriter, once the project got underway. Having worked with him before, Thompson was well aware of his professional skills and political sentiments. She had been Hughes's typist for his novel *God Sends Sunday* and later worked with Hughes and Zora Neale Hurston on their *Mule Bone* collaboration. She had also pulled Hughes into the International Labor Defense's fight to free the Scottsboro Boys.[38]

Thompson's and Hughes's stories were quite similar. Both were trying to make a life for themselves at a time when there were limited opportunities for black intellectuals. Despite an undergraduate degree from the University of California at Berkeley and graduate work in both Chicago and New York, Thompson could find jobs only in the service or "helper" category. "[She was] a fiercely intelligent woman at the center for New York's African-American intellectual scene during the final days of the Harlem Renaissance. . . . A cum laude graduate of Berkeley with a degree in economics, Patterson [Thompson] had taught at several colleges before coming to New York. . . . With her literary connections and leftist politics, she was the obvious choice to lead the group."[39] She was definitely more politically active than Hughes, and nonsupporters accused her of giving speeches that were "harangue mixed with social service and lynching statistics and . . . Communist platitudes about the solidarity of black and white labor."[40]

When Thompson cabled Hughes about the project's approval, Hughes was doing a poetry-reading tour on the West Coast. He had taken the advice of Mary McLeod Bethune, president of Bethune-Cookman College, who suggested that he take his poetry to the people as a way of making a modest living and of giving others hope in difficult times. He, too, had been unable to find steady work following his graduation from Lincoln University in Pennsylvania in 1929. "When I was twenty-seven the stock-market crash came. When I was twenty-eight, my personal crash came. . . . Almost all the young white writers I'd known in New York in the 'twenties had gotten good jobs with publishers or magazines as a result of their creative work. . . . But they were white. I was colored."[41] Hughes quickly responded to Thompson's cable: "Hold that boat, cause it's an ark to me."[42] He was not going to miss this opportunity, "Hollywood was still a closed shop—with the Negroes closed out. . . . I thought if I were ever to work in motion pictures . . . it would have to be abroad."[43]

But Thompson's goal to build tangible support for the project was not an easy one to achieve. Although two prominent blacks had been involved in the film project from the Soviet side—Fort-Whiteman and James Ford—Thompson knew the project required support on the U.S. side as well.[44] It needed patrons who could attract the kind of financial and other resources necessary to maintain a New York office as well as to draw in actors and writers.

A largely unsung activist, Thompson's political credentials were long established; she had been hosting Soviet Friendship Society meetings in her home for quite some time.[45] She also had the skills necessary for working with people of diverse interests and backgrounds. The job required attention to a myriad of logistics: the fund raising, the vetting of potential participants, the sorting of applications, the submission of requests to the Soviets, and the coordination of the group's travel abroad.

Her acumen could be seen in a number of strategic moves made at the onset. Rather than position herself as the committee head, she named herself the secretary and kept largely in the background.[46] For the head, she drew in W. A. Domingo, a Jamaican activist who had been close to the Garvey campaign.[47] She then drew in other well-known and highly respected members of the black community, making sure the committee was interracial and international and included women.[48] Thus, she managed to avoid factional bickering and to deflect some of the negative energies that might have impeded the committee's work. She needed people from the progressive, intellectual, and artistic communities, who usually had the will but few monetary resources. She also needed people from the business and middle-class communities, whose monetary resources and social networks could be tapped. This group was particularly important if the committee was to have any longevity. Ultimately, Thompson found ways for people to support the project without getting mired in their own particular political camps.[49] Smith noted committee members as diverse as "Bessye Bearden [wife of artist Romare Bearden], George S. Counts, Malcolm Cowley, Rose McLendon, John B. Hammond, Jr. and Will Vodery."[50] Kate Baldwin added, "William H. Davis (owner and publisher of the Amsterdam News) . . . Floyd Dell, and Waldo Frank" and noted that Thompson found "people who joined [and] supported the film project while representing a broad range of views regarding socialism."[51]

Assembling a Group

Thompson then turned to assembling the group that would travel to the Soviet Union. She wanted at least fifteen people, most of whom, she felt, should be actors or involved with the theater.[52] Besides word of mouth, notices were posted in the newspapers. But they produced little success. A disappointed Moon noted that the "publication of the story aroused little interest in Harlem."[53] No doubt the fact that they had to pay their way over and concerns about Communism and stories of privation in the Soviet Union inhibited some. Nonetheless, Thompson prevailed and pulled together a group, sometimes accepting people whose credentials might not have been up to her original standards. These recruitment problems account for the facts that most had no experience in theater and a significant number were loathe to get involved in political activities. Additionally, they might explain the frequent reference to a group of twenty-two Negroes (the projected number) when, in fact, the group turned out to be twenty-one Negroes and McKenzie, who was white.[54]

Some, like Hughes, Miller, and Crawford, had been primed and were eagerly awaiting the project's start. Miller and Crawford had accompanied Hughes on the California leg of his tour. They, too, had a keen interest in the Soviet experiment. Thompson had contacted Miller directly. A member of a John Reed club, Miller was " a young black lawyer . . . a brilliant speaker, merciless in debate, [and] committed to racial socialism without being a party member; the resolutions of the Sixth World Congress of the Comintern, when the cause of black self-determination had been first raised by communists, had become his Bible."[55] Crawford's place in the group had come about differently. Crawford was not known to the political community; however he was "a cheerful, light-complexioned chiropractor and insurance clerk who liked poetry in general but revered Hughes's 'The Negro Speaks of Rivers.'"[56] In fact, because of Crawford's admiration for Hughes he was able to convince Thompson to let him go. Crawford's sojourn to the Soviet Union did dramatically change his life; within two years of his return, he took on a major role in the Communist-backed League of Struggle for Negro Rights and other political activities.[57]

Moon also remembered discussing the Soviet Union and the potential project with Ford in the early months of 1932. "What would it be like to live in a world free of poverty and Jim Crow—the 'classless society' he called it. . . . I thought of all . . . the incidents—each petty in and of itself, but all cumulative, setting me apart from my classmates, my fellow students, from humanity."[58] He worried that he might need previous acting experience, but "[Ford said] Soviet directors were skilled in developing good films out of raw materials. . . . This condition left the door wide open. I had long wanted to make a trip to Russia to see for myself what was happening in that country."[59]

Project Miscues

Once installed in their Moscow hotel, all eagerly signed their contracts. Thompson had promised them "round-trip passage (to be reimbursed at the project's end) and 'guaranteed expenses and salary.'" All received "400 rubles per month, accommodations at the Grand Hotel, and ration books to shop in the stores."[60] They had ample invitations for the theater, clubs, and other outings. Hughes wrote, "We were almost nightly guests of one or another of the great theatres, the Moscow Art Theatre, the Vakhtangov, the Meyerhold, the Kamerny, or the Opera."[61] But although they did not lack opportunities for amusement, problems eventually arose around the lack of food choices and project delays. The Meschrabpom officials tried their best to make them comfortable, but the country was going through food shortages, and it was difficult to "[cater] to American appetites." Now, the Soviets went to even greater lengths than they had before to please them. Observed Smith, the Soviets "dispatched trucks into the nearby countryside to forage for food. . . . [And] with full stomachs, ample supplies of vodka, and with keys to the city, the Negro[es] . . . settled down to enjoy themselves."[62]

However, as the days stretched into a month and rehearsals had not started, the group again became restless. The diversions had continued. "They were invited to receptions, museums, factories, schools. Hughes was interviewed on the radio. Negro residents of Moscow invited them to their homes, and the great Russian film director, Sergei Eisenstein, gave a party in their honor."[63] But their rising discontents were not based on the lack of entertainment or on whether they were paid or well-housed, but on their aspirations to do the film. Hughes was obviously busy in the Meschrabpom offices, but he offered few details about his work and the reasons for the delay. In fact, Hughes was concerned as well but chose not to worry the others.[64]

Burdened with an enormous script in Russian, Hughes spent several weeks arranging for translations. He engaged in various negotiations around suggested changes. "At first I was astonished at what I read. . . . The writer meant well, but knew so little about his subject. . . . His concern for racial freedom and decency had tripped so completely on the stumps of ignorance that his work had fallen as flat as did Don Quixote's value when good intentions led that slightly demented knight to do battle."[65] Thompson concurred, "It began in Africa and featured wailing villagers, Arab slave traders in fezes, a naïve missionary, and the greedy, cruel captain of a slave ship. The scene shifted to an auction block in the U.S. South where a family was being torn asunder and then to a Civil War battle scene. . . . [The] main action of the script revolved around a labor dispute in a factory. . . . [One] version of the script had the Red Army arriving to assist the anti-lynching forces."[66]

But there were rising concerns, as the group had been given contracts and paid for work yet to be done. In fact, Hughes was being paid "at a salary which, in terms of Russian buying power, was about a hundred times a week as much as I had ever made anywhere else,"[67] and he was reluctant to forfeit either the pay or the possibility of working on a major production. Instead, he tried discussing the script with the officials. But he was crossing both language and pride barriers "in English, scanty French and bad German."[68] At first, he was met by blustery reactions, and then, after weeks of no official word on the film, a request came through that he rewrite the script. Hughes had painstakingly pointed out the problems with the previous script, but he was not willing to write the new one. "I couldn't. . . . I've never lived in the South [the film's location], never worked in a steel mill and know almost nothing about unions or labor relations."[69]

Misinformation in the Soviet Group

There were other problems as well. Each group had misjudged the other. The Soviets had terribly misunderstood the cohort they would be hosting, expecting professional actors and singers. Meschrabpom also expected that blacks from the United States would have the appropriate class solidarity. They were not prepared for such an eclectic group.

First, there was the question of skin color. "There before the astonished Russians stood twenty-two men and women ranging in color from dark brown to high yellow. 'We needed genuine Negroes and they sent us a bunch of metisi (mixed bloods),' one disturbed Russian remarked in an undertone. Another puzzled official shook his head after shaking hands with several members of the group. 'Their hands, so soft, they don't feel like workers' hands.'"[70] Thompson complained, "We have had to argue at great lengths to tell them we are all Negroes." Montero commented, "In appearance, ours was a very mixed group of people . . . from Wayland Rudd, who was as black as Paul Robeson, to a person like myself, who could be regarded as Hispanic."[71] Virtually a case of racism in reverse, the very characteristics used to denigrate blacks in the United States—dark skin color and worker status—were the ones valued for this project. The filmmakers had assumed this cohort would naturally have dark skin and be workers.[72] The original plan was to use Russian actors with their faces blackened, but later the filmmakers decided they wanted black actors from the United States, but these did not seem "black" enough.[73]

Part of their concern was based on the visual effect of the film. The black people needed to look black on screen. These were the same contradictions faced in 1922 by Claude McKay and Otto Huiswood, the first blacks to formally attend Comintern meetings. Despite the light-skinned Huiswood's Communist credentials, the Soviets chose dark-skinned McKay for the propaganda photos and public platforms.[74] Interestingly, Joanne Van Tuyl, who has done considerable work on the origins of the *Black and White* project, noted that an earlier screenplay done by Constantine Grebner had included notes to the effect that not all American Negroes were dark-skinned and could, in fact, have skin of various shades.[75] Grebner also noted that these lighter-skinned Negroes could still encounter racism and like their darker brethren were fighting against Jim Crow.[76] But, by the time Hughes and his group arrived in Moscow in 1932, a different team had taken charge of the project, and a young, relatively inexperienced German director, Karl Yunghans, had been brought in. Yunghans had worked with Africans before but had never met American Negroes, nor been to the United States. Thus, he too had limited knowledge about black Americans. Hughes reported that Yunghans fretted that he was saddled with a cast that "looked more white than black, did not know Negro work songs, and . . . had not a tired, aging worker in it."[77] In the end, these were people several generations away from their African ancestors. Their faces and features represented blends of the New World. So the Soviets' quest for "visual authenticity" could not be met without darkening make-up.

Second, there was the question of class. Although the group was now in the "class-less" Soviet Union, they carried with them social structures from the United States. The Soviets assumed that a certain class solidarity prevailed across African America, but this group, made up primarily of college graduates and professionals and virtually all Northern, urban residents, did not consider itself a group of workers. Any jobs that they might have heretofore condescended to do that might be classed in the worker category were, to their minds, only temporary. Their ambitions were to move on to endeavors more in keeping with their perceptions of their station in life. Smith worked in the post office, although he had trained to be a journalist. Patterson was a housepainter, although he was an artist. So, again, the contradictions surfaced. Fighting their way out of worker and, hence, lower-class status in the United States, many of them were nevertheless moved by the solidarity banner "Workers of the World Unite" at the border crossing. However, although they welcomed the international solidarity inspired by the Soviet experiment, within the denigrating context of a racist United States the label *worker* did not sit so well.

Furthermore, the Soviets appeared not to realize that ordinary workers in the United States would have trouble going abroad to participate in such a project. They would not have the funds to pay for the journey and, in the Great Depression, neither the leisure nor the confidence that a job would be waiting for them until their return to the United States.[78] Workers' priorities would be to stay in the United States and to hold on to whatever jobs they had.

Third, in their quest for authenticity, the Meschrabpom officials also expected this group to demonstrate other stereotypical behavior, such as singing and dancing. Hughes wrote, "The first rehearsal of the music was funnier than anything in the script. . . . [The Meschrabpom officials were] victims of that old cliché that all Negroes just naturally sing. . . . Being mostly Northerners, only a few of us had ever heard a spiritual outside a concert hall, or a work song other than 'Water Boy' in a night club. . . . They were too intellectual for such old-time song, which to them smacked of bandannas and stereotypes."[79]

Misinformation in the Black and White *Group*

The U.S. group was also misinformed. First, they were amazed to find other blacks or darker-skinned people living in the Soviet Union. Few realized that there were other peoples of color among the many nationalities of the Soviet Union.

Some had heard about the Afro-Russian poet Pushkin and were pleased to see his statue prominently displayed in Moscow.[80] Hughes's best friend, Arna Bontemps, had received *Opportunity* magazine's Pushkin prize twice in the mid-1920s.[81] Others, especially those in theater, had heard about the nineteenth-century black American Shakespearean actor Ira Aldridge, who was known as the "African Roscius" and was celebrated throughout Europe. But, although Pushkin and Aldridge were celebrated, both were long gone.

Members of the group might also have heard stories about previous sojourners who had gone for short stays or political training, but they did not realize that some were still there. Hughes remarked, "Among the crowd of Russian actors and writers who greeted us at the [Moscow] station . . . were also four Negroes: a very African-looking boy named Bob, a singer called Madam [Coretta] Arle-Titz, a young man named Robinson who was a technician, and Emma Harris."[82] Arle-Titz and Harris, both former entertainers, had been in the country since the early part of the century. Bob was likely Robert Ross, a political trainee in the 1920s; and Robert Robinson was a tool-and-die specialist drawn to the Soviet Union from the Ford Motor Company in 1930. All these people, who were sojourners for different reasons, had remained. And there were more. After stating that "there were in 1932 to my knowledge, not more than a half-dozen American Negroes in Moscow, with the exception of our movie group," Hughes acknowledged that there were "colored students said to be in residence at the Lenin School . . . which foreign visitors never saw."[83]

Second, the *Black and White* group was equally ill-informed about living conditions. They had packed extra provisions to share with their hosts as well as to have on hand for themselves through difficult times. "[They brought] canned goods, sugar, coffee, soap, toilet paper—but they were mistaken."[84] The people around them were not showing signs of suffering; they were not "pale and undernourished or in need of the canned goods [they] had brought."[85] Despite the ongoing rationing, their Meschrabpom hosts made enormous sacrifices of time, effort, and money to ensure their comfort. The average Russian might have had to live under the restrictions of the time, but these special guests would not. As with other specialists invited to the Soviet Union to share their skills, orders had come from the highest levels that the groups were to be treated with special care. Robinson, who had been living in the Soviet Union for two years by the time the film group appeared, observed somewhat bitterly. "As so-called official representatives of black America, the artists and intellectuals were given the red carpet treatment. Their Soviet hosts escorted them around town to showcase the positive changes in the lives of Soviet people that had resulted from the revolution. The entire group was housed at the Grand Hotel in Moscow and that is where I first met Hughes."[86] Arnold Rampersad noted, "Normally reserved for visiting upper-rank provincial officials, the Grand Hotel stood only a block from the Kremlin and the fabulous domes of St. Basil's on Red Square. . . . At the Grand Hotel, Hughes, Loren Miller, and Matt Crawford shared a suite handsomely furnished in pre-Czarist style . . . with ancient beds, heavy drapes and thick carpets."[87]

Smith, curiously recounting the story as if he had not been a part of the group, did seem to be particularly sensitive to the poverty he observed on the streets. While Hughes and the others were living well as guests of Meschrabpom, Smith contended he found "hungry men and women" and "food was also scarce in my second-class hotel."[88] It is possible that Smith was relaying his experiences after the group left and he was no longer being hosted by Meschrabpom. By that point, as was true for *Black and White* group members Patterson and Rudd, who also stayed behind, these black sojourners were shifting from being special guests to being foreigners living in and among ordinary Russians. On the one hand, they retained their access to the special shops that took foreign currency. But, on the other, they had to find accommodations among those facilities that were not already set aside for special guests of the government or government officials. This was also the case for Robeson's brothers in-law, Frank and John Goode, who, unlike Robeson, the special visitor, had to fend for themselves after they arrived in 1933.

Moon also noted some of the difficulties faced by the Russians in contrast to the special treatment the film group received, but he observed as well that "poverty [was] tolerable in the Russia of 1932 [because of] its universality." Continued Moon, "There was plenty of poverty in Moscow and Leningrad and Odessa . . . more indeed than in New York or Cleveland. . . . You could see it in their homes [and] in their dress. You could see it in the scarcity of consumer goods and in the relative high prices. The Communists had not liquidated poverty . . . they had [spread] poverty so that the people as a whole were equally deprived." He was also amazed at the different lifestyles of Hollywood's directors and of the Soviet director Sergey Eisenstein. "In Hollywood, directors of Eisenstein's eminence live[d] in enviable luxury, even during the Depression. I remember the night we were guests in the apartment of Sergei M. Eisenstein, the world famous Russian film director. . . . I was amazed by the barren and outmoded quarters which this great director occupied. . . . This was dramatic demonstration of the leveling impact of the Soviet regime. It was a stimulating evening we spent there and no one seemed dismayed by the paucity of creature comfort." For Moon, though, the lesson was that despite "the paucity of creature comfort," the people he met in the Soviet Union were not suffering from "defeatism and spiritual decay." To Moon's mind, Jim Crow, discrimination, and poverty made life in Harlem worse. "The Great Depression [subverted] the living standards of millions more. . . . I saw and knew the fearful cost of poverty. I saw the frustrations, rooted in poverty and nourished by discrimination . . . driving some to defeatism . . . [and] crime."[89]

The Project Collapses

After nearly three months of negotiations, uncertainty, and script changes, and, most particularly, the fight against being constrained by stereotypical images of black life, the project finally collapsed. Moon and Hill took credit for alerting the others that things had gone awry. "[All] but two . . . had left Moscow for Odessa. . . . When Hill and I caught up with the company in Odessa the would-be players were stunned. . . . I broke the silence with harsh words: 'Comrades, we've been screwed!'"[90] There was no question that the group knew cancellation was a possibility, but once it happened, "hell broke loose," according to Hughes. "Hysterics took place. Some of the girls really wanted desperately to be movie actresses. . . . The whole Negro race had been betrayed by Stalin. Some said the insidious hand of American race prejudice had a part in it all—that Jim Crow's dark shadow had fallen on Moscow, and that Wall Street and the Kremlin now conspired together never to let the world see in films what it was like to be a downtrodden Negro in America."[91]

The knowledge that they had apparently not escaped racism plus the fact they would have to return to the United States with little to show for their efforts spurred their anger. Journalists Poston and Moon hoped to use this opportunity to gain recognition by the white press in the United States. Tony Scherman noted that they staged a protest over the debacle. "[Intent] on denouncing their hosts' cowardice and duplicity, Poston and a few others demanded an audience with Stalin."[92] Together with disaffected members Alberga and Thurston McNairy Lewis, they were also quick to spread the news to the international press. Wrote Moon, "Although we had been in unanimous agreement in Odessa, back in Moscow the group split wide open. The Communist sympathizers, after consulting with party leaders . . . accepted the official version. Poston and four others joined me in protesting the deal as a compromise with American anti-Negro prejudice."[93]

Moon rushed off a telegram to the *Amsterdam News*, and he and Poston sent an even longer missive from Berlin after they left the Soviet Union. It was published on October 4, 1932, under the title "Amsterdam News Reporters Tell Why Soviet Russia Dropped Film."[94] A report on the article appeared in the October 5th *New York Times* under the heading "Say Race Bias Here Halted Soviet Film."[95] Leading off with the subhead "Harlem Writers Who Went to Russia with Negro Troupe Send 'Inside Story,'" the article continued, "According to the Moon-Preston [sic] story, Colonel Hugh Cooper . . . [prevailed] upon Stalin to order cancellation of the film."[96]

Ironically, it was through this controversy that Moon's and Poston's dreams of appearing in the *New York Times* were fulfilled. This was just the kind of news the *Times* wanted. Moon and Poston later also wrote or inspired a spate of articles on the debacle that appeared in the black press, such as "Soviet Abandons Negro Photoplay" and "Claims Russians Will Make Film" in the New York *Amsterdam News* and "Newspaper Men Expose Tactics of Soviet in Making Film" in the Baltimore *Afro-American*. Four months after the "hopeful" announcement of their impending journey, the *Black and White* film group appeared again in the press, only now it was as a victim of an international racist conspiracy.[97]

Hughes and Thompson, along with fifteen other members of the group, tried to counter the negative publicity. However, few of these arguments were published in the mainstream press.[98] Commented Thompson, "Many statements have been issued collectively and individually by the majority of our group and have been steadily ignored by the representatives of the press through whom adverse statements were released."[99] Hughes had immediately sent out a counter statement to the *New York Herald Tribune*, but the article, entitled "Negroes Adrift in 'Uncle Tom's Russian Cabin': Harlem Expeditionary Unit Is Stranded in Moscow," appeared only in the *Daily Worker*.[100] "Newspaper reports that I and other members are adrift . . . are absolutely untrue. Our contracts and salaries . . . continue to October 16. The return passage . . . is guaranteed. Several members of the group intend to remain in the Soviet Union. Many have already secured positions here."[101] Trying to save face, Hughes continued, "the Meschrabpom officials finally informed the group officially that the scenario was inadequate. They said it was unfortunately not worthy of the kind of picture they had hoped to make. They also indicated politely that the Negro actors were not quite what they had expected."[102] Only one small piece appeared in the *New York Times* supporting Hughes's position. Quoting information from Cyril Lambkin, national secretary of the Friends of the Soviet Union, the article stated that the charges were unfounded and that the project had been cancelled because of "scenario and technical difficulties."[103]

Why the Project Failed

But Moon's allegations were correct. The *Black and White* film project fell through more for strategic reasons than for artistic ones.[104] One sector of Soviet officialdom might have been focusing on the propaganda benefit of exposing U.S. racism, but other sectors were far more interested in the economic benefit of currying favor with U.S. businessmen and technical experts, as an August 30, 1932, letter from the U.S. consul general, George S. Messersmith, to the U.S. Secretary of State indicated: "I have the honor to report that Col. Hugh L. Cooper of New York, returned from Russia several days ago and gave the

Consulate General certain information with reference to conditions in Russia. Col. Cooper has been particularly agitated over the reception and kindly treatment which American negroes have had in Russia. . . . He was much exercised over the much advertised film which was to be taken in Russia to show the ill treatment of negroes in various parts of the world."[105]

Underscoring the point, Robinson noted, "The [film] project eventually was scrapped, either because of pressure from the US government, or from white American businessmen who enjoyed lucrative contracts with the Soviets, or both."[106] There was far greater need for Colonel Cooper's dam-building expertise and for maintaining good relations with industrialists such as Ford, who was backing the construction of a plant in Magnitogorsk and other plants than for making a film about the treatment of blacks in the United States. Moon's bitter assessment of the project's demise read the political climate correctly. "The Comintern has accepted this compromise."[107]

The Meschrabpom officials continued to try to distract the *Black and White* film group. There was a previous diversionary holiday in the Black Sea region. "As guests of the Theatrical Trade Unions we were invited on a pleasure cruise of the Black Sea, a gay and pleasant trip around the Crimean Peninsula to Sebastopol, Yalta, Gagri, Sochi, Sukhum, and down the coast almost to Turkey."[108] Now, the Soviets offered not only to continue to cover the group's accommodations for the duration of their stay in the country but also to pay for a tour of several European capitals on their return to the United States or to extend their sojourn in the Soviet Union.

Those with the least political sophistication and those most disappointed to have not been able to follow through with the original agreements happily jumped for the European tour and left the country almost immediately. These were: Poston, Moon, Montero, Hill, Alberga, Garner, and T. M. Lewis. Fifteen others—Hughes, Smith, Thompson, Crawford, Miller, McKenzie, West, Rudd, Patterson, Jones, Sample, White, Jenkins, J. Lewis, and M. Lewis—decided to extend their sojourn in the Soviet Union. They had come a long way to see the Soviet experiment at work, and as long as the Soviets would host them, they were happy to sample more.

Touring Soviet Asia

Given the opportunity to see other parts of the Soviet Union, several immediately asked to visit Soviet Central Asia. This request took their Soviet hosts by surprise as this part of the country was normally closed to foreigners. As Hughes noted, "This gave our trade-union hosts pause."[109] The Soviets would have preferred to show off the European section of the country, which was rapidly industrializing. As to Soviet Central Asia, "Only a very few selected journalists, and no tourists, were permitted there. It was said to be a land still in flux, where Soviet patterns were as yet none too firmly fixed."[110] But, for blacks, temporarily relieved of Jim Crow, it was important to see how other people of color were faring. They did not immediately realize that progress in Soviet Central Asia was a process that affected not only people of color but also people whose religion and customs were based on Islamic tradition. Change here would of necessity be more complex than that for the peasants of European Russia.

The combination of the embarrassment of the film debacle and the negative press in the West encouraged the Soviets to give in to this request.[111] It would also be advantageous to have this Soviet-friendly group spread positive comments to counter the negative images elsewhere. Hughes's request for a permit "not only to tour, but to remain in Central Asia long enough to write about it for publications in America" was especially appealing.[112] Thus, when they loaded Hughes and ten others onto a special train car on September 22, 1932, they ensured that the group had plenty of supplies and a support team to help smooth the way.[113] "Hughes, Thompson, Miller, Crawford, and Alan [Allen] McKenzie; Katherine Jenkins and her fiancé George Sample; and Connie White, Mollie Lewis, Juanita Lewis, and Mildred Jones [went]. With them was a small supporting group, including their interpreter Lydia Myrtseva, a political guide, and Otto Huiswood of *The Negro Worker*."[114] This was the same Huiswood who had initially gone to the Soviet Union in 1922, at the time of the Fourth Comintern congress. In the late 1920s and early 1930s Huiswood returned frequently to the Soviet Union, where he worked on a number of Comintern projects. Now, Huiswood served as a bridge between blacks (the guests) and the various people they would meet in the Central Asian parts of the country. As editor of the *Negro Worker*, a publication targeted at African and other colonial peoples, he might also have been charged with writing pieces for this publication.

For the duration of the five-day-journey, they enjoyed their private train car and an easy familiarity with the diverse group of travelers elsewhere in the train.

> We had the run of the train, soon knew everybody and everybody knew us. . . . Russian travelers, men and women, are great joke tellers. . . . Their jokes often put translators at a loss to convey the point. . . . The first day everybody talked politely about such things as the Five Year Plan, Voroshilov's horse, [Kliment Voroshilov, along with Semyon Budyonny, were extremely loyal to Stalin and served as marshals in the Red Calvary. Hughes's reference, however, would have been more appropriate to Budyonny, who was recognized for having created a special breed of high-performance horse.[115]] or the new ballet at the Bolshoi. The next day folks inquired about the conditions in "starving America" where, they had heard, the depression had reduced everyone to skin and bones. But the third day as the train rocked along into Asia such tame subjects had worn thin. . . . I had brought along my victrola with Louis Armstrong and Ethel Waters, so I contributed some lusty canned music to the long ride. . . . With our new and interesting companions, the days on the road passed quickly.[116]

As the journey progressed, Hughes mused, "I am riding South from Moscow and am not Jim-Crowed, and none of the darker people on the train with me are Jim-Crowed, so I made a happy mental note in the back of my head to write home to the Negro papers: 'There is no Jim Crow on the trains of the Soviet Union.'"[117]Others were equally impressed with dramatic changes in the region. Wrote Crawford, "There is an exact parallel between the condition of these people during the czarist regime and the position of Negroes in the States now"; and yet, as noted by Baldwin, "[the group saw] the introduction of compulsory education, and industrialization as hallmarks of a new era, new way of living, and 'new people.'"[118]

At each stop, they were taken on tours of farms, factories, and other projects as demonstrations of the improvements to the region. Samarkand was typical. "A few . . . lovely sites were granted to us. But most of our time was taken by a visit to the University, an inspection of the first medical school in Central Asia, then under construction, and by trade-union teas where statistics galore were relayed from one language to another, and expectantly aimed at our nonabsorbent heads by enthusiastic Communists."[119] After a week, the group prevailed on their hosts to cut the journey short. "After the free and easy life we'd led in Moscow and Odessa . . . the earnest and intense hospitality . . . with its day-long schedule of planned activities was almost too much to take."[120] They had seen the Soviet experiment's effect on the lives of peoples of color, but now they were worn out. Rather than spend the few last days in the historic city of Ashkhabad (Ashgabat), the group left Hughes behind to continue the journey on his own. The rest returned to Moscow.

Back in Moscow at the end of September 1932, the group split again. Thompson, Sample, Miller, and Crawford left for the United States. The remaining cohort joined those who had stayed behind in the city earlier. Of those, Hughes was pleased to note, "Dorothy West was writing, Mildred Jones taking screen tests for a new picture. Long, tall Patterson who paints houses had married a girl who paints pictures. . . . Wayland Rudd was studying singing . . . and taking a role in a new Meyerhold play. McKenzie stayed in the films, working for Meschrabpom. And Homer Smith [was working] as a special consultant in the Central Post Office. . . . So the Negroes made themselves at home."[121] But, by January 1933, all, save Patterson, Rudd, and Smith had returned to the United States. "So of the twenty-two of us, three adopted the soil of the Soviets as a permanent homeland."[122] Hughes himself stayed almost a year, until late spring of 1933.

Following his sojourn in the Soviet Union, an energized Miller wrote several articles for the *Daily Worker*. Under the title "How the U.S.S.R. Wiped Out Oppression," he observed, "The Soviet Union is the best friend of the Negro and all oppressed people."[123] Both Miller and Crawford joined the national council of the League of Struggle for Negro Rights and then campaigned for Hughes to take over the presidency later.[124] Smith and West also wrote of their experiences for U.S. audiences. Smith, who stayed behind, sent a number of dispatches back during his fourteen years under the pen name "Chatwood Hall."[125] West wrote a number of pieces under the pen name "Mary Christopher." Two of those, "A Room in Red Square" and "Russian Correspondence," appeared in *Challenge* magazine after her return to the United States.[126] Interestingly, both West and Smith used pseudonyms, suggesting that they were concerned about the effect their Soviet connections might have on future job prospects. Moon and Poston, however, whose dispatches were more critical of the experience, never seemed to have thought about using pen names or disguising their identity.

Hughes, Staying On to Investigate the Soviet Experiment

Hughes had secured various projects and was glad to continue his travels in the Soviet East. "After three months of the movies, I was delighted to pack my bags and go off on a plain prose-writing assignment to Central Asia."[127] He wanted to see "socialism tearing down the customs of ages" and to "compare their [the peoples of Central Asia] existence with that of the colored and op-pressed peoples I had known under capitalism in Cuba, Haiti, Mexico and my own United States."[128]

A special thrill for all was to learn how the Soviet experiment worked for peoples of color swept up into the new Soviet Union. Uzbekistan was emblem-atic, as Hughes noted in a 1946 *Chicago Defender* article. "So from Jim Crow cars to freedom, from helplessness to the ballot, from ignorance to school, from scorn . . . to having a part in their own government."[129]

After visiting Tashkent, Samarkand, and Bokhara (Bukhara), Hughes believed that women, in particular, had become particular symbols of these changes. As he told his *Chicago Defender* readers, "Most of the women of So-viet Central Asia now have thrown away their veils . . . and are being educated in Soviet schools in ideals of freedom for all. From a land of Jim Crow, exploi-tation, and harems, Soviet Central Asia had become the most advanced portion of the Orient and an equal part of the entire great Soviet Union."[130] As Baldwin concurred, "The unveiling of Muslim women resonated not only with Hughes's general desire for an end to segregation . . . but with a more specific longing to escape from a 'life beneath the veil' [which, with] the publication of W.E.B. Du Bois's *The Souls of Black Folk*, . . . had established itself in black American consciousness."[131]

With his freshly minted understanding of the Soviet system, plus a per-sonal history of Jim Crow, Hughes wanted to make sure people in the provinces were equally as accommodating as those in Moscow. He worried that his status as a black guest of Meschrabpom might not get him into all the places he wanted to visit because he would be traveling largely on his own. Obtaining a Soviet press pass and a contract from *Izvestia* for a series of articles, he also made sure to carry letters of introduction from the Soviet Writers' Union. "I was glad I belonged to the International Union of Revolutionary Writers. Credentials were far more important than rubles."[132]

But he did not expect to be left so abruptly in Ashkhabad, the group's last stop together. Hughes thought that the group would stay for a few days and that the Meschrabpom representatives would make other arrangements for him. "With the help of our guides and translators, I expected in two days to be safely settled in a hotel with contacts made for a more extensive exploration of the region." But his traveling companions were eager to get back to Moscow. "They tried to persuade me to give up my idea of remaining in Soviet Asia. For them a week had proved sufficient. . . . [I got] angry with the others . . . jumped off the train without handshakes or farewells. A couple of fellows were decent enough to toss my bags down. With a hoot, the train pulled away, gathering speed across the sands."[133] Always resourceful, Hughes did find others to help him, including the black engineer Bernard Powers and the black agricultural specialists with whom he spent the Christmas holidays.

Over the next weeks, he observed, kept notes, and sent articles back to Moscow, many of which were published in *Izvestia* and *Innostranaiya Literatura*.[134] He also kept a journal with the thought that he would eventually do a book. Some of these notes served as the kernel later for several chapters of *I Wonder as I Wander*.

He liked the fact that the arts being were being marshaled for social change. "Even propaganda in talented hands took on dramatic dimensions. In Tashkent, talented Russian directors were using all the folk elements of Uzbek music, poetry and dance in aiding to create an Uzbek national theatre where there had been none before. . . . Dramatist Ismailov . . . told me, 'We try to use the theatre to teach people how beautiful life can be if we destroy the old ugly selfish customs of the past. And we try to show our varied nationalities [ethnic groups] how to get along together. . . . We must all be comrades.'"[135] And it never ceased to amaze Hughes how American technology was being used to bolster Soviet development. "All the world [had] heard of American machines and technical knowledge, and some collective farms near Samarkand used Chicago tractors."[136] On the eve of his departure for Moscow, his Uzbek hosts insisted that he accompany them to see a special example of progress in their city. "Finally I went with them. They took me a few blocks away to a big garage that housed the municipal buses, and there they proudly pointed, 'Amerikanetz! See!' They wanted to show me that their buses were from my country. They went inside and spoke to a driver and in a very short time one of the big buses rolled out. I was helped in and, as the only passenger, driven to the very door of my hotel—as a gesture of hospitality toward a stranger."[137]

In all, Hughes spent three extra months, from the end of September to early January in Soviet Central Asia before returning to Moscow. He wrestled with split emotions: he looked forward to returning to Moscow and the conveniences of the fancy hotels; but he regretted leaving his new friends behind, "I said that unfortunately I was leaving that night to return to Tashkent. 'They want you,' said the translator, 'to accept the hospitality of the Uzbek workers. They want you to stay a long time in Samarkand, so that when you go back to

America, you will remember their city with pleasure.' 'Only with pleasure could I remember Samarkand,' I said."[138]

Meeting Other Black Artists and Expatriates

Two other black artists, Arle-Titz and Harris, had been living in the country for decades by the time Hughes and the *Black and White* film group arrived, and their personal histories both amazed and amused this new group of black sojourners. Enormously resilient, the women had experiences that stretched from tsarist days through the travails of the Civil War and into the later adjustments of the Soviet regime.

Hughes described Harris as "Emma Harris who's lived in Russia for thirty years, sings, and makes the best apple pies in the world."[139] An invaluable bridge for blacks trying to settle into their new life in the Soviet Union, Harris sought out any newcomers and invited them to her apartment. Because of this hospitality, Soviet authorities were willing to turn a blind eye to her black-market connections and occasional anti-Soviet comments. Hughes first saw her when she was singing at a massive Scottsboro rally and witnessed other public occasions. "Emma would be introduced to a cheering audience as 'our own beloved Negro comrade, Emma.' . . . [She] must have been in her early teens when she [left Dixie]. But she could denounce race prejudice in no uncertain terms [and] in fluent Russian [and then] walk off the platform to bravos." That she survived through such different times was also remarkable, as she told Hughes. "I'm like a cat with nine lives, honey. . . . I always land on my feet—been doing it all my life wherever I am. These Bolsheviks ain't gonna kill me!"[140]

Harris was born in Kentucky around 1875 and had gone to Europe as part of a singing troupe, the Louisiana Amazon Gods. The group toured Germany and then split into smaller groups. Harris traveled with one of these groups, the Six Creole Belles, on an extended tour of Russia and Poland. Later leaving that group, she formed her own trio, with which she continued to perform at various locations inside and outside of Russia. Her fortunes reversed, and she found herself stranded in Siberia, where she taught English until she was able to return to Moscow and resume her theatrical work.[141] Harry Haywood, who met her in the mid-1920s, noted, "Being Black wasn't a liability, but on the contrary, a definite asset [and she] parlayed this asset into a profitable position." She subsequently married a wealthy Russian who helped her set up a fancy house of prostitution, where her clients were the "wealthy and nobility."[142] In fact, as Allison Blakely added, she also had six servants and a footman to help look after her large house and other interests.[143] A test of her value to the Russians came during the early years of the Civil War, when she was arrested and thrown in jail along with the White Guard soldiers who were hiding in her house.

They were taken to the Lubyanka Prison and some of the more notorious White Guardists were summarily executed. Emma remained in a cell for days. Finally she was called upon before a Cheka official. He told her that they were looking into her case. Many of the people who had been arrested at her place were counter-revolutionaries and conspirators against the new Soviet state. . . . Emma disclaimed knowledge of any conspiracy. . . . "You know the only reason we didn't shoot you was because you are a Negro woman," the official said. To her surprise, he added, "You are free to go now. . . . Try to find some useful work."[144]

Harris served as a nurse for the troops and later worked with the American Relief Association. By the mid-1920s, when Haywood met her, she was working in a textile factory and living in modest surroundings. Instead of her mansion, she now lived in a two-room apartment that she shared with a young Russian woman whom Haywood suspected was one of her previous prostitutes.

Haywood and his fellow students happily pooled their funds so that Emma could prepare meals at her house. "Soon after the first Black students arrived, she sought them out . . . like long lost kinfolk. At least once a month, we students would pool part of the small stipends we received and give Emma money to shop for and prepare some old home cooking for us. On these occasions, she would regale us with stories from her past life. At time one could detect a . . . nostalgia for her old days of affluence. . . . She was not an ardent partisan of the new regime [and] knowing our sentiments, she avoided political discussion."[145]

By the time the *Black and White* film group arrived in 1932, seven years later, her accommodations were still Spartan but no worse than that of the average Russian. Noted Smith, "Emma's one room was in an old building near three railway stations." When he asked her why she stayed there, she replied, "Man, you ain't seen no rooms for rent signs in Moscow, have you?"[146] Importantly, though, she now had her own place and was not required to share the space with anyone else.

Harris had been cautious with the political studies students like Haywood and Golden in the mid-1920s, but now she knew she occupied a special niche in the society and could relax somewhat. Noted Smith, "Having been well-to-do before the Revolution, Emma was now listed in the category of declasse bourgeoisie. She expressed undisguised bitterness over her present lot, and criticism of prevailing conditions and the Soviet regime was sharp. . . . If made by a Russian, her remarks would have landed [her] in Siberia."[147] But, as Hughes noted, Harris's hospitality clearly shielded them from the day-to-day realities of most Russians. "Living in the Grand Hotel and eating well, or accepting Emma's black-market hospitality, I never would have known there was hunger a few hundred miles South of Moscow."[148]

Harris told Hughes that she worked as a translator, but, he noted, "[I] never observed her at work, never found her without the time to cook a feast. . . . She had some of the best food in Moscow . . . [and yet] had only an ordinary worker's ration card. But she knew all about black markets and speak-easies. In a city where almost nothing was open after midnight, Emma could always find a place to buy a drink."[149] Smith added, "Her clientele was strictly American, however, because her Russian neighbors had no money with which to supply the ingredients. 'Just supply me the rubles, I'll find the stuff,' Emma would say." He last saw her just after World War II. She was in her early seventies and about to return to the United States.[150]

The other long-time black expatriate was Arle-Titz. Noted Hughes, "She had toured the Soviet Union in concert with great success. Her scrap books are full of critiques and testimonials from workers and Red Army men. She has known many of the leading revolutionists and is a friend of Maxim Gorky."[151] Arle-Titz had been a part of Harris's trio, and after the group disbanded, she entered formal studies at the St. Petersburg Conservatory.[152] Robinson contended that she had been married and that when the marriage broke up, she decided to stay on. "By then she was enrolled at the Imperial Conservatoire—an opportunity for formal musical training which was unavailable to her in America."[153] Like Harris's, Arle-Titz's career showed the possibilities for American blacks in Russia. Not technically African American, Arle-Titz was born in Mexico but raised in New York. Still, she suffered some of the same discrimination as blacks and was not sorry to leave the United States. Harris was often referred to as "the Mammy of Moscow, but Arle-Titz represented herself as 'nobility.'[154] Her married name came from her second husband, Boris Arle-Titz, a professor of piano instruction, "a courtly and cultured gentleman of the old school of Russia intellectuals."[155] The first marriage ended bitterly when her husband gave into the pressure of his family and friends who ostracized him for marrying a black person. She told Robinson that her relationship with Boris developed differently. "I turned him down four times. When he would not give up, I finally told him about my first marriage. He just said that I should not think that all men are alike, that he would never allow anyone to interfere with his private life, and that the color of a person's skin color had nothing to do with the color of one's spirit. . . . My race was irrelevant." Continuing her story, Robinson noted that "Boris warned Coretta that she would face anti-Red prejudice if she returned to America, and that establishing her school might be more difficult than she thought." Ultimately, the two settled into a comfortable life in Moscow, and her new husband's family did not seem to have any qualms about her being black or foreign. Her family in the United States was not so accommodating, for she never heard from her parents again after she told them about her first marriage.[156]

Like Harris, Arle-Titz's living arrangements were far less commodious than either Robinson or Smith would have expected. When Smith met her in 1932, she and her husband lived in "two small, dingy rooms in the western section of Moscow near Kropotkinskaya Square." She had "a huge, aging grand piano [occupying] one-third of one room and the Russian servant girl [occupying] most of the other, which served as the kitchen and dining room." Although he considered "these cramped quarters wholly inadequate," from his observations of the circumstances of other Moscow residents, he felt they were fortunate in having them."[157]

Reflection on the Experience

Hughes spent nearly a year in the Soviet Union, returning to the United States by way of Siberia, China, and Japan. Many of the people he met and the events that occurred during his travels were later immortalized in his poetry, reportage, and prose work. His Soviet sojourn had brought out a new self-assurance in him. As Rampersad commented, "[Hughes] was tremendously alive. With critical and financial success that had come not from godmotherly patronage but from radical work."[158] Noted Hughes, "Not that I write more here than I do elsewhere, but I am paid better, and there is a wider market. . . . Most coloured writers [in the United States] find their work turned down with a note that the files are already full of 'Negro material,' or that the subject is not suitable. . . . In Moscow, on the other hand, the editors welcome frank stories of American Negro life. They print them and pay for them. . . . There is a tremendous reading public buying millions of books." It delighted him that the Soviet appreciation of writers and other artists meant that they had decent housing and other accommodations. "[There are] cooperative dining rooms for writers, specially built modern apartments with very low rents, excellent clubs. . . . As for me, I received for one edition of my poems in translation more money in actual living value than I have yet made from the several editions of my various volumes of poetry in America."[159]

Like Rudd, Patterson, and Smith, Hughes had made his peace with the Soviet bureaucracy because of the hospitable society in which he found himself. "There are often mountains and swamps of red tape that would drive you crazy, were it not for the gentle patience and kindnesses of the ordinary citizens and simple workers. . . . So in spite of the entirely new routine of life which Moscow offers, it does not take long to feel at home."[160]

Hughes began his autobiographical work, *I Wonder as I Wander*, while he was still in the Soviet Union; however, the document he was writing in the 1930s and into the early 1940s was dramatically altered before it finally appeared in the 1950s. Observed Baldwin, "As Hughes' correspondence of the 1950s makes evident, there is a portion of the author's work that he excised in response to perceived pressures to disassociate himself from the USSR."[161] Yet Hughes did leave in brief glimpses of the uniqueness of his and others' experiences. There was something special about the Soviet experiment for blacks. "Maybe the fact that I was colored, too, made a difference. . . . Some things irritated [other] people much more than they did me. . . . Dirt without Jim Crow was bad—but dirt with Jim Crow, for me, would have been infinitely worse. . . . If, rather than a Negro, I had been a Russian of the old school, like Grasdani, [the formerly aristocratic Russian woman whom Hughes hired to cook for him in Tashkent; she hated the term *comrade* and asked that he call her Grasdani, which meant citizen] or a famous Berlin journalist like [Arthur] Koestler, or a comfortable white American tourist affording twenty dollars a day for a room, or a highly skilled foreign engineer impatient with lesser skilled men and bungling red tape . . . maybe I would have become quickly disillusioned, too." And, for an addendum in anticipation of the anti-Communist tenor of the times, he drew on the words of the famed black abolitionist Frederick Douglass: "As to the purge trails, the liquidation, the arrests and censorship, deplorable as these things were, I felt about them in relation to their continual denunciation in the European and American press, much as Frederick Douglass felt before the Civil War when he read in the slave-holding papers that abolitionists were anarchists, villains, devils, and atheists. Douglass said he had the impression that 'Abolition—whatever else it might be—was not unfriendly to the slave.' After all, I suppose, how anything is seen depends upon whose eyes look at it."[162]

CHAPTER 9

Paul Robeson's Search
for a Society Free of Racism

ତ୍ୟୌ

I was not prepared for the feeling of safety and
abundance and freedom that I find here.[1]
—Paul Robeson (1935)

*R*ecalling his first visit to the Soviet Union, black cartoonist Ollie Harrington wrote, "I was invited by the satirical *Krokodile* [journal] to see the Soviet Union." He was in Tashkent and mapping out a scene in his mind:

> I sat on a parkbench where I could drink in the breathtaking oriental beauty of the opera house. I was thinking of coming back the next day with my sketchpad when a little Uzbek girl came to me holding out a flower. Of course, I couldn't understand what she was saying but Yuri, my interpreter explained, "She asks if you are Paul Robeson?" Her mother appeared and suddenly it seemed there were hundreds of Uzbek children with their mothers, all carrying hastily picked flowers. I was terribly flustered but I managed to explain that I wasn't Paul Robeson but that he was my friend. And then one Uzbek mother, proud of her English said, "Here, he is our beloved Pauli."[2]

For the Uzbeks, some of the many people of color of the Soviet Union, Paul Robeson was almost a saint, and even those black visitors who might only vaguely resemble him became "our beloved Pauli" in the minds of ordinary people. For many of these visitors, it was at first perplexing but also, as is evident in Harrington's telling of the story, it was an honor and a pleasure to enjoy some of the adulation Robeson engendered.

Myth versus Reality

Robeson has been associated with the Soviet Union and the Russian people more than any other black person, both in the United States and around the world. Yet Robeson was far from the first black person to do a sojourn there. People whom he admired, like McKay, Du Bois, William L. Patterson (who went in the 1920s), and Hughes (who went in the early 1930s) helped draw his attention there. In England, too, he heard accounts of the Soviet experiment that intrigued him. Over the years of travel back and forth, Robeson clearly developed an intense interest to settle in the Soviet Union and talked freely about the warmth of the Russian people, but he never stayed longer than several months at a stretch. Despite repeated returns to the Soviet Union, England ultimately became his permanent residence away from the United States.[3]

Robeson was also both the subject of and the manipulator of a vast media campaign in the East and in the West that brought his ideas, image, and story into people's living rooms. Although he ultimately fell victim to the anti-Communist pressures in the United States and his memory was virtually erased in the mainstream American mind, his persona continued to grow in other parts of the world. His campaigns in support of the world's oppressed, no matter their color, religion, or location, made him the model of global solidarity for all peoples. The occasion of his sixtieth birthday, in April 1958, gave nations as diverse as Japan, South Africa, the Soviet Union, Mexico, England, Hungary, East Germany, and India, along with twenty-seven others, the opportunity to show him their gratitude. Among the many messages and tributes came a proclamation from Prime Minster Jawaharlal Nehru of India: "Paul Robeson is [not only] one of the greatest artists of our generation, but also . . . has represented and suffered for a cause which should be dear to all of us—the cause of human dignity."[4] And support for Robeson meant support for those whom he admired. As he continued to express solidarity with the Soviet experiment, other peoples began to look favorably on the Soviet Union too.

Attraction to the Soviet Experiment

Many have speculated about Robeson's interest in Russian culture and the Soviet experiment. He had once stated, "I came in contact with Russians at college [Rutgers University]. I heard them sing their native songs and was struck by their likeness to Negro music." This encounter made him reflect on the difference between the Russian's appreciation of their music and the disparaging attitudes toward black music. "What was wrong with our despised music if it was akin to the revered Russian? Had we a value that had been passed by?"[5]

No doubt he had read the many accounts of McKay's and Du Bois's 1920s sojourns.[6] He even spent his holidays with McKay in France in the mid-1920s. His son, Paul Jr., noted that he "had always been attracted by McKay's overt challenges to white racism . . . [and] went out of his way to spend time talking with McKay about race and radicalism."[7]

Friends William L. Patterson, Slava Tynes, and Wayland Rudd all had their personal perspectives on Robeson's earliest exposure. Patterson and Robeson had been close friends since the early 1920s, when Robeson married Eslanda and Patterson was then married to one of Eslanda's closest friends, Minnie Sumner. Recalled Patterson, "I saw a great deal of Paul Robeson. We became lifelong friends. Paul and I argued over the nature of the Black man's struggle."[8] Left-leaning from his law school days, Patterson had discovered Emanuel Levine's progressive bookshop in Berkeley.[9] Then, there were his experiences with the Sacco and Vanzetti case.[10] "What they had said would live with me forever. . . . The significance of the case was tremendous. Sacco and Vanzetti belonged to white and Black, Italian, German, English, Jew, Russian, American—they belonged to progressive mankind. . . . This kind of belonging led to unity."[11] When Robeson and his wife, Eslanda, made their first trip to the Soviet Union in 1934, they made a point of visiting Patterson, who was back in Moscow for medical treatment and to visit his Russian family.[12] In a 1951 tribute, Robeson acknowledged Patterson's influence on him. "One thing that comes to my mind . . . is thinking of the Sacco and Vanzetti case. I was then finishing school and beginning to think of my career. I didn't know much of what was behind the political things of the time. I remember reading in the paper that Elizabeth Gurley Flynn and Patterson were up in Massachusetts defending the rights of Sacco and Vanzetti. I remember also Pat's struggles around the ILD [International Labor Defense] and the Scottsboro case. . . . I know as a young man I was tremendously inspired."[13]

Afro-Russian journalist Slava Tynes, son of agricultural specialist George Tynes, contended that Robeson's early introduction occurred elsewhere. Tynes asserted that Robeson had met Russians who were visiting a Harlem nightclub in the 1920s: "One was Eduard Tisse, the well-known Soviet cameraman. The other man was Sergei Eisenstein, his countryman, and a world famous film director. Robeson was struck by their simple manner, friendliness and sincerity. They found common ground very soon [and this] turned into [a] real creative friendship."[14]

Robeson's friend and fellow artist Rudd also insisted on taking credit. Chiding Robeson years later, Rudd wrote, "I'll never forget the ring in your voice, Paul, when you said: 'Way [Wayland] I'll come!' Man of your word, that you are, you came."[15] The Robesons' arrival was commemorated in a photo showing Rudd, Paul and Eslanda Robeson, Eslanda's brother Frank, filmmaker Eisenstein, Marie Seton, and others shortly after they arrived that December.[16]

England, Africa, and the Soviet Union

But Robeson also pointed to his years in England as furthering his political savvy and interest in world affairs. An African friend of his had pointed to the similarity of opportunity under the Soviet experiment and the desires of the many colonial peoples to gain their freedom. "He had traveled east and had seen the Yakuts, a people who had been classed as a 'backward race' by the Czars. He had been struck by the resemblance between the tribal life of the Yakuts and his own people of East Africa. What would happen to a people like the Yakuts now that they had been freed from colonial oppression and were part of the construction of a socialist society. Well, I went to see for myself."[17]

It was also in England that Robeson began systematic studies of leftist thought. As Phillip Foner noted, " [Robeson's] radicalism antedated his first visit to the Soviet Union. . . . His radical stance on political and economic issues was largely shaped under the influence of the British working class." Robeson himself told an interviewer in 1960, "I came here unshaped. Great parts of my working class roots are here."[18] He became close friends with anarchist Emma Goldman, who gave him a wide range of books to read. And although Goldman became disenchanted with the Bolsheviks after they came to power and imprisoned many of her anarchist friends, the books she and Robeson discussed left an indelible mark on him.[19] If nothing else, he had imbibed the credo that change was inevitable and that the individual had a key role in pressing for this change.

The Pairing of Eisenstein and Robeson

But it was the invitation of famed filmmaker Eisenstein that resulted in Robeson's first trip to the Soviet Union. Eisenstein had been keen on finding a way to work with Robeson since their chance encounter in Harlem. With Seton acting as a go-between, Eisenstein sent Robeson a note: "I never had an opportunity to meet you and I was allways [sic] sorry of it because you are one of the personalities I allways [sic] liked without knowing them personally. [I am] extremely pleased to hear from Mary [sic] that you get really interested in our country."[20] Robeson did not yet know Eisenstein, but he had confidence in Seton. She had been among the first to welcome him to England, and they had stayed close.[21] She was so happy to put the two together that she accompanied Robeson and his wife on that first journey.

As much as Robeson had been curious to see the country he had heard so much about, he, like Du Bois before him, could not shake doubts over whether the promise of a nonracist society could be achieved. He confessed this doubt to Eisenstein toward the end of that first visit. "I hesitated to come; I listened to what everybody had to say but I didn't think this would be any different from any other place. But—maybe you'll understand—I feel like a human being for the first time since I grew up. Here I am not a Negro but a human being. . . . Here, for the first time in my life, I walk in full human dignity."[22]

The Robesons had been living a comfortable life in England and enjoying Robeson's rising prominence, but an incident at a German train station en route to the Soviet Union reminded them that there were still hazards to being black. He, his wife, and Seton were en route and had a day's layover in Berlin. Duberman noted that while they waited for their train, Robeson saw a group of men looking at them with "real hatred in their eyes."[23] According to Paul Jr., these were "brown-shirted storm troopers." They formed a "rough semi-circle around them [and cut] them off from the other passengers. . . . Paul explained to Marie [Seton], who knew no German, that [the men] thought she was German. As their epithets became louder and more provocative, Paul told her to stay outwardly calm. 'This is . . . how a lynching begins. . . . If either of us moves, or shows fear, they'll go further.' "[24] Duberman continued the account, " 'I took a step forward,' Paul told a reporter many years later, and 'they could read something in my eyes.' For whatever reasons of their own, the men moved off." Seton, in her account of the incident, observed later, "For a long time after the train moved out of Berlin . . . Paul sat hunched in the corner of the compartment staring out into the darkness."[25]

This memory was still fresh when the Robesons arrived in the Soviet Union, but the warm reception accorded him everywhere they went assuaged his fears. It also comforted him that he and Eisenstein were kindred spirits. Both were trying to make use of their creative talents in environments that seemed designed to deny their skills and abilities. Both were struggling with the contradiction of receiving adulation and acclaim for their talents while falling prey to the petty bickering of bureaucrats on the other.

Eisenstein found his experiences in the United States confusing. Celebrated for directing the Russian films *Strike* and *The Battleship Potemkin*, he had been invited to Hollywood, but there his every suggestion was turned down by people uneasy with his avant-garde style.[26] The final blow came when the American backers of his projected film, *Que Viva Mexico*, withdrew their support and the Stalinist government summarily ordered him to return to the Soviet Union. Despite this precipitous fall from grace, he still hoped that his previous successes would lead to directing new films in the Soviet Union, but the Soviets were not pleased about the negative publicity he had attracted. Noted Paul Jr., "[Eisenstein] had returned to Moscow in disgrace in April 1932. Now still in the Soviet filmdom's doghouse, Sergei had no assurance that the cinematic authorities would sanction one of his films."[27]

Eisenstein and Robeson wanted to collaborate on a film about the Haitian revolution based on the play *Black Majesty* by C.L.R. James. Both men thought the Haitian revolution offered useful lessons about the potential of oppressed people to rule themselves. Eisenstein wanted Robeson to play either Henri Christophe or Jean-Jacques Dessalines, leaders in the Haitian fight for independence.[28] Robeson had also spent years trying to find just the right script and backers to do the story justice but had been unable to do so.[29] But the project never came off because by the time Eisenstein had finally made the arrangements to make the film, Robeson had already signed a contract with Sir Alexander Korda to play the lead in the film *Saunders of the River*. As Robeson told writer Jan Carew later, he could not get out of the Korda contract, and "it was one of the great mistakes of my life."[30] The opportunity for Eisenstein and Robeson to work together never arose again, although Robeson and Eisenstein remained friends and continued to discuss projects for years afterward.[31] It is questionable whether *Black Majesty* could have been completed, despite Eisenstein's and Robeson's enthusiasm. After Eisenstein returned to the Soviet Union from the United States, the Soviet censors, notorious for their unpredictability in deciding what was and was not Socialist Realism, also found much of Eisenstein's work to be too avant-guard.[32]

The Soviet interest in black film projects waxed and waned. Although the projected Eisenstein-Robeson *Black Majesty* had trouble finding support from the authorities, the Soviets were ready to back the earlier antiracist *Black and White* film project. This program had lured Hughes, Lloyd Patterson, Rudd, Smith and a number of other blacks to the Soviet Union. The Soviets went to great lengths—and expense—to bring in this group of twenty-two a mere two years earlier. But a shift in priorities caused that film to be cancelled. One might also question whether a film highlighting a successful slave rebellion might not have shown blacks as having too much liberty and as being able to overthrow their oppressors by themselves. As much as the Soviets professed solidarity with the struggles of peoples of color, they retained the view that these nascent societies would need the help, if not the guidance, of European (read Soviet) peoples. This paternalistic attitude would disrupt relationships with many black progressives in future decades.

A Whirlwind of Solidarity

Robeson's first visit was filled with receptions and political and cultural events. Technical specialist Robinson was also invited to one of those events. "I received an invitation to attend a reception given in [Robeson's] honor by the prestigious All Union Society for Cultural Relations with Foreign Countries. . . . The reception excelled by far anything I had attended thus far in the Soviet Union. Men were dressed in tuxedos and women wore evening gowns."[33] Treated like royalty, Robeson was greeted not only by Eisenstein and Soviet officials but also by the public, both as an artist and as a symbol of the potential achievements of all black people.

He was also profoundly struck by the examples of the black sojourners he met during that first visit, two of whom were his wife's brothers. Duberman noted they were "sympathetic to the Soviet experiment [and] had decided to try living in a socialist land and thus far were enthusiastic over the experiment. John had gotten work as a bus driver at the Foreign Worker's Club garage, and Frank, more recently arrived, had—as a powerfully-built man—the prospect of being billed as a 'Black Sampson' in a wrestling troupe tour of circuses and carnivals."[34] Paul Jr. also noted, "Frank, who traveled to rural as well as urban areas with the circus, was especially emphatic on this point [no race prejudice], announcing that he had decided to become a Soviet citizen and marry a Russian woman."[35]

Frank was the more easy going and adaptable of the brothers.[36] He had already attended university in the United States but did not complete his studies because he was trying to support his elderly mother and help Eslanda pay her college expenses.[37] But, as was true for most blacks, he could only find jobs that required his brawn, not his brain. Thus, despite his college studies, he had to take on disparate jobs, such as lumberjack and Pullman porter on trains. At the same time, this earlier flexibility made it easier for him to accept the Soviets' proposal that he be a wrestler in the traveling circus troupe. Frank had not done wrestling professionally before, but, as Smith noted, he was so large and threatening that he had little difficulty defeating all those who wanted to take him on. "One day, shortly after his arrival in Moscow, a sharp-eyed scout for the Moscow Circus caught sight of Goode and knowing an unmistakable attraction when he saw one, made him an attractive offer to join a string of husky Russian wrestlers then touring the country. . . . The circus scout felt that . . . Goode would prove a great box-office attraction. His guess proved correct for [there were] packed houses in every city where Goode appeared."[38]

Although Frank was doing well, John was not. Noted Duberman, "[Eslanda] didn't like the looks of John—'cold, and worn, and old.' During their stay, Essie loaded him up with warm underwear and a heavy leather coat, paid rent for six months on a room he could have to himself, and left him enough foreign money to buy scarce eggs, meat and vegetables till Spring."[39]

Nonetheless, the total effect of the trip was a positive one as the Robesons were mollified by the testimonials of other black sojourners. "The black community itself feted the Robesons. . . . All the black Americans expressed deep contentment with life in the Soviet Union, a society, they told Robeson, that was entirely free of racial prejudice."[40]

The Family Settles In

Robeson returned to the Soviet Union four times through the mid-to-late 1930s.[41] He was in constant demand for concerts, speeches, and solidarity appearances, and he happily accepted invitations to take his holidays there as a guest of the Soviet government. He also began seriously contemplating moving there himself, but these intentions were diverted by the expansion of his career in Europe. Ultimately, London was a better staging area, and he could easily get around Europe and return to the Soviet Union as often as he chose. Also, as noted by Paul Jr., "From his conversations with Sergei [Eisenstein], as well as from his own observations, Paul came to realize that, despite his optimistic statements about making his home in the Soviet Union, he could never live there permanently. It was a great place to visit."[42]

Nonetheless, Robeson's fascination with the Soviet experiment grew. He went to stay "with friends on film location at a collective farm and [had an] 'idyllic' time, 'astonished' at how well informed the village children were about 'the American Negro problem'—and how free of racial prejudice." He also spent time at John's workplace. On New Year's Day in 1935, "[making] rounds at John Goode's garage, Paul sang and got a raucous welcome."[43]

In January 1936, he formally established an apartment in the Hotel Nationale in Moscow, and the extended family spent the Christmas holidays there. By that point too, Robeson had decided that the environment would be better than that of the United States for his son. Installing his mother in-law, Eslanda Cardoso Goode, in the apartment as the boy's guardian, as she had done in other countries over the many years of his young life, he then enrolled Paul Jr. in a special Soviet school.[44] Thus, by late 1936, Robeson had four family members who had joined the black sojourner group: his mother in-law, his two brothers in-law, and his son.

In making the decision to leave Paul Jr. in Moscow, the Robesons drew on the experiences of others who had made similar decisions. They knew about Williana Burroughs's satisfaction in leaving her two boys in the Soviet Union. They also knew, though, that unlike the clandestine movements of Burroughs and others who left children there, their actions would be watched by the rest of the world. A *Life* magazine feature piece, "Robeson in Moscow," commented, "Slav admiration so touched Robeson that . . . he announced he would send his son Paul Jr. . . . to Soviet schools." An article in the New York *Amsterdam News* stated, "The nine-year-old son of Paul Robeson will not grow up in the preju- diced atmosphere of America."[45] And, in an article entitled "Robeson Puts Son in Soviet School," the *New York Times*, announced that Robeson "does not want [the] boy to have to contend with race prejudice until he is older."[46] Paul Jr. did not yet know Russian; years later he wrote, "My parents enrolled me in the equivalent of an American fifth-grade class in a 'model school.' Despite its official public status (all schools in the Soviet Union were public by law) this school was the equivalent of the most exclusive private school in the United States (Stalin's daughter and Foreign Minister [Vyacheslav] Molotov's son at- tended it along with the children of other high Soviet officials). My classmates went out of their way to be helpful . . . and within a month, with an ear for language and after-school tutoring in Russian, I was in every way included as one of the group."[47] Years later, Robeson commented, "[Paul Jr.] said that he had good teachers and good playmates. . . . Why should that disturb anybody?"[48]

The Robeson Effect

Frank and John Goode had preceded Robeson in moving to the Soviet Union and, thus, had not initially benefited from his presence. However, once the Robesons began to make frequent visits, the Goodes found certain advantages to their family ties. The Soviet authorities helped Eslanda find John better accom- modations than he had had at first. By 1935, Robeson observed, "I visited the home of my brother in law. . . . His apartment had plenty of light, fresh air and space. Believe me he is very happy."[49] Eslanda was also satisfied that all were well settled. Paraphrasing her diary entries in late 1935, Duberman wrote, "On New Year's Eve the family gathered together in Moscow—Ma Goode, Pauli, Paul, Essie, Essie's brothers, John and Frank, Larry [Brown], and William Pat- terson. They had a 'high old time;' three days later, Essie felt 'still full of vodka, caviar, champagne and Russian cigarette smoke.'"[50] Frank's daughter, Eslanda, remembered that in the late 1950s, when the Robesons were again traveling to the Soviet Union, Frank, as Robeson's brother in-law, found the authorities much more receptive to his requests than they were at other times.[51]

Smith also found a way to take advantage of the extended Robeson family presence. He prevailed on Robeson's mother-in-law to give him some of
Paul Jr.'s hand-me-down clothing for Russian children he knew. "Two of my
neighbor's boys, I explained, were desperately in need of shoes and clothes.
They were about the same size as Paul, Jr.; did young Robeson have any extra
clothes or shoes he could spare?" Smith neglected to tell Mrs. Goode that these
children were not his neighbor's children but distant relatives of the celebrated
poet Pushkin. He was uncertain whether Mrs. Goode would have been so ame-
nable to helping them in view of their family's former elite status.[52] However,
Smith underestimated Robeson and, by extension, his family's attitudes toward
Pushkin. Robeson himself regularly celebrated Pushkin, both as a symbol and
as an artist like himself. "When I approached Russia, I found that I was interested in the Eastern part. I can't read Turgeniev, whose language is influenced
by French and the West . . . but I am interested in Gogol and Pushkin, who show
more Eastern [Russian] and Tartar influence."[53] He probably would have liked to
have known some of Pushkin's descendants.

Paul Jr. did well at the Soviet model school; however, by 1938, the rum-
blings of war had grown louder, and the Stalinist regime had begun to treat foreigners with increased suspicion. John was worried about this development and
left for the United States in 1937.[54] The Robesons decided to move Paul Jr. and
his grandmother back to London but worried about Frank's safety as he had become a Soviet citizen.[55] They knew that the removal of Paul Jr. had to be done
delicately so as not to anger the Stalinist government, which, in turn, might direct
its ire to Frank. Wrote Paul Jr., "The Soviet Union felt it was already in a situation
that was to them 'the equivalent of war.' . . . They could not tolerate any kind of
dissent. . . . Uncle Frank, who had forfeited his American citizenship to become
a Soviet citizen, was vulnerable to arrest and even execution. . . . So my father
felt it was time to . . . enlist Patterson's help."[56] Patterson was close to the highest
echelons and thus could put in a special word on their behalf. Using Eslanda as a
go-between, Patterson encouraged her to demonstrate her support of the Stalinist
regime in her letters to him. Noted Paul Jr., "She supported the purge to the hilt,
and denounced Ignaty Kazakov."[57] They were right to try to shield Frank because
"Uncle John's timely departure had saved him from arrest and probable execution. . . . [In] a copy of a 1938 Soviet secret police file . . . Arthur Talent, a twenty-
five-year-old art student from Moscow . . . from whom John had rented a room,
falsely denounced John as a British spy. Talent had been arrested in January 1938
solely because he had emigrated from the United States with his parents in the
1920s. . . . Terrified of his interrogators, Talent denounced everyone he could
think of, including John, whose other " 'crime' was that he spoke German."[58]

Ten Years Later

Robeson did not return to the Soviet Union until after the war, in 1949,
when he gave a number of concerts and was an honored guest for the 150th

anniversary of Pushkin's birth.[59] The blacks he met now were no longer sojourners but expatriates and their families. He also met Lily Golden; she was now a university student, no longer the small girl he had first seen in the 1930s.[60] In a 1953 article for the *New World Review*, Robeson noted her father's contributions to the Soviet experiment and his amusement at meeting her as a grown woman. "And an old friend of mine, Mr. Golden, trained under Carver at Tuskegee, played a prominent role in cotton production. In 1949, I saw his daughter, now grown and in the university—a proud Soviet citizen."[61]

Robeson's 1949 return to the Soviet Union came on the heels of a major storm swirling around him. He and Du Bois had just addressed the Congress of World Partisans of Peace in Paris in April. Noted Duberman, there were two thousand delegates from over fifty nations. "Robeson sang to the gathering and then made some brief remarks, most of them unexceptional echoes from a dozen previous . . . speeches. . . . But then he tacked on a less familiar refrain[:] . . . the wealth of America . . . had been built 'on the backs of the white workers from Europe . . . and . . . millions of blacks. . . . Our will to fight for peace is strong. We shall not make war on anyone. We shall not make war on the Soviet Union.'"[62]

This statement in itself would have been alarming to the United States and its allies, which considered the Paris Peace Congress a Soviet ploy, but the Associated Press report misrepresented Robeson's words by printing a different text. This version was even more inflammatory: "We denounce the policy of the United States government, which is similar to that of Hitler and Goebbels. . . . It is unthinkable that American Negroes would go to war on behalf of those who have oppressed us." As Duberman continued, "The outcry was immediate . . . The white press rushed to inveigh against him as a traitor; the black leadership hurried to deny he spoke for anyone but himself."[63] Despite the furor in the United States, none of Robeson's international concerts were canceled. In Europe, which was surfacing from World War II, any talk of peace was welcomed. In fact, Robeson went on to give a series of sold-out concerts before thousands of people in London, Copenhagen, Stockholm, Oslo, and Prague.

For Robeson, then, the 1949 Pushkin celebration was more than a celebration of a single historical figure, it was emblematic of a larger pact. Speaking at a welcome-home rally in New York on June 19, 1949, Robeson stated, "Here is a whole one-sixth of the earth's surface, including millions of brown, yellow and black people who would be Negroes here in America and subject to the same awful race prejudice. . . . In this Soviet Union, the very term 'backward country' is an insult, for in one generation former colonial peoples have been raised to unbelievable industrial and social levels. . . . These achievements make completely absurd the . . . pronouncements that it will take several generations, maybe hundreds of years, before we Negro people in the West Indies, Africa, and America can have any real control over our own destiny." Furthermore, he continued, "here is a whole nation which is now doing honor to our poet Pushkin—one of the greatest poets in history—the Soviet people's and our proud world possession."[64]

Less than a month after his return to the United States, a massive slander campaign was launched by the U.S. government. Smear articles spread around both the white press and the black under titles such as "Why Doesn't Paul Robeson Give More to His Own Negroes Instead of Russian Reds?" and "'I Love Above All, Russia,' Robeson Says."[65] Clamped into internal exile, he was shut off from audiences at home by fear of association, and he was prevented from traveling to his international engagements by the cancellation of his passport.

A Year of Renewal

It took nine long years to win the appeal to have his passport returned. Once the ruling came down in June 1958 through the concurrent Supreme Court case of Rockwell Kent and Walter Briehl, Robeson and Du Bois, who also lost his passport, were exonerated. As Duberman noted, the court ruled "that the Secretary of State had no right to deny a passport to any citizen because of his political beliefs [and] that the Passport Division had no right to demand that an applicant sign an affidavit concerning membership in the Community Party. Suddenly it was all over."[66]

When Robeson set foot in the Soviet Union in the fall of 1958, he was still savoring this new climate of goodwill, and the Soviets were determined to lionize him. They housed him and his wife in the finest of accommodations and made sure he had access to the most senior of Soviet officials. The black expatriate community also made special pilgrimages to see him, as Eslanda's diary noted: "[August 19 was spent] with Negroes in Moscow, who came in a body to the Hotel to greet and welcome Paul."[67]

Most important, the Soviets made arrangements for him to speak at a number of special venues and, through radio broadcast, ensured that his words reached into the farthest sectors of the country and abroad. Soviet television broadcast a live twenty-minute interview and showed a documentary about his work. His concert at the Lenin Stadium for eight thousand people was also televised.[68] Thus, wherever Soviet TV and radio reached, so did Robeson's larger-than-life persona and voice. He had become a beacon of hope not only for people in the Soviet Union but also for others in the developing world. Noted Duberman, Robeson was moved. "Robeson was shown as 'visibly affected' by his reception, weeping openly, and immediately . . . bursting into the Russian patriotic song 'Shiroka Strana Moya Rodnaya' ('My Broad Native Land'), singing twice the refrain, 'I know no other land where people breathe free.'"[69]

The visit to Uzbekistan as a guest of the International Festival of Films of Africa and Asia was no less thrilling. Robeson looked forward to seeing the effects of the agricultural specialists' "transforming of the desert in Uzbekistan into blooming acres of cotton."[70] Eslanda wrote in her diary, "When our motorcycle escort stopped momentarily so that the way could be cleared, people peered into the car and the shout went up . . . 'Pol Robeson is here!' And crowds seemed to materialize out of nowhere to shout, 'Preevyet! Welcome.'"[71]

Following the festival, Robeson flew to Yalta on the Black Sea, where he gave concerts and visited one of the children's Pioneer camps, a particular delight of his.[72] Khrushchev was also vacationing in the area and invited the Robesons to join him. As Duberman noted, "[They] were driven for half an hour to a hunting lodge in the hills above Yalta, where they were greeted by the Khrushchevs, the Voroshilovs, the Mikoyans, Tupolev (the airplane designer) and others. . . . [They] then proceeded in another line of cars to a further retreat . . . [where] they met . . . the current 'leaders of the German, Italian, Rumanian, Bulgarian, Polish, Czech, Hungarian governments and their wives.' . . . At dinner, toasts were made all around—Paul's was so moving, Essie reported, that it produced tears."[73]

Later in that same year, in December 1958, the Robesons returned to the Soviet Union just in time for a special New Year's Eve dinner with Khrushchev. As Eslanda noted, it was a "formal affair, with engraved invitations to dinner at eleven at the Kremlin."[74] This was a year of 'return' for both Robeson and Du Bois, who, like him, had weathered the firestorm of the McCarthy era. Shirley Graham Du Bois described the poignant meeting of the two men during that special dinner. "Both men rose simultaneously [at this point, Du Bois was ninety] and began threading their way through the maze of tables toward each other. The going was a bit difficult; chairs were pushed out of the way and waiters with loaded trays had to sidestep them. . . . But the two seemed unaware of the commotion they were causing. When they finally did meet, big Paul and small Du Bois threw their arms around each other in a bear hug and Mr. Khrushchev rose to his feet applauding. Then everybody in the hall was up, applauding and shouting their names."[75]

Illness and Recovery

Unfortunately, Robeson fell ill shortly thereafter and was forced to spend months in a Soviet hospital. This development caused no small amount of consternation because Du Bois, too, had been ill earlier that fall and had spent an extended time in a Soviet sanitarium. Their illnesses portended the loss of two invaluable allies who crossed national and racial boundaries. The Soviets were particularly worried because African and other developing nations were gaining their independence and the Soviets had hoped Du Bois and Robeson could help foster alliances with these nascent states. In a sense, it this urgency may have led to the Robeson's and Du Bois's illnesses because both were plunged into demanding travel and work as soon as their passports were returned.

Robeson's illness also interfered with his plans to finally do a major production of *Othello* in England and with his plans to do a Russian production

later.[76] He had done the play at the Savoy Theatre in England thirty years earlier—in 1930—to great acclaim, but the 1959 production was to be at the famed
Shakespeare Theatre in Stratford-upon-Avon. Remarkably, Robeson recovered.
Rehearsals began in April, opening night was in early May, and the production
ran to November. But the physically challenging acting, concerts, and political
activities ultimately broke Robeson's health, and he had to return to Moscow
for further treatment. Like Patterson and Du Bois, the Robesons were more
comfortable with the security and attention they received in the Soviet Union
than with the attention they would have received in the United States. They
frequently returned to the Soviet Union for medical care, and in the latter part
of the 1950s and early 1960s, both Paul and Eslanda were treated by Soviet
doctors.

Although ill in 1960–1961, Robeson did participate in a few events. One
was to accept Robinson's request that he visit the First State Ball Bearing Plant.[77]
Robinson noted that his co-workers were ecstatic. "As soon as we entered the
shop, the workers broke into thunderous applause. . . . Robeson captivated the
workers with his voice and personal magnetism." But, then, he was amazed to
hear Robeson sing a Jewish song. "Robeson began another one that startled me.
It was a song [from] the Jewish tradition that decried their persecution through
the centuries. I knew this song would alienate party officials in the audience.
I wondered whether Robeson . . . was even aware of Soviet anti-Semitism. I
decided that he must be, and that perhaps he knew what he was doing. As he
sang, there was a cry in his voice, a plea to end the beating, berating, and killing
of Jews."[78] This was not the first time Robeson defied growing anti-Semitic attitudes. Ten years earlier, at the end of his 1949 Moscow concert, he sang a song
in honor of Jewish friends who had suddenly disappeared. Noted Duberman,
"Asking the audience for quiet, he announced that he would sing only one en-
core. Then he expressed with emotion the sense he had of the deep cultural ties
between the Jewish peoples of the United States and the Soviet Union. . . . [He]
referred to his own friendship with [Solomon] Mikhoels and [Itzik] Feffer . . .
then sang in Yiddish, to a hushed hall." These were subtle messages. Robeson
purposefully avoided publicly expressing any disappointment with the Soviet
experiment because he felt other goals were more important. Observed Duberman, he never went "further than to make the barest suggestion that the best
chance for reaching his primary goal—improving the condition of oppressed
people—lay with the egalitarian impulses originally unleashed by the Russian
Revolution."[79]

Robeson also felt compelled to recognize Soviet solidarity by participating in the celebrations for the renaming of the Soviet Peoples' Friendship
University after Patrice Lumumba.[80] Lumumba's assassination in January 1961
infuriated him, and now he knew his presence would help to honor the slain
Congolese leader and to encourage African and other youth to take advantage
of studying in the Soviet Union. Although never able to revisit the Soviet Union
after he left for the last time in 1961, he was pleased to know that thousands

of African and other Third World students would have the opportunity for this advanced education.

The Visitor versus the Expatriate

Robeson's many trips to Soviet Union were those of a "special guest." Observing his visits from the Russian perspective, Slava Tynes noted, "Now arriving in the Soviet Union Paul Robeson was not merely a visitor, but a great friend of the Soviet people. . . . And every time when [he] came to the USSR again photographs appeared in the Soviet press with warm words addressed to the dear and welcomed friend." Continued Tynes, Robeson was an "unbending heroic character [and] example for their children and . . . [they wanted] to commemorate for the generations to come the image of this extremely humane man."[81] It was also significant that as Carew noted from his visits to the Soviet Union, officials allowed his photograph to hang alongside that of Stalin in government offices when no other photographs were allowed.[82] The Soviets even named a mountain peak in the western Tyran-Shan and Trans-Ili Ala-Tau of Central Asia after him in 1953.[83]

But Robeson was also shielded from dealing with the day-to-day life of residents of the Soviet Union. He was invariably housed in the finest hotels and whisked around comfortably to his various engagements. The Soviet authorities were also most accommodating to his every wish. They made sure that Robeson's path intersected with one or another of the black expatriates, some of whom were always in the groups that greeted him on his many arrivals.[84] In the early, pre–World War II period, his enthusiasm was largely confirmed by theirs, as all were pooling their talents and energies with their Russian counterparts. However, this convergence began to end in the latter part of the 1930s, as Stalinism calcified and the purges began. By the time Robeson returned in 1949 and during his visits in the late 1950s and early 1960s, his experiences as a visitor and those of the blacks living there increasingly diverged.

The Robesons had gotten some indication of the hardships of living under the Soviet experiment as early as 1936, when their son developed problems because of his limited diet. Noted Duberman, "They found Pauli and Ma Goode 'very well' (except that Pauli had developed an intestinal problem calling for a special nonfat diet, which necessitated finding them a flat with kitchen facilities for preparing his special meals)."[85] But as they had the money and influence, they could make special arrangements to help resolve this problem; thus the boy and his grandmother stayed on.

They also knew that John was having trouble accomplishing his goal of studying to be an engineer. According to his niece, Eslanda, John was frustrated at not having been able to match his aspirations to the reality of living in the Soviet Union. Although, as Paul Jr. noted, "[he] was mechanically inclined— always tinkering with machines," John found it was difficult to balance the need to make a living with formal studies of the Russian language.[86] Engineering courses were usually offered in special institutes where English was not being used. Foreigners could attend some institutions, like KUTVA, which was specifically designed for foreigners doing political training; however, the technical institutes were populated by Russians, and so no special language support was available. Also, as John came to understand, the informal Russian he was learning as a mechanic was not sophisticated enough for formal technical studies. John stayed for three years and helped "reorganize the bus repair system" at his workplace, but he was never able to move on to advanced studies. Continued Paul Jr., in early 1937, "when Paul and Essie headed back to London [for] four days ... Uncle John accompanied them, carrying just one suitcase, ostensibly for a short vacation. ... In fact, Uncle John had no intention of coming back. ... He deliberately left most of his belongings behind so as not to raise suspicion."[87]

Eslanda also wanted her brother Frank to leave as they were making plans to take Paul Jr. and his grandmother out. Wrote Paul Jr., "Worried about Frank's fate if a major European war broke out [Eslanda] made a quick trip ... to see him. [She also tried to see] Dr. Kazakov, our good friend from the Kislovodsk days. She was deeply worried to learn that he had been one of the first arrested in the latest purges. Uncle Frank was still determined to take his chances in the Soviet Union; he wanted no part of a return to the United States."[88]

Frank, like most of the black expatriates, married and settled down with his Russian family. And, despite occasional brushes with the Soviet authorities, all but one of the sojourners/expatriates, Lovett Fort-Whiteman, eluded the purges.[89] By the time of Khrushchev's refutation of Stalinism and establishment of the program of peaceful coexistence in the late 1950s, there remained fourteen families, including Frank Goode's, extending from this 1920s and 1930s group of black sojourners.

PART IV

❧

The Expatriates and New Sojourners

CHAPTER 10

The Expatriates

THE PURGES, THE WAR YEARS, AND BEYOND

൙

The harshness of the regime, of course, could not be overlooked;
but this did not affect me or other Negroes directly.[1]
—Homer Smith (1964)

*W*hen Homer Smith downplayed his and other blacks' brushes with the Soviet secret police by stating that it "did not affect" them, he was basically right. Only one of this small remaining group of black sojourners, Lovett Fort-Whiteman, was known to have been purged. If, however, Smith wanted to indicate that they had only minor encounters or were minimally aware of what was happening to others, then he is seriously misleading. Many of them were challenged by experiences that were traumatizing. As Smith himself had observed, "My boss . . . was liquidated along with several other postal officials. . . . Many disappeared without a trace. . . . Employees had begun talking in whispers."[2] And, Robert Robinson had speculated, " 'How really secure am I?.' . . . Russians and foreigners at the factory—including my shop—were disappearing."[3]

Smith's first, direct encounter occurred when he went to meet a potential news source:

> I had noticed two husky men in black overcoats and black fur caps pacing back and forth across the square. . . . Instead of by-passing us as they had been doing previously, they met us head-on. Tapping me on the shoulder, they said, "Come along with us. . . ." The linings of my overcoat, jacket and fur cap were ripped open. . . . The soles and heels and inner soles of my boots were then thoroughly examined. . . . [I] was carefully frisked. . . . When I went next day to a tailor, the old man seemed quite unconcerned over the condition of my clothes. . . . "It looks as if you have fallen into the hands of the Black Ravens." . . . Russians . . . referred to their Secret Police Agents as Black Ravens. . . . Though nothing had really come of my brush with the MVD [Ministry of Internal Affairs], it was for me . . . the end of the beginning.[4]

Smith was taken aback by the tailor's reaction, but even he had to admit that all was not so simple. He too found he was willing to accommodate these difficulties in light of his larger ambitions to be a foreign correspondent. "I had begun to question the intelligence of remaining. . . . My disappointment had grown with the passing years. [But] this did not directly affect me. . . . As always, I traded in well stocked shops where only valuta (foreign money) was accepted. These shops were out of bounds for the Russian citizen. . . . I, as a foreign newsman, fared well enough."[5]

Ten of the black sojourners, including Smith and Robinson, were still in the Soviet Union after the end of the 1930s: Lovett Fort-Whiteman and Robert Ross of the fellow travelers; Oliver Golden and George Tynes of the agricultural specialists; Lloyd Patterson and Wayland Rudd of the *Black and White* film group, and Frank Goode.[6] Golden's Jewish American wife, Bertha Bialek Golden, also remained. An eleventh black sojourner, Williana Burroughs, who had visited the country several times since the late 1920s and then moved to the Soviet Union in 1937, stayed through the war, but she was not an expatriate and left in 1945. Neither Smith nor Fort-Whiteman took up Soviet citizenship either.[7]

Smith's and Robinson's memoirs, together with books by Lily Golden and Yelena Khanga, provide insights into the challenges and compromises many in the black sojourner group faced. By the latter part of the 1930s, communication with families and friends in the United States had fallen off considerably, and the blacks remaining in the Soviet Union were thrown more and more on their own resources. Wrote Khanga, "From 1931 until 1936, letters from America got through with some regularity. After that [1937 onwards], nothing arrived until the thaw after Stalin's death."[8] Communication had moved regularly back and forth between the United States and the Soviet Union, either carried by frequent visitors or mailed. But, with the hardening of the Stalinist regime and growing war tensions, these lines were cut, and the disruption continued for decades. Added Khanga, "[When] Bertha . . . received a letter from Viola, Oliver's youngest sister, [in 1988] . . . it was the first communication from the Chicago Goldens in more than twenty years."[9] The only exception was during World War II, when Bertha occasionally received food packages from the United States.[10]

During the initial period, when the sojourners' skills were helping to build the country, the Soviets encouraged goodwill between the two countries. The Soviet government itself maintained lines of contact by collaborating with U.S. industrialists who were establishing plants in the Soviet Union and paying part of the foreign specialists' salaries directly into U.S. banks. Additionally, as the sojourners' initial contract periods were coming to an end, the Soviets not only offered the option to renew their contracts but also agreed to cover the expense of holiday trips back home. The bargain was clearly honored by both, for there were no reports of black specialists refusing to return to the Soviet Union to take up their renewed contracts. Indeed, many found that the U.S. trip only confirmed what they feared. Glad to see family and friends and taste foods from home, they found the job situation and racism the same as when they left. As Robinson commented, following his six-week holiday, "[I] was physically rested, spiritually replenished, yet eager to get back to what I enjoyed most—my work."[11]

By the latter part of 1936 and rise of 1937, the black sojourners had at least two compelling reasons for agreeing to take up Soviet citizenship: first, the guarantee of employment and other social supports and, second, their Russian families. Fort-Whiteman, Goode, Patterson, Ross, Rudd, Smith, and Tynes married Russians or other women whom they met in the Soviet Union. Golden had gone there with his wife, Bertha. All but Smith and Fort-Whiteman had children. Robinson, who finally left the country after forty-four years, never admitted to a serious relationship or to having any children. However, Frank Goode's daughter, Eslanda, indicated that he may have fathered a child, Robert Zotov, out of wedlock.[12] Black sojourners Henry Scott, Dick Williams, and John Sutton started families as well, but they were not willing to renounce their U.S. citizenship and were forced to leave their families behind when they returned to the United States in the late 1930s. Joseph Roane, who had arrived in the Soviet Union with his wife, Sadie, had a child, and the three of them returned to the United States during this same time.

The sojourners had been content to tap into the benefits of being foreign specialists in the Soviet Union, including access to better housing and food-stuffs than ordinary Russians had access to. However, many found that once they took Soviet citizenship, their status as specialists began to change.[13] Both the Soviet and the U.S. governments looked at them differently. They might not have always enjoyed full support from U.S. officialdom before, but now, as Soviet citizens, they were certain that the U.S. government would do little to help if they got into difficulty with the Soviet authorities. Soviets also expected them to adjust their lifestyle to more closely match that of the Russians among whom they were living. Wrote Robinson, "The day I became a Soviet citizen, I felt no different. I was the same Robert Robinson: toolmaker, inventor, aspiring mechanical engineer, trying to survive in an alien culture. . . . I did have to give up the foreign specialist card that admitted me into the elite shops that carried western-style goods. Now I had to eat at a smaller, plainer-looking restaurant that catered only to Russian technical personnel. . . . I had to accept a less comfortable lifestyle for a greater sense of security."[14] The point about security was key: the Soviet experiment was giving them a certain security, while returning to the United States promised only the combined struggles of Jim Crow, the Great Depression, and anti-Communist attitudes. They might have let go of their individuality, but, as members of designated workers' groups, they now had guaranteed access to medical facilities, vacation resorts, and other social benefits.

The war and its aftermath placed new demands on these sojourners-turned-expatriates. Although most survived this trying period, one profited from it: Smith, the foreign correspondent, built his new career on the good fortune of being in the right place at the right time. The wartime adjustments were trying for all, Russian or non-Russian, and the black sojourners could understand this. What they had not anticipated was that in the lead-up to the war and for many years afterward, their being foreign presented problems as well. Because they were outsiders, they were also suspected of being spies. Despite their Soviet citizenship, they retained aspects of their foreignness because they were Negroes and had come from the United States. It is safe to assume that all underwent secret police scrutiny in the worst of the Stalinist years and beyond and that files were kept by the infamous NKVD (People's Commissariat of International Affairs) or the MVD, which were early versions of the KGB (Committee for State Security).[15]

They were saved from the worst of the terror, though, because most of them studiously avoided getting involved in Soviet politics. Robinson stated, " I just kept doing what I could do, which was to put in sixteen-hour days. I had no time during the week to do anything but go home and rest."[16] At the same time, the politically active, such as Burroughs, Golden, and Ross, may have found their distant posts or the nature of their jobs helped them avoid some of the worst effects of the purges. Golden and Burroughs were located far from the centers of power. Ross's role as an official propagandist was useful to the Soviet authorities. Finally, they all were Negroes, which, although it still labeled them as foreigners, did have certain political advantages in the Soviets' parallel anti-racist propaganda war against the United States.[17]

Oliver Golden and His Family

In her book Khanga told the story of the event that caused the Goldens to stay in the Soviet Union:

> On July 19, 1934, my mother, Lily, was born in Tashkent. This was the decisive event in my family's history; without a child, my grandparents would have returned to the United States in 1937 . . . [but] they did not want to raise a racially mixed child in America. . . . Regardless of the strong prejudices Russians might hold toward various ethnic minorities, and those minorities toward one another (and toward Russians themselves), there would at least be no legal discrimination against their daughter. . . . What they could not have realized at the time was how much discrimination my mother would encounter not because she was dark-skinned but because she was the child of foreigners.[18]

The act of taking up Soviet citizenship in 1936 was a confirmation of the Goldens' earlier decision that the Soviet experiment offered a better future for blacks and their families than did the situation in the United States. They were not willing to return to a country where their child would be subject to the double discrimination of having a black father and an association with Communists.

They had another reason to take comfort in their decision because, by now, they had settled into a comfortable life in Tashkent. The government had assigned them a large apartment in the House for the Foreign Specialists, a four-story structure reserved for foreign specialists and minor diplomats.[19] They also had three servants to help them manage the apartment and maintain their various political and personal duties. "One woman came in every day to clean up after the constant flow of guests, and cooked for the family. A second woman came to sew clothes for my mother and friends. . . . The third woman was my beloved 'Auntie Nadya.' . . . My parents never really lived a normal Soviet life, with all its difficulties, problems and hardships."[20] Auntie Nadya managed the house and the other servants, stood in long lines for food, and generally oversaw all that needed to be done. Not having these day-to-day responsibilities, Bertha and Oliver Golden were free to concentrate on other duties: Golden taught at the Irrigation and Mechanization Institute and frequently went out of town on lecture tours, and Bertha gave English lessons.

In 1937 they felt the first of the Stalinist suspicions. Khanga noted that after a month's holiday with Robeson and his family, "My grandparents returned home to a shocking sight at the House of Foreign Specialists. . . . They saw that the door next to theirs was sealed with strips of paper. Those paper strips were a dreaded sight throughout the country during the Stalin years. They meant . . . that the apartment's occupants had been arrested. . . . And that wasn't all. While the family was away in Kislovodsk, the police had also come in a dark unmarked car for my grandfather himself."[21] As her mother, Lily, continued the story, "When my father heard that the unmarked car had come for him . . . he [went] to the office of the NKVD. 'You came for me,' he said, 'Arrest me if you think I'm an enemy of the people.' The genial police official replied, 'Comrade Golden, don't get so upset. We've already fulfilled the plan of arrests for your area. Go home and work in peace.'"[22] Golden discovered that the specter of an arrest could as easily dissipate as loom up. Many agencies followed the industrial template of using plans and target numbers. Thus, it was possible that the police, recognizing that they had achieved their goal for the period, did not feel particularly compelled to return for him. It could also have been an instance of trying to avoid political fallout. Golden probably realized this possibility, and his confrontation with the secret police in their offices was a challenge. As Khanga observed, "It's also possible . . . that some official thought better of arresting a well-connected black American communist."[23] After his death in 1940, he could no longer protect his wife and child directly, although the occasional reference to his contributions could pave the way for other dispensations.

Bertha and Lily remained in Tashkent through World War II, facing the combined ordeals of the war years and suspicion of foreigners. Ironically, although the main difficulties for blacks living in the United States were their race and color, in the Soviet Union, these sojourners found their main challenges were that they were foreigners or were in contact with foreigners. Lily might have been born in Uzbekistan and have been brown like the Uzbeks, but her face did not have the Asiatic features common to the region. Her surviving parent, Bertha, white and Jewish American, was just as suspect.[24]

Khanga noted that it was also not a simple question of color or race or of looking different to the Russians. As her mother observed, many of those who were treated differently looked like the average Russian. "People avoided us because we were of foreign origin. . . . Many of those arrested in the purges had been accused of contacts with 'foreigners.'"[25] Antipathy toward Jews was a version of this discrimination, as Khanga's grandmother discovered despite her years of devoted service to the country. "In 1948, my grandmother was fired from her job as an English teacher at Tashkent's Institute of Foreign Languages and . . . told that her 'American credentials' weren't good enough. . . . Never mind that she was one of the few people at the institute with any knowledge of the spoken language. . . . Universities were ordered by the political authorities to fire thousands of distinguished teachers in the sciences and humanities. Most were Soviet Jews, whom Stalin had come to regard as a Fifth Column, but many non-Jews with foreign associations were also fired."[26]

The day-to-day business of survival took on enormous complexity. "[Bertha] could never have raised my mother during those years if she had made any excuses. [She] held down several jobs. She taught English at Central Asian State University in Tashkent, gave private lessons at home, and translated articles for the Soviet radio network's English broadcasting service [and] worked as an announcer on broadcasts aimed at India." A stalwart supporter of the Soviet experiment, she even sacrificed her last set of funds in support of the War effort. "When the Nazis were overrunning the Ukraine and laying siege to Leningrad, my grandmother gave her last $600—she had brought it from America [in 1931] and saved it for an emergency—to help pay for a Soviet tank."[27]

Lily was about seven when the war broke out, and even as a small child she had wartime responsibilities. She waited in the lines for their daily bread ration and held their spot for their weekly turn to do their bathing and washing at the public baths. Also, as she got older, she joined other children to pick cotton. Cotton was important for the war effort, and every able-bodied person participated in the cotton picking.

> At 11, at last we were permitted to go to a kishlak [Uzbek settlement] some 60 miles from Tashkent to pick up cotton. . . . We slept in a cow barn. . . . I suffered terribly from deep scratches, torn flesh around the nails and bleeding fingers. . . . Another problem was food. There was nothing to eat except what we could forage ourselves. Because I spoke Uzbek more fluently than any of my classmates [who were Russians or the children of other expatriates], it became my responsibility to get bread for the kids. . . . The Uzbeks were especially kind and friendly to me. They seemed to enjoy my command of their language, and almost invariably produced other presents for the kids besides the bread.[28]

It was not easy work, and yet there was a camaraderie among the children as they pooled their efforts. Furthermore, Lily, a mixed-race child of black and white sojourners, was serving as a bridge between the Russians and the Uzbeks. She would play a similar role bridging the Russians and African peoples twenty years later.

Despite the difficulties, there were some unexpected benefits to living so far from Moscow. "The war was not such a disaster for me personally. My mother and Auntie Nadya protected me from much of the hardship." Over four thousand miles away from the front, Tashkent was a major evacuation destination. "Life in Tashkent . . . was exciting culturally and intellectually. Professors from Moscow, Leningrad, and other [cities] were evacuated to Tashkent. . . . I was going to a lot of concerts, plays and meetings with the brightest intellects of the USSR."[29] Lily had music and German lessons and was introduced into a concentrated intellectual milieu that would have been difficult to find elsewhere.

By the 1950s, like all provincial children, Lily was eligible to go to a regional university and would have done so but for the intercession of Rudd. A good friend of her parents, Rudd was visiting Tashkent at the time and insisted that she attend the best university in the country: Moscow State University. Rudd knew that provincial students were not usually let into Moscow State, but he had solid political connections and expected that Lily could benefit from them. "My mother said 'no way.' She could never permit me to venture so far away from home and her care. Rudd argued that . . . he would be nearby, would help me and generally keep an eye on me."[30]

By the time Lily finally arrived in Moscow, though, Rudd was on the verge of an extended concert tour, and he did not have the time to make the necessary introductions. Thrown on her own resources, Lily was made painfully aware of how important connections could be. Trying to get permission to take the university entrance exam, she found not only the problem of being a provincial but also the hazards of being the daughter of foreigners and a Jew. "People like you are not accepted in this University!" shouted the University interviewer. University applications, like those for jobs, included a number of questions to ferret out key information. "What is your nationality? Do you have relatives abroad? Where were your parents buried? Do you have contacts with foreigners?"[31] Golden might have been a celebrated black agricultural specialist in the 1930s and early 1940s, but, now, he and his wife were liabilities to their daughter.

Rudd returned to Moscow but died suddenly. Not knowing what else to do, Lily went his funeral and there discovered the rest of the black expatriate community. "Many unknown faces. Black and white. A big white man approached me. . . . He was surprised that I knew no one among the crowd."[32] This was Ralph Parker, an Englishman who had adopted Henry Scott's two Afro-Russian daughters after Scott left the country.[33] Parker introduced Lily around. A special delight for her was to meet Tynes, who had known her father well as he had first come to the Soviet Union as part of Golden's agricultural specialist group. Tynes had not met Lily because she was born in Tashkent after the other members of the group were reassigned to other parts of the country.

Lily also met Ross and his daughters, Ella and Ina. "Bob [Ross] explained that Wayland Rudd had been the leader of the Black community in Moscow, but that position had now fallen to him. As such, he was ready to help me."[34] Ross had good connections. As Smith noted, "It was generally assumed that [Ross] had been brought over by the American Communist Party. . . . He maintained close relations with influential Communists and Communist Youth Organizations."[35] Bypassing the university interviewers, Ross arranged for her to take the entry exams for Moscow State University directly. Successfully enrolled, Lily completed her degree in history and music. "I was the first ever Black student of Moscow State and the second Black to get an [advanced] education in Russia; the first was . . . Alexander Pushkin."[36]

Lily's life of relative comfort in Tashkent, followed by her admission to the most sought-after university in the country, contrasted greatly with the experiences of her stepbrother, Ollava. Whereas Lily's life was relatively sheltered, her stepbrother's was quite the opposite. Lily and her mother were aware that Golden had another child somewhere in the country, but they did not meet him until Lily moved to Moscow. A friend had asked her, "Are you aware that, in Leningrad, there lives a man who looks like you and has your name?"[37] Lily was delighted at the discovery, and Bertha was equally accepting of these new members of the extended Golden family. "I wrote to Leningrad and within a few days, Ollava Golden came to see me in Moscow." A short time later, Ollava's mother, Anya, came too. "I very much liked my newfound relatives, as did my mother. . . . I called Anna [Anya] 'Mamanya.' . . . She called me 'my dear daughter.' My mother called Anna 'Dear sister.' Mamanya was often to live in my home, particularly when my daughter was born [1962]."[38] Like Auntie Nadya when Lily was growing up in Tashkent, Anya frequently took over the responsibilities of looking after the house, cooking, and cleaning. Khanga remembered that the "third important woman in my life [was] my Baba Anya, grandmother Anya."[39]

Ollava was twenty-four and Lily was nineteen when they finally met in 1953.[40] Lily had the careful supervision of family and friends and was now attending the university. Ollava had an uncertain and difficult childhood, had never completed higher education, and was now working as a dance instructor. He never got to know his father and, during the war, also temporarily lost his mother.

Ollava was born out of wedlock after his mother had nursed Golden back to health following his depression over losing Jane. Although they maintained some contact after Golden moved back to the United States, they lost track of each other before Golden returned in 1931. Despite Oliver's repeated attempts, the authorities insisted that Anya and Ollava could not be found. "The authorities finally told my grandfather that Anya was dead and Olava had disappeared after being sent to an orphan's home."[41] Golden died before they were located.

Anya knew that links to foreigners could cause her expulsion from the party, if not banishment back to Siberia, but, as Khanga noted, "Anya loved Oliver so much that she had wanted to have his child even though she knew he was leaving. She gave birth to a son [and] named him after his father." Furthermore, continued Khanga, she insisted on formally registering the baby. "It took great courage to register the name of an American on her child's birth certificate. She could easily have put down someone else's names, or no name at all, and spared herself the attentions of the secret police."[42]

At the same time, Anya was an extremely loyal Communist and threw herself into the struggle wherever and whenever the Soviet authorities directed her. In fact, her activities at the Russian front resulted in many commendations. Still, as she told Khanga, she tried to keep son with her. "Ollava stayed in the camp in the forest with me. . . . We lived on berries we could gather in summer, on rabbits and squirrels we shot. Sometimes we were very hungry, because the Germans had taken everything from the farms." But the demands of her undercover work made it difficult to look after a child at the same time. She was forced to place him in a home for foreign children for safekeeping. They were reunited after the war, but it had been a rough time for the boy, as it was for other children in similar orphanages. "It was extremely difficult to locate a child assigned to a state home. Institutions were overloaded and many children simply ran away."[43]

Describing their first meeting, Lily wrote, "Ollava was a thin man, dark with curly hair and the Mongolian eyes that I remembered from [my father's] photo." The "Mongolian eyes" came from his mother, who was from one of the northeast Asian groups swept up into the new Soviet Union. Ollava's passion was dance. "Ballet was such an obsession that he would think about it all the time." His avocation was the care of animals and a special garden in his home city. Continued Lily, "The city [Vladimir] allowed him to create a garden with fountains, a lake and waterfalls. This was where he kept his animals—dogs, cats, rabbits, hedgehogs."[44]

Although neither Lily nor Ollava had the opportunity to fully grow up in the presence of their father, they shared the bond of being children of the same man and had their father's image in their own features. Also, their understanding of him was filtered through the fond memories of their mothers and others with whom he worked. As a result, they shared the problem of trying to locate themselves as Afro-Russians in the Soviet ethnic system. Unlike Ollava, though, Lily benefited from her early years with her father and the many visits of Robeson and others who tied her, even tangentially, to other black expatriates.

The extended black expatriate community and other friends of her parents often stepped in on her behalf as she negotiated the bureaucratic maze of trying to relocate permanently to Moscow. Lia Gavurina, a white American expatriate and friend of her mother, helped her find accommodations and gain the powerful Komsomol Central Committee's permission to work in the city. Ross helped her find a position with Ivan Potekhin in the African Studies division of the Oriental Studies Institute. "Ross helped me many times, as did many of my father's old friends in Moscow. Because of them, I was never allowed to feel that I was all alone in this great city." Watching Ross plead her case, she also increased her understanding of the legacy bequeathed to her by the early sojourners. "Robert told this famous specialist on Africa about my background and story, ending with the plea, 'Only you can help her! Lily's father made a big contribution to the development of the cotton industry in the USSR. She dreams of studying African history, but she does not have Moscow registration.'"[45] She got her job and access to the senior-most Africanist as she did her graduate research at the university.

Frank Goode and His Family

Frank Goode and his brother John began their sojourn in the Soviet Union in 1934, some months before their brother in-law Paul Robeson made his first trip there. Like Robeson, they were in search of a place where they could "breathe freely," but, after a few years, a disappointed John returned to the United States. However, Frank, who had found a special niche as a state-sponsored wrestler, decided to stay. Noted Smith, "The wrestling troupe traveled all over Russia with tremendous success. Goode had plenty of loose money, and a way with buxom Russian women."[46] Convinced that he had a much better chance under the Soviet experiment than in the United States, Goode took up Soviet citizenship in the mid-1930s.[47] He also married, but the union was short-lived, as he found his wife more interested in the easy living at his expense than in being loyal to him.[48]

Once the war broke out, though, there was little interest in wrestling troupes. "Goode's wrestling troupe was disbanded and the wrestlers were left to shuffle for themselves. . . . There was no time or money now to be devoted to . . . wrestling activities."[49] Like many escaping from the fighting, he stayed in the provincial regions to the east of the Urals mountains where he hoped to make do, living off the remainder of his previous income. He sold many of the things he had collected over the years to get additional money but discovered later that the peasants were not interested in money when he wanted to buy items from them. He then turned to making shoes to barter for food. He also did demonstration feats of strength, lifting and wrestling with inanimate objects, to earn extra money.

When he suddenly appeared at Smith's doorstep in 1945, people had only recently been allowed back into Moscow. Goode was in dire straights. "On a bitter-cold January evening in 1945 . . . the doorbell of my Moscow apartment rang. . . . In the doorway loomed a huge figure in a coarse black cotton padded overcoat, black fur cap with the earflaps dangling loose and wearing valenkis, the knee-high felt Russian boots. The caller turned out to be Paul Robeson's brother-in-law. It was a hungry and cold and depressed American Negro whom I let into my apartment. . . . His former bulk had shrunken to smaller proportions. . . . I helped him pull off his valenkis and instead of wearing socks, his feet were wrapped in pieces of rags."[50]

Smith asked him what he planned to do. "Well, Frank, it now looks as if the war will soon be over. . . . What are your after-war plans?" To which Goode replied, "Brother, I wouldn't mind going home [to the U.S.] . . . but I now have a Soviet passport; do you think they would let me leave? . . . Just look at me now—dressed like most Russians, worse than some. It never crossed my mind before the war that I would ever come to this." Smith gave Goode a good meal, supplied him with warm clothes and food. Reflecting back in the mid-1960s, Smith wrote, "I never saw Frank Goode again before I left Russia after the end of the war. I understand he returned to wrestling . . . and again began wearing quality clothes and shoes sent him by Paul Robeson and his sister Eslanda."[51]

By the end of the 1950s, Goode was living with his second wife and daughter on his state pension in the town of Gorki.[52] Goode's daughter, Eslanda, was born in 1950. Eslanda noted that her father had originally been offered an apartment in Moscow but chose Gorki for his retirement so his wife could be near her family. He also thought that living in a provincial area was more conducive to a quiet life and he could avoid state assignments to deliver lectures on racism in the United States. This plan was not always successful, and Goode, like many others, was occasionally sent to talk to groups about the plight of blacks in the United States. Goode died in 1967.[53]

Lloyd Patterson, Wayland Rudd, and Their Families

Both Lloyd Patterson and Wayland Rudd, who arrived in 1932 with the *Black and White* film group, married early and started families. The Soviet experiment's promise of a nonracist society had allowed them to follow their hearts rather than worry about the racist strictures of the society from which they came. Noted Smith, "[Patterson and his wife] became parents of three sons, one of whom [James] I understand has graduated with honors from the Naval Academy."[54] This same, son, James, went on to become a well-known poet. Tom became a TV cameraman.[55] Junny died prematurely in a car accident.

According to Tynes's daughter, Amelia, Rudd, like Patterson, welcomed the opportunity to cross the color line and married a white woman with whom he had been in love in the United States. They had a child, Lolita, and then the three went back to the United States in 1934. Two years later, Rudd returned to the Soviet Union, but, this time, he was alone.[56] Rudd was still frustrated with the lack of opportunity in the United States and looked forward to returning to what he termed the "liberated" theater in the Soviet Union.[57] He never went back to the United States, renounced his U.S. citizenship, and subsequently re-married and had two other children, Victoria and Wayland Jr.

Although both Patterson and Rudd spent the 1930s working in the theater in Moscow, their paths split during the war. Patterson became one of several expatriates who helped with the English-language broadcasts; he died at the front during the war.[58] Before his death, he and another American expatriate, Ann Stanley, had been evacuated to Komsomolsk-na-Amure. Here, they continued their English-language broadcasts to Japan, China, India, and other parts of Asia. Like many Soviet-era cities and towns of strategic importance, this town was closed to the general public during and after the war. Later, Komsomolsk-na-Amure became a tourist destination, and, in commemoration of the fiftieth anniversary of D-Day, advertisements highlighted the work done by Patterson and Stanley. "[In Komsomolsk-na-Amure is] one of the best museums in the Russian Far East. . . . Of interest are the photos and documents of two Americans, Ann Stanley and Lloyd Patterson, who ran the English language propaganda during the Great Patriotic War [World War II]."[59]

Rudd stayed in theater work through the 1930s and into the early 1940s, acquiring a range of parts and responsibilities. Both Smith and Robinson did not feel he gained the recognition he deserved. Noted Smith, "[Rudd] discovered that the road of a thespian is a rocky one, whether it be in Moscow or on Broadway, U.S.A."[60] Robinson complained that although "Rudd had obtained his diploma as an actor/director from one of Moscow's best drama institutes, and was well known by the authorities to be living in Moscow," he did not get the part of Bret, a black character in the production *Deep Are the Roots*; "he was never even allowed to audition. . . . [They had a] white actor playing the part."[61] Allison Blakely saw Rudd's trajectory differently. According to him, Rudd not only acted in the play *Deep Are the Roots* but wrote it. In addition, he acted in theater and film, graduated from the prestigious Theatrical Art Institute, and later joined not only the well-known Meyerhold Theatre but also the famous Stanislavsky Opera and Drama Theatre. "Rudd was mesmerized by all the excitement of experimentation current in Soviet theatre at the time. Most impressive . . . was the fact that here there was an equal role for the Negro."[62] Toward the end of his life, he headed a drama company, directed plays, and frequently gave lectures on U.S. racism. A special achievement was that "[Rudd] . . . became the first Negro actor to play [Othello] in Russian."[63] The Russians had memories of Ira Aldridge's work, but unlike Aldridge, who performed all his parts in English while the Russian company did theirs in Russian, Rudd performed his parts in Russian. That Rudd could do the part in Russian spoke not only to his acting talents but also to his linguistic ones.

Patterson and Rudd shared a similar encounter with Stalinist suspicions when Vsevolod Meyerhold became a special target of Stalin and the Meyerhold Theatre was shut down. However, as Blakely noted, "The disfavor into which the Meyerhold School fell in the 1930s did not adversely affect Rudd. . . . [He] seemed to find no difficulty in associating with opposing schools of theatre. . . . He joined the Stanislavsky Opera and Drama Theatre. (Meyerhold's approach to theatre opposed Stanislavsky's in many respects.)"[64]

Following the German invasion in 1941, Rudd joined a theater company that performed at the Russian front. At his death in 1952, Rudd, like Golden, was given a special honor when a grateful Soviet government arranged for him to lie in state in the Union Hall of the Theatrical Trade Union.[65]

Robert Robinson

Technical specialist Robinson lived and worked in the Soviet Union from 1930 to 1974. In contrast to the intellectuals, artists, and journalists, Robinson had a job that placed him squarely among workers, not among elites. Still, as a foreign specialist and part of the black sojourner community, he was able to participate in activities and have access to certain facilities that ordinary workers could not. Also, because of his special skills and talents, he developed his own notoriety, which brought both benefits and liabilities.

Despite his having taken up Soviet citizenship, Robinson always planned to return to the United States. He enjoyed the kind of work he was doing and was glad to use his time in the Soviet Union as a "safety net." But, as the purges were beginning to affect those around him, he began to see that he, too, might be in a perilous state. "From 1934 to 1936, more than twenty people in our shop suddenly disappeared. They were engineers, toolmakers, foremen, even party members. . . . [Also,] being from another country became a mark of suspicion." Conversely, though, being a foreigner and a black man may have saved him—at least temporarily—during his first brush with the secret police. "Only once did the police knock on my door. It was in 1943, at about 12:30 A.M. When I opened it and they saw my dark-skinned, non-Russian face, they excused themselves. I obviously was not the person they were looking for."[66] Robinson's color probably saved him. Either the police were so confused by seeing Robinson that they did not arrest him or they were savvy enough to recognize that Robinson would be much more useful to the propaganda efforts if he were left alone to do his work.

During the war years, Robinson was evacuated to Kuibyshev. His preeminence as a foreign technical specialist in tool-and-die technology called for his continued service in a secure location. "I had figured correctly that in the midst of a war, when the factory was straining to support the military effort, [senior authorities] would not look kindly on the thought of loosing me." On the day of the impending move, the authorities announced, "Comrades, our factory does not exist anymore. All the machine tools are being sent to Kuybyshev. All of you will have to travel to that city and start working anew. Each and every one of you will receive in advance three months' salary and three kilos of flour. . . . By six o'clock tonight the train will come for you all." The extra pay and food were good enticements, as life in Moscow had become increasingly precarious. "The Germans continued their advance on Moscow. The closer they came, the more difficult it was to find food. A supper of black bread, dried fish, and tea without sugar was considered a treat."[67]

Robinson and his fellow First State Ball Bearing Plant co-workers were among the first technicians to be evacuated to Kuibyshev. "It took us about two months to assemble the factory. Although it was a far cry from the one we had left behind in Moscow, it was operational."[68]

Although well-known and liked in Moscow, particularly among his fellow workers, Robinson found his foreignness a hazard at the plant in Kuibyshev.

> One morning when it was at least twenty-two degrees below zero, I
> trudged to the plant along with hundreds of other workers, anxious only

to get in out of the cold. . . . The guard made little real effort to check our passes, since he was no more anxious than we were to spend any unnecessary time out in the cold. I was past the gate . . . when I heard someone shouting, "Stop that foreign spy!" I looked over my shoulder to see him approaching me, his bayonet fixed and his finger on the rifle's trigger. I did not dare move a muscle. . . . Two Russians who knew me from Moscow quickly came to my rescue. One of them shouted at the guard, "Stop! Do you know what you are about to do?." . . . The other Muscovite added, "This comrade has been working in our factory for over ten years and he has always proved himself to be a reliable person."[69]

At first, Robinson was housed with the rest of the industrial workers. "Our new so-called industrial complex had in reality been a center for training horses. These stables were turned overnight into living quarters. . . . More than seventy people had to share one toilet and one washbasin." His specialist status helped and the Soviets later found him improved accommodations. "Fortunately, the administration soon found living quarters for me in a two-room log house, inhabited by an elderly couple whom I came to call Uncle Misha and Aunt Olga." His hosts were able to help him in another way as well. When he fell ill and had to be sent back to Moscow for treatment, they packed special food bundles for his long journey. "[They gave me] two bags of food that [included] a roasted chicken, a few slices of bread, two bottles of melted butter, several pounds of sugar, boiled carrots, and eight soft rolls."[70]

But Robinson's circumstances worsened after his return to Moscow. Sent back because he would have access to improved health care, he was still expected to continue working at a plant. This job was also key because it gave him access to his much-needed food ration card. "I rushed off to the factory to get my bread card, which entitled me to my daily ration of six hundred grams (21.1 ounces) of black bread a day. When I went to the store for the bread, I was shocked to see that the only other food available was potatoes, and that a sack cost nine hundred rubles, the equivalent of $180. At the time I was making eleven hundred rubles a month. So for the next few days I lived only on black bread. . . . I was soon to learn that food shortages, which before the war were frequent enough, were now acute. During 1942, I was hungry all the time."[71]

One of his doctors took pity on him. Although Robinson had a medical authorization for additional food, an intractable Soviet bureaucracy and greatly weakened physical constitution made it impossible for him to use it. So the doctor invited him to eat with her family once a week. "Comrade Robinson, my husband and I have discussed your situation and we would like you to join us for dinner on Sundays." Robinson was overwhelmed, "I would have wept.'" It also amazed him to see how small her apartment was and yet how much food was being served. "[The room was] barely large enough for the four of us to sit around the table. I admired the spread of food. . . . There was such variety, none of it available in the Moscow stores, which were only selling black bread and mustard. They must have gone by commuter train twenty or so miles outside the city and bartered for the food on the black market." Later, Robinson commented, "I survived the purges, unbearable cold, hunger, the loss of friends, serious illness, the war, the Soviet bureaucracy, and the secret police."[72] But even he had to acknowledge that it was the occasional acts of kindness that helped him survive.

Robinson also appreciated being recognized for his talents. On the eve of his departure in 1974, he was still working on a difficult technical problem that only he could solve. His supervisor had approached him with the good news about his request for a vacation abroad. "Congratulations on being allowed to go abroad," he said, but quickly added a caveat: "But I must tell you that I cannot let you go until you finish your job on your drawing board." Robinson had been an expert problem solver for forty-four years and was still needed. As he noted, it was "a complicated job. . . . I had to design 162 parts . . . [and] every design and set of tolerances had to be checked and approved by the senior designer. Only then would the shop superintendent sign a form releasing me. . . . The Communist party of the entire factory had met to approve my vacation, but [he] still had the power to block my trip."[73]

After years of unsuccessful attempts to leave, Robinson was finally called into the Visa Division office on December 18, 1973. "On . . . a bitterly cold day, I came home and found a post-card in my apartment mailbox. It was from the visa division." Later, he described meeting the official who would give him the permission he sought. "Finally, he pulled out a red passport. What a relief! My trip to Africa suddenly became more concrete." But before handing the passport over to Robinson, the official admonished him. "You must always uphold the integrity of the Soviet Union; you must be presentable at all times—always sober; you must shave daily; and you must not allow yourself to be in doubtful company."[74]

Robinson left the Soviet Union after forty-four years for a forty-five-day visit to Uganda. But, through the intersession of President Idi Amin, he was given permission to stay in Uganda indefinitely. As an aide told him, "President Amin has . . . told his Minister of Foreign Affairs to advise the Soviet ambassador to Uganda that you will be staying here to teach."[75] He professed amazement that the Soviets did not raise a serious protest about this change in his status, but there can be no doubt that they were well aware of his persistent attempts to leave. They would have anticipated that he would subsequently find an excuse to stay away and might also have determined that Robinson could be a de facto "ambassador" of the Soviet Union and its technical expertise. Robinson married, and he and his wife finally settled in the United States in 1978 through the help of American friends.

Homer Smith and His Family

Homer Smith, resident in the Soviet Union for fourteen years from 1932 to 1946, initially went as a member of the *Black and White* film group like

Patterson and Rudd, but he spent most of his working life as a foreign correspondent. Looking back over his many years in the Soviet Union, he noted, "Quite frankly . . . I still have a certain lingering nostalgia for Russia—but for a Russia far different from that Russia that I came to know so well. . . . This book . . . represents a long cherished desire to set down some of my intensive and extensive Russian experiences, observations and impressions."[76]

Like other black sojourners, Smith was glad to be living in a society that did not discriminate against blacks (and in the early days, Jews). Yet he was disappointed that this was also a society that increasingly encouraged people to suspect and spy on one another. Still, despite this rising climate of hostility and uncertainty, he wrote "[I decided to] cast my lot with news reporting. Besides it was in that year I first met Marie Petrovna."[77] Although he was initially pushed by his professional ambitions, it was also evident that his personal life became a strong motivation for remaining in the Soviet Union.

Smith was at once the object of suspicion and incredibly lucky. On December 5, 1936, he was covering the deliberations for the new Soviet constitution. Stalin and all the senior governmental officials were in attendance at the meeting. But the security police purposefully delayed Smith's entry, despite his credentials. "My press card, which had to be accompanied by a special ticket for this occasion, had been closely examined at least five times by uniformed NKVD men before I was finally admitted to the press box." After observing the congress for a while, Smith decided he needed to change his location to get a close view of Stalin when he left the hall.

> I had learned from a Russian journalist that at the close of the congress Stalin would not leave through the side-door . . . but would pass through the meeting hall and enter the delegate's lounge adjoining it. But this lounge was out-of-bounds for non-delegates. . . . There was no visible stairway . . . leading down to it. Yet I was determined somehow to get down in to that lounge. . . ." I want to see Tovarish [Comrade] Stalin," I entreated, showing [the guard] my press card. . . . He waved me in the direction of the delegates' lounge. . . . [When I got there] no one was in the lounge . . . because the delegates were still inside the meeting hall, since under the rules of precedence, nobody could precede Stalin. This gave me the opportunity of taking up a vantage point close to the door. . . . Just as I approached it, it was opened and I almost met Stalin head-on.[78]

Smith did not get a personal interview, but his luck was with him again. Instead of calling for his arrest, he recalled, "Stalin turned his cold, steely eyes in my direction, and I felt as if I was being turned into a statue. They seemed to go right through me. . . . After Stalin and his retinue had passed into the lounge, the delegates surged in." Smith too was "swept along with them as they followed him into the adjoining . . . St. George's Hall."[79] Not only had Smith personally witnessed a momentous event, the formation of the Soviet constitution, but he had come closer to Stalin and the highest Soviet officials than any foreign journalist.

Smith's personal encounters with the Stalinist terror network seemed to decrease with his rising responsibilities as a foreign correspondent. This lack of harassment was no doubt encouraged by his generally positive reportage. "I and many of my journalistic colleagues wrote favorably of the new charter in our dispatches. It seemed to us at least a start in the right direction." However, the pressures on his wife and her family increased. "The times were inauspicious for a foreigner to become a member of a Russian family. The bloody purges were still on and all foreigners, white or black, were suspected of engaging in espionage. . . . Marie soon lost her job and could not find another. Every application blank that she filled in had to show the name of Smith—and that obviously was a foreign name. She and her parents came under Secret Police surveillance because a foreigner was now a member of the family. . . . It was not my color, for a change. In Moscow, my nationality was quite enough."[80]

Although sobered by these experiences, Smith knew he was in the Soviet Union at a key point in world history. Furthermore, these opportunities far outnumbered any he might have had in the United States as a Negro. From 1935 to 1938, his pieces had been published in the black press and the NAACP's *Crisis* magazine. Now, Smith's dispatches were being picked up by the Associated Press (AP) news service. Once World War II spread into the Soviet Union in 1941, his prominence grew. As the only foreign correspondent behind Soviet lines, he had access to information that few others had. He was officially brought onto the AP staff in Moscow, a position that would have been impossible for a black man in the United States to obtain. The Soviet experiment and then the war had changed his life forever. Of the AP's willingness to jump the color bar, Smith wrote, "I had just happened to be on the scene when the shooting started and all of the civilian correspondents were placed on war footing. Early in 1944 I joined the staff of the Associated Press, Moscow Bureau, by invitation and with approval from the New York office and on a salaried basis."[81] Smith had hoped that the Soviet experiment would at least allow him access to the profession of journalism, but, even in his wildest of dreams, he could never have envisioned that he would rise so far.

When the front got close to Moscow, he and his wife were evacuated to Kuibyshev along with the other correspondents and Soviet officials.[82] Two other blacks had been sent there from Moscow as well: the technical specialist Robinson and the English-language broadcaster Burroughs; their jobs were also of strategic importance. By this point, those who could get out of Moscow were walking or taking whatever transport was available. "Reports were circulating everywhere that the Germans were still advancing and Russian defenses [were] melting away like icicles. . . . Most Russians had serious doubts that Moscow could be held." Smith was eligible for the government-coordinated evacuation, but he and his wife had to get on a train, if they could find one that had space. They missed the designated train, which carried most of the Soviet officials and other foreign correspondents, and had to take another, less regulated one. "The stampede to board the coach . . . was worse than the rush hour on the New York subway. The coach, with all the shades sealed down for blackout purposes, was quickly filled with a motley array of Russians. . . . A place meant anywhere one could wedge into. . . . The only standing room was in front of the smelly toilet at the end of the corridor. We resigned ourselves to the circumstances. . . . The train crept along slowly . . . at what seemed like ten miles an hour—a sitting duck for a Luftwaffe bomber."[83] Still, Smith's luck was with him. He came across a friend and his wife on the same train, and the two sets of them alternated standing and sitting for the remainder of the eleven-day journey.

Smith and his wife had carefully packed items that could be used to get food and other necessities along the way. They had no way of knowing how long or how difficult the journey might be, but they knew that money alone would not suffice. Once their personal supplies ran out, they could get fresh food and drink only from peasant farmers along the route. In fact, these farmers were, for the first time in their lives, in total charge of all transactions. Anticipating that the Germans would be victorious, they had no use for Russian rubles. "We had packed our suitcases with certain articles that we knew would be in short supply in the countryside—sugar, tea and coffee, soap, nylon stockings and woolen socks, shirts and underwear, towels, and handkerchiefs. We felt that such commodities might outrank in purchasing power, and we were soon to learn that they did. The few thousand rubles I had in my pocket held no attraction for the peasants." As a result of their good planning, the Smiths ate "boiled chickens, roasted meat, milk and honey, boiled eggs, fruit, baked bread and other foodstuffs."[84]

Relieved to finally arrive in Kuibyshev, they still had to fend for themselves. "Normally the city had a population of about three hundred thousand. Evacuees had now swollen the population to almost one million and this rapid population increase had created frightful congestion. The problem of feeding this influx was serious." Smith was assigned a room in the overcrowded Grand Hotel. But his wife found them other accommodations. "Some of the minor diplomats and the foreign correspondents were packed into this dingy pre-Revolution building. But through friendly contacts, my wife and I managed to find quarters elsewhere in the city." In addition to Marie Petrovna's skills at bartering and finding various supports, Smith also had access to the diplomatic shop.[85] There, he found food, vodka, and clothes, as well as other items that could be used to barter for fresh foodstuffs at the peasant markets on the edge of town.

Throughout Smith's fourteen years in the Soviet Union before, during, and after the war, no matter where he went, he had passes to the special food shops. Even when reporting from the front, he and the other foreign correspondents could get special food and other comforts that regular Russians could not. In the fall of 1941, when he went with the Soviet military back to Moscow, he found some of these special arrangements still in place. "Moscow was like a deserted city, with the feel and smell of war everywhere. . . . With their great talent for improvisation, the Russian authorities had managed to provide and stock a special food shop for the Allied foreign military mission men who had arrived in the city. The foreign correspondents were also provided with passes to this shop—besides access to a special dining room in the Metropole Hotel."[86]

By the summer of 1946, the purge climate and constant battles with the Soviet bureaucracy helped Smith decide it was time to leave the country. But he was not ready to return to the United States. He accepted an invitation from the Ethiopian government to work in their Press and Information Office. He also planned to continue his work as a foreign correspondent for the Negro press and the AP. Because he was a foreign correspondent and not a Russian citizen, he did not anticipate that he would have any difficulty leaving. "I could continue to write for AP and the Negro Press and most important of all, as a foreign correspondent, the Russians could not very well place any obstacles in the way of my leaving the country to take up another assignment." His wife was another matter. She was Russian, and exit visas were not given to Russians to go abroad, not even the wives of American correspondents."[87]

Smith was more than aware that wives and family were some of the main reasons why some black expatriates settled in the country. There were stories about others who had left with the intention of returning or of bringing their families out, but they were then totally cut off from them. As Khanga noted, the Soviet government was an active player in spreading misinformation about family members. "There were other tragedies among Russian wives and children left behind in 1937. When the women tried to reestablish contact with their husbands in the United States, Soviet authorities told them the men had been arrested . . . and died. . . . After the war, a number of American men, in turn, tried to locate their wives and children—only to be told by the Soviets that their families were dead."[88]

Smith made many attempts to gain permission to take his wife with him prior to leaving in 1946. But it took another year of appeals from abroad before he could secure permission for her to join him in Ethiopia. In 1947 Marie Petrovna went to Ethiopia, where they lived for fifteen years. In 1962, Smith finally returned to the United States, bringing his wife and two children.[89]

George Tynes and His Family

In the early 1980s, during what would be his last visit to the United States, Tynes told Blakely, "Down there [Uzbekistan] they thought I was an Uzbek, a little bigger and a little darker than most, but they tried to talk Uzbek to me."[90] The message was that Tynes was not singled out from the people around him in Uzbekistan. If he were thought to be something other than a Russian, at least it was not to be a denigrated black man as he was in the United States. Tynes was, in fact, a mix of Dakota Indian and black and quite familiar with U.S.-style second-class citizenship.

He had returned to the United States briefly in 1936, five years after he left with the agricultural specialists. By this time, he was married to a Ukrainian he had met in Uzbekistan, and the two of them had a two-year old child. Noted

Blakely, Tynes was not sorry to go back to the Soviet Union, where "he found life to be much more congenial for him as a Negro."[91] Over twenty years would pass before he returned for a series of visits between 1960 and 1980, under the sponsorship of a cousin.[92] His last visit was in 1980, two years before he died.

Like several other agricultural specialists, Tynes had happily renewed his contract in 1934. He had good jobs, was recognized for his work, and had a child. In 1939, Tynes decided to take up Soviet citizenship, and over the next eight years he and his wife had two more children.[93] Each child was born at a different location to which Tynes and his wife were posted in the 1930s and 1940s. Vyacheslav was born in Tashkent, Amelia in the Cossack region in 1941, and Ruben in the Crimea in 1947.[94] In addition to these sites, the family was also sent to collective farms in Soviet Georgia, the Ukraine, Estonia, and finally a project just outside Moscow.

The Soviet Ministry of Agriculture moved the specialists to different sites for two- to three-year periods. This schedule provided the specialists time to help design and establish agricultural systems and procedures for which they were responsible, train local farmers and technicians to use the new techniques, and see some results of their efforts. Tynes's expertise was in fisheries and duck breeding. Robinson noted, "[The Soviets] gave Tynes the novel title of zoo technician. [He helped] the Soviet Union produce more and healthier ducks. From Central Asia, he was transferred to Simferopol in the Crimea. After the war, he landed on an experimental farm a few miles outside of Moscow."[95]

When World War II broke out, Tynes was drafted into the Soviet army but, rather than doing traditional military service, spent his service time as the director of collective farms.[96] This was fortuitous for the Tynes family, in that they lived on farms where they continued to have access to food and other comforts. Yet, as is evident from the seven-year gap between their first and second child, the war apparently did effect the Tynes family. Unlike the Goldens, far to the east in Central Asia, the Tyneses were in the Cossack region, which often fell within the battle lines. Even when moving to the Crimea later, they were still relatively close to the front.

Tynes's prominence grew with each new posting. His final post was the most prestigious: head of the new experimental fish and duck farm outside Moscow. Robinson wrote, "Because of him, the Soviet poultry exhibition won first prize in an international fair in Belgium in the mid-fifties. . . . Tynes was . . . proud of his medals and wore them whenever he came to Moscow."[97] Tynes retired in 1974, and the government assigned him an apartment in Moscow, where he lived for the remainder of his life.[98] When he died in 1982, he was the oldest surviving black male sojourner.

Williana Burroughs

When Williana Burroughs obtained permission to work for the Soviet government in 1937, she probably did not consider whether she would formally resettle there. She also did not intend to be apart from her husband, Charles, forever.[99] But she was already in her mid-fifties and wanted to spend time near her two youngest children, Neal and Charles, who had been resident in the country for nearly ten years. She had managed to see them sporadically over the years when conducting party business in Moscow, but she regretted that her visits had been short; they were now fourteen and eighteen years old.

A longstanding member of the New York Teachers' Union, Burroughs was an active Communist and, under the name Mary Adams, often returned to Moscow to make reports to the Comintern. Thus, it was not hard to gain the CPUSA leadership's support in requesting a move to Moscow. "Please communicate to the Radio Centre . . . our recommendation for the post of editor of Comrade Mary Adams [Wilhemina [sic] Burroughs]. . . . [She] had been active in a leading capacity in the New York District for many years."[100]

For the next three years, she dutifully served as a radio announcer and editor for the Radio Committee in Moscow. But, by 1940, like Robeson, who had withdrawn his son from the Moscow school a few months before in light of the increased wartime pressures in Europe, she began to think that it would be safer if she took her sons back to the United States than if they stayed in the Soviet Union. But the Soviets prevailed on her to remain, stating that there was a shortage of Americans who could perform Comintern duties at that vital time. She and her sons stayed on, but over the next two years, with the strains of the job and worsening work and living conditions, her health began to fail. She made another appeal to leave. "For over five years I have been working in the V.R.K. as an announcer and editor. I am a Negro woman, a U.S. citizen, member of the U.S. Communist Party. . . . I have questions connected with my work, as well as personal concerns that require your attention." This letter was sent to the higher echelons with the comment "Com. Burroughs came to me with a request to forward you the enclosed. . . . Throughout her stay in Moscow, especially during the last two years, she has been dissatisfied with her financial situation, and in the last year she has suffered from impaired health. (She is 61 years old). During the last several months she has applied personally to the Comintern for help."[101] But, again, her request was denied. When Smith met her, she had been evacuated to Kuibyshev.

Kuibyshev served not only as the administrative center for the country but also as one of the sites for the foreign-language broadcasts. Like Patterson in Komsomolsk-na-Amure, Golden in Tashkent, and other English-speaking expatriates, Burroughs was a pivotal person in this enterprise of maintaining contacts with other countries. Other personnel were used too, and by 1942 broadcasts were being done in twenty-nine languages. An article based on a "Voice of Russia" program commemorating the seventy-fifth anniversary of Radio Moscow stated, "The role of Radio Moscow increased immensely in the war years. For people in many countries of the world radio broadcasts from Moscow became an important, and in some cases, the only channel through which they could get information on the developments at the fronts. . . . The announcers, translators and correspondents worked non-stop for hours on end." Veteran radio announcer Joe Adamov noted, "We had an Afro-American working for us, Williana Burroughs. She spoke very bad Russian, and she used to break her tongue trying to pronounce the names of these Russian villages. . . . [But] she sympathized with us and stayed here for the duration of the war voluntarily and shared with us all the hardships and even the workers' food card that we had."[102]

As there was only one hotel in Kuibyshev, and that was reserved for Soviet officials, the diplomatic corps, and foreign correspondents, others were assigned elsewhere and shared rooms and flats. Most of these flats were unheated or had a single heat source; many did not have indoor plumbing. As Smith observed, "She [Burroughs] and a British woman announcer had been provided with a small room in a cold basement on Kuibyshev Street. The old Negro woman was obviously undernourished and inadequately clothed—as, of course, were tens of thousands of other evacuees in Kuibyshev—to face the bitter cold that had begun sweeping down from Siberia and across the Volga River onto the city."[103]

Burroughs did not have the social cushions that Smith enjoyed as a foreign correspondent, so she welcomed Smith's help in using his access to the diplomatic shop to get items she could sell. "Feeling sorry for the old woman, I often bought a few bottles of vodka in the special Diplomatic Shop. . . . She did not drink, but used [the vodka] more profitably to trade for food [and] clothes."[104]

After the war, Burroughs was sent back to Moscow, where she was reunited with her son, Neal. Her older son, Charles, had been called up into the Russian Army. She was finally able to return to the United States a few years later with Neal, then seventeen, but she died shortly afterward. Noted Smith, "The neglect and hardships she had experienced during the war undoubtedly hastened her death."[105]

Charles was twenty-one when she left. After completing his secondary school studies, he worked variously as a toolmaker and a trapeze catcher in a Soviet circus. Called into service in 1942, he was a truck driver for the Soviet army. Interestingly, Burroughs never applied for Soviet citizenship for either of the boys, and, as a result, Charles was still eligible to be called into the U.S. army. Thus, Charles ended up serving in two armies: the Russian and the American. "Charles Burroughs . . . received a draft notice [in 1943, and] early in 1945 he reported to an American base in Teheran, Iran, and was inducted." When Charles got his notice in 1943, he was in the Soviet Union and waited to see after his mother before going into the U.S. army. They both left the Soviet Union in 1945. After World War II, Charles also returned to the United States.[106]

In 1987, on the eve of Gorbachev's *glasnost*, Charles returned to the Soviet Union after forty-two years.[107] He was nearly seventy. Jack Houston wrote, "[Charles] described himself as 'pro-Soviet' and stated that 'you could say I'm pro-Communist' although not a member of the CPUSA." Fleshing out the details of life under the Soviet experiment, Charles continued, "The Soviets were very cordial because they needed workers for the revolution. . . . Unemployment was high in the U.S., and there were more Americans over there than you can think of. Thousands upon thousands, making money. My mother didn't go over there to make money, as most of the foreigners did, but because she was a Communist and wanted us to be educated by Communists."[108]

Interestingly, the fact that Charles was U.S. citizen who grew up in the Soviet Union and then later served in the U.S. army shielded him somewhat from the more arduous duties in either army. He was not given particularly sensitive roles either. The Russians had him driving trucks. The U.S. army in Iran and Germany kept him in an office. He noted, "They thought, and rightly so, that I was pro-Soviet. . . . So they were not going to give me any important job. I was just a private, just operating in an office of my company in Munich, though I did do some translating." Although his translating might not have appeared significant, he was fluent in Russian, and his language skills were definitely more useful in administrative units than at the front.[109]

Forty years later, he went back to the Soviet Union under the aegis of the Chicago Center for U.S./U.S.S.R. Relations and Exchanges. Reflecting on the experience and his fifteen years spent there as a boy growing into manhood, he said, "What stirred inside me . . . was that I was back. . . . [and] I went because I was going home."[110]

Lovett Fort-Whiteman

Lovett Fort-Whiteman was the only black expatriate known to have died in the Stalinist purges. In his early period in the Soviet Union, when he was heading the ANLC, he happily traveled back and forth to the United States as he took on the responsibility of drawing other blacks to the Soviet Union. Some of his early recruits were Otto Hall, Harry Haywood, Roy Mahoney, William Patterson, and Kweku Bankole. But, his 1928 return to the Soviet Union proved fateful, for he was never able to leave the country again.

He had intended to stay for a while and then return to his ANCL work in the United States. But he did not understand that his flamboyance and independent streak were starting to work at cross-purposes to Comintern policies and the interests of the powerful black members of the CPUSA leadership. Fort-Whiteman had not been enthusiastic about the Comintern's call for black self-determination, and the Comintern removed him from the leadership of the ANCL. Having lost this important position, he was seen by the black leadership in the United States as a liability. "The new black leaders [in the CPUSA] did not enjoy having a defeated rival around, so to get him out of the way—and as consolation in view of his past service—the Comintern gave him work in Moscow."[111]

Fort-Whiteman told Smith he had "[come] home to Moscow" and that he had studied at "the Armour Institute of Technology in Chicago and was currently doing fish-breeding research for the University of Moscow."[112] Fort-Whiteman also gave regular lectures on U.S. racism and was teaching at various institutions.[113] Observed Smith, "He was often sent on speaking tours to Russian industrial and farming centers. . . . He was always well dressed in clothes of good quality and the sort of shoes that were unobtainable in Russia."[114]

Fort-Whiteman was married when he first went to the Soviet Union in 1924, but his wife, Olivia, did not accompany him.[115] When he returned to the Soviet Union in 1928, he was also alone. Settling into his new role as black sojourner, it was not long before he remarried. This time, it was to a Russian Jew who also worked at a Moscow research institute. At this point, Comintern policy was to immediately chastise anyone who expressed anti-Semitic attitudes; thus, his marrying a Russian Jew was not deemed a liability. Anti-Semitic attitudes would arise toward the end of World War II. Fort-Whiteman also began to adjust his clothing and personal style. Continued Smith, "He had adopted the practice of many Russian Communists of shaving his head, and with his sallow brown complexion and his finely-chiselled nose set into a V-shaped face, he resembled a Buddhist monk."[116] Smith's observation of Fort-Whiteman's choice of clothing also pointed up the contradiction in his roles: on the one hand, he was to "sell" the Soviet experiment to foreigners who visited the city or to the sojourners—hence the Russian-style clothing; on the other, he was to "sell" modernization to provincial people who came to his lectures—hence the wearing of Western-style suits when on lecture tours. Smith, too, was impressed. "I admired his excellent clothes and shoes."[117]

But, by 1933, despite his apparent ease with the sojourner life, Fort-Whiteman wanted to return to the United States. "After three years in Moscow, Fort-Whiteman decided that he would like to return to the United States (of which he was still a citizen) and applied for permission to do so from the CPUSA. His request was not granted."[118] Fort-Whiteman probably did not know that the CPUSA had been behind his exile to the Soviet Union. Its leaders, working with the Comintern, had absolute control over the movements of people back and forth, and there was little likelihood that their opinions had changed over this period. Occasionally, the CPUSA and the Comintern could relent, as they did when they allowed Burroughs to return to the United States in the mid-1940s because of her poor health. But Comintern documents indicated that Fort-Whiteman was under close scrutiny and in serious danger because of several miscalculations on his part.[119]

Fort-Whiteman's first mistake was to reenter the Soviet Union under a false name. This was a serious offence in the Comintern. Instead of using a passport issued in his name, he entered under the name Eugene Norris. Entering the country in this way put him in a delicate position, for not only had he misrepresented himself to the Soviets but he was now completely dependent on the Soviet government. In a way, the person known as Lovett Fort-Whiteman did not officially exist in the Soviet Union because no documents attested to his entry. At first, this lack of an official identity did not appear to matter. Fort-Whiteman joined the Communist Party of the Soviet Union in 1929 and assumed his teaching duties. However, three years later, in 1932, he was forced out of the Soviet party because he was not paying his dues.

Fort-Whiteman's second mistake was being outspoken on political matters. Most of the black expatriates learned to keep their political opinions private
and concentrated on their jobs and families. Fort-Whiteman however, having
developed a notion of self-importance in the heady days of his ANLC work in
the United States and in his new role as a lecturer in Moscow, conducted his
business as though he were above secret police scrutiny and criticism. He made
it a point to meet incoming blacks at the train stations and was quick to represent
himself as an important figure. As Smith observed, "Lovett Forte-Whiteman
considered himself the mentor of this group [the Negro American colony in
Moscow] and did his best to proselytize and indoctrinate them. He often invited
them, singly or in groups, to have lunch with him and unfailingly he channeled
the conversation around to political subjects."[120]

Unfortunately for him, Smith, William Patterson, and James Ford were
not particularly supportive of his self-aggrandizement and, in clandestine reports to the Comintern, alleged that he was taking positions that were counter
to Comintern policy.[121] Robinson noted, "[Fort-Whiteman] offered some criticism of a book by Langston Hughes, *The Ways of White Folks*, during a discussion at the Foreign Club. A black lawyer[122] from the upper echelon of the
Community [Communist] Party USA was in the audience . . . [and] he stated
. . . that the criticism of the book was counter-revolutionary."[123] To be "counter-
revolutionary" was treasonous in the Soviet Union, for it meant that one was
going against Comintern and Communist Party policies. Smith also complained
that Fort-Whiteman had a habit of bragging about his contacts within the inner
circle of the Comintern. "[He] often referred to his friends whose names were in
the Communist 'Who's Who,'" suggesting they fully supported his work.[124]

Not long afterward Fort-Whiteman was summoned to the NKVD offices. Many speculated about what happened to him. Smith discovered that he
had mysteriously disappeared when he went to visit him in early 1937. "About
a year after the beginning of the great Moscow purge trails in 1936, Lovett
Forte-Whiteman disappeared. One day I called at his home. There was no answer to my first knocks, but I persisted. Finally, Mrs. Lovett Forte-Whiteman
cracked the door open. 'Is Gospodin [Mr.] Forte-Whiteman at home?' I asked.
'No, he isn't, and I beg you never to come here looking for him again,' she
replied tartly. I had been living in Russia long enough to understand the
implications."[125]

Fridrikh Firsov was among the first to reprint a number of memos about
Fort-Whiteman, exposing a whole network of communications and collaborations in the Comintern and in the CPUSA that led to his demise. A January
1935 memo accused him of trying to organize and indoctrinate other blacks.
"Not long ago there was created a group of some blacks who live in Moscow.
This group aims to set up an organization under the condition of its complete
indifference to politics [Comintern policies]." The files also indicated that "the
leadership perceived the attempt of Lovett and his friends to set up the group
besides [outside of] the official organizations as an affair directed against the

Communist Party. . . . The Comintern letter had to attract [the] attention of the NKVD to Lovett."[126]

These documents also pointed to some of the internecine struggles among the black expatriates and the black leadership of the CPUSA. The "black lawyer" Robinson mentioned was William Patterson. Patterson's role as a conduit of information to the authorities was perfectly logical, as he was staunchly supportive of Comintern policy. Patterson was probably the person who submitted the statement about Fort-Whiteman's crimes to the ECCI in the first place. In Firsov's documents, Patterson warned, "To my knowledge he openly professes an anti-Comintern line on the National Question and had propagated this among the Negro comrades here and abroad. . . . I am [of] the opinion that Whiteman's main task is the corruption of the Negro elements and . . . there is the possibility that Whiteman is used by . . . the American Consulate as [its] man among the Negroes here."[127]

This file also listed the names of other blacks in attendance, including John Goode, Lloyd Patterson, Coretta Arle-Titz, Rudd, and Smith. The remaining names (which could be pseudonyms), Aimes, Qoo, and Sylestin, were persons on whom there was no further information. Patterson also worried about Fort-Whiteman's effect on others. "At the present time, he has under his influence Robert Robinson, a very fine worker in the Ball bearing plant and member of the Moscow Soviet. Robinson has deep rooted bourgeois national tendencies which Whiteman [is] playing upon. . . . Something should be done to remove him."[128]

Firsov contended that a March 20, 1936, letter from the Comintern sealed Fort-Whiteman's fate. "The letter contained all the information received from Patterson. The ending gave the answer of the Comintern. . . . 'The representative of the [Communist Party] believes that Fort-Whiteman must not come back to the USA.'" This was effectively a death sentence or, at least, a sure sign that Fort-Whiteman would be arrested.[129] Patterson had enormous prestige among the members of the Comintern, and his allegations of Fort-Whiteman's complicity in trying to undermine the relationship between the Soviets and blacks could not be ignored.

Smith stated that Fort-Whiteman disappeared from Moscow in 1937.[130] Harry Klehr, John Earl Haynes, and Kyrill Anderson listed Fort-Whiteman's dates in the book's "Glossary of Individuals and Organizations" as 1894–1939, suggesting that he died two years later, in 1939. "In 1996, records about Fort-Whiteman compiled by the NKVD, the Soviet political police, in the late 1930s surfaced in the archive of the internal security service of the newly independent nation of Kazakhstan." Following his arrest warrant in 1937, Fort-Whiteman was sent to a village in Kazakhstan where he worked in the schools for a while. But this punishment was not enough because, in 1938, "an NKVD board changed Fort-Whiteman's punishment to five years' hard labor [and] he was sent to the Sevostlag prison labor camp near Magadan, in northeastern Siberia. . . .

Fort-Whiteman's official NKVD death certificate [stated] that he died on 13 January 1939 at the Sevostlag labor camp."[131]

In summing up Fort-Whiteman's "crimes," Smith noted that Fort-Whiteman's habit of stressing race consciousness was another source of his downfall—from the perspective both of the Soviets and of the black expatriates. "[He] committed . . . the greatest faux pas of all. He advised and insisted . . . that the group should maintain a high degree of consciousness of their color and always remember that they were Negroes. But the complete absence of any racial prejudice or discrimination and the almost total lack of color consciousness in Russia made Lovett Forte-Whiteman's advice extremely unpalatable [to the Comintern officials]." No less important, the black expatriates were equally unhappy with his emphasis on race. Continued Smith, "As a matter of fact, a Negro in Russia had no reason at all to think of color. Most not only wanted to, but were fast forgetting about their color, escaping if you will."[132]

CHAPTER 11

William "Bill" Davis, the American National Exhibit, and U.S. Public Diplomacy

ତଡ

Who are the Negroes in Russia? How did they get there? How are they treated? How do they live? Are they really free?[1]
—William Davis (1960)

*I*n late July 1959, William "Bill" Davis was serving as one of seventy-five guides at the American National Exhibit in Moscow when another black man approached him. Davis was perplexed. He knew the three other black guides and the four black models in his group, but who was this fellow? To Davis's amazement, it was Robert Ross, a black man from Montana, who had been living in the Soviet Union for over thirty years. Ross was an actor and lecturer.[2] But, as Davis would learn, Ross was not alone; many other blacks had gone to the Soviet Union in the 1920s and 1930s, and at least four were still there at the end of the 1950s.[3] Davis was determined to learn about these "Negro former Americans and others who were born in Russia" and to find out whether life was better for them under the U.S. or the Soviet system.[4]

Continued Davis, "I asked Bob how he earned his living when he was not actually engaged in making a movie. Up to the time, he had not acted in a movie in more than three years. He said he received pay for lecturing to various groups on the life of Negroes in America, and on the 'struggle' of Negroes like Paul Robeson and W.E.B. DuBois [sic]."[5] Ross was doing well. Besides his salary, he tapped into a range of other social benefits as a member of the theatrical workers' trade union and special friend of the Soviet government. As technical specialist Robert Robinson observed, "[Ross was] the Kremlin's expert lecturer on social conditions in the United States [and would] host visiting American Blacks . . . [treating] them . . . like dignitaries."[6] He had easy access to any visiting blacks and frequently feted these visitors at his well-appointed apartment. More than mutual gestures of hospitality, these meetings provided Ross with useful information about the country he had left in the 1920s, and the visitors were, for the first time, introduced to the subject of the black diaspora in Soviet Russia.

Over the two months of Davis's stay in Moscow, he and Ross met over twelve times. Davis also met three other original sojourners: Robinson, agricultural specialist George Tynes, and Paul Robeson's brother in-law Frank Goode; and he also met eight descendants, some of whom were children of other black sojourners or expatriates.[7]

Blacks and the American National Exhibit

After World War II, the Cold War made communication between the peoples of the United States and the Soviet Union difficult. The McCarthy hysteria not only stopped Robeson and Du Bois from traveling to the Soviet Union, but prevented others from doing so as well. It also prevented other forms of communication. However, in the latter part of the 1950s, the climate changed. With McCarthyism discredited and Khrushchev's "peaceful coexistence" providing for a new openness, people on both sides took steps to remedy the situation. So, not only were Robeson and Du Bois returning to the Soviet Union, but many others—white and black—also wanted to see what life was like on the other side of the Iron Curtain. An exchange of national exhibits gave rise to exchanges and other visits of educators, artists, and other professionals.[8] As Walter Hixon noted, the year 1959 itself saw ten thousand to fifteen thousand American citizens taking advantage of these increased opportunities.[9] Besides the American National Exhibit staff itself, the larger delegation traveling along with them included a cross-section of journalists and entertainers, some of whom were black. John H. Johnson, the African American publisher of *Ebony* and *Jet*, was among them. He had been among the few blacks invited to do a Voice of America segment representing the "other side" of the United States some years before, and he was curious to see the country himself. He asked Russian-speaking Davis to help him meet some of the members of the black expatriate community and commissioned Davis to do a piece for *Ebony*.[10]

The American National Exhibit organizers were eager to show a specific kind of United States to the Soviets. The exhibit would demonstrate "Western ideas, symbols and consumer culture."[11] It would also represent an inclusive country. The guides had been carefully selected, and Davis's place, along with that of other blacks, though fortuitous on the surface, had not been coincidental. The Soviet Cold War media barrage represented the United States as a racist country, and the State Department organizers correctly anticipated that the Soviets would criticize the exhibit for not having blacks. So they planned to use a few as models in the tableaux of typical American scenes.[12] However, these models were not Russian-speaking. When a fresh opportunity presented itself in the form of Russian-speaking black candidates for exhibit guide positions, the plan was altered to include them as well.

Davis wrote, "Early in 1958, the U.S. Government was in need of young Russian-speaking Americans to serve as guides at the American National

Exhibition in Moscow. Eight hundred young men and women applied; 75 were selected. Among this number were four Negroes. I was one of them."[13] Once Davis and the three other blacks passed the qualifying requirements, the U.S. organizers began to envision a double benefit. Not only could they demonstrate their particular exhibit or object for the passersby, they could also discuss— in Russian—the improved race relations in the United States. Coupled with an elaborate display of the "comforts" of the U.S. lifestyle, these special guides were sure to defuse some of the Soviets' negative opinions of the United States.

Starting a new wave of verbal Cold War skirmishes, Khrushchev had grabbed the lead when, on June 2, 1957, he announced to his *Face the Nation* audience in the United States that "broadened trade and cultural ties were keys to improved East-West relations."[14] He was well aware that this broadcast, estimated to reach five million Americans, would be a prime opportunity to enter directly into U.S. households. Accusing the U.S. government of impeding the development of peaceful ties, he adjured his listeners to "do away with your Iron Curtain."[15]

The U.S. government was not pleased. Here, in the form of an interview on national TV, the Soviet premier represented his government as welcoming a less hostile political climate, while casting the United States as the reluctant participant. In truth, despite the call for improved international relations, the United States was still actively searching for ways to undermine the Soviet system. Hoping to turn the cultural agreements to U.S. strategic advantage, then Senate majority leader Lyndon Johnson, called for an " 'open curtain' that would allow Western ideas to 'cleanse evil' inside the USSR."[16] Then, teams of U.S. and Soviet negotiators began the laborious task of trying to find some mutually agreeable means to lead off these cultural agreements.

But, four months later, the Soviets sent out another challenge: Sputnik. With the successful launch of this satellite on October 4, 1957, the U.S.S.R. officially entered the space race, again taking the lead. Furthermore, Sputnik provoked the worry that if the Soviets could send rockets into space, they could also fire missiles against the United States. This was yet another painful reminder that the Soviet experiment could not be ignored or downplayed. Noted Ronald Grigor Suny, "When the Soviet Union launched the first space satellite, called sputnik (fellow traveler), on October 4, 1957, a shock passed through the Western nations. When that success was followed by a rocket orbiting the Earth, carrying the dog Laika and later (April 1961), the first human in space, Yuri Gagarin, a deep panic spurred Americans and West Europeans to invest in rockets and scientific education."[17]

The Exchange Agreement

Returning to their work with renewed fervor the U.S. and Soviet team members signed the Agreement between the United States of America and the Union of Soviet Socialist Republics on Exchange in the Cultural, Technical and

Educational Fields on January 27, 1959. Among other items, the signatories agreed to "reciprocal exchanges of radio and television broadcasts, feature and documentary films, students and professors, artists and writers, scientists and agricultural experts, athletes [and] youth."[18] Six months later, in June 1959, the Soviets opened their National Exhibit in New York and President Dwight D. Eisenhower was the first to enter.[19] When the United States opened its exhibit in Moscow on July 24, 1959, Khrushchev was there. This exchange agreement was renewed over the next twenty-seven years until 1985, when the last two to sign were U.S. President Ronald Reagan and Soviet Premier Mikhail Gorbachev.[20]

The Soviets had achieved a major coup: they had enhanced their country's image in the global community by entering into negotiations with the United States and forcing that country to agree to a series of reciprocal relationships. Noted Hixon, the Soviets saw the agreement as "[enhancing] Soviet capabilities in agriculture, industry, medical and technical fields."[21]

Equally keen to target audiences beyond the Soviets, the U.S. government also perceived these ties victoriously. Continued Hixon, it had increased "its ability to appeal to the peoples behind the Iron Curtain."[22] This exchange agreement enabled both a movement of people back and forth and a movement of ideas. Furthermore, through the extension of the international media, the United States would impress not only Soviet audiences but also those who would hear and read about the exhibits in other parts of the world. This global quest for "hearts and minds" was not "propaganda"—which the United States accused the Soviets of promulgating—but "public diplomacy" designed to bypass the regular politicians.[23] The American National Exhibit and other exchanges would "tell several million average [Soviet and other] citizens directly the story of the United States."[24]

Exhibit as Propaganda

The Soviets led off the exhibit exchange in June 1959 by highlighting their new space technology in a three-story space in the New York Coliseum. The U.S. visitors saw "machinery, science and technology." Continued Hixon, "Computers, farm machinery, and televisions were featured. Playing the October 1957 *Sputnik* launch for its maximum propaganda value, the Soviets suspended several model satellites from the ceiling."[25] Eisenhower, as a former military man, was understandably curious and spent an hour touring the facility. Remarked Christian Herter, the Secretary of State, "It remains a fascinating and convincing show. Those sputniks suspended from the ceiling alone would carry the message of progress and achievement."[26]

The American National Exhibit opened on July 24, 1959, in a large park just outside Moscow with displays scattered around the grounds. The exhibit included two specially constructed buildings. A huge geodesic dome was placed at the center of the exhibit and served as the information building. Another featured technical advancements, including exhibits on "labor, agriculture, public health and medicine, education, space research." Elsewhere, the attendees saw "colorful displays of food, clothing, toys, sporting goods, travel information, art, books, newspaper[s], musical instruments . . . a model kitchen and a color television studio."[27] Smarting from the Soviets' unexpected show of technological advances, the U.S. government brought its most dazzling array of technical and consumer products. For their part, the Soviets were glad to be able to closely observe items and, perhaps, copy those they found useful.

Although U.S. consumer goods and technology were the advertised features of the exhibit, a secondary, but no less important, contest in comparative race relations was being waged. When photos of the Little Rock confrontations circled the globe two years before, Eisenhower complained that "[a] tremendous disservice . . . has been done to the nation *in the eyes of the world.* . . . Our enemies are gloating over this incident and using it everywhere to misrepresent our whole nation." John Foster Dulles, the Secretary of State at that time, added that these internecine struggles were "not helpful to the influence of the United States abroad" and that "Radio Moscow [had] been chirping happily about the troubles of integration."[28] Even Washington, D.C., the "capital of the free world," could be an embarrassment. Officials lamented the "prejudice and humiliation experienced by non-white visitors . . . [demonstrating] to the world American hypocrisy about freedom."[29] Both Cold War antagonists were keen to win allegiances within the growing anticolonial community, of which Africa was a major part. Thus, Davis and the other blacks were part of the race-relations exhibit for the United States. At the same time, Ross and the other black expatriates living in the Soviet Union became part of the Soviet display.

It was no accident, therefore, that at the opening of the exhibit and in the pictures that circled the globe to mark this event Davis was prominently displayed. Recalling the event, Davis wrote, "On July 24 Vice President Richard M. Nixon arrived Sokolniki Park with Soviet Premier Nikita Khrushchev and gave what many of us felt was the best speech of his career. The National Hymn and Star Spangled Banner were played by a Russian band. As they did so, I helped Herbert Howard, a guide from Boston, to raise the American flag. Mr. Nixon cut a ribbon and the American National Exhibition in Moscow was officially open."[30]

The Robeson and Du Bois Mystique

People flocked to the exhibit, eager to learn about the opposing society and as well to enjoy the talents being displayed. But the United States was still troubled by one artist who did not travel under U.S. government auspices: Paul Robeson. Indeed, Robeson's influence could not be ignored. Almost as soon as he retrieved his passport from a reluctant U.S. government in 1958, he had returned to the Soviet Union. "Robeson received a frenzied public welcome when he arrived in Moscow. . . . Enthusiastic, bouquet-throwing crowds greeted

Robeson and his wife at each stop on their tour of Soviet Central Asia, the Caucuses, and the Crimea."[31]

Much of the Soviets' view of race relations was framed by their relationship with Robeson and Du Bois. For nearly a decade, the Soviets had been active members of the international campaign to have these two men released from the internal exile imposed by the U.S. government. Their support of Robeson and Du Bois not only annoyed the United States and its allies but also enhanced the Soviets' image among other peoples of color. People from colonial and former colonial societies admired these men, and, by extension, they respected those these men admired. Robeson had credited African students he met in London for directing his attention to the Soviet experiment and now, in the late 1950s and early 1960s, his continuous support of Soviet policies toward peace and national liberation was drawing in new generations of African admirers.

Davis observed, "Mention his [Robeson's] name and Russians will turn toward you and smile. They think of him as a downtrodden Negro who has been exploited by white American capitalists."[32] He tried to disabuse his visitors of the notion that blacks were still suffering from discrimination and noted that Robeson, in particular, had done quite well. Noticing that his visitors had a special interest in how much money Americans made, he pointed out that "[Robeson] earned thousands of dollars with his great singing voice in America."[33] He purposefully avoided acknowledging that Robeson had only recently been freed from an eight-year period during which the government-led campaign had severely damaged his professional career. But Robeson's Soviet fans would not let Davis evade the full story, and frequently countered, "Why didn't the United States give Robeson a passport several years ago?"[34]

Surmounting the Foreign Service Barriers

When Davis submitted his application to be a guide for the planned exhibit in Moscow, he was eager to try out his Russian and hoped his position at the exhibit would help him enter the Foreign Service.[35] He had managed to get into the federal government as a narcotics agent, but the Foreign Service was only for elites, and blacks at the time were decidedly not eligible.[36] At the time, Davis was thirty-three. He had an undergraduate degree in anthropology from Boston University, an M.A. in sociology from Rutgers, seven years of experience as a narcotics agent, and a young family to support.

Davis's fascination with different cultures and languages had served him well at a certain level. His job with the narcotics division had occasionally sent him outside the United States for investigations in France, Germany, Belgium, and Holland, but these were infrequent and had only whetted his appetite for overseas assignments. As a result, he learned a number of other languages;[37] that way—should the opportunity present itself—he would be ready to make the shift to another branch. The addition of Russian was a perfect strategic move.[38]

Davis knew that by winning a position in this State Department–sponsored program, he could demonstrate to a recalcitrant U.S. government that blacks had the ability to represent the United States in the international arena. He had the expertise, including reliable service in another branch of the U.S. government, linguistic skills, and previous experience in an international context. Ultimately, this unusual personal opportunity for Davis became an invaluable boon for the U.S. government.

Years later, when describing the group's meeting with Eisenhower, Davis remarked that the president seemed perplexed with the black presence in the guide group. Eisenhower even stopped to ask Davis a few questions.[39] The president wanted to know how blacks were eligible to be in the pool of those applying, not to speak of being among those selected. The exhibit guidelines stated that the team should be made up of people "fluent in [the] Russian language, well adjusted, well educated, and of good appearance,"[40] but blacks were not commonly thought of in this way. State Department notes from the meeting underscored the importance of this group.

> Aware of the crucial role the guides would play as direct representatives of American society, Eisenhower summoned the young people [they were twenty to thirty-five years old] for a personal meeting before they departed for Moscow. The president's desire to meet with the guides stemmed in no small part "because he was so curious as to why four Negroes should have studied Russian well enough to act as interpreters." Eisenhower could not have been oblivious to the fact that should any one of the African-American youths emerge as a critic of the United States while in Moscow, the action would deliver the Russians a propaganda bonanza. "I just would like to ask a question first of the four Negroes here. . . . How did you happen to get interested in Russian?"[41]

Besides Davis, the other guides were Norris Garnett and Herb Miller.[42] The fourth has not yet been identified.

In addition to the four black exhibit guides, Soviet audiences saw four black models included in the team of forty-seven used in the various tableaux.[43] Davis noted that two of those models were husband and wife Norma and Galbert Noble, but he did not name the other two.[44]

The proposal to use these models caused some concern in the United States as well. The exhibit designers were wrestling with the contradiction of having to present an appealing face to a highly critical international community while being responsive to a powerful southern constituency. When word got out that some of the projected tableaux included an integrated cast, South Carolina Senator Strom Thurmond raised a vigorous protest, demanding that they cut "fashion shows which misrepresent life in the homes of the typical American families."[45] Forty-one fashion editors submitted a petition with similar concerns. In an attempt to assuage the fears of these influential people while not loosing the propaganda advantage, the organizers dropped some of the controversial scenes. Evidently, the image of blacks and whites mingling as equals at a back-yard barbecue and a wedding was too much for some even as late as 1959.[46]

Nixon and Khrushchev Debate

The American National Exhibit also presented a special opportunity for Nixon to "lay to rest some of Khrushchev's misconceptions about America."[47] Like Davis, Nixon hoped to use the American National Exhibit to gain additional notice. The State Department noted, "When Nixon brought up the possibility of opening the American National Exhibition in Moscow [both the] Secretary of State John Foster Dulles [and the] USIA endorsed the proposed trip. . . . [And] . . . Ambassador Llewellyn E. Thompson . . . advised the Department of State that he favored Nixon's visit [but] opposed a formal Soviet invitation. . . . [Thompson also] suggested the United States try to obtain a commitment from the Soviet Government for a broadcast of a speech by Nixon nationwide to the Soviet people."[48] Diplomatic protocol constrained official representatives; they were expected to employ the language and manner of diplomats. But if Nixon went simply on behalf of the United States, he could be outspoken and direct.

Thus, during frequent interactions at various sites around the exhibit, Nixon proceeded to engage Khrushchev in an ongoing debate over the relative merits of the U.S. and Soviet systems. One of those discussions, in the General Electric exhibit, was known as the "kitchen debate." Pointing to the shiny equipment, Nixon said, "This is the newest model. This is the kind which is built in thousands of units for direct installation in the houses. . . . Our steel workers, you know, are on strike. But any steel worker could buy this house. They earn $3 an hour. This house costs about $100 [a] month to buy on a contract running 25 to 30 years." Countering this remark, Khrushchev observed, "The Americans have created their own image of the Soviet man. . . . But he is not as you think. You think the Russian people will be dumbfounded to see these things, but the fact is that newly built Russian houses have all this equipment right now. Moreover, all you have to do to get a house is to be born in the Soviet Union. You are entitled to housing. I was born in the Soviet Union. So I have a right to a house. In America, if you don't have a dollar—you have the right to choose between sleeping in a house or on the pavement. Yet you say that we are slaves of communism."[49]

Davis Explains a Computer and African America

The records do not indicate whether Nixon and Khrushchev specifically discussed race relations. However, the topic frequently came up in other parts of the American National Exhibit. Davis was to demonstrate the state-of-the-art IBM-RAMAC 305 "electronic brain," a computer that had been specifically donated for the exhibit. The machine had been programmed to answer in ten different languages, and over the span of the exhibit it answered 15,381 questions.

Among the twenty most-asked questions were several about black culture and race relations in the United States. such as the "origins of American jazz," "How old is Louis Armstrong?" and "How many Negroes have been lynched in the U.S. since 1950?"[50]

Davis was frustrated that people seemed more interested in knowing about him than about the technology he was demonstrating.[51] "As usual, a large group of Soviet citizens were gathered around listening to my commentary and poised to ask questions not about the computer, but about the price I paid for my shoes or my suit, or how much salary I earned. . . . The crowd asked me a lot of personal questions."[52] Two other guides reported that they, too, were often challenged by questions that went far beyond the duties of their specific posts. One of the other black guides, Herb Miller, stated, "You get one or two questions about a particular exhibit you happen to be standing by and 99 questions about America." Another guide, a Russian émigré, noted, "About 10 percent of my time is devoted to explaining American agriculture. Most of the time I find myself answering questions about everything under the sun . . . [the] American education system, the problem of racial discrimination, and comparative wage scales."[53]

Although the guides expressed amazement, the U.S. State Department organizers had clearly anticipated these sorts of questions. In preparation for the tour, the guides were briefed not only on the equipment and other items they were to show at the exhibit but also on the appropriate ways to respond to social questions. Noted Hixon, "Training focused on preparing the guides on ways to respond to questions that Soviet visitors were likely to ask. The panel asked prospective guides how they would handle questions about school desegregation in the wake of the highly publicized clash in Little Rock in 1957. . . . Preparers tested the guides on 'their ability to reply in a calm, objective manner.' . . . [They were taught to admit] that the United States had yet to afford equality to Blacks, while stressing that progress was being made."[54] The exhibitors were not to deny that racism still existed but to state that the United States was correcting the problem. The presence of the black models and guides was a demonstration of these improved relations, but, at the same time, it might have encouraged some of these questions on race. Had all the exhibitors been white, race issues might not have surfaced so often. Nonetheless, the exhibitors—black and white— "peppered with questions about segregation, slums, and poverty," dutifully responded that "amelioration was the hallmark of American democracy."[55]

Attracting a New Generation of Black Sojourners

Davis was also amazed to see African students in Moscow. At the time of the American National Exhibit, the Soviets had given university scholarships to three hundred Egyptian students and thirty students from other African nations. "The Russian government is investing a great deal in these African students. . . . The African students are grateful for the opportunity to study in Moscow. . . . It is reasonable to assume that the best educated Africans will be key figures in their native governments in the future."[56] Within a year, the Soviets would establish the Soviet Peoples' Friendship University specifically to host this growing international student cohort, and over the next decades thousands of students would come to the Soviet Union to study.

A corollary to these initial 1959 contacts between black guides and the African students in Moscow was the incident that arose around exhibit team member Garnett a few years later. Garnett's sojourn to the Soviet Union to work at the exhibit also opened doors to the Foreign Service for him. In 1964, he was named the first black assistant cultural officer to be posted to the Soviet Union. But Garnett's tenure was cut short when the Soviets accused him of fomenting discontent among African students.[57] A telegram from the U.S. embassy in Moscow stated, "On May 11 the [Soviet] Foreign Ministry has declared Norris D. Garnett, Assistant Cultural Officer at the U.S. Embassy and the first African-American assigned there, *persona non grata* for carrying on work hostile to the USSR among African students. . . . [The] Soviets undoubtedly hope by their move re Garnett and lurid publicity being given to the case in Soviet media to discourage African students in Moscow from further contacts with the U.S. and other embassies."[58] Garnett's specific duties were not made public, but it is likely that the U.S. government wanted him to develop a rapport with African and other students of color in Moscow. That these relationships might undermine relations between the Soviets and the students was ultimately the cause for his expulsion.[59] Despite the occasional student discontents, though, the increasing numbers suggest that the students and their sponsoring countries placed greater value on the long-term benefits of this training than on the short-term problems of living in the Soviet Union.

Sampling Black Expatriate Life

The black expatriate community made a pilgrimage of its own to the exhibit to see U.S. technology, but they were even more keen to compare their lives with those of the U.S. blacks working at the exhibit. They or their parents had left the United States in the 1920s and 1930s because of the humiliations and limitations of Jim Crow, thus, as noted by Davis, they knew "about racial discrimination in New York City." But it amazed Davis that "they had never heard that a Negro [Hulan Jack] was president of the Borough of Manhattan in New York. They did not know about Negro members of Congress and Negro judges."[60] Davis's choice of Jack as a sign of progress for blacks was ironic because a subsequent Manhattan Borough president, Percy Sutton (who served from 1966 to 1977), had direct connections to the black sojourners. His older brother, John, was one of the agricultural specialists who went to the Soviet Union in the early 1930s. Percy was ten when his brother left the United States; but even after his brother returned in 1937, he knew he had an Afro-Russian cousin, Juan. Percy eventually met Juan in the 1970s, decades after the family lost touch with him.[61]

Davis was equally clueless about the kinds of opportunities these blacks had under the Soviet experiment and clearly expected that they would have had many fewer than they did. The Cold War images promulgated by the U.S. and other Western-oriented media repeatedly portrayed Soviet people as suffering from a lack of political freedom and social comforts. Conversely, Davis observed that although this image might be correct for ordinary Russians, the blacks he met there were quite well off within the Soviet system. They often lived in more comfortable surroundings or had access to more stores and people than did the ordinary (white) Russian.

Davis visited a number of the expatriates in their homes or at other sites. Others he accompanied on errands. His article suggested he was relatively free to move about Moscow and to go out to the nearby rural areas, but there can be no question that the Soviet authorities were aware of his movements. No doubt, they had decided that these visits would show the Soviet experiment in a favorable light. Otherwise, he and the expatriates might have encountered difficulties. As Hixon noted, "Striving to discourage and intimidate citizens, CPSU [Soviet Communist Party] officials thoroughly toured the [American National] exhibition themselves and reported to their superiors on what they found."[62] Added Richmond, "Interaction with [Soviet] people was not without its hardships . . . in the early years of the [student and scholar] exchange. . . . You knew that much of what you said or did would be reported to the KGB . . . [and you] had to be constantly on the alert."[63]

The expatriates' lives offered a striking contrast to life for the average black person in the United States. "For the most part, Negroes in Russia are given the same freedom as other citizens. . . . In some cases, a dark face in Moscow has a[s] much advantage as it would have a disadvantage in Mississippi."[64] Davis accompanied an unnamed black expatriate to have a watch repaired. "People were lined up waiting to get in. It was during the lunch hour and although a repairman was inside, he had the door closed." Davis was sure that they would have to wait too. " 'Not at all,' my friend replied, 'We will go in immediately.' He walked to the head of the line and knocked on the door. The door was opened and he beckoned me to join him inside. When the lunch hour was over, the door was opened to the public. However, my friend who had gone in ahead of the line was served first. The repairman even refused to accept payment for his services. I asked my friend why he would not wait his turn like everyone else. He answered, 'Well, the Russians are very sympathetic towards Negroes.' "[65]

Davis admitted that he did not witness any signs of racial prejudice. "I found no public display of racial prejudice in Moscow. Such would be a criminal offense."[66] Still, he felt compelled to add that others had reported certain incidences. "It is my understanding that the Russian women are sometimes taunted and made the butt of jokes when they have Negro husbands or boy friends."[67] He also noted that although he saw Ross over ten times, he found it strange that he never saw Ross's Russian wife. Conversely, though, he also saw Tynes frequently, and Tynes's wife, Maria Alexandrovna, was always with him.[68] Perhaps, because dark-skinned Ross made his living critiquing the mistreatment of blacks by whites, having his Russian wife nearby might complicate this position. Tynes, however, who was lighter-skinned and often taken for an Uzbek, seemed happy to blend into the local society.

Some black expatriates seemed to have better housing than others. "Bob Ross lives better than the other Negroes in Moscow. His apartment is in a newly constructed building in a nice section of the city. He also has a kitchen and a private bath. Well furnished, the space is adequate."[69] The comment about "adequate" space was based on U.S. standards, not Russian. That Ross had been assigned a unit that included a private kitchen and bath (full toilet and bathroom) more than proved his special status. Few Russians, other than elites, had such facilities at the time.

Visiting Tynes and his family at the duck research preserve on the outskirts of Moscow, Davis conceded that the Tynes too was "more fortunate than most Russians." Tynes and the other agricultural specialists had been posted to Uzbekistan in the early 1930s for their first assignments. There, their lives had been much more rudimentary than they were almost twenty years later. Now, in 1959, Tynes was a senior statesman in his field and was "considered the leading authority on fish and ducks in the Soviet Union."[70] The average Russian living in the city had to wait hours in lines before selecting items from a limited range of food. Tynes had no such problems. It was no accident, therefore, that the Tynes family could host the black expatriate gatherings, and, as Lily noted, a "rich table would be spread."[71]

Housing in the Soviet Union was an important social measure. Although all Soviet citizens were guaranteed housing, it might take many years before a unit was available, depending on the location. Davis noted that the Tynes family "had two bedrooms, a living room, dining room, kitchen and bathroom. This is very important in Russia when you consider that most of the people in Moscow live in only one or two rooms." In Moscow, "most people go to a public shower once a week because they do not have suitable bathing facilities at home."[72] At the time of Davis's visit and well into the 1980s, apartment dwellers in the majority of the older apartment complexes continued to share a kitchen and bathroom facilities. As Lily explained, "Apartments could not be bought in the Soviet Union. The government, to be precise, Moscow City Council, usually gave them free and people waited for them for several years." She noted that when she married and became pregnant in the 1960s, she needed additional space for herself, the baby, and her mother, who was moving to Moscow to help out. "I could exchange my mother's apartment with three rooms in Tashkent and my [earlier] apartment [in Moscow] with one room [for] a bigger apartment in Moscow. . . . [With] great difficulties, I began the adventure of changing apartments."[73]

But Davis found it perplexing that although Tynes held a certain status in Soviet society, he and his children were still known as Negroes. He wondered whether this label was a vestige of the same racism that faced blacks in the United States. "I asked many Russians this question: 'If a Negro who has become a Russian citizen marries a Russian woman and they live in Moscow, what will be the nationality of their children?' The answer is always 'Negro.' . . . 'How long then does it take a Negro to become a plain Russian?' I suspect it will take him as long as it will take to become a plain American without a racial tag."[74] Not understanding the Soviet system, Davis not realize that the label *Negro* was more an ethnic designation than a racial one. The use of the term was similar to the Soviets' use of the terms *Uzbek* and *Chechen*. In fact, the descendants of the black expatriates seemed to have preferred to retain this term as a link to their fathers and their U.S. heritage. An example occurred when Lily applied for her passport in 1950:

> I am 16 and must get my Soviet passport. I went to the police, who gave me a passport that recorded my nationality as "American." I told him that "American" was a term of citizenship, while I was "Soviet." The officer explained that "Soviet" did not mean nationality. After that complaint, they gave me another passport that stated that I was "Uzbek." Again I complained that I had no Uzbek blood in my veins [although Lily was born in Uzbekistan]. Then they wrote that I was "Russian." . . . I refused to take this passport. . . . You must write that I am a "Negro." . . . The policeman explained that there was no such nationality [in the Soviet system].[75]

In face of her persistence that they record her as a Negro, the suspicious authorities ordered her to prove she was a Negro. "How will you prove that you are a Negro? One can come and say he is Negro. Others will come and say that they are something else. . . . You think that, by stating you are a Negro, you will be able to leave the country?"[76] She then produced a 1931 article from the New York *Amsterdam News*, which stated that her father was from the United States and a Negro. The next time she went to collect her passport, "Negro" was written in it. "Thus I became the only person in the world with a passport in which it was written that I was a 'Negro.'"[77] Once she established the precedent, other Afro-Russian children from the black sojourner/expatriate group followed her example.[78]

The Soviet official who challenged Golden was quite prescient. These Afro-Russians descendants seeking passports did intend to travel, and, in some cases, that travel was to see the land of their American father.[79] The possibility of having these blacks "leaving" the Soviet Union for the United States could also result in a propaganda advantage for the United States and disadvantage for the Soviet Union. In fact, as several of the Afro-Russian descendants ultimately discovered, having the nationality of Negro recorded in their official Soviet documents, a nationality that did not officially exist in the Soviet system of classification, did make it easier for them to obtain a U.S. passport later.[80]

Tool-and-die specialist Robinson was the only openly discontented black expatriate Davis met. Although many decades apart, Davis and Robinson had both come from Detroit and looked to their Soviet sojourns as a means to realize their professional ambitions. Robinson had been there for nearly thirty years by the time Davis met him. "He approached and looked at me quizzically. Finally, in polite but crisp Russian language, he said, 'Hello.' I responded in Russian. He then asked where I was from. I replied 'Detroit.' The serious expression that had been on his face gave way to a smile."[81] Davis was impressed with Robinson's accomplishments. "[Robinson] worked hard for his adopted country and has produced not less than 27 industrial inventions which the Soviet government has used. [Robinson] is a senior engineer [and] has more than 25 years of service to his credit." But now Robinson wanted Davis to help him leave the country. Knowing he was under suspicion, he insisted that no substantive talk occur in his apartment or any other enclosure. As Davis noted, "We never discussed anything serious inside a room in any building. He was taking a chance in sharing his story with me and placing his confidence in me."[82] But Davis was not in a position to help at that time. Although Davis returned to the Soviet Union some years later in another capacity, he still could not help. "There was nothing more I could legitimately do to get him out." Not until 1974, after Robinson had managed to leave the country for a visit to Uganda, could Davis intercede on his behalf. "I began working through contacts in the White House and the U.S. Immigration and Naturalization service." Four years later, when Robinson finally returned to the United States, Davis helped him get settled and find a publisher for his memoirs.[83]

The Afro-Russian children intrigued Davis in a different way. None of these young people had had any personal experience with Jim Crow or other U.S.-style racism. Many were enrolled in highly-regarded schools or universities, like Vyacheslav Tynes at the Air Force Academy and Lily at Moscow State University, or had become professionals, like Margaret Scott, who was a ballerina with the Bolshoi Ballet.[84] These slots were not generally open to average Russians but were available only to those with a high commitment to the Soviet system, excellent qualifications, and important connections. That the descendants of blacks fleeing Jim Crow could tap into these opportunities in the Soviet Union spoke volumes about the differences in the opportunities available to blacks in the United States and in the Soviet Union at the time.

Meeting Goode, Robeson's brother in-law, gave Davis a glimpse at a third possible trajectory for the black expatriates. Ross had gone in the 1920s as a fellow traveler; Tynes had gone with the waves of technical agricultural specialists of the early 1930s. Goode had gone because he was tired of Jim Crow. He had neither a political agenda nor a special skill to share. When Davis met him, he was living on his pension in the town of Gorky, about two hundred miles away from Moscow. "A big, powerful handsome man named Frank Goode lives quietly with his wife and nine-year-old daughter."[85] Davis was impressed with his effort to come to Moscow, noting that the Soviet bureaucracy often made these journeys difficult. "If you get permission to take a trip to another city, you must report to the police in that city and let them know where you will stay, the length of time you expect to be there and why you are there in the first place."[86] But

Davis may not have realized that Goode, as Robeson's brother in-law, did enjoy certain privileges. His daughter, Eslanda, commented that he could travel to Moscow quite easily and that he and his family often made trips to join Robeson when he and his wife were in the country.[87]

In the end, Davis wished to know whether the expatriates wanted to return to the United States. Goode expressed interest in seeing the changed country but, like the others, was not willing to leave his family. Davis then speculated whether people could be truly free in the Soviet Union. For him, freedom was measured by the ability of a man to "read what he wants . . . to listen to what he wants" and especially to travel. Davis had "been to 11 countries (nine at my own expense)," whereas the Russians were not so free to move outside their country.[88] To his mind, therefore, the fact that the Russians and the black expatriates did not travel—whatever the reason—suggested a "failure" of the Soviet experiment. "The real test of freedom in Russia is directly connected with the government's lack of faith in its people to return home after seeing the 'outside world.' I will believe that George Tynes is a free man in Russia only when . . . he is permitted to visit America on vacation with his *entire* family. I will believe that Robert Robinson is a free man if I see him paying a social call on friends . . . in America. The same thing goes for Bob Ross and Frank Goode."[89]

Bringing the Black Expatriate Story Home

Davis's 1960 *Ebony* article was designed to accomplish two tasks: to enlighten black America about blacks living in the Soviet Union and to catch the notice of the U.S. government. To capture the attention of blacks, he wrote, "In the East-West struggle for world power, it is perhaps important for the average American—black or white—to know what life is like on the other side.[90] And, to capture the notice of the U.S. government, he inserted other comments: "When a Russian says he wants peace he really means it. . . . They are a very proud people who want more than anything else for their country to be really great in everything. . . . People all over the Soviet Union want the meeting between President Eisenhower and Premier Khrushchev to be a great success."[91] He purposefully stretched his story from the particular accounts of black expatriates into the larger question of peace negotiations so his piece would not be overwhelmed by the news of Khrushchev and Nixon's encounters. This article was published in a popular black magazine, but Davis trusted that the Cold War "listening posts" were tuned in to publications directed to people of color, especially those articles that referred to the Soviet Union. Davis not only was positioning himself within black America but also was hoping this article might help with his intentions to join the international-affairs community.

The 1959 American National Exhibit did affect Davis's future. In subsequent years, he would join the Foreign Service, and over his twenty-eight-year career he represented the United States in the Soviet Union and various African nations. Among his many posts were Ghana, Ethiopia, Guinea, and Senegal.

Davis's presence at the exhibit, along with that of his black co-workers, also influenced the aspirations of a number of Afro-Russian descendants he met. Although fully Russian in culture, they nursed secret aspirations to know about the culture of their black fathers. Many of these potential "reverse" sojourners saw the American National Exhibit as an opening to visits they might someday make themselves. Many thus maintained contact with Davis but had to wait for a change in political climate before they found ways to act on these plans.[92] Of these descendents, Lily was among the first to see the United States when she arrived in 1987 under the auspices of the Soviet Peace Committee.[93] Others followed in the 1990s.

Khrushchev Makes His Sojourn to the United States

The American National Exhibit whetted the appetite not only of the Afro-Russian descendants but also of Khrushchev to visit the United States. Khrushchev had already expressed his interest but to no avail, largely because of Secretary Dulles's reluctance to pursue further ties with the Soviet Union. As Hixon noted, "Dulles considered Khrushchev 'the most dangerous person to lead the Soviet Union since the October Revolution.'"[94] But, in addition, Eisenhower wanted to visit the Soviet Union and was willing to take the gamble. Less than a month after the close of the American National Exhibit in Moscow and four months after Dulles's death, Khrushchev made his landmark visit. Noted Suny, "In September 1959 the Soviet Union's most enthusiastic tourist traveled from Washington [D.C.] to New York, from California to the corn fields of Iowa."[95] Du Bois, hailing this visit, noted that "the Soviet Union has successfully established a socialist state. . . . This state is one of the greatest industrial states of the world and likely soon to lead all others. . . . [And] as proof of this the First Minister of the Soviet Union has visited the United States, has been received with courtesy and in places with enthusiasm. . . . This alone marks an era. It would have been impossible ten years ago. Yet Nikita Khrushchev did it."[96] The white and black members of the American National Exhibit team returned to the United States with new perspectives on the Cold War. The Soviet Union was no longer an abstraction. They had lived there for several months, met Russians, and debated issues with them. Davis and the other blacks had made the corollary discovery of the black sojourner presence in the Soviet Union. They discovered blacks who had moved there thirty years before and had remained, tying their futures to the Soviet experiment and raising their families. And they discovered the new post–World War II black sojourners arriving from countries on the verge of their independence, coming in with their own desire to share in the Soviet promise.

CHAPTER 12

The Cold War, Solidarity Building, and the Recruitment of New Sojourners

ତ୦ର

Before our eyes, Africa was gaining freedom. We could never
have guessed [that the] next year, in 1960, on the initiative of
the Soviet Union at the United Nations, more than 30 African
colonies would be granted their independence and the year
would be declared "The Year of Africa." . . . The general
enthusiasm knew no bounds when legendary figures like
Dr. Du Bois and Paul Robeson, appeared in our midst.[1]
—Lily Golden, 2002

*I*t was the fall of 1958. Robeson had re-
turned to Moscow in August, and Du Bois followed shortly thereafter. In October, both would meet a grown Lily Golden in Tashkent at the Asian and African
Writers conference. It was the first time in over ten years that Lily had seen the
city of her birth, her "beloved Tashkent." Happy to have the excuse to return, she
was also under assignment from Professor Ivan Potekhin. "Potekhin proposed
that I should go . . . as a delegate to the first Conference of Asian and African
Writers. He said that he expected Paul Robeson and Dr. Du Bois, 'your friends,'
to attend. 'Try to talk to them about opening . . . an Institute of African Studies
in Moscow. I hope their authority will help us.'"[2] Potekhin had good reason to
hope that Du Bois and Robeson's reappearance in the Soviet Union could push
this agenda. For one, they were Pan-Africanists, and, for another, they were
good friends of the Soviet government and, with their high-level intercession,
the government was sure to act.

Potekhin, like Lily, was resurfacing from the cataclysmic revelations of
Stalinist atrocities at the Twentieth Communist Party Congress in 1956. Lily
noted there was a general "sense of renewal" and people were enjoying "a slight
thaw in the ice of rigid conformity."[3] Some of the Cold War tensions were re-
laxing, and she began to notice that more and more Africans were making their
appearance in the Soviet Union. Some of the earliest visitors of the era—two
Sudanese and one Libyan—arrived in 1957. These were the first Africans Lily
met. Little did she realize that this small delegation would lead to other contacts

and even to meeting men whom she and many other Afro-Russian daughters of her generation would marry.

A year later, Lily was nominated to the committee hosting African delegates for the World Festival of Youth. "During my last year in Moscow State, there was a major historic event. Khrushchev decided to open a window to the outside world, and so we had the 'World Festival of Youth.' . . . I was nominated to be responsible for all the delegates from African countries. . . . There were several thousand Africans with thousands of problems. . . . We had to do everything, including taking care of the plane tickets, finding books on Russian art . . . organizing meetings between Black Americans and Africans." Indeed, the Russians, although they opened their doors to these delegates, actually knew little about them. Lily remembered people asking her, "What do they eat? How do they dress and behave?" But, throughout the city, the general response to the many international visitors was a combination of wonder and enthusiasm. "Many Soviet people were in cultural shock at meeting Africans. The majority of Muscovites, and especially those who had come from the distant provinces for the festival, had never seen Africans before. Some had never seen foreigners, because of the 'Iron Curtain.'" At the same time, the visitors were thrilled to be so warmly received. "The guests from Africa had never encountered such success. They told me that no other country had ever offered them such admiration and attention."[4]

The festival itself was quite a coup for Khrushchev. These international gatherings, which drew the world's future leaders together, had been taking place in various countries every two years since 1947. The 1957 festival in the Soviet Union not only signaled the Soviet support of the festival's goals of fighting fascism and solidifying peace but also had the largest attendance ever, with thirty-four thousand people representing 131 countries.[5] A significant number of the assembled youth came from the Soviet Union, but the fact that 130 other countries sent delegates spoke to a strong commitment to the festival goals and to curiosity about the Soviet experiment. Importantly, as Lily noted, Khrushchev was not only opening the door to these latter-day sojourners but also permitting increased contact between the Russians and outsiders. Putting the West on notice, the Soviets, by example and invitation, were embarking on a campaign to win over new generations of hearts and minds. Lily, like so many other participants—both Russians and visitors—was filled with great optimism. The fact that Guinea gained its independence during the time of the festival added to the excitement. As Lily put it, "The spirit of self-determination filled the air." Many thought "the entire continent would soon be free of colonialism . . . [and] all Africa's problems would be solved automatically. There would be no wars, no poverty, and no hunger."[6]

For their part, Robeson and Du Bois, quickly returning to the Soviet Union, also called on other peoples of the world to come sample the Soviet experiment. In January 1960, Robeson announced, "Come and see this exciting Socialist land. . . . You will see something extraordinary. You will see a new kind of human being—one shaped in conditions where deep concern for others is basic. . . . We know that the power and influence of the Soviet Union and the Socialist world will support the struggles of people everywhere."[7] Du Bois offered his admiration. "It came to be the firmly held accusation of the Western world that Russian socialism was . . . a deliberate attempt to turn the clock of human progress backward. . . . Today, what a change! . . . Until the launching of Sputnik in 1957, it was customary in the West to regard all Soviet claims of social, scientific, and industrial accomplishment as exaggerations or plain lies. Today . . . the Soviet Union is already leading in education and science and has met the problem of poverty as no other nation. Of its future as a great nation, there is today no doubt."[8] They were no less thrilled with Khrushchev's call for the freedom of all colonial and dependent nations at the fifteenth session of the General Assembly of the United Nations.[9] Robeson commented, "This is certainly one of the most important pronouncements that could be made in our time. Clearly if these nations were independent the danger of war would be lessened greatly. . . . But from the point of view of people like my own in Asia, in Africa and in Latin America, who have been a subject people, stepped upon and persecuted literally for centuries, we are certainly deeply thankful to Mr. Khrushchev's suggestion."[10]

A Confluence of Forces

The late 1950s brought a confluence of global forces. Having now consolidated his power after the Twentieth Congress, Khrushchev was pushing his policy of peaceful coexistence and reaching out to new populations. The Bandung Conference of 1955, which had brought together twenty-nine countries containing over two-thirds of the world's developing societies, was calling for new kinds of global relationships.[11] African nations were gaining their independence, with seven attaining it in the 1950s alone.[12] And Robeson and Du Bois, now exonerated, were—by word, deed, and photo—linking the Soviet experiment with the aspirations of people of color around the globe.

The response of white and black Communists to the 1956 revelations about Stalin could not have been more different. As Duberman noted, "Many white Communists . . . went to pieces over the Khrushchev report, deserting the CPUSA in droves." Conversely, "few black members left the Party, preferring to read Khrushchev's revelations as a sign of renewed hope, an indication that the U.S.S.R. was about to return to the purity of its earlier revolutionary goals."[13] The two foremost black supporters of the Soviet experiment—though neither was a member of the CPUSA at the time—were suddenly forced into a delicate position.[14] These trail blazers and role models for millions of blacks in the United States and elsewhere had for decades represented the Soviet model as a beacon of hope. What would these stalwart apologists have to say?

Robeson made the decision not to comment publicly and, instead, "maintained an outward equanimity."[15] In a provocative *Ebony* article, Carl T. Rowan asked, "Has Paul Robeson betrayed the Negro?" Then, discussing efforts to understand Robeson's opinions, he described Robeson as "a sad-voiced martyr" and a "singer who had forgotten his lyrics" but conceded that Robeson was sincere, and "even Negroes who consider Robeson politically naïve and tactically dumb find reasons to sympathize with him."[16]

Unlike Robeson, Du Bois decided to meet the exposé head on. He did not speak to the acknowledgement of Stalin's crimes but situated his analysis in a different context. Noted Lewis, "Du Bois adjusted the Russian casualty table in light of the Atlantic slave trade, the scramble for Africa, the needless First World War, Nazi death camps. And the color-coded poverty. . . . To Du Bois, the degradation of the communist ideal in Soviet Russia was philosophically irrelevant to the expiation of sins of American democracy, whose very possibility he now deeply doubted."[17] In a 1956 article, he commented, "Under the leadership of Joseph Stalin, the Soviet Union proceeded to build the first modern socialist state without consenting to share with the West the loot of colonial peoples. It was the astonishing and increasing success of socialist Russia which helped liberate Asia and is today forcing the liberation of Africa. . . . We could wish that all the men who in blood and tears have helped raise mankind out of the gutter had been scholars and gentlemen. But usually they have not been." Finally, he noted, "When at last Africa is emancipated the credit should go in no little degree to the vast influence of Lenin, Stalin and Mao Tse-tung on the thoughts of men."[18]

The Bandung Challenge

Both Du Bois and Robeson had sorely regretted not having attended the April 18, 1955, Bandung Conference of Asian and African Nations, but their state-imposed internal exiles were still on. The twenty-nine nations in attendance announced that they were forming new allegiances in view of the bipolar split of the larger, industrialized nations. The First World comprised the United States, its European allies, and Japan. The Second World was made up of the Soviet Union, the Eastern Bloc nations, and other Communist allies. The remaining nations, feeling squeezed between the two and yet being pressured to join one or the other camp, decided the time had come to choose a third path. As Paul Gorden Lauren noted, "They wanted to be 'neutral,' 'non-aligned' states forming their own 'Third World.'"[19]

Robeson sent his greetings and support. "How I should have loved to be at Bandung! The time has come when the colored peoples of the world will no longer allow the great natural wealth of their countries to be exploited and expropriated by the Western world while they are beset by hunger, disease and poverty." Taking his observations further, he pointed out that positive models existed. "The whole economic, social and cultural advancement of whole populations of hundreds of millions of people can be rapidly achieved. . . . The possibility and practicability of such rapid social advancement had been attested

[to] by those who have objectively examined the history of the Soviet Union since 1917 and developments during the last decade in the countries of Eastern Europe, in China, and in newly emancipated Asian countries such as India."[20]

Du Bois, too, sent a solidarity message. "Because of my fifty years of service in the cause of twenty-five million colored peoples of America, I venture of my own initiative to address you in their name, since the United States will not allow me to attend this meeting. We colored folk of America have long lived with you yellow, brown and black folk of the world under the intolerable arrogance and assumptions of the white race. We beg you to close ranks against men in America, Britain, France, Spain, Belgium, and the Netherlands, so long as they fight and scheme for the colonial system, for color, caste and class exploitation."[21]

Khrushchev's Moves: Aswan and Other Projects

Du Bois observed, "Africa is not inviting Communism, [but] what state or nation today offers Africa what the Soviet Union does?"[22] The Soviet programs of support for infrastructure building and education fed directly into the interest of these developing societies in having the equipment and personnel to advance. A prime example was the Aswan High Dam project in Egypt. Egypt expected the full backing of the United States and other nations. However, the Western nations withdrew in a dispute over the Egyptians' refusal to sever ties with the Soviets.[23] At the same time, the Soviets recognized the U.S. withdrawal as an opportunity not to be missed. Khrushchev immediately responded to President Gamal Abdel Nasser's request for help; Khrushchev correctly surmised that this support would solidify the Soviets' friendship not only with the Egyptians but also with other Arab nations.[24] The project took over ten years to complete, and the Soviets spent one billion dollars;[25] but the larger goal of gaining an expanded network of relationships was also achieved. In 1956, the Soviet Union had formal relations with only one country in Africa—Ethiopia. Within ten years, that number had increased to twenty-six. A 1969 conference report by K. S. Kremen stated, "[The Soviet Union has provided] assistance in the training of Africa's expert personnel, in developing her health services and public education. In January 1967, the Soviet Union trained five thousand students from nearly all African nations. . . . Medical colleges are training over 700 Africans, which is equal to nearly half of African physicians today."[26] By 1970, as Allison Blakely noted, the spread of Soviet technical and other support had increased to the point that there were "around eight thousand" nonmilitary personnel working in Africa alone.[27]

Twenty-five years after the first groups arrived in the Soviet Union at the end of the 1950s, P. Ya. Koshelev noted, "The training of skilled native manpower at different levels is an object of great concern in Soviet co-operation with African countries. During the years this co-operation has been in progress Soviet specialists have trained close on 150,000 skilled workers through on-the-job [and other] training at various projects. . . . Manpower training for African countries has assumed large-scale proportions at enterprises and at higher schools of the Soviet Union as well. To meet the wishes of many nations, Soviet educational institutions have, in recent years, been admitting foreign students for specialized training."[28]

New Sojourners to the Soviet Union

When William Davis met African students in 1959, he was correct when he observed that "the Russians are leaving no stones unturned in their attempt to make reliable friends in Africa." The Soviets extended a wide range of inducements to enhance the attractiveness of their scholarship programs.

> Russia pays for the transportation . . . from Africa. . . . They receive 3,000 roubles ($300) as an allotment for winter clothes. Each student receives 900 roubles a month while he is a student. The average Russian worker makes only 800 roubles a month . . . and thus [they are] paid more than Russian citizens. . . . When the African students are on vacation they continue to collect the 900 roubles a month and are given a bonus of 1,500 roubles for extra spending. Every two years the Soviet government pays [their] passage to [and from] their native country.[29]

Additionally, the students benefited from free room and board and health care. When Davis questioned them about their ties to Communism, these pragmatic sojourners told him they were more "interested in clothes on their backs and shoes on their feet than they are in any kind of 'ism.'"[30] Jan Carew's 1960s-era students stressed similar aspirations. "So, we arrive in Russia with expectations heightened by decades of propaganda for Russia. Those who returned from Youth Congresses . . . had glowing tales to tell of prodigal hospitality and an absence of racial discrimination. . . . And in backward countries like mine where, not so long ago, there was one university scholarship a year for the whole country, our need for large numbers of educated people is greatest of all. For us, winning our independence is just one great step forward in a race for life. Our need is so great that if the devil in hell offered us a chance for an education we would take it."[31]

The first groups of students attended Moscow State University. Within a year, the scholarship program was expanded and the new Peoples' Friendship University (later, Lumumba University) was founded specifically to train people from Africa, Asia, and Latin America. From its beginnings to the collapse of the Soviet Union at the end of the 1980s, the university attracted students from all over the globe. As Blakely observed, in the mid-1980s, there were "approximately six thousand graduate and undergraduate students at Lumumba University, with the largest contingent from Africa. Each year, thousands more apply for seven hundred available openings."[32] Besides the large cohort of foreign students, a select number of Soviet students were allowed entrance. Robeson's niece, Eslanda, was one of them.[33]

Renaming the university in 1962 after the recently martyred Patrice Lumumba helped solidify the ties between the Soviet Union and the peoples of newly independent nations.[34] Even after the collapse of the Soviet Union, at the end of the 1980s, when the new Russian government again renamed the university as part of its campaign to shed references to its Communist past, people would not let the name—or linkage—die. Although officially renamed the Russian Peoples' Friendship University," many in the developing world have insisted on calling it Lumumba University, and Lumumba alumni associations continue to maintain ties through a far-flung global network.[35]

The Black Expatriates and African Visitors, Students, and Dignitaries

Golden's work in the newly established Africa Institute of the Academy of Sciences brought her into direct contact with African students and dignitaries arriving in the country. Other daughters of the black sojourners/expatriates who were studying or working in Moscow also encountered these incoming students. For these young, unmarried Afro-Russians, the interaction with Africans was new and exciting. Although their skin might have been darker than the average Russian's, the lives of most of them had been shaped by their Russian mothers or by Russian culture. Meeting the incoming Africans offered a whole new set of experiences and, indirectly, a tie to their African American fathers. As Lily pointed out, it frustrated her that she was constantly called on as the "spokesperson" for all black people. "I was the only black-skinned student in a [Moscow State] University population of 12,000."[36]

The African students also presented fresh perspectives on the larger world in which people of color were integral players. Recounting her encounters with the Ghanaians at the Asian and African Writers conference, Lily wrote, "They were representing the first nation of [sub-Saharan] Africa to achieve independence in 1957 [and] theirs was the most numerous delegation."[37] She also met people from many other countries who would later take on prominent roles. "Some of these African and Asian writers . . . were to become famous figures in world politics and literature. I soaked up the heady atmosphere."[38] Despite the beautiful clothing and forthright manner of many of the delegates, Lily was put to task when one asked her, "Why do the Uzbeks look at me so strangely, as if some of them pitied me?" She tried to explain the legacy of Soviet propaganda that placed Africans, like black Americans, among the wretched of the earth. "As far as most Soviet people had been informed by the mass media, the Africans were poverty stricken, non-educated, deprived of everything. . . . They [the Russian people] had expected to see hungry people dressed in tatters. Instead they had met affluent students who spoke several foreign languages [and] were European dressed."[39]

Later, she was intrigued to benefit from global African diasporic solidarity when some of her African visitors were ready to fight on her behalf. When the attentions of a highly placed member of the Soviet Writers' Union caused her embarrassment, members of the Ugandan delegation immediately offered help. "At one point, three writers from Uganda approached me and asked, openly, whether [his] attentions were disturbing me. I was surprised, and wanted to know how they noticed this. The answer was 'Sister, if you get tired of him, just tell us.'"[40]

The thrill and excitement of having Africans present, plus the prospects of an exciting future, led many of the Afro-Russian daughters to marry African students. "I must mention that all of the Black Soviet girls, including me, eventually married Africans. . . . This was the end of the 1950s, the beginning of the 1960s. It was the dawning of a new epoch in Africa and we were in euphoria over the beginnings of self-determination. We felt that we must go to Africa and, having a good education, we must help the continent to build a new life." The Afro-Russians held a romantic notion of extending the missions of their fathers, who, as African American specialists, had arrived in the Soviet Union some thirty years earlier to help build the new Soviet Russia. Unfortunately, romantic notions could not withstand the later realization that the Russian and African cultures could not mesh. Noted Lily, "All of us who went [to Africa] ended up returning to the Soviet Union. . . . They appreciated the fact that we were educated, black-skinned, and of African origin . . . [but we] could not adjust. . . . [We] could not compromise with polygamy and found that there was no possibility of employment, despite [our] education."[41] Although their future spouses were apparently happy with them while still in the Soviet Union, being independent Soviet women was incompatible with the paternalistic and often feudal surroundings into which they moved in African societies. This incompatibility not only symbolized a contest of social structures but also a challenge along racial lines. Racist behavior was prohibited in the Soviet Union but remained a vestige of the African countries' former colonial status.[42] Continued Lily, "One after another, my girlfriends of African [American] origin were marrying Africans. Ella and Ina Ross followed hard in my footsteps. After them Amelia Tynes, and then Victoria Rudd. Yelena [Scott], Parker's adopted daughter . . . [married] a man from India. All followed their husbands. Soon, one by one, they began to reappear again in the Soviet Union. . . . This was no mean feat. . . . Visas to return to the USSR were not easily obtained, but some of them were prepared to face prison in order to return."[43] Children were often the final reason they chose to leave, as these mothers determined the Soviet Union would be a better environment than Africa in which to raise them. Lily, although one of the earliest to marry an African, never moved to the continent. This was not for lack of trying, but various problems, both in the Soviet Union and in Zanzibar, continued to delay her. Still planning to join her husband in Zanzibar, though, she began to worry about her daughter's future. "I dreamed of giving her the best possible education with opportunities in music and sport. But Zanzibar, with its Muslim traditions and restrictions on the freedom and equality of women, was hardly the appropriate place compared with the possibilities of the Soviet Union. It was difficult to discuss this with a devout Muslim who truly believed what he said 'We respect women so much that we do not even look at them.'"[44] Later, when many of these Afro-Russian women remarried, it was to Russians or men from Eastern Bloc nations.[45] In this case, their Russian cultural background proved stronger than any historical link through the African diaspora.

Solidarity, Scholarships, and the Future

The Cold War solidarity efforts of the Soviets provided signal opportunities for developing special relationships with nations of Africa and other parts of the Third World. The multiyear Soviet, and later Eastern Bloc, scholarship programs were extremely attractive to newly industrializing nations in need of skilled personnel, and they produced new generations eager to partake in what they hoped would be a nonracist society. Many had been impressed by the Soviets' willingness to work alongside them on various projects in their home countries, and they anticipated a similar spirit of friendship and solidarity when they went to the Soviet Union.

This sense of solidarity not only affected potential students from Africa but also inspired young Soviet teachers and other professionals to want to go abroad to work on Soviet projects in other countries. Two of those who went abroad were Eslanda Goode, who taught in Cambodia, and Valentina Abdelrahim-Soboleva, a former Russian colleague at Lincoln University who married a Sudanese student and went with him to teach in Africa.[46]

Unanticipated problems began to surface with the African students in the Soviet Union as the years progressed. In addition to adjustment issues in Moscow, students began to experience tensions around dating patterns and male-female relationships. The student group was overwhelmingly male, and growing numbers were developing liaisons with young Russian women they met. As Lily, Eslanda, and Amelia observed, Russians found it exciting being around exotic foreigners, many of whom brought gifts from their trips to Europe over the holidays and had nice housing in the university quarters. The districts around the universities also began to see increasing numbers of mixed-race children.[47]

Toward the end of the 1980s, the social, political, and ideological fabric holding the Soviet system together fell apart. It had been fraying for years but was bolstered largely by policies and procedures that provided "patches" to any problems that surfaced. For the most part, incidents were not acknowledged to be racism per se but were considered signs of "hooliganism" or of tensions fueled by alcohol.[48] Earlier, Soviet authorities moved swiftly to correct racist behavior, and there was a concerted effort to match the solidarity rhetoric with action. But, by the late 1980s, with *glasnost* and *perestroika*, many of the top-down checks and balances that kept order in the society at-large fell by the wayside. The official pronouncements and the day-to-day experiences of foreign students living in certain parts of the Soviet Union moved further apart. With the dissolution of the subsidized economy in the last part of the 1980s and early 1990s, ordinary Russians increasingly acted out their frustrations against foreigners, and disinterested police ignored complaints. Before, people were encouraged to—and for the most part did—submerge their personal aspirations under the general goal of societywide access to certain creature comforts. And a high value was placed on state planning and the notion of an equitable sharing of resources, such as employment, health care, education, and housing. With the dramatic shift from a centralized, command economy to one structured around capitalist models, people who managed heretofore with relatively little income were now being forced to pay for items formerly subsidized by the government. Jobs were being lost, and incomes could not keep up with expenses. In the face of these problems for ordinary citizens, the foreign students, whose numbers had grown into the thousands, continued to stand out because of their darker skin color and the fact that their lives seemed still heavily subsidized at the expense of Russian citizens.

Yet, in the midst of the increasing tension, students from developing societies continued to arrive up to and through the collapse of the Soviet Union. The educational program was a good one, and the examples of the many thousands who had successfully completed these programs in the past continued to be a strong motivator. In a 1996 *New York Times* article, Rachel Swarns interviewed an eighteen-year-old law student in Russia who noted that her father did his engineering studies at the former Lumumba University and retained his enthusiasm about the solidarity and friendship he experienced during his tenure there. The reporter added, "The [University] still attracts foreign students because its diplomas still carry prestige in parts of the third world and because its tuition is only $2,000 a year. . . . Even students who complain about crumbling dormitories and Communist professors still commend the university's academic rigor [and] many [graduates] have become respected political and scientific leaders in their countries. They include doctors in Japan, economists in Chile, politicians in Mexico and engineers in Nigeria."[49]

The black expatriate community discussed in this book, whose tenure in the Soviet Union has stretched from the 1920s through the dissolution of the Soviet Union, did not suffer from these same problems. First, their numbers were relatively small.[50] Khanga estimated that in the 1990s the total black-Russian group (descending from black sojourners/expatriates) numbered five thousand to ten thousand; "there were too few of us to attract the kind of bigotry directed towards larger minorities." However, the African student population at the time was estimated at forty thousand.[51] Second, by the mid-1990s, all the original sojourner/expatriates discussed here had died, and their Afro-Russian children, representing fourteen family lines, had spent most of their lives in the Soviet Union.[52] Fully acculturated, they also benefited from their family's decades-long tenure in the country and the fact that their parent or grandparent had come to the country under different auspices than had the African students. Many of these earlier blacks had come to train the Russians and shared their skills building the Soviet experiment. Khanga, whose experiences stretch from Soviet into post-Soviet Russia and who has lived in the Soviet Union, in the United States, and, more recently, in post-Soviet Russia, speaks for many Afro-Russian descendants of the black sojourner/expatriate group when she compares U.S.S.R. and U.S. life. "I never felt like a stranger in my black skin. Unlike many African-Americans [in the United States], I was never made to feel less intelligent, less capable, less likely to achieve than my white schoolmates. . . . Was my family, by virtue of its descent from one of the few American blacks who came to the Soviet Union in [the] thirties, a special case? Yes and no. . . . I was insulated from . . . prejudice [because] there are too few of us. . . . When I was growing up, I thought of my color not as a target for discrimination but simply . . . as a mark of separateness. No racist taunts were aimed at me, but I did attract persistent, usually polite curiosity."[53]

What does this comparison suggest for those who still look to the country, now Russia, as a source of opportunity? It is clear that many of the issues that propelled peoples of color to look to the Soviet model in the early years remain, despite the fact that the global political landscape has changed and only one superpower remains. The search for opportunity, in the form of education, training, and productive work, still encourages ambitious young people to look to Russia and other former Communist nations as offering steps toward their future. Students also continue to go to the remaining Communist states, such as Cuba and China. The formal Cold War may have dissolved with the collapse of the Soviet Union, but there remains an undercurrent of desire to locate alternatives to the Western, capitalist model embodied by the United States and its allies. For some, therefore, Russia still carries a legacy of some of the best parts of a social experiment. They continue their quest for a place where white and black can live and work together for the common good, as so expressively described by James Patterson, the Afro-Russian son of Lloyd Patterson of the *Black and White* film group:

> But I recall
> How two old women anxiously
> sang something beside my cradle
> and they bent over me, their skins different in color
> somehow very similar and dissimilar
> and their hands rocked me as one.[54]

APPENDIX: FAMILY LINES OF SOJOURNERS/EXPATRIATES

NOTE: This chart includes seventeen spouses/partners of the initial set of fourteen black sojourners/expatriates (not all the sojourners/expatriates married the mothers of their children). Their children, grandchildren, and great-grandchildren, along with all their spouses/partners, constitute another sixty-nine people. In total, this chart shows one hundred people, with some sojourners/expatriates and some of their children having more than one spouse/partner. Robert Robinson *(Black on Red)* mentions sixteen bi-racial children of the first generation of Afro-Russian descendants. He does not name them all, but of those listed in this chart (which shows twenty-four, born from the late 1920s to mid-1950s, in the second column), the only ones he may not have known of were Ollava Golden (b. 1929), Joseph Roane Jr. (b. 1932), and Dick Williams's child, all of whom lived far from Moscow; Lolita Rudd (b. 1933), who returned to the United States with her American mother in 1936; Smith's two children, who were born in Ethiopia after he left the Soviet Union in 1946; and Robert Zotov (b. c1955). Although Robinson knew John Sutton, he did not mention Sutton's son, Juan. The thirty-two Soviet and American spouses/partners listed here are described as either American (Polish/American Jew, American Jew, African American) or by their "nationality" as given in the Soviet system (Udmurt, Russian, woman from Batum, Lithuanian, Tatar, Bulgarian, Jewish Russian, Ukrainian). Other sources for the names and dates are Eslanda Goode (interviews), Amelia Tynes (interviews), William Davis (interviews), Allison Blakely *(Russia and the Negro)*, Yelena Khanga *(Soul to Soul)*, Homer Smith *(Black Man in Red Russia)*, William Patterson *(The Man Who Cried Genocide)*, and Lily Golden *(My Long Journey Home)*.

211

Sojourner/Expatriate	First Generation	Second Generation	Third Generation

Column headers: Sojourner/Expatriate — First Generation — Second Generation — Third Generation

(1) Lovett Fort-Whiteman (d. c1939)

Russian Jew

(2) Oliver Golden (d. 1940)

Anya (Udmurt)

Ollava Golden (b. 1929)

Oliver Golden (d. 1940)

Bertha Bialek (Polish/American Jew) (d. 1985)

Leah (Lily) Golden (b. 1934)

Abdullah Hanga (Khanga) (Zanzibari)

Yelena Khanga (b. 1962)

Russian

Liza (b. 2002)

(3) Frank Goode (d. 1967)

Woman from Batum

Frank Goode (d. 1967)

Alexandrovna Gushova (Russian)

Eslanda Goode (b. 1950)

Lithuanian

Alexander

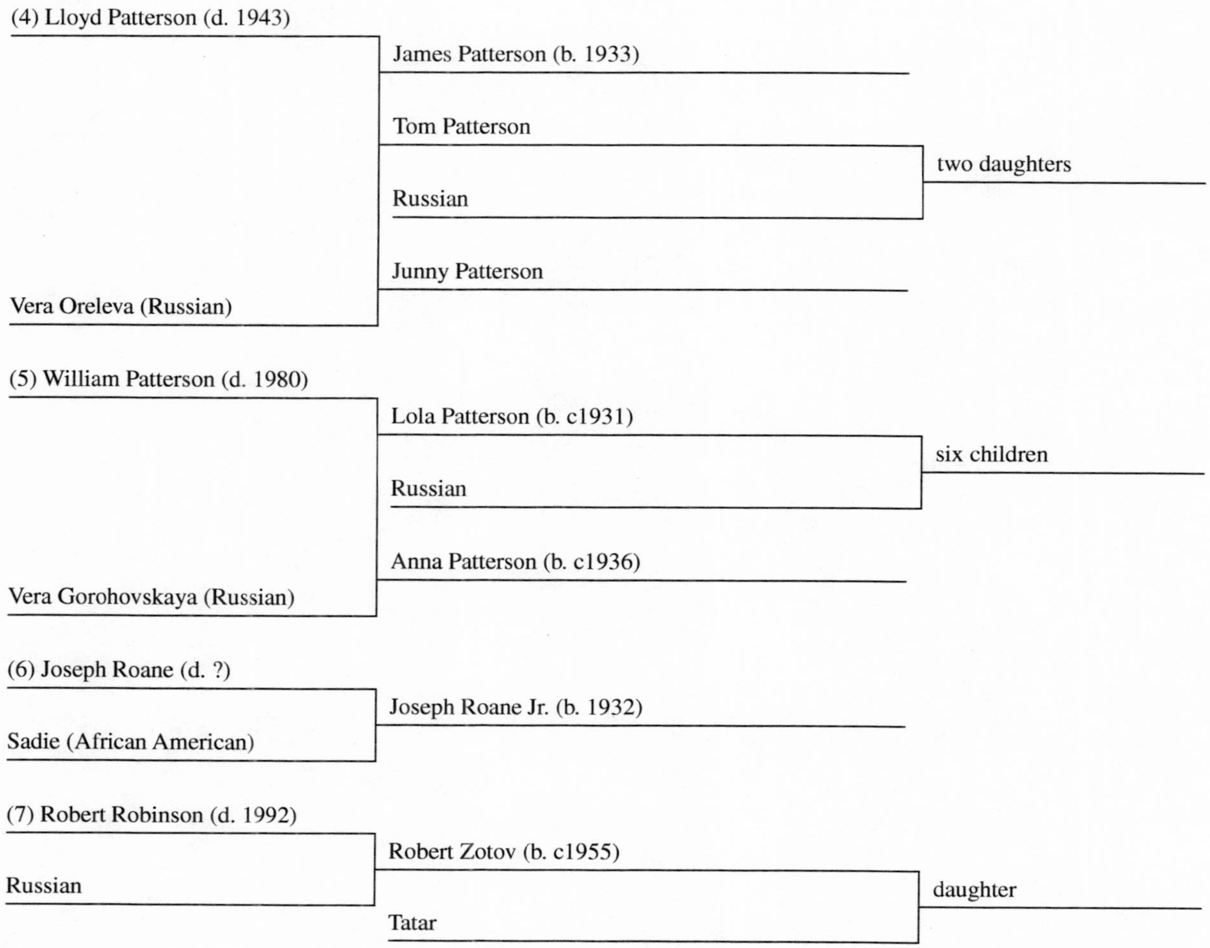

(4) Lloyd Patterson (d. 1943)

James Patterson (b. 1933)

Tom Patterson

Russian

two daughters

Junny Patterson

Vera Oreleva (Russian)

(5) William Patterson (d. 1980)

Lola Patterson (b. c1931)

Russian

six children

Anna Patterson (b. c1936)

Vera Gorohovskaya (Russian)

(6) Joseph Roane (d. ?)

Joseph Roane Jr. (b. 1932)

Sadie (African American)

(7) Robert Robinson (d. 1992)

Robert Zotov (b. c1955)

daughter

Tatar

Russian

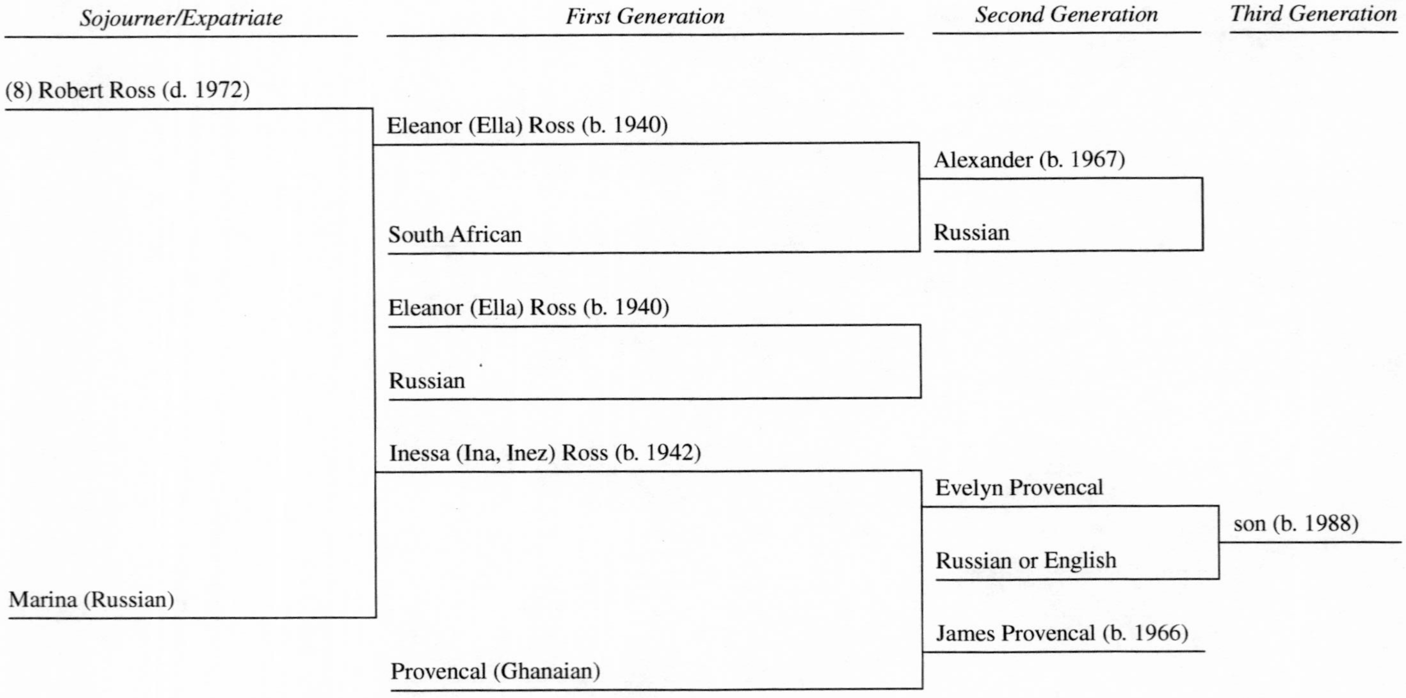

Sojourner/Expatriate   _First Generation_   _Second Generation_   _Third Generation_

(8) Robert Ross (d. 1972)

Eleanor (Ella) Ross (b. 1940)

South African

Alexander (b. 1967)

Russian

Eleanor (Ella) Ross (b. 1940)

Russian

Inessa (Ina, Inez) Ross (b. 1942)

Evelyn Provencal

Russian or English

son (b. 1988)

James Provencal (b. 1966)

Marina (Russian)

Provencal (Ghanaian)

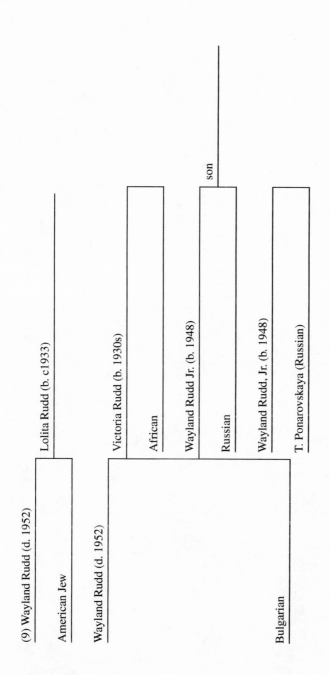

(9) Wayland Rudd (d. 1952)

American Jew

Lolita Rudd (b. c1933)

Wayland Rudd (d. 1952)

Bulgarian

Victoria Rudd (b. 1930s)

African

Wayland Rudd Jr. (b. 1948)

Russian

Wayland Rudd, Jr. (b. 1948)

T. Ponarovskaya (Russian)

son

Sojourner/Expatriate	*First Generation*	*Second Generation*	*Third Generation*
(10) Henry Scott (d. early 1940s)			
	Margaret (Marjorie, Margie, Ulamei) Scott (b. c1931)		
	Russian		
	Yelena (Lena) Scott (b. c1933)		
Valya (Russian)			
	Indian		
(11) Homer Smith (d. ?)			
	two children born in Ethiopia		
Marie Petrovna (Russian)			
(12) John Sutton (d. ?)			
	Juan Sutton (b. c1936)		
Russian			

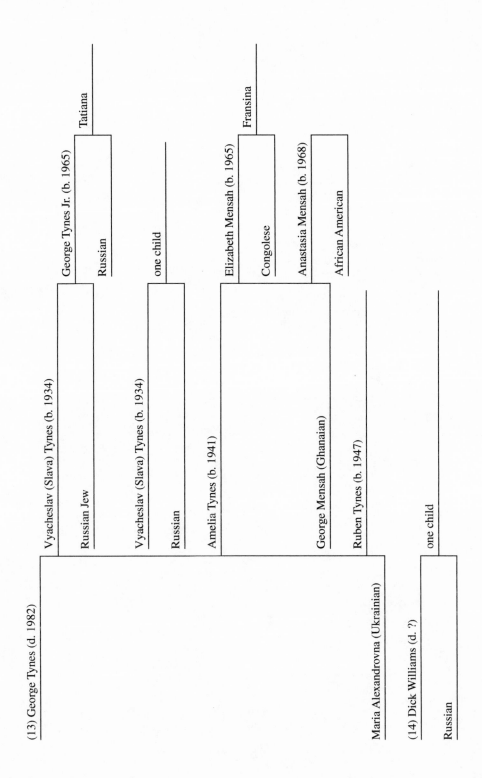

(13) George Tynes (d. 1982)

Vyacheslav (Slava) Tynes (b. 1934)

Russian Jew

George Tynes Jr. (b. 1965)

Russian

Tatiana

Vyacheslav (Slava) Tynes (b. 1934)

Russian

one child

Amelia Tynes (b. 1941)

George Mensah (Ghanaian)

Elizabeth Mensah (b. 1965)

Congolese

Fransina

Anastasia Mensah (b. 1968)

African American

Ruben Tynes (b. 1947)

Maria Alexandrovna (Ukrainian)

(14) Dick Williams (d. ?)

Russian

one child

NOTES

PREFACE

1. Fyodor Mikhailovich Dostoevsky, "The Grand Inquisitor," in *The Brothers Kara-mazov*, trans. Andrew R. MacAndrew (New York: Bantam Books, 2003), 340.
2. The city of Kiev is now in the independent country of Ukraine.

CHAPTER 1 *A Journey Begins*

1. Oliver Golden to George Washington Carver, December 12, 1930, quoted in Lily Golden, *My Long Journey Home* (Chicago: Third World Press, 2002), 199.
2. Carver to Oliver Golden, January 24, 1931, George Washington Carver Papers at Tuskegee Institute (hereafter, Carver Papers), National Historical Publications and Records Commission, Microfilm Collection, Library of Congress, Reel 12, #720.
3. The Golden story is told in detail in subsequent chapters.
4. Yelena Khanga, *Soul to Soul: A Black Russian American Family, 1865–1992* (New York: Norton, 1992), 48.

CHAPTER 2 *Early Sojourners Claude McKay and Otto Huiswood*

1. Claude McKay, "Soviet Russia and the Negro—An Essay by Claude McKay" [1922–1923], in *The Crisis Reader: Stories, Poetry, and Essays from the N.A.A.C.P.'s Crisis Magazine*, ed. Sondra Kathryn Wilson (New York: Modern Library, 1999), 276, 285.
2. Quoted in Wayne F. Cooper, *Claude McKay: Rebel Sojourner in the Harlem Renaissance* (New York: Schocken Books, 1987), 100.
3. Quoted in Wayne F. Cooper, "Claude McKay and the New Negro of the 1920's," *Modern American Poetry* <http://www.english.uiuc.edu/maps/poets/m_r/mckay/cooper.htm> (April 8, 2007).
4. Kate Baldwin, *Beyond the Color Line and the Iron Curtain: Reading Encounters between Black and Red, 1922–1963* (Durham, N.C.: Duke University Press, 2002), 14. Although the formal establishment of the U.S.S.R. (Union of Soviet Socialist Republics) was on December 30, 1922, Americans continued to refer to it as Soviet

Russia into the 1930s. Even as late as 1932, members of the *Black and White* film group were still using this term; Homer Smith, *Black Man in Red Russia: A Memoir* (Chicago: Johnson, 1964), 2. However, other sources began to use the terms *Soviet Union* and *U.S.S.R.*, more often in the latter part of the 1920s, and I have chosen to use *Soviet Union* when discussing those who went to study from the mid-1920s onward.

5. Quoted in Cooper, *Claude McKay*, 65.
6. George Hutchinson, *The Harlem Renaissance in Black and White* (Cambridge, Mass.: Harvard University Press, 1997), 414.
7. Quoted in Cooper, "Claude McKay and the New Negro."
8. Cooper, *Claude McKay*, 66.
9. Faith Berry, *Before and Beyond Harlem: Langston Hughes, a Biography* (New York: Citadel Press, 1992), 140–142. In the Scottsboro case (March 1931), nine boys riding on a crowded freight train traveling from Chattanooga to Memphis, Tennessee, were dragged off the train in Alabama and accused of raping two white women who had been riding on the same train. The boys were tried, and all but one were sentenced to death. International campaigns focused attention on their case and prevented the United States from following through with the death sentences. All remained on death row for years and some for decades. The last one was exonerated in 1976.
10. Tyrone Tillery, *Claude McKay: A Black Poet's Struggle for Identity* (Amherst: University of Massachusetts Press, 1992), 21–23.
11. Cooper, *Claude McKay*, 68.
12. Ibid.
13. Ibid., 71–72 and 90–91.
14. Hutchinson, *Harlem Renaissance in Black and White*, 263.
15. Haywood, whose political sensibilities developed in this same period, notes that "Blacks were needed to fill the labor vacuum caused by the war boom" and that thousands moved north "eager to escape the conditions of plantation serfdom. . . . The war and the riots left me bitter and frustrated." Harry Haywood, *Black Bolshevik: Autobiography of an Afro-American Communist* (Chicago: Liberator Press, 1978), 84, 87.
16. Cooper, *Claude McKay*, 100.
17. Ibid., 92–93. Also, see Hutchinson, *Harlem Renaissance in Black and White*, 264.
18. Tillery, *Claude McKay*, 41.
19. McKay claimed to have never formally joined the Communist Party. Cooper notes that he was on record as having been a member of the ABB, which was heavily influenced by Communists and which was known to have served as a conduit for blacks entering the Communist Party. Also, letters written by McKay while he was in the Soviet Union stated that he was a member of the Workers' Party and the ABB. Cooper, *Claude McKay*, 176, 184.
20. Cedric J. Robinson, *Black Marxism: The Making of the Black Radical Tradition* (Chapel Hill: University of North Carolina Press, 1983), 216–217.
21. The Comintern forced Reed's Communist Labor Party to merge with Charles Ruthenberg's United Communist Party. This merged party was later known as the Communist Party of the United States of America.
22. Baldwin, *Beyond the Color Line and the Iron Curtain*, 35–36.
23. Lenin (1870–1924) was the founder and first leader of Soviet Russia, later known as the Union of Soviet Socialist Republics.

24. Quoted in Harry Haywood, "The Struggle for the Leninist Power on the Negro Question in the U.S.A.," in *American Communism and Black Americans: A Documentary History, 1930–1934*, eds. Philip S. Foner and Herbert Shapiro (Philadelphia: Temple University Press, 1991), 96.

25. From "Draft Theses on the National-Colonial Question," as noted in Haywood, *Black Bolshevik*, 223.

26. Abel Startsev, "Notes by Lenin and an Unknown Soldier," in *Sputnik, Monthly Digest*, March 1969, 54–55, from an article that originally appeared in *Literaturnaya Gazetta*, based on research in the John Reed papers in the Houghton Library at Harvard University.

27. Cooper, *Claude McKay*, 107.

28. Ibid., 129.

29. Ibid., 133.

30. McKay, "Soviet Russia and the Negro," 280–281.

31. Baldwin, *Beyond the Color Line and the Iron Curtain*, 29, 28.

32. Allison Blakely, *Russia and the Negro: Blacks in Russian History and Thought* (Washington, D.C.: Howard University Press, 1986), 82.

33. Ibid., 82–83.

34. Cooper, *Claude McKay*, 171–172.

35. Blakely, *Russia and the Negro*, 84.

36. Baldwin, *Beyond the Color Line and the Iron Curtain*, 55.

37. Ibid., 29–30.

38. Ibid., 55.

39. Cooper, *Claude McKay*, 174.

40. Haywood, *Black Bolshevik*, 656, note 5.

41. Blakely, *Russia and the Negro*, 83.

42. Baldwin, *Beyond the Color Line and the Iron Curtain*, 37. Baldwin incorrectly identified the publication as "The International Press Correspondent." Other sources indicate it was the *International Press Correspondence*. See copy of speech at the Marxists Internet Archive, which lists the publication as the *International Press Correspondence*, 3 (January 5, 1923), 16–17 <www.marxists.org/history/usa/groups/abb/1922/1100-mckay-cominternspeech.pdf > (July 18, 2006). Baldwin (37–38) further raises concern that the translations, although disseminated rapidly, did not reflect the full implications of the original text.

43. McKay, "Soviet Russia and the Negro," 280.

44. Ibid., 280–281.

45. According to Harry Klehr, John Earl Haynes, and Kyrill M. Anderson, *The Soviet World of American Communism* (New Haven, Conn.: Yale University Press, 1998), 15–18, Reed, Benjamin Gitlow, and a group of disaffected members of the Socialist Party, who had been thrown out of the party, formed the Communist Labor Party on August 31, 1919. In response, another group in the Socialist Party, composed of Ruthenberg and Louis Fraina, joined left-wing socialists in forming an alternative to the Communist Labor Party—the Communist Party of America—almost immediately afterward. Although both parties professed loyalty to the newly formed Comintern, they adamantly refused to work together in the United States. Eventually, the Comintern prevailed and forced them to combine into one party. This new party was originally named the Workers Party; later it became the CPUSA.

46. Haywood, *Black Bolshevik*, 140.

47. Robinson, *Black Marxism*, 209.
48. Otto Huiswood (1893–1961) went to the Soviet Union first in 1922 and then returned to study and do Comintern work in 1927.
49. Foner and Shapiro, eds., *American Communism and Black Americans*, 358. Many delegates used pseudonyms to avoid detection by the U.S. or other non-Communist authorities.
50. Robinson, *Black Marxism*, 220.
51. Quoted in Baldwin, *Beyond the Color Line and the Iron Curtain*, 54, 50.
52. Foner and Shapiro, eds., *American Communism and Black Americans*, 358.
53. Quoted in Baldwin, *Beyond the Color Line and the Iron Curtain*, 55.
54. Blakely, *Russia and the Negro*, 84.
55. Baldwin, *Beyond the Color Line and the Iron Curtain*, 50.
56. Quoted in ibid., 49.
57. McKay, "Soviet Russia and the Negro," 281.
58. Baldwin, *Beyond the Color Line and the Iron Curtain*, 59–60.
59. Cooper, *Claude McKay*, 181–182.
60. Blakely, *Russia and the Negro*, 85.
61. Earl Ofari Hutchinson, *Blacks and Reds: Race and Class in Conflict, 1919–1990* (East Lansing: Michigan State University Press, 1995), 15.
62. McKay, "Soviet Russia and the Negro," 278–279.
63. Wilson Record, *The Negro and the Communist Party* (Chapel Hill: University of North Carolina Press, 1951), 22.
64. Robinson, *Black Marxism*, 220.
65. Haywood, *Black Bolshevik*, 225.
66. Quoted in Robinson, *Black Marxism*, 221.
67. Claude McKay, *A Long Way from Home* (New York: Arno Press and the *New York Times*, 1969).
68. Blakely, *Russia and the Negro*, 90. The Lenin School was set up in 1926 to serve the advanced students coming from the United States and Europe. Haywood was one of the first blacks to attend.
69. Baldwin, *Beyond the Color Line and the Iron Curtain*, 49–50. Also, see Blakely, *Russia and the Negro*, 84.
70. Haywood, *Black Bolshevik*, 147.
71. Foner and Shapiro, eds., *American Communism and Black Americans*, 358.
72. Blakely, *Russia and the Negro*, 92.
73. Haywood, *Black Bolshevik*, 147.
74. Blakely, *Russia and the Negro*, 85.
75. Ibid.
76. Cooper, *Claude McKay*, 180–181.
77. Cyril Briggs and Richard Moore, both of whom were active in the ABB and the CPUSA, were from Barbados.
78. McKay, "Soviet Russia and the Negro," 279, 286.

Chapter 3   *Harry Haywood, KUTVA, and Training Black Cadres*

1. Haywood, *Black Bolshevik*, 149, 151.
2. Ibid., 148.

3. Ibid., 148, 20. The Communist Party in the United States in the 1920s was known by various names: Communist Party, Workers Party, Workers "Communist" Party. See Harry Klehr, John Earl Haynes, and Fridrikh Igorevich Firsov, *The Secret World of American Communism* (New Haven, Conn.: Yale University Press, 1995), xxiv.
4. Haywood, *Black Bolshevik*, 117.
5. Ibid., 205–206.
6. Ibid., 24–25.
7. Ibid., 27, 80.
8. Ibid., 39.
9. Ibid., 42.
10. "Houston Riot of 1917," *The Online Handbook of Texas* <http://www.tsha.utexas.edu/handbook/online/articles/HH/jch4_print.html> (September 9, 2005).
11. Haywood, *Black Bolshevik*, 79.
12. Ibid., 54–55.
13. Ibid., 55, 64.
14. Ibid., 118.
15. Ibid., 84
16. Ibid., 1, 4.
17. Ibid., 96.
18. Ibid., 121.
19. Ibid., 129.
20. Haywood's sister, Eppa Hall; ibid., 140.
21. Robinson, *Black Marxism*, 216–217.
22. Haywood, *Black Bolshevik*, 131.
23. Ibid., 124.
24. Ibid., 126.
25. Ibid., 132.
26. Ibid. Haywood does not identify H. V. Phillips's first name(s).
27. Ibid., 134.
28. Fort-Whiteman was the first black American to receive political training when he went to the Soviet Union in 1924.
29. They would be at the University of the Toilers of the East, or KUTVA, a special political-training school run by the Comintern.
30. Haywood, *Black Bolshevik*, 146.
31. Hutchinson, *Blacks and Reds*, 16.
32. Haywood, *Black Bolshevik*, 144.
33. Hutchinson, *Blacks and Reds*, 43.
34. Haywood, *Black Bolshevik*, 147, 144.
35. The *New York Times* article, dated January 17, 1926, and entitled "Communists Boring into Negro Labor," does not identify the ten people.
36. Ibid.
37. Hutchinson, *Blacks and Reds*, 31.
38. Haywood, *Black Bolshevik*, 145, 146.
39. Ibid., 149.
40. Ibid., 153.
41. Ibid., 153, 155.

42. Blakely, *Russia and the Negro*, 82. In Russian, the name is Universitet Trydyash-chiysya Vostoka Imeni Stalina. Many institutions and people were named after Sta-lin. This institution was also often referred to as "the University of the East."

43. Haywood, *Black Bolshevik*, 155.

44. Ibid., 155–156.

45. Haywood does not give the full names of some of the students. In most cases, these are the only data available. Where available, I have added their full names in the footnotes. There is some confusion here about Mahoney. Mahoney was also identi-fied as a classmate of Otto's and as having come the year before. It is possible that his studies overlapped the two training periods.

46. Haywood, *Black Bolshevik*, 148. Otto also had a pseudonym, John Jones. Claude McKay, who had gone in 1922, used the pseudonym Eli Edwards. "Party Pseud-onyms" <http://www.marxists.org/subject/usa/eam/pseudonyms.html> (July 10, 2005). One should note that party pseudonyms were not exclusive and could be used by different persons in different periods.

47. Haywood, *Black Bolshevik*, 167. Haywood does not list all these blacks, but they most likely were Haywood, Bankole, and Williams, and in Otto's group: Otto Hall, Golden, Mahoney, Patterson, and either Denmark Vessey or Maude White, who were mentioned in William L. Patterson's book *The Man Who Cried Genocide* (New York: International, 1971), 103.

48. Blakely, *Russia and the Negro*, 144; also, Haywood, *Black Bolshevik*, 167–168; Smith, *Black Man in Red Russia*, 34–39.

49. Robert Ross (Johnson) and Henry Scott were among those identified; they were expelled after two years of study at KUTVA. See chapter 3, note 86.

50. Among the African Americans, Haywood identified Otto Hall (aka John Jones), Mahoney (aka Jim Farmer), Oliver Golden, Jane Golden, White, Fort-Whiteman, Philips, Leonard Patterson, William L. Patterson, James Ford, Helen McClain, Ma-rie Houston, Ike Hawkins, William S. Patterson (different from William L.), Bennet (aka N. Petrovsky), John Henry, Edward Welsh, Herbert Newton, Arthur Murphy, Charles Young, Mother Wright, Homer Smith, Lloyd Patterson, Langston Hughes, Louise Thompson, Wayland Rudd, Henry Lee Moon, Ted Poston, Loren Miller, Cyrill Briggs, Harris, and Arli-Titz.

51. Woodford McClellan, "Africans and Black Americans in the Comintern Schools, 1925–1934," *International Journal of African Historical Studies* 26, no. 2 (1993): 375.

52. For example, McClellan noted that "also in the group were the African 'Sone' (or 'Sonne,' real name Thomas Odabor), who came via England; 'Robert' (Pierre Kal-mek or Kalmak), via France"; ibid., 381.

53. Ibid., 373.

54. Blakely, *Russia and the Negro*, 90.

55. Fort-Whiteman announced that he had a group of ten, seven of whom were women, studying in Moscow in 1925. The *New York Times* article with this information, "Communists Boring into Negro Labor," appeared on January 17, 1926. The state-ment made here stems from data collected from Haywood, Robinson, Robeson, and others who mention predominantly male sojourners.

56. Haywood, *Black Bolshevik*, 217.

57. Patterson, *The Man Who Cried Genocide*, 91, 92. Sacco and Vanzetti were con-victed and electrocuted in 1927 for alleged robbery and murder. However, the case

was never conclusively proved and stands as an example of virulent xenophobia and antianarchist sentiments.

58. Ibid., 95–96.
59. Ibid., 97. After Ruthenberg's death, Lovestone was slated to take over the leadership of the CPUSA. He was expelled from the party on Stalin's orders two years later, when he would not agree to a transition. See Klehr, Haynes, and Firsov, *Secret World of American Communism*, 7.
60. Patterson, *The Man Who Cried Genocide*, 96.
61. Ibid., 98–99, 118.
62. For the Scottsboro case, see note 9 in Chapter 2.
63. Patterson, *The Man Who Cried Genocide*, 138.
64. Haywood, *Black Bolshevik*, 345.
65. Foner and Shapiro, eds., *American Communism and Black Americans*, 364, note 8.
66. Haywood, *Black Bolshevik*, 163–164.
67. Blakely, *Russia and the Negro*, 92, See also George Padmore, *Pan Africanism or Communism?* (New York: Doubleday, 1971), 297.
68. Haywood, *Black Bolshevik*, 160.
69. Ibid., 161.
70. Ibid., 212–213.
71. Ibid.
72. Ibid., 170–171.
73. Ibid., 340.
74. Ibid.
75. Ibid., 198.
76. Blakely, *Russia and the Negro*, 90.
77. Haywood, *Black Bolshevik*, 161.
78. McClellan, "Africans and Black Americans in the Comintern Schools, 1925–1934," 376.
79. Haywood, *Black Bolshevik*, 167.
80. McClellan, "Africans and Black Americans in the Comintern Schools, 1925–1934," 375–376.
81. See Chapter 5.
82. Quoted in McClellan, "Africans and Black Americans in the Comintern Schools, 1925–1934," 385.
83. Ibid., 384–385.
84. Ibid., 377, 375.
85. McClellan, "Africans and Black Americans in the Comintern Schools, 1925–1934," 377.
86. Robert Robinson, *Black on Red: My 44 Years inside the Soviet Union* (Washington, D.C.: Acropolis Books, 1988), 302–303. McClellan, "Africans and Black Americans in the Comintern Schools, 1925–1934," writes that "two whites and one black, Gary Johnson ("Robert Ross") . . . were expelled" (377). He does not identify the white students.
87. Robinson, *Black on Red*, 303.
88. William Davis, "How Negroes Live in Russia," *Ebony*, January 1960, 66.
89. Robinson, *Black on Red*, 303–304. More information about Robinson is given in Chapters 5 and 10, and additional information about Scott can be found in Chapter 10.

90. Klehr, Haynes, and Anderson, *Soviet World of American Communism*, 41.
91. Blakely, *Russia and the Negro*, 111. Also, see Haywood, *Black Bolshevik*, 218–280.
92. Haywood, *Black Bolshevik*, 219, 124–125, 219–220.
93. Haywood, *Black Bolshevik*, 291–292.
94. Blakely, *Russia and the Negro*, 125.
95. Haywood, *Black Bolshevik*, 329.
96. Ibid., 328, note 662.
97. Padmore, *Pan Africanism or Communism?* xv.
98. Hutchinson, *Blacks and Reds*, 53.
99. Harry Haywood, "Against Bourgeois-Liberal Distortions of Leninism on the Negro Question in the United States," in Foner and Shapiro, eds., *American Communism and Black Americans*, 26–27.
100. Ibid., 18.
101. Robinson, *Black Marxism*, 223.
102. Padmore, *Pan-Africanism or Communism?* 293.
103. Robinson, *Black Marxism*, 182, 255.
104. Blakely, *Russia and the Negro*, 91. Blakely also contended that Padmore's activism as a student leader had probably attracted the ire of the Ku Klux Klan, which was another reason for his hasty departure.
105. Padmore, *Pan-Africanism or Communism?* xxv.
106. Blakely, *Russia and the Negro*, 91.
107. Ibid., 112.
108. Ibid., 92.
109. Ibid., 91.
110. Ibid., 125.
111. Padmore, *Pan Africanism or Communism?* xxviii.
112. Ibid., 292.
113. Ibid., xxviii.
114. Haywood, *Black Bolshevik*, 338.
115. Ibid., 338–339.
116. Ibid., 389. Patterson was well aware of the problems as he and his Russian wife had decided not to fight this battle. Although they did not divorce when Patterson was ready to leave the Soviet Union in the late 1920s, they did amicably divorce years later. Patterson, *The Man Who Cried Genocide*, 109.
117. Haywood, *Black Bolshevik*, 339, 387–390.
118. Ibid., 312.
119. Haywood does not provide Nasanov's first name, but this was probably N. Nasanov per Klehr, Haynes, and Anderson, *The Soviet World of American Communism*, 359.
120. Haywood, *Black Bolshevik*, 332.
121. Ibid., 350.
122. Hutchinson, *Blacks and Reds*, 74.
123. Haywood, *Black Bolshevik*, 628, 630.
124. Ibid., 441. The Politboro consisted of the executive leadership of the CPUSA.
125. Haywood (*Black Bolshevik*, 468) noted that three thousand Americans volunteered for the Lincoln Brigades and of these about one hundred were black.
126. Ibid., 467–469.

127. Ibid., 500.
128. Ibid., 628.
129. Ibid.
130. Ibid., 630. Haywood died in 1985.

CHAPTER 4 *W.E.B. Du Bois and the Soviet Experiment*

1. Quoted in David Levering Lewis, *W.E.B. Du Bois: The Fight for Equality and the American Century, 1919–1963* (New York: Henry Holt, 2000), 203.
2. Ibid., 203.
3. W.E.B. Du Bois, "On the U.S.S.R.," *Labor Defender* (New York), November 1928, 248.
4. W.E.B. Du Bois, "Colonialism and the Russian Revolution," *New World Review* (November 1956): 18–21, in Herbert Aptheker, ed., *Writings by W.E.B. Du Bois in Periodicals Edited by Others*, vol. 4, *1945–1961* (Millwood, N.Y.: Kraus-Thomson, 1982), 275.
5. Blakely, *Russia and the Negro*, 102.
6. Ralph Ellison, *Invisible Man* (New York: Vintage Books, 1952).
7. Lenin started the New Economic Policy program in 1921 to encourage foreign investment and spur growth in the agrarian sector as the country emerged from its civil war.
8. Quoted in Baldwin, *Beyond the Color Line and the Iron Curtain*, 175.
9. The National Association for the Advancement of Colored People's journal *The Crisis: A Record of the Darker Races* was begun in 1910. Du Bois was its editor from 1910 to 1934.
10. Robeson also credited his African friends in England with having directed his attention to the developments under the Soviet experiment. Du Bois's Pan-African congresses were held in London in 1921 and 1923.
11. Herbert Aptheker, ed., *The Correspondence of W.E.B. Du Bois*, vol. 1, *Selections, 1877–1934* (Amherst: University of Massachusetts Press, 1973), 251–252.
12. Quoted in Lewis, *The Fight for Equality*, 195.
13. Jackson's visit predated the formal training programs established in 1926. However, he may have been one of the ten persons to whom Lovett Fort-Whiteman referred when he returned to the United States in 1925 to recruit others. (For additional information on Fort-Whiteman, see Chapters 3 and 10.)
14. Aptheker, ed., *The Correspondence of W.E.B. Du Bois*, 1:289–290.
15. Quoted in Lewis, *The Fight for Equality*, 197.
16. Quoted in ibid., 194–195.
17. Du Bois writes of attending the University of Berlin in 1892 (*In Battle for Peace: The Story of My Eighty-Third Birthday*, special ed., printed exclusively for the Committee for the Du Bois Foundation (New York: Masses and Mainstream, 1952), 20.) He completed two full years there but could not raise the funding to finish his studies toward a Ph.D. He returned to Harvard, where he completed his Ph.D. He returned in 1958 to the university in Berlin (then renamed Humboldt University), where he received an honorary doctorate. Lewis, *The Fight for Equality*, 560.
18. Lewis, *The Fight for Equality*, 199.
19. Quoted in ibid., 200, 201.

20. Du Bois published two other pieces in the *Crisis* in this early period: "My Recent Journey" (December 1926) and "Judging Russia" (February 1927).
21. Herbert Aptheker, ed., *The Correspondence of W.E.B. Du Bois*, vol. 2, *Selections, 1934–1944* (Amherst: University of Massachusetts Press, 1976), 76.
22. Ibid., 92.
23. Lewis, *The Fight for Equality*, 261.
24. Patterson had assumed the leadership of the ILD in 1931, after J. Louis Engdahl, its former leader, left on an extended international solidarity tour with the mothers of two of the Scottsboro Boys.
25. David Levering Lewis, *W.E.B. Du Bois: A Reader* (New York: Henry Holt, 1995), 583, 586.
26. Lewis, *The Fight for Equality*, 257.
27. Ibid., 258.
28. For Pickens's recantation, see Patterson, *The Man Who Cried Genocide*, 132.
29. Lewis, *The Fight for Equality*, 258–259.
30. Quoted in ibid., 259.
31. Ibid., 258–259.
32. Aptheker, ed., *The Correspondence of W.E.B. Du Bois*, 1:475, 482.
33. Lewis, *The Fight for Equality*, 405.
34. Aptheker, ed., *The Correspondence of W.E.B. Du Bois*, 2:137.
35. Lewis, *The Fight for Equality*, 389. See also Aptheker, ed., *The Correspondence of W.E.B. Du Bois*, 2:121–126, and Herbert Aptheker, *Writings by W.E.B. Du Bois in Periodicals Edited by Others*, vol. 3, *1935–1944* (Millwood, N.Y.: Kraus-Thomson, 1982), specifically, "Neuropa: Hitler's New World Order," 132–138, and "Prospect of a World without Race Conflict," 184–192.
36. Lewis, *The Fight for Equality*, 406.
37. Ibid., 390, 406. William Burroughs might have been Williana Burroughs, who worked for Radio Moscow.
38. Robinson's technical specialists went in 1930, Golden's agricultural specialists in 1931, the *Black and White* film group in 1932, and Paul Robeson in 1934.
39. Lewis, *The Fight for Equality*, 407.
40. Ibid., 408.
41. Ibid., 412–418.
42. Aptheker, ed., *Writings by W.E.B. Du Bois in Periodicals Edited by Others*, article published in *Soviet Russia Today* 17 (November 1949), 4:14–15, 32, 128.
43. Aptheker, ed., *The Correspondence of W.E.B. Du Bois*, 2:413.
44. Ibid., 378. Also, Du Bois had been the principal convener of the early Pan-African congresses of 1919, 1921, 1923, and 1927, held in Paris (1919) and London (1921, 1923, 1927).
45. Padmore, *Pan Africanism or Communism?* 148. Nkrumah's Ghana would be the first country to fully embrace the notion of Pan-Africanism. Both Padmore and Du Bois would eventually move there as well.
46. Herbert Aptheker, ed., *The Correspondence of W.E.B. Du Bois*, vol. 3, *Selections, 1944–1963* (Amherst: University of Massachusetts Press, 1978), 196, 260, 264.
47. Quoted in Lewis, *The Fight for Equality*, 544–545.
48. Quoted in ibid., 545.
49. Aptheker, ed., *Writings by W.E.B. Du Bois in Periodicals Edited by Others*, 4:129.
50. Quoted in Baldwin, *Beyond the Color Line and the Iron Curtain*, 169.

51. Aptheker, ed., *Writings by W.E.B. Du Bois in Periodicals Edited by Others*, 4:131, 132.

52. Quotes from Lewis, *The Fight for Equality*, 542, 545–547.

53. Ibid., 548.

54. See #2063 Foreign Agents Registration Act (Department of Justice, *USAM, Title 9, Criminal Resource Manual*) <http://www.usdoj.gov/usao/eousa/foia_reading_room/usam/title9/crm02063.htm.> (September 9, 2005). Also, by way of further background, in a 1953 letter to the prosecuting attorney, W. R. Cole, Attorney General Don Easvold wrote, "The Foreign Agents Registration Act (22 U.S.C.A. § 611 *et seq.*) . . . requires every agent of a foreign principal to file a registration statement with the Attorney General. The matters to be covered in the registration statement and the procedure to be followed are set forth in long and involved detail in the first sections of the act. Finally it provides that failure to register shall be a crime and imposes penalties. . . . After reviewing the act in its entirety, the court [in *United States v. Peace Information Center*, 97 F. Supp. 255 (1951)] conceded that, in borderline cases, certain persons may have doubt whether they are within the terms of the act. But it was held that such a circumstance is not sufficient to vitiate the law. The cited case is authority for the proposition that the crime denounced need not be defined so precisely that the application of the statute is clear beyond doubt in every case." Source: <http://www.atg.wa.gov/opinions/1951-53/opinion_1951-53_491.html> (September 9, 2005).

55. Lewis, *The Fight for Equality*, 550.

56. Aptheker, ed., *Writings by W.E.B. Du Bois in Periodicals Edited by Others*, 4:274–275.

57. Kent, a photographer who had traveled to the Soviet Union previously, had been denied a passport to travel to London for the World Peace Conference and had been required to sign an affidavit that he had no affiliation with the Communist Party. Briehl, who was a physician, was also required, upon applying for his passport, to produce an affidavit that he was not a member of the Communist Party.

58. Lewis, *The Fight for Equality*, 559. See also Martin Duberman, *Paul Robeson: A Biography* (New York: New Press, 1989), 463.

59. Quoted in Lewis, *The Fight for Equality*, 558.

60. Aptheker, ed., *The Correspondence of W.E.B. Du Bois*, 3:420–421.

61. Baldwin, *Beyond the Color Line and the Iron Curtain*, 176. Baldwin, 197, has Du Bois receiving the Lenin award before he left for the Soviet Union in 1958; Blakely in *Russia and the Negro*, 102 and 177, note 37, puts the award in 1959, after Du Bois returned to the United States.

62. Langston Hughes, *I Wonder as I Wander* (1956; repr., New York: Thunder's Mouth Press, 1989), 102.

63. Quoted in Lewis, *The Fight for Equality*, 561.

64. Quoted in ibid., 560–561.

65. Gerald Horne, *Black and Red: W.E.B. Du Bois and the Afro-American Response to the Cold War, 1944–1963* (Albany, N.Y.: State University of New York Press, 1985), 9.

66. Aptheker, ed., *Writings by W.E.B. Du Bois in Periodicals Edited by Others*, 4:290.

67. Quoted in Baldwin, *Beyond the Color Line and the Iron Curtain*, 198, 199.

68. Khanga, *Soul to Soul*, 21.

69. Golden, *My Long Journey Home*, 87.

70. Duberman, *Paul Robeson*, 473.
71. Lewis, *The Fight for Equality*, 413–414.
72. Ibid.
73. Lewis, *Du Bois Reader*, 626–630.
74. W.E.B. Du Bois, "China and Africa," speech given at Pekin University, in *The World and Africa: An Inquiry into the Part Which Africa Has Played in World History* (New York: International Press, 1965), 311.
75. Ibid.
76. Lewis, *The Fight for Equality*, 564.
77. Ibid., 566.
78. Du Bois, "China and Africa," 313, 315–316.
79. Du Bois, *In Battle for Peace*, 163–164.

CHAPTER 5 *Robert Robinson and the Technical Specialists*

1. Robinson, *Black on Red*, 81.
2. Ibid., 26, 37.
3. Smith, *Black Man in Red Russia*, 208.
4. Smith had three jobs over his fourteen-year tenure: he went as part of the *Black and White* film group, worked as a postal-systems specialist, and finally became a foreign correspondent.
5. Robinson, *Black on Red*, 62.
6. Quoted in Ronald Grigor Suny, *The Soviet Experiment: Russia, the USSR, and the Successor States* (Oxford: Oxford University Press, 1998), 62–64.
7. Ibid., 233.
8. Roy Medvedev, *Let History Judge: The Origins and Consequences of Stalinism* (New York: Columbia University Press, 1989), 248.
9. Robert Service, *A History of Twentieth-Century Russia* (Cambridge, Mass.: Harvard University Press, 1998), 170, 177. See also Vincent Baker, "American Workers in the Soviet Union between the Two World Wars: From Dream to Disillusionment" (master's thesis, College of Arts and Sciences, West Virginia University, 1998), 9. Baker noted that according to the July 1931 *Business Week*, forty-four companies were doing business in the Soviet Union with products "ranging from rubber to radios to fertilizer." He further commented, "The magnitude of Soviet purchases in the U.S. is difficult to estimate[; however] the *Business Week* article raises two interesting points—first, the economic benefit to the U.S. of Soviet purchases was seen as being significant, and, second, Soviet business seemed good, even to such a conservative publication."
10. Smith, *Black Man in Red Russia*, 209–211.
11. Hughes, *I Wonder as I Wander*, 188.
12. Other agencies included the Society for Technical Aid to Soviet Russia and the American-Russian Chamber of Business; Baker, "American Workers in the Soviet Union," 9. Amtorg handled both individual American workers and groups. It also dealt directly with corporations. Baker "American Workers in the Soviet Union," 7.
13. Ibid., 4, 9.
14. Ibid., 6.
15. Service, *A History of Twentieth-Century Russia*, 177.
16. Baker, "American Workers in the Soviet Union," 8.

17. Ibid.
18. Smith, *Black Man in Red Russia*, 210.
19. Baker, "American Workers in the Soviet Union," 12.
20. "Americans Essay Color Bar in Soviet," *New York Times*, August 10, 1930, 9.
21. "Reds Send Three to Russia," *Amsterdam News*, 1931 (specific date unknown).
22. Robinson, *Black on Red*, 85–86.
23. Ibid., 24.
24. LeRoi Jones, "The City," in *Afro-American History: Past to Present*, ed. Henry Drewry and Cecilia H. Drewry (New York: Scribner, 1971), 366.
25. Robinson, *Black on Red*, 23–24.
26. Ibid., 28–29.
27. Ibid., 25, 26, 63, 28.
28. Ibid., 29.
29. Ibid., 27–28.
30. Ibid., 29–30.
31. Ibid., 30–31.
32. Ibid., 35.
33. Ibid.
34. Quoted in ibid., 36.
35. Ibid., 37–42.
36. Ibid., 37, 39.
37. Ibid., 66.
38. Ibid.
39. Ibid., 67.
40. Ibid., 68.
41. Haywood, *Black Bolshevik*, 339–340.
42. "Americans Essay Color Bar in Soviet," "Attack on Negro Red Still Stirs Moscow," and "Apologizes to Russians," *New York Times*, August 10, August 11, and August 22, 1930, respectively.
43. Robinson, *Black on Red*, 108.
44. Langston Hughes, "Moscow and Me," *Innostranaiya Literatura* (*International Literature*, Moscow), July 1933, in Faith Berry, ed., *Good Morning Revolution: The Uncollected Social Protest Writing of Langston Hughes* (New York: Lawrence Hill, 1973), 74.
45. Hughes, *I Wonder as I Wander*, 87.
46. Robinson did not decode the acronym but stated that this organization handled the travel arrangements for the workers.
47. Ibid., 79–81.
48. Ibid., 25, 128.
49. Ibid., 82, 29.
50. Ibid., 82.
51. Ibid., 84.
52. Wayland Rudd of the *Black and White* film group went home for a period in 1934, and George Tynes of the agricultural specialist group went home briefly in 1936.
53. Robinson, *Black on Red*, 104.
54. Ibid., 312.
55. Quoted in ibid., 317.
56. Quoted in ibid., 317–318.

57. Ibid., 108.
58. Ibid.
59. Ibid., 109.
60. Ibid., 110.
61. Ibid., 107, 112.
62. Ibid., 343.
63. Ibid., 251.
64. Additional information on the agricultural specialists appears in Chapters 6 and 7.
65. Smith, *Black Man in Red Russia*, 2.
66. Haywood, *Black Bolshevik*, 98.
67. Smith, *Black Man in Red Russia*, 2.
68. Ibid.
69. Smith, *Black Man in Red Russia*, vii.
70. Ibid., 2.
71. For example, see Berry, *Before and Beyond Harlem*, 183 and 346, note 9.
72. Baldwin, *Beyond the Color Line and the Iron Curtain*, 96–98.
73. Hughes, *I Wonder as I Wander*, 101–102.
74. Smith, *Black Man in Red Russia*, 9–10.
75. Ibid., 10.
76. Ibid., 12.
77. Ibid., 5–6, 17.
78. Ibid, 18.
79. Ibid., 17.
80. Ibid., 56, 76.
81. Ibid., 58.
82. Ibid.
83. Ibid, 60.
84. Robinson, *Black on Red*, 109–110.
85. Smith, *Black Man in Red Russia*, 67.
86. Ibid., 96.
87. Ibid., 172.
88. Ibid., 105.
89. Ibid., 101.
90. Ibid., 202–203.
91. Ibid., 213.
92. Ibid.
93. The following discussion is extracted from Smith, *Black Man in Red Russia*, 127; Klehr, Haynes, and Firsov, *Secret World of American Communism*, 199–202; and a letter from Charles Burroughs Sr. to Mrs. Charles Young, Colonel Charles Young Collection, 1897–1931, Manuscript Collections, The African-American Experience in Ohio, 1850–1920, Ohio Historical Society (hereafter, Young Collection), letter #17 <http://dbs.ohiohistory.org/africanam/mss/831.cfm> (August 7, 2006).
94. Jack Houston, "Going Home . . . to the USSR/ Chicagoan Returns to Boyhood Residence after 42 Years," *Chicago Tribune*, May 17, 1987, Chicagoland Section, 3.
95. Letter from Charles Burroughs Sr. to Mrs. Charles Young, Young Collection, letter #17.
96. Houston, "Going Home . . . to the USSR," 3.

97. Hutchinson, *Blacks and Reds*, 96–97. See also Klehr, Haynes, and Firsov, *Secret World of American Communism*, 199.

98. Quoted in Klehr, Haynes, and Firsov, *Secret World of American Communism*, 200.

99. Hughes, *I Wonder as I Wander*, 104.

100. Berry, ed., *Good Morning Revolution*, 80. See also Blakely, *Russia and the Negro*, 96.

101. Hughes, *I Wonder as I Wander*, 165.

102. Ibid., 163–164.

103. Ibid., 176.

104. Ibid., 179.

105. Ibid., 177–180.

106. Ibid., 181.

107. Ibid., 148.

108. Charles H. Nichols, ed., *Arna Bontemps—Langston Hughes Letters, 1925–1967* (New York: Dodd, Mead, 1980), 435.

109. Smith, *Black Man in Red Russia*, 208–209.

110. Ibid., 64.

111. Robinson, *Black on Red*, 13–14.

112. Ibid.

CHAPTER 6 *George Washington Carver, Oliver Golden,
and the Soviet Experiment*

1. Oliver Golden to George Washington Carver, April 18, 1931, quoted in Golden, *My Long Journey Home*, 203.

2. Golden to Carver, December 12, 1930, quoted in Golden, *My Long Journey Home*, 199.

3. Carver to Golden, January 24, 1931, Carver Papers, Reel 12, #720.

4. Golden to Carver, April 18, 1931, quoted in Golden, *My Long Journey Home*, 202.

5. Service, *A History of Twentieth-Century Russia*, 153.

6. Medvedev, *Let History Judge*, 202.

7. Ibid., 248, 227.

8. For the Alabama work, see Marc S. Miller, ed., *Working Lives: The Southern Exposure History of Labor in the South* (New York: Pantheon Books, 1981), 121.

9. Golden to Carver, December 12, 1930 and April 18, 1931, quoted in Golden, *My Long Journey Home*, 199, 202–203.

10. Quoted in Khanga, *Soul to Soul*, 77.

11. Ibid., 84.

12. *Guide to the Microfilm Edition of the Carver Papers*, Reel 9, correspondence, 22.

13. "Colored Chemist Thrills Br'water [Bridgewater]," *Daily News Record*, Carver Papers, Reel 60, #899.

14. Ibid. See also "Legends of Tuskegee," George W. Carver Museum at the Tuskegee Institute National Historic Site <http://www.nps.gov/history/museum/exhibits/tuskegee/gwcgallery.htm> (November 25, 2007).

15. "Roosevelt Medals Presented to Three: Carver, Sandburg, and General McCoy Praise Late President," *New York Times*, October 28, 1939, 7 <http://select.nytimes.com/gst/abstract.html?res=F40C17F63B5E10728DDDA10A94D8415B898FF1D3> (November 25, 2007).

16. Carver to Messrs. McNeill and Libby of Honolulu Limited, Libby's Pine Apple Products, March 4, 1929, Carver Papers, Reel 11, #730.
17. Carver to Dr. C. F. Andrews, February 24, 1929, Carver Papers, Reel 11, #704. Extracts of this correspondence also appeared in several newspapers, such as the Tulsa, Oklahoma, *Eagle* (December 27, 1930) and the Moultre, Georgia, *Observer* (December 15, 1930), Carver Papers, Reel 60, #1058.
18. *Guide to the Microfilm Edition of the Carver Papers*, 13.
19. Carver to Robert Moton, February 27, 1929, Carver Papers, Reel 11, #712.
20. Marlene Park, "Lynching and Antilynching: Art and Politics in the 1930s," *Prospects*, no. 18 (1993): 311.
21. *Guide to the Microfilm Edition of the Carver Papers*, 21.
22. Quoted in "Enthusiasm of Hearers Stirred by Dr. Geo. W. Carver's Address," *Columbus Inquirer* (Georgia), June 18, 1929, Carver Papers, Reel 60, #981.
23. "Colored Chemist Thrills Br'water."
24. Quoted in "Russia Seeks Doctor Carver's Aid for Cotton," *East Tennessee News*, January 22, 1931, Carver Papers, Reel 61, #002.
25. Carver to John Sutton, January 26, 1931, Carver Papers, Reel 12, # 731.
26. Carver to Golden, January 24, 1931, Carver Papers, Reel 12, #720.
27. Golden to Carver, April 18, 1931, quoted in Golden, *My Long Journey Home*, 202.
28. Ibid., 202–203.
29. Langston Hughes, " Cowards from the Colleges," *Crisis*, August 1934, in Berry, ed., *Good Morning Revolution*, 55, 62.
30. Carver was engaged in a number of projects prior to World War I, including not only in Japan and Korea but also in Liberia, Sierra Leone, Kenya, Malawi, and the southern African region. "The Tuskegee Idea—Past," *Tuskegee Idea* (magazine published by Tuskegee University Press), c. 1990.
31. Golden's granddaughter raised this question as well; Khanga, *Soul to Soul*, 76.
32. "Russia Seeks Doctor Carver's Aid for Cotton," *East Tennessee News*, January 22, 1931, Carver Papers, Reel 61, #002.
33. "Russia Calls Carver," *Christian Index* (Baptist Convention of the State of Georgia), March 19, 1931, Carver Papers, Reel 61, #0021.
34. Quoted in Golden, *My Long Journey Home*, 206.
35. Charles Burroughs Sr. to Mrs. Young, Young Collection <http://dbs.ohiohistory.org/africanam/mss/831.cfm> (December 3, 2005).
36. Blakely, *Russia and the Negro*, 96–98. Also, Langston Hughes, "Going South in Russia," *Crisis*, June 1934, in Berry, ed., *Good Morning Revolution*, 80.
37. Information on Young in "Son of Colonel Charles Young Off to Russia," *Baltimore Afro-American*, October 17, 1931.
38. Golden to Carver, quoted in Golden, *My Long Journey Home*, 207.
39. Some sources list the group as having fourteen members; others, sixteen. None of the sources identifies all sixteen people; however, the *Baltimore Afro-American* article published on October 17, 1931, noted that there were "eleven cotton specialists" and "a civil engineer and four other workers" ; "Son of Colonel Charles Young Off to Russia." Although Khanga (*Soul to Soul*, 72) states the number as fourteen, including Golden and his wife Bertha, she does not identify all those who went in this group. A photo in Lily Golden's book *My Long Journey Home* (unnumbered page between pages 88 and 89) shows fourteen people of whom five are women and nine are men. The only women identified in any sources were Bertha

Bialek Golden, Sadie Roane, and Frank Faison's wife (unnamed); the other two women in the photo are unidentified. For more details on this group, see Chapter 7.

40. Blakely, *Russia and the Negro*, 96–98. See also Khanga, *Soul to Soul*, 72.

41. One of these was Bertha Bialek Golden, Golden's second wife, who was a Polish Jewish immigrant to the United States. She met Golden when he returned from his studies in the Soviet Union. Khanga, *Soul to Soul*, 61.

CHAPTER 7 *The Agricultural Specialists Journey to the Soviet Union*

1. John Sutton to Carver, January 7, 1932, Carver Papers, Reel 13, #532. Permission granted by Sutton family.

2. Ibid.

3. For a discussion of the actual number of blacks in the group, see Chapter 6, note 39.

4. Golden, *My Long Journey Home*, 6–7.

5. Quoted in Khanga, *Soul to Soul*, 61.

6. Ibid., 59.

7. Golden, *My Long Journey Home*, 9.

8. Khanga, *Soul to Soul*, 61–70.

9. Golden, *My Long Journey Home*, 10, and Khanga, *Soul to Soul*, 70, questioned whether Bertha and Oliver formally married, maintaining that they had a common-law union. In any case, they lived together continuously until Golden's death in 1940.

10. Golden, *My Long Journey Home*, 10; Khanga, *Soul to Soul*, 63.

11. Khanga, *Soul to Soul*, 76

12. Golden, *My Long Journey Home*, 11–12.

13. Blakely, *Russia and the Negro*, 96–99. Golden, *My Long Journey Home*, has a photo showing fourteen people (unnumbered page between pages 88 and 89). A 1932 telegram in support of the Scottsboro Boys in the same book (197) lists the names: "Mr. and Mrs. O. J. Golden, Joseph Roane, J. B. Sutton, Mr. and Mrs. Frank Faison, B. C. Curry, Bernard C. Powers, George Tynes, A. M. Overton, Frank Gordon, Mr. and Mrs. B. L. Hopkins, Miss Charlotte B. Hopkins." The name B. L. Curry appears here rather than the Welton Curry of the newspaper article; this discrepancy may reflect an error on the part of the article writer. Note that Roane's name was also misspelled in the article. Charles Young's name does not appear on this telegram, perhaps an indication that he was posted elsewhere at the time.

14. "Son of Colonel Charles Young Off to Russia."

15. Ibid. The initials given for Hopkins in the article, B. L., match those given in the telegram sent from Uzbekistan. Although Blakely (*Russia and the Negro*, 960) gives the initials as C. T., he does not provide a direct source. He also does not list all eleven members.

16. "Son of Colonel Charles Young Off to Russia."

17. Khanga, *Soul to Soul*, 74. Though Khanga stated that Golden was the only card-carrying Communist, it was known that her grandmother had joined the CPUSA with her brother.

18. Ibid., 77.

19. Ibid., 78.

20. Quoted in ibid., 78–79.
21. Golden, *My Long Journey Home*, 12.
22. Khanga, *Soul to Soul*, 79.
23. The Soviets changed their calendar from the Julian calendar to the modern one, used by most Western nations, in the 1920s. The difference between the two ranges around eleven days. Thus, October 25 in the Julian calendar became November 6 in the new dating system. The name of the holiday, the October Revolution, has remained, although its commemoration occurs in November.
24. Golden, *My Long Journey Home*, 12. Hughes, *I Wonder as I Wander*, 103, recorded his journey as having taken five days; however, he took the train from Moscow, not Leningrad, which was further west, on the Russian coast.
25. Hughes, *I Wonder as I Wander*, 103–104.
26. The tsarist presence began officially with the assumption of Ivan "the Terrible" to the throne in 1547. The tsars ruled Russia up to the Bolshevik Revolution in 1917, almost four hundred years. See David MacKenzie and Michael W. Curran, *A History of Russia, the Soviet Union and Beyond* (Belmont, Calif.: Wadsworth, 2002), 118–119.
27. Hughes, *I Wonder as I Wander*, 174.
28. Khanga, *Soul to Soul*, 80.
29. "History of Tashkent," *The World of Central Asia with Advantour* <http://www.advantour.com/uzbekistan/tashkent/history.htm> (September 2, 2006).
30. Hughes, *I Wonder as I Wander*, 142.
31. Eslanda Goode interviews, Lincoln University, Lincoln University, Pennsylvania, 1993.
32. Khanga, *Soul to Soul*, 126.
33. Hughes, *I Wonder as I Wander*, 181.
34. Ibid., 177–178.
35. Ibid., 179.
36. Ibid., 178–179.
37. Ibid., 180.
38. Ibid., 176.
39. Golden, *My Long Journey Home*, 12, had a different spelling of the town name. Other sources, including her daughter, Khanga, *Soul to Soul*, 80, spelled it Yangiyul.
40. Golden, *My Long Journey Home*, 12–13.
41. Hughes (*I Wonder as I Wander*, 180) mentioned meeting "three or four jovial colored wives." Blakely (*Russia and the Negro*, 97) stated, "Roane and Faison were accompanied by their wives. Golden brought along his second wife [Bertha], who was of Polish-American descent." Frank Faison's wife is never named and remains a shadowy figure.
42. Khanga does not provide a last name for Pearl.
43. Quoted in Khanga, *Soul to Soul*, 60–61.
44. Quoted in Blakely, *Russia and the Negro*, 98.
45. Ibid.
46. Ibid., 97.
47. Robinson, *Black on Red*, 29.
48. Quoted in Khanga, *Soul to Soul*, 79.
49. Blakely, *Russia and the Negro*, 98.
50. Khanga, *Soul to Soul*, 78.

51. Blakely, *Russia and the Negro*, 98.
52. Ibid.
53. Khanga, *Soul to Soul*, 83–84.
54. Ibid., 80.
55. Ibid., 83–84.
56. Ibid., 73.
57. Ibid., 80.
58. Ibid.
59. Suny, *The Soviet Experiment*, 181. Also see Khanga, *Soul to Soul*, 80.
60. Khanga, *Soul to Soul*, 80.
61. Blakely, *Russia and the Negro*, 97.
62. Quoted in Khanga, *Soul to Soul*, 84.
63. Ibid., 86.
64. Golden to Carver, August 19, 1931, and Sutton, telegram to Carver, October 15, 1931, in Golden, *My Long Journey Home*, 207–208.
65. Sutton to Carver, January 7, 1932, Carver Papers, Reel 13, #532. Mrs. Sutton's name is unknown.
66. Ibid.
67. This address suggests a version of Krasnodar, which is in the northern region of the Caucuses district. The second part of the address, Ceb-Kab, appears to represent Sev(r)-Cav, which could mean Northern Caucasus (Sevr Kavkaz in Russian).
68. Robinson, *Black on Red*, 323. Blakely, *Russia and the Negro*, 99, confirms this assessment.
69. Blakely, *Russia and the Negro*, 99.
70. Robinson, *Black on Red*, 323.
71. Ibid., 323–324.
72. Khanga, *Soul to Soul*, 79.
73. Ibid., 91.
74. Ibid., 92.
75. Ibid., 86.
76. Golden, *My Long Journey Home*, 9.
77. Khanga, *Soul to Soul*, 77.
78. Hughes, *I Wonder as I Wander*, 176.

CHAPTER 8 *Langston Hughes and the* **Black and White** *Film Group*

1. Hughes, *I Wonder as I Wander*, 73.
2. Ibid., 65.
3. Smith, *Black Man in Red Russia*, 1.
4. Henry Lee and Mollie Moon Collection (hereafter, Moon Collection), Schomburg Center for Research in Black Culture, New York Public Library, Box 14, Memoirs folder.
5. Berry, *Before and Beyond Harlem*, 156.
6. Hughes, *I Wonder as I Wander*, 65, 70; Smith, *Black Man in Red Russia*, 23, 24; Berry, *Before and Beyond Harlem*, 346, note 9. Berry contends that Hughes confused Winwood with Garner, both of whom were well-known performers.
7. Blakely, *Russia and the Negro*, 93, and Amelia Tynes interviews, Washington, D.C., 2001.

8. Hughes, *I Wonder as I Wander*, 70.
9. Moon Collection, Box 14, Memoirs folder.
10. Berry, *Before and Beyond Harlem*, 154–155.
11. Hughes, *I Wonder as I Wander*, 69.
12. Quoted in Khanga, *Soul to Soul*, 78.
13. Berry, *Before and Beyond Harlem*, 155, 105, 112, 157.
14. Hughes, *I Wonder as I Wander*, 71.
15. Ibid., 72.
16. Ibid, 73.
17. Ibid.
18. Mezhabpomfilm was the full name of Meschrabpom.
19. *Komsomolskaya Pravda* (issue no. 147), in War Department of the Legation of the United States of America (in Riga, Latvia), report from Charge d'Affairs Felix Cole, to the Secretary of State in Washington, D.C. (Doc. # 537, July 8, 1932). This is an English version of the original Russian article.
20. Ibid.
21. Hughes, "Moscow and Me," 67.
22. Smith, *Black Man in Red Russia*, 25.
23. Berry, *Before and Beyond Harlem*, 158.
24. Hughes, "Moscow and Me," 67.
25. Ibid., 68. Also, see Berry, *Before and Beyond Harlem*, 158.
26. Report from Charge d'Affairs Cole.
27. Hughes, *I Wonder as I Wander*, 87.
28. Ibid., 87.
29. Ibid., 74. The campaign had been being waged since the spring of 1931. This was the same case that inspired the agricultural specialist group in Uzbekistan to send a support telegram in April 1932 (Golden, *My Long Journey Home*, 197).
30. Quoted in Berry, *Before and Beyond Harlem*, 142. The poem and article appeared in the June 25, 1932, *Baltimore Afro-American*.
31. Hughes, "Moscow and Me," 73.
32. Berry, *Before and Beyond Harlem*, 161.
33. Ibid., 146.
34. Smith, *Black Man in Red Russia*, 22.
35. Berry, *Before and Beyond Harlem*, 160.
36. Ibid., 157.
37. Ibid.
38. Ibid., 152, 153. See also Smith, *Black Man in Red Russia*, 23; Arnold Rampersad and David Roessel, eds., *The Collected Poems of Langston Hughes* (New York: Vintage Books, 1994), 10.
39. Robert S. Boynton, "The Red and the Black," *New York Times Magazine*, January 2, 2000, 22.
40. Berry, *Before and Beyond Harlem*, 129.
41. Hughes, *I Wonder as I Wander*, 3–4.
42. Quoted in Berry, *Before and Beyond Harlem*, 152.
43. Hughes, *I Wonder as I Wander*, 65. Some black writers, like Wallace Thurman, found ways to work but only as ghost writers. See Berry, *Before and Beyond Harlem*, 152.

44. Ford was credited with proposing the original idea of the film when he was visiting the Soviet Union earlier. He considered this a logical extension of the Negro Question. But although the Comintern liked the idea in Moscow, it got little support from the CPUSA.
45. Baldwin, *Beyond the Color Line and the Iron Curtain*, 96. Also, see Arnold Rampersad, *The Life of Langston Hughes*, vol. 1, *1920–1941, I, Too, Sing America* (New York: Oxford University Press, 1986), 235.
46. Thompson did not want the fact that she was female to get in the way of the Co-operating Committee's work. Stereotypical views of the time devalued projects headed by women.
47. Domingo was a prominent West Indian, the first editor of Marcus Garvey's *Negro World*. See also Berry, *Before and Beyond Harlem*, 155.
48. Baldwin, *Beyond the Color Line and the Iron Curtain*, 96.
49. Ibid.
50. Smith, *Black Man in Red Russia*, 23.
51. Baldwin, *Beyond the Color Line and the Iron Curtain*, 96, 97.
52. Ibid., 96. In letters between Arna Bontemps and Hughes, it is clear that Bontemps also speculated about joining the group; see letter dated April 25th (1932) from Bontemps to Hughes, in Nichols, ed., *Arna Bontemps—Langston Hughes Letters*, 24.
53. Moon Collection, Box 14, Memoirs folder, 12.
54. One can understand the errors in reports by members of the Soviet press because they were not going on the experience of meeting the group but on previous notices that Meschrabpom had given them. As to Moon's press statement issued on June 11, three days before the ship departed, it is likely that he and the others in the group did not meet until the time of departure.
55. The John Reed clubs were linked to the Communist Party, and although not all members formally joined the party, these clubs often served as a training ground for young activists.
56. Rampersad, *The Life of Langston Hughes*, 1:236, 238.
57. Ibid., 240.
58. Moon Collection, Box 14, Memoirs folder, 12, 3.
59. Ibid., 12.
60. Berry, *Before and Beyond Harlem*, 159.
61. Hughes, *I Wonder as I Wander*, 76.
62. Smith, *Black Man in Red Russia*, 26.
63. Berry, *Before and Beyond Harlem*, 159.
64. Hughes, *I Wonder as I Wander*, 77.
65. Ibid., 76.
66. Quoted in Baldwin, *Beyond the Color Line and the Iron Curtain*, 99.
67. Hughes, *I Wonder as I Wander*, 75.
68. Ibid., 90.
69. Ibid., 79.
70. Smith, *Black Man in Red Russia*, 25.
71. Quoted in Jack El-Hai, "Black and White and Red," *American Heritage* 42, issue 3 (May/June 1991)<http://www.americanheritage.com/articles/magazine/ah/1991/3/1991_3_83.shtml> (August 2, 2006).

72. Berry, *Before and Beyond Harlem*, 158–159.
73. Smith, *Black Man in Red Russia*, 22, 23.
74. See Chapter 2 for additional information about McKay and Huiswood.
75. Joanne Van Tuyl, "Soviet Scripting of Race: Examining the 1932 Screenplay of Grebner's Blacks and Whites," presentation given at the Association for the Study of World Wide Diaspora conference, Brazil, October 7, 2005.
76. Ibid.
77. Quoted in Berry, *Before and Beyond Harlem*, 158–159.
78. It is possible that in mounting the Co-operating Committee, Thompson had also hoped to raise funds to help underwrite the costs for some members of the group.
79. Hughes, *I Wonder as I Wander*, 79–80.
80. Ibid., 87.
81. See Chidi Ikonne, "*Opportunity* and Black Literature, 1923–1933," *Phylon* 40, no. 1 (1979): 86–93.
82. Hughes, *I Wonder as I Wander*, 82.
83. Ibid., 86.
84. Berry, *Before and Beyond Harlem*, 158.
85. Hughes, "Moscow and Me," 67.
86. Robinson, *Black on Red*, 320.
87. Rampersad, *The Life of Langston Hughes*, 1:245.
88. Smith, *Black Man in Red Russia*, 17.
89. Moon Collection, Box 14, Memoirs folder.
90. Ibid.
91. Hughes, *I Wonder as I Wander*, 95.
92. Tony Scherman, "Poston of the Post," *American Legacy*, Fall 2001, 24. See also Berry, *Before and Beyond Harlem*, 164.
93. Moon Collection, Box 14, Memoirs folder, 23.
94. Berry, *Before and Beyond Harlem*, 166.
95. "Say Race Bias Here Halted Soviet Film," *New York Times*, October 5, 1932, 26.
96. Ibid.
97. Berry, *Before and Beyond Harlem*, 346, notes 17, 18, 20.
98. The *Daily Worker* published "Soviet Film Policy Refutes Slanders about Negro Movie" (October 15, 1932) and "Langston Hughes Spikes Lies on Negro Film" (September 8, 1932).
99. Quoted in Berry, *Before and Beyond Harlem*, 166.
100. Hughes, *I Wonder as I Wander*, 96.
101. Quoted in Berry, *Before and Beyond Harlem*, 167.
102. Hughes, *I Wonder as I Wander*, 97–98.
103. *New York Times*, October 6, 1932, 10.
104. Although the film *Black and White* was never realized, the basic theme of the potential of socialism to cross the racial divide continued to be exploited into the end of the twentieth century. A number of productions appeared with a similar theme. Hughes, working with the translator Lydia Filatova in Moscow, was commissioned to translate a number of poems by the Russian poet Vladimir Mayakovsky, one of which, "Black and White," was written in 1925 in response to racism observed in Cuba. Some contended that this poem was one of the inspirations for the original *Black and White* film project. Mayakovsky used as the title for his poem the English words *Black*, *and*, and *White* transliterated into Russian rather than the

Russian words *chorny*, *i*, and *biely* (communication from Professor Joanne Van Tuyl, October 2005). See also Rampersad, *The Life of Langston Hughes*, 1:266. Further information can be found in the online "Encyclopedia of Soviet Writers" <http://www.sovlit.com/bios/mayakovsky.html> (October 15, 2005). Also, Soviet textbooks, depicting the unfair conditions under which blacks lived in the United States, used this theme. One lesson in *English: A Textbook of the English Language for the 7th Grade in 7-Year and Secondary Schools* (3rd ed.), published by the Ministry of Education in 1952, contained a story under the title "White and Black" that read, "The mill-owners in the United States exploit the workers and especially the Negro workers. They teach the white people to hate the coloured workers." The two-part story described the painful experiences of the white and Negro children in this mill town and then ended with "So that is how Charlie and Myrtle, like Sam and Billy, had their first lesson in race hatred. People of different races can live and work happily together in our country, because our country is a Socialist country." Hugo S. Cunningham, "US Racism as Presented to Seventh-Graders in Stalinist Russia" <http://www.tiac.net/users/hcunn/rus/eng/eng-white.html> (October 15, 2005). Even as late as 1991, just after the collapse of the Soviet Union, a new film appeared under the title *Black and White*. It was a U.S./Russian coproduction set in New York rather than in the U.S. South. The two central characters were a Soviet émigré and the black man she fell in love with. As the film promo read, "An interesting perspective is brought to the screen with the cityscape as a dramatic backdrop to a classic romance." "Black and White," *1-World Festival of Foreign Films* <http://www.1worldfilms.com/Russia/blackandwhite.htm> (October 15, 2005). This careful wording could not hide the suggestion that only someone raised outside the racist United States would be able look beyond the racial barriers.

105. Quoted in Berry, *Before and Beyond Harlem*, 168–170.
106. Robinson, *Black on Red*, 320.
107. Quoted in "Say Race Bias Here Halted Soviet Film," 26.
108. Hughes, *I Wonder as I Wander*, 94.
109. Ibid., 102.
110. Ibid.
111. Articles that exemplified the bad press were "Negroes Adrift in 'Uncle Tom's Russian Cabin': Harlem Expeditionary Unit Is Stranded in Moscow" and "Amsterdam News Reporters Tell Why Soviet Russia Dropped Film"; Hughes, *I Wonder as I Wander*, 97.
112. Hughes, *I Wonder as I Wander*, 102.
113. Patterson, Rudd, Smith, and West remained in Moscow.
114. Rampersad, *The Life of Langston Hughes*, 1:254. Most sources spell McKenzie's first name as Allen; however, Rampersad and Baldwin spell it Alan.
115. See Suny, *The Soviet Experiment*, 146. Also, Budyonny's horses were immortalized in many of Isaak Babel's stories.
116. Hughes, *I Wonder as I Wander*, 103–104.
117. Hughes, "Going South in Russia," 77.
118. Baldwin, *Beyond the Color Line and the Iron Curtain*, 100 (Crawford quote from same source).
119. Hughes, *I Wonder as I Wander*, 105–106.
120. Ibid., 105.
121. Hughes, "Moscow and Me," 70.

122. Hughes, *I Wonder as I Wander*, 102.
123. Quoted in Berry, *Before and Beyond Harlem*, 171.
124. Rampersad, *The Life of Langston Hughes*, 1:286. Also, see Berry, *Before and Beyond Harlem*, 167. The League of Struggle for Negro Rights was a 1930s version of the ANLC and was, like the ANLC, to be an organizing arm of the CPUSA to recruit blacks to the party. Besides Hughes, Harry Haywood and other blacks who trained at Comintern schools in Moscow were assigned to this wing of the party. Haywood, *Black Bolshevik*, 343.
125. See, for example, Chatwood Hall, "Soviet's Ace 'Black Tartar' Scourges Nazi Luftwaffe," in *Chicago Defender*, January 22, 1944; *Chicago Defender* Black Aviation Historical Archive <http://www.blackaviation.com/tartar.html> (November 27, 2007).
126. *Challenge* 1, no. 1 (March 1934) and *Challenge* 2, no. 2 (September 1934). Notes Baldwin (*Beyond the Color Line and the Iron Curtain*, 266, note 24), "'A Room in Red Square,' is accompanied by the following note: 'Mary Christopher is, we believe, a pseudonym for a woman who went to Russia a year ago with an acting company. If she has written more, we hope she will send [it].'"
127. Hughes, "Going South in Russia," 70.
128. Ibid., 75–76.
129. Christopher C. De Santis, ed., *Langston Hughes and the Chicago Defender: Essays on Race, Politics, and Culture, 1942–1962* (Chicago: University of Illinois Press, 1995), 172.
130. Langston Hughes, "The Soviet Union and Health," *Chicago Defender*, July 20, 1946, in Berry, ed., *Good Morning Revolution*, 88.
131. Baldwin, *Beyond the Color Line and the Iron Curtain*, 102–103.
132. Hughes, "Moscow and Me," 71.
133. Hughes, *I Wonder as I Wander*, 106–107.
134. *International Literature* journal.
135. Hughes, *I Wonder as I Wander*, 173.
136. Ibid., 188. Smith, in *Black Man in Red Russia*, also noted that several projects were underway that not only were funded by Americans and Germans but were also staffed by them (210–211).
137. Hughes, *I Wonder as I Wander*, 189. For further details on collaborations between U.S. industrialists and the Soviets, see Suny, *The Soviet Experiment*, 87–88.
138. Hughes, *I Wonder as I Wander*, 189.
139. Hughes, "Moscow and Me," 68.
140. Hughes, *I Wonder as I Wander*, 84.
141. Langston Hughes, "Negroes in Moscow," *Innostranaiya Literatura* (*International Literature*, Moscow), 1933, 80.
142. Haywood, *Black Bolshevik*, 168.
143. Blakely, *Russia and the Negro*, 95.
144. Haywood, *Black Bolshevik*, 168.
145. Ibid., 169.
146. Smith, *Black Man in Red Russia*, 35.
147. Ibid., 35.
148. Hughes, *I Wonder as I Wander*, 85.
149. Ibid., 84–85.
150. Smith, *Black Man in Red Russia*, 36, 38.

151. Hughes, "Negroes in Moscow," 80.

152. Ibid.

153. Robinson, *Red on Black*, 322. Robinson spelled her name Arle-Titzs.

154. Smith, *Black Man in Red Russia*, 34, 36.

155. Ibid., 36.

156. Robinson, *Black on Red*, 322.

157. Smith, *Black Man in Red Russia*, 36–37.

158. Rampersad, *The Life of Langston Hughes*, 1:268.

159. Hughes, "Moscow and Me," 72. Although the *Black and White* group was paid well in rubles, this money could be spent only in Russia. No funds could be taken out of the country. Writer Jan Carew, who was a guest of the Soviets in the 1960s, also received large amounts of royalties that could be spent only in the Soviet Union. Many Third World writers complained that although their works were doing well in the Soviet Union, the Russians needed to sign the Berne Convention (which provided international protection for the works of writers and other artists) so that they could take their royalties outside the country.

160. Ibid., 73.

161. Baldwin, *Beyond the Color Line and the Iron Curtain*, 86–87.

162. Hughes, *I Wonder as I Wander*, 212.

CHAPTER 9 *Paul Robeson's Search for a Society Free of Racism*

1. Philip Foner, ed., *Paul Robeson Speaks: Writings, Speeches, Interviews, 1918–1974* (Secaucus, N.J.: Citadel Press, 1978), 95.

2. Ollie Harrington, *Why I Left America and Other Essays* (Jackson: University of Mississippi Press, 1993), 43.

3. Duberman, *Paul Robeson*, 795. Duberman noted that Robeson traveled to the Soviet Union in 1934–1935, 1936–1937, 1949, 1958–1959, 1960, 1961.

4. Quoted in ibid., 461.

5. Foner, ed., *Paul Robeson Speaks*, 92.

6. McKay published "Soviet Russia and the Negro" in two parts in *Crisis* magazine (December 1923 and January 1924). Du Bois wrote various pieces for *Crisis* as well as articles for the *Pittsburgh Courier* under the title "Forum of Fact and Opinion" (1936). Lewis, *The Fight for Equality*, 389.

7. Paul Robeson Jr., *The Undiscovered Paul Robeson: An Artist's Journey, 1898–1939* (New York: Wiley, 2001), 96.

8. Patterson, *The Man Who Cried Genocide*, 65.

9. Ibid., 30.

10. Duberman, *Paul Robeson*, 41, 106–107. The Sacco and Vanzetti trial was originally about a robbery and a murder, but it turned into a public discussion of politics, the rising radicalism in the post-World War I era, calls for a more equitable shaping of society than currently existed, and the subsequent "Red scare." The demand for the execution of Sacco and Vanzetti on flimsy charges was to serve as a warning to others who might want to try to move society toward socialism.

11. Patterson, *The Man Who Cried Genocide*, 89.

12. Duberman, *Paul Robeson*, 187. Also see Robeson Jr., *The Undiscovered Paul Robeson*, 222–223.

13. Foner, ed., *Paul Robeson Speaks*, 283.

14. Slava Tynes, Editors of Freedomways, *Paul Robeson: The Great Forerunner* (1965; repr., New York: International, 1985), 94.
15. Duberman, *Paul Robeson*, 628, note 59.
16. Susan Robeson, *The Whole World in His Hands: A Pictorial Biography of Paul Robeson* (Secaucus, N.J.: Citadel Press, 1981), 59. See also Robeson Jr., *The Undiscovered Paul Robeson*, 251.
17. Paul Robeson, *Here I Stand* (New York: Othello Associates, 1958), 41, 43.
18. Foner, ed., *Paul Robeson Speaks*, 3.
19. Duberman, *Paul Robeson*, 89.
20. Quoted in ibid., 182.
21. Robeson Jr., *The Undiscovered Paul Robeson*, 151. In fact, Seton later wrote an English biography of Robeson: *Paul Robeson* (London: Denis Dobson, 1958).
22. Quoted in Susan Robeson, *The Whole World in His Hands*, 58.
23. Duberman, *Paul Robeson*, 184.
24. Robeson Jr., *The Undiscovered Paul Robeson*, 218.
25. Quoted in Duberman, *Paul Robeson*, 185.
26. "Sergei Eisenstein Biography," in *Baseline's Biography of Film*, Carleton University <http://www.carleton.edu/curricular/MEDA/classes/media110/Severson/bio.htm> (July 9, 2007).
27. Robeson Jr., *The Undiscovered Paul Robeson*, 213.
28. Duberman, *Paul Robeson*, 182, 190.
29. Ibid., 196.
30. Interview with Jan Carew, Louisville, Kentucky, 2002, from conversations with Robeson in England in 1958. The Eisenstein film *Black Majesty* was never produced, but a version of the story came to fruition later when Robeson was asked to act in a London production of the play in 1936. See also Duberman, *Paul Robeson*, 196–197.
31. Robeson Jr., *The Undiscovered Paul Robeson*, 243–245.
32. Duberman, *Paul Robeson*, 182–183, 222.
33. Robinson, *Black on Red*, 311.
34. Duberman, *Paul Robeson*, 185.
35. Robeson Jr., *The Undiscovered Paul Robeson*, 221–222.
36. Ibid., 47.
37. Goode interview, 1994. Also in D. Beliayebsky, "Vibori bez vibora" [A Choice with No Alternative: As Told by Former U.S. Citizen Frank Goode], *Gorbigovoki Rabochii*, March 1962, 3.
38. Smith, *Black Man in Red Russia*, 197.
39. Duberman, *Paul Robeson*, 185.
40. Ibid., 189.
41. Ibid., 795.
42. Robeson Jr., *The Undiscovered Paul Robeson*, 246.
43. Duberman, *Paul Robeson*, 206, 187.
44. Ibid., 209. Smith (*Black Man in Red Russia*, 47), recalled their living in the Metropole Hotel.
45. Robeson Jr., *The Undiscovered Paul Robeson*, 280.
46. "Robeson Puts Son in Soviet School," *New York Times*, December 21, 1934, 18.
47. Robeson Jr., *The Undiscovered Paul Robeson*, 280.
48. Robeson, *Here I Stand*, 44.

49. Foner, ed., *Paul Robeson Speaks*, 107.
50. Duberman, *Paul Robeson*, 208.
51. Goode interview, 1995.
52. Smith, *Black Man in Red Russia*, 47.
53. Foner, ed., *Paul Robeson Speaks*, 101. In the Soviet Union, people of color, primarily Asian peoples, were often referred to as those living in the "Eastern part" of the country.
54. Goode interview, 1996.
55. Robeson Jr., *The Undiscovered Paul Robeson*, 306.
56. Ibid.
57. Ignaty Kazakov was a physician whom the Robesons knew in Moscow; he was imprisoned in the late 1930s after he "confessed" to the murder of the chairman of the Unified State Political Administration (Duberman, *Paul Robeson*, 221).
58. Robeson Jr., *The Undiscovered Paul Robeson*, 306.
59. Susan Robeson, *The Whole World in His Hands*, 166.
60. Robeson Jr., *The Undiscovered Paul Robeson*, 262. Also, see Golden, *My Long Journey Home*, 19.
61. Foner, ed., *Paul Robeson Speaks*, 348.
62. Duberman, *Paul Robeson*, 341.
63. Ibid.
64. Foner, ed., *Paul Robeson Speaks*, 209.
65. Duberman, *Paul Robeson*, 342, 359.
66. Ibid., 463.
67. Quoted in ibid., 465.
68. Ibid., 468. Robinson (*Black on Red*, 317), stated that the crowd was thirteen thousand.
69. Duberman, *Paul Robeson*, 468. The title of this song is also translated as "My Broad Homeland" or "My Great Homeland."
70. Foner, ed., *Paul Robeson Speaks*, 348.
71. Quoted in Duberman, *Paul Robeson*, 468.
72. Susan Robeson, *The Whole World in His Hands*, 222, 252.
73. Duberman, *Paul Robeson*, 469–470.
74. Quoted in ibid., 473.
75. Quoted in Lewis, *The Fight for Equality*, 562.
76. Robeson was honored to be carrying Aldridge's mantel after he met with Aldridge's daughter in London and received the earrings Aldridge used when playing Othello almost a century earlier. In the latter part of the 1950s, Robeson would also be invited to perform *Othello* in Moscow. See Duberman, *Paul Robeson*, 91.
77. Robinson, *Black on Red*, 317–318. Also see Susan Robeson, *The Whole World in His Hands*, 228.
78. Robinson, *Black on Red*, 318.
79. Duberman, *Paul Robeson*, 353–354.
80. Susan Robeson, *The Whole World in His Hands*, 233.
81. Slava Tynes, "Paul Robeson: Great Friend of the Soviet People," in Editors of Freedomways, *Paul Robeson*, 98–99.
82. Carew interview, 2002.
83. Tynes, "Paul Robeson," 99. Also, see Foner, ed., *Paul Robeson Speaks*, 39.
84. Goode interview, 1994.

85. Duberman, *Paul Robeson*, 209–211.
86. Robeson Jr., *The Undiscovered Paul Robeson*, 47. Also Goode interview, 1996.
87. Robeson Jr., *The Undiscovered Paul Robeson*, 219, 281.
88. Ibid., 304. Paul Jr.'s comment that Eslanda was searching for Kazakov is curious in that Duberman quotes a letter from Eslanda to Patterson in which she denounced Kazakov as a means to shield her brother Frank; see Duberman, *Paul Robeson*, 220–221.
89. Khanga, *Soul to Soul*, 91.

CHAPTER 10 *The Expatriates*

1. Smith, *Black Man in Red Russia*, 207.
2. Ibid., 96.
3. Robinson, *Black on Red*, 112.
4. Smith, *Black Man in Red Russia*, 94–96.
5. Ibid., 104.
6. Black sojourner John Sutton, who had a child, Juan, returned to the United States in 1937, leaving the boy behind with his mother.
7. The records are not conclusive on Fort-Whiteman, but, apparently, because he reentered the country in 1928 under a fictitious name, he was in a kind of legal limbo.
8. Khanga, *Soul to Soul*, 228.
9. Ibid.
10. Golden, *My Long Journey Home*, 22.
11. Robinson, *Black on Red*, 84.
12. Goode interviews, 1993. Also, William Davis interviews, Washington, D.C., 2001, 2006. Attempts were being made to reestablish contact between Robinson and the estranged child in the 1980s, just before Robinson died.
13. Smith, as a foreign correspondent, was able to avoid being forced to take Soviet citizenship.
14. Robinson, *Black on Red*, 112.
15. Klehr, Haynes, and Anderson, *Soviet World of American Communism*, 218–227.
16. Robinson, *Black on Red*, 88.
17. By the 1960s, the status of Negro became a liability, as xenophobic reactions to outsiders rose again.
18. Khanga, *Soul to Soul*, 86, 87.
19. Golden, *My Long Journey Home*, 16–17.
20. Ibid., 17–18. Auntie Nadya was Ukrainian, but the Goldens did not know enough about the different nationalities at the time to distinguish her from a Russian.
21. Khanga, *Soul to Soul*, 89–90.
22. Quoted in ibid., 90–91.
23. Ibid., 91.
24. Ibid., 300–301. Bertha Bialek (Golden) had originally immigrated from Poland but had obtained American citizenship before she left the United States.
25. Golden, *My Long Journey Home*, 20.
26. Khanga, *Soul to Soul*, 102.
27. Ibid., 97. Although there is a slight inconsistency (see Golden, *My Long Journey Home*, 23, which stated that the amount was $700), this was an enormous amount of money for the time.

28. Golden, *My Long Journey Home*, 29–30.
29. Ibid., 23–25.
30. Ibid., 39.
31. Quoted in ibid., 41, 20.
32. Ibid.
33. One of the daughters was named Yelena. Lily identified the second daughter as Mardji (probably Marjorie); Golden, *My Long Journey Home*, 45. Parker married Afro-Russian descendant Marjorie Scott's Russian mother after her divorce from Henry Scott; Robinson, *Red on Black*, 304. Marjorie Scott and Yelena could be the two Afro-Russian girls mentioned by Lily.
34. Golden, *My Long Journey Home*, 42.
35. Smith, *Black Man in Red Russia*, 201.
36. None of the blacks from the United States or Africa who studied in the Soviet Union in the 1920s and 1930s went there for a regular university education; they were involved in two- to four-year political training programs at KUTVA or the Lenin School. The Africans and other people of color who went to the Soviet Union in the late 1950s were there for eight to ten years before they were ready to graduate. Thus, Lily, one of the oldest Afro-Russian descendants, who was fortunate to get into Moscow State University in 1952, was, in 1957, the first black person to graduate from that university. Her mention of Alexander Pushkin (1799–1837) takes account of the fact that Pushkin, an Afro-Russian descendant of an Ethiopian brought to Russia in 1700, was educated at the most elite institution of his time, the Lyceum in St. Petersburg, having graduated in 1817.
37. Golden, *My Long Journey Home*, 55.
38. Golden, *My Long Journey Home*, 56. Khanga in *Soul to Soul* used the Russian version, Anya. Even Lily Golden uses a version of this spelling in her affectionate name for Anya, Mamanya.
39. Khanga, *Soul to Soul*, 117, 119.
40. Ibid., 118. Lily spelled his name Ollava, in *My Long Journey Home*, 56, which may be a Russian-style spelling; Khanga, *Soul to Soul*, from which most of the quotes are taken, used an English-style spelling. The sound is the same; it replicates Oliver Golden's name.
41. Khanga, *Soul to Soul*, 118.
42. Ibid., 68, 119–120.
43. Ibid., 118, 119. Khanga's book contains a photo of Anya with Golden in the 1920s, a second taken forty years later with Ollava, and a third showing her with her World War II medals.
44. Golden, *My Long Journey Home*, 56.
45. Golden, *My Long Journey Home*, 42, 70–71. The Afro-Russian descendants often benefited from their fathers' notoriety and could gain access to various privileges. Grateful Soviets were willing to show their appreciation for the fathers' early contributions by helping their children.
46. Smith, *Black Man in Red Russia*, 198.
47. Robeson Jr., *The Undiscovered Paul Robeson*, 221–222.
48. Smith, *Black Man in Red Russia*, 198.
49. Ibid., 198.
50. Ibid., 198–199.
51. Ibid., 200–201.

52. Ibid., 200.
53. Goode interviews, 1993.
54. Smith, *Black Man in Red Russia*, 64–65.
55. Madeline Murphy, "To Be a Poet, Russian, and Black," *New World Review*, March–April 1974, 12.
56. Tynes interviews, 2002.
57. Blakely, *Russia and the Negro*, 146.
58. Ibid., 155.
59. Travel2Russia, *Destination Guide: Komsomolsk-na-Amure* <http://www.travel2 russia.com/destguide/komsom.htm> (July 9, 2007).
60. Smith, *Black Man in Red Russia*, 66.
61. Robinson, *Black on Red*, 226.
62. Blakely, *Russia and the Negro*, 146, 147.
63. Smith, *Black Man in Red Russia*, 65–66. Also, see Blakely, *Russia and the Negro*, 147.
64. Blakely, *Russia and the Negro*, 146–147.
65. Tynes interviews, 2002.
66. Robinson, *Black on Red*, 116–123.
67. Ibid., 155–158. Robinson's transliteration of the city name differs from that in most other sources, which write it Kuibyshev.
68. Ibid., 169.
69. Ibid., 170.
70. Ibid., 169, 177.
71. Ibid., 182.
72. Ibid., 192, 405.
73. Ibid., 375.
74. Ibid., 372.
75. Ibid., 399.
76. Smith, *Black Man in Red Russia*, 67, xvi, xv. Smith's pieces (written under the pseudonym Chatwood Hall) regularly appeared in the *Chicago Defender*, the *Afro-American*, and the *Crisis*.
77. Ibid., 96.
78. Ibid., 67–68, 75.
79. Ibid., 75–76.
80. Ibid., 76, 104. It is interesting to note the parallels to the repercussions of the McCarthy inquisitions in the United States, when persons who were known to have (or who were suspected of having) ties to the Soviets were shunned.
81. Ibid., 67, 172.
82. Ibid., 138. This city was formerly known as Samara; it was renamed after the Russian Civil War to honor one of Lenin's commissars.
83. Ibid., 124.
84. Ibid., 124–125.
85. Ibid., 139, 140, 138–139, 127.
86. Ibid., 150.
87. Ibid., 202, 213.
88. Khanga, *Soul to Soul*, 92.
89. Smith, *Black Man in Red Russia*, 217.
90. Blakely, *Russia and the Negro*, 97.

91. Ibid.
92. Tynes interviews, 2001. The name of the cousin is unknown.
93. Blakely, *Russia and the Negro*, 97.
94. Tynes interviews, 2001.
95. Robinson, *Black on Red*, 324. Zoo technician was short for zoological technician.
96. Blakely, *Russia and the Negro*, 97.
97. Robinson, *Black on Red*, 342.
98. Blakely, *Russia and the Negro*, 97.
99. Houston, "Going Home . . . to the USSR," 3.
100. Quoted in Klehr, Haynes, and Firsov, *Secret World of American Communism*, 199, 200.
101. Quoted in ibid., 201–202.
102. Quoted in Voice of Russia, "Our Station Is 75 Years Old: Radio Moscow in the War Years," *Voice of Russia: World Service in English* <http://www.vor.ru/English/75/program_5.html> (September 13, 2006). The effectiveness of these broadcasts, which were done in native languages and by native speakers, was shown when an anti-Communist radio station set up in the United States in 1951 took some of its model from the Radio Moscow broadcasts. See "January 18, 1951: American Committee for Liberation from Bolshevism (Amcomlib) Incorporated," in *Radio Liberty: 50 Years* <http://hoorferl.standford.edu/rlexhibit/timeline.php> (September 13. 2006): "George Kennan, former U.S. ambassador to the Soviet Union, began to discuss using a radio station as a tool in the ongoing ideological struggle with the Soviet Union. . . . By drawing on the population of Soviet émigrés . . . the station would be able to address Soviet citizens in a familiar tone, not as outsiders."
103. Smith, *Black Man in Red Russia*, 127.
104. Ibid.
105. Ibid.
106. Klehr, Haynes, and Firsov, *Secret World of American Communism*, 199.
107. Ibid.
108. Quoted in Houston, "Going Home . . . to the USSR."
109. Ibid.
110. Ibid.
111. Klehr, Haynes, and Anderson, *The Soviet World of American Communism*, 218.
112. Smith, *Black Man in Red Russia*, 77.
113. Robinson, *Black on Red* ("teaching English . . . at the Anglo-American school"), 361. See also Hutchinson, *Blacks and Reds* ("teaching political science . . . at the Cercerin Institute near Moscow"), 54; and Fridrikh Firsov, "Black American 'Pilgrims' in the Soviet Union and the Comintern: New Documents (The Fate of Fort-Whiteman Lovett)" (paper presented at the conference of the American Association for the Advancement of Slavic Studies, Boca Raton, Florida, September 24–27, 1998) ("a teacher at the first MGU [Moscow State University] and of the English School"), 7.
114. Smith, *Black Man in Red Russia*, 77, 79.
115. Fort-Whiteman was known to have been married in 1924 to Olivia Fort-Whiteman, a fellow communist. She and he were on record as having been representatives of the party at a United Negro Improvement Association meeting with Garvey in 1924. Olivia Fort-Whiteman had been assigned to speak on behalf of the party. Hutchinson, *Blacks and Reds*, 45.

116. Smith, *Black Man in Red Russia*, 78.
117. Ibid., 79.
118. Klehr, Haynes, and Anderson, *Soviet World of American Communism*, 219.
119. Firsov, "Black American 'Pilgrims' in the Soviet Union and the Comintern"; also, personal communication with author.
120. Smith, *Black Man in Red Russia*, 80. Smith spelled the name Forte-Whiteman.
121. Klehr, Haynes, and Anderson, *Soviet World of American Communism*, 223.
122. This is William Patterson.
123. Robinson, *Black on Red*, 361.
124. Smith, *Black Man in Red Russia*, 81.
125. Ibid., 83.
126. See Firsov's paper "Black American 'Pilgrims' in the Soviet Union and the Comintern," 1, 6, 8. Also, see Klehr, Haynes, and Anderson, *Soviet World of American Communism*, 6, 218–226. Both works were based on investigations of Comintern and CPUSA documents that offered behind-the-scene details on Fort-Whiteman's case. Firsov had worked in the inner sanctum of Soviet secrets. Firsov had been the director of the Department for Publication of the Documents of the World Communist Movement at the Russian Center for the Preservation and Study of Documents of Recent History in Moscow. This institution was, in Soviet days, the central archive of the Institute of Marxism-Leninism at the Central Committee of the Communist Party of the Soviet Union.
127. Firsov, "Black American 'Pilgrims' in the Soviet Union and the Comintern," 12.
128. Quoted in ibid., 7, 12.
129. Ibid., 13.
130. Smith, *Black Man in Red Russia*, 83.
131. Klehr, Haynes, and Anderson, *Soviet World of American Communism*, xxv, 222–223. The discussions also mentioned Homer Smith and Robert Ross (Johnson). But the actions taken against them were not injurious.
132. Smith, *Black Man in Red Russia*, 81.

CHAPTER 11 *William "Bill" Davis, the American National Exhibit, and U.S. Public Diplomacy*

1. Davis, "How Negroes Live in Russia," 65.
2. Ibid., 66.
3. Davis met Robert Ross, Robert Robinson, George Tynes, and Frank Goode of the 1920s and 1930s sojourner group.
4. Davis, "How Negroes Live in Russia," 65.
5. Ibid., 66. Also, Davis interviews, Washington, D.C., 1999.
6. Robinson, *Black on Red*, 305. Ross and the other black expatriates did not work for private companies but were paid by the Soviet government through one of its many trade unions. Everyone who worked in the Soviet Union was paid by the government through the trade-union structure because the Soviet system did not support private enterprises.
7. The descendants were Vyacheslav Tynes, Amelia Tynes, Ruben Tynes, Eleanor Ross, Inez (Inessa) Ross, Margaret Scott, Wayland Rudd Jr., and Lilly (Lily) Golden. Davis also met Maria Tynes, the wife of George.

8. Walter Hixon, *Parting the Curtain: Propaganda, Culture and the Cold War, 1945–1961* (New York: St. Martin's Press, 1997),153.

9. Ibid., 161.

10. Davis interviews, Potomac, Maryland, 2006. Johnson worked on Voice of America broadcasts in the late 1940s as a demonstration of improved U.S. race relations.

11. Hixon, *Parting the Curtain*, 155.

12. Previous opportunities for Negroes to visit the Soviet Union occurred in the U.S.-sponsored jazz tours of the 1920s and the 1950s. Both integrated and all-black tours were sponsored. A jazz troupe had been suggested for the American National Exhibit, but the Soviets turned it down. At the same time, the State Department did not press for the jazz group because although such groups were good for their "emotional" appeal, the American National Exhibit was supposed to highlight the intellectual and technical strengths of the United States.

13. Davis, "How Negroes Live in Russia," 65–73.

14. Hixon, *Parting the Curtain*, 151.

15. Quoted in Hixon, *Parting the Curtain*, 151.

16. Quoted in ibid.

17. Suny, *The Soviet Experiment*, 409.

18. Quoted in Hixon, *Parting the Curtain*, 153.

19. Ibid., 170.

20. Yale Richmond, *Cultural Exchange and the Cold War* (University Park: Pennsylvania State University Press, 2003), 15.

21. Hixon, *Parting the Curtain*, 153.

22. Ibid., 154.

23. See ibid.

24. Ibid., 161.

25. Ibid., 170.

26. Quoted in ibid.

27. Ibid., 175.

28. Quoted in John Hope Franklin and Isidore Starr, eds., *The Negro in Twentieth Century America; a Reader on the Struggle for Civil Rights* (New York: Vintage Books, 1967), 289–290, 496.

29. Thomas Borstelmann, *The Color War and the Color Line: American Race Relations in the Global Arena* (Cambridge, Mass.: Harvard University Press, 2001), 90–91.

30. Davis, "How Negroes Live in Russia," 66. The U.S. State Department would sponsor a number of other interracial tours through the 1960s; they were designed to "promote a vision of a color-blind American democracy"; Penny M. Von Eschen, *Satchmo Blows Up the World: Jazz Ambassadors Play the Cold War* (Cambridge, Mass.: Harvard University Press, 2004), 4.

31. Hixon, *Parting the Curtain*, 156–157.

32. Davis, "How Negroes Live in Russia," 69.

33. Davis, "How Negroes Live in Russia," 69. Davis noted that visitors often asked him how much money he made; William Davis, "Afterword," in Robinson, *Black on Red*, 429.

34. Davis, "How Negroes Live in Russia," 69.

35. Davis interviews, Washington, D.C., 2001.

36. Davis's post as a narcotics agent was in the Treasury Department. Ralph Bunche could be considered an exception, although his route to the Foreign Service

occurred in the war years. Bunche had joined the Office of Strategic Services (the early version of the Central Intelligence Agency during World War II); his primary responsibility was Africa. He was later directly involved in the initial negotiations for the formation of the United Nations, which he formally joined as a staff member in 1946 at the special request of the secretary-general, Trygve Lie. For seven years (1947–1954), he was director of the Department of Trusteeship and Information from Non-Self-Governing Territories and was directly involved with the process of decolonization. In 1955, he was assigned to another post at the U.N., that of undersecretary for special political affairs. In this capacity, he was directly involved in the Suez Crisis. Kwame Anthony Appiah and Henry Louis Gates, eds., *Africana: The Encyclopedia of the African and Black Experience* (New York: Basic Civitas Books, 1999), 328.

37. Davis interviews, Washington, D.C., 2001. and curriculum vitae.
38. Davis, curriculum vitae and interviews, Potomac, Maryland, 2006. Davis also subsequently learned Portuguese and Japanese. See also Bob Massey, "Dancing with the Devil," *Washington Post*, July 5, 1998 <http://www.washingtonpost.com/wp-srv/style/features/klan.htm> (July 9, 2007). In 1958, while J. Edgar Hoover was investigating Martin Luther King Jr.'s alleged Communist ties, Davis was in Chicago studying Russian. His mastery of Russian had won him the temporary assignment as a guide and translator in Moscow. There Davis caught the attention of the deputy director of the U.S. Information Agency—and, by 1961, he had his first posting as a diplomat, in Ghana.
39. Davis interviews, Lincoln University (Lincoln University, Pennsylvania), Washington, D.C., and Potomac, Maryland, 1995–2006.
40. Quoted in Hixon, *Parting the Curtain*, 171.
41. Ibid., 171 and 268, note 66.
42. Davis did not identify the guides except for Norris Garnett ("How Negroes Live in Russia," 66). Hixon identified another guide as Herb Miller (*Parting the Curtain*, 196).
43. Hixon, *Parting the Curtain*, 205.
44. Davis, "How Negroes Live in Russia," 69. Davis identified them as having been married at the time. Hixon (*Parting the Curtain*, 172) noted that they were engaged to be married. A photo in the collection of Amelia Tynes shows Davis with four black models—two women and two men—at the duck farm with George Tynes and his wife, Maria. Davis does not mention the black models in the text of his *Ebony* article, other than in a photo showing a group leaving a Baptist church in Moscow. Here, he identified them as "Norma Noble, who with her husband, Galbert (carrying travel case) was a model at American Exhibition" (69). The distinction between guides and models is significant, as the guides spoke Russian and were to interact directly with the Soviets. The models stayed in the background, although Davis was accompanied by the four models during at least one of his visits to the Tynes farm.
45. Quoted in Hixon, *Parting the Curtain*, 172.
46. Ibid.
47. Office of the Historian, U.S. Department of State, "July-August 1959: Visit to the Soviet Union of Richard M. Nixon," *Foreign Relations of the United States* 10, part 1: *1958–60: E. Europe Region; Soviet Union; Cyprus*, 6 <http://dosfan.lib.uic.edu/ERC/frus/frus58-60x1/10soviet4.html> (July 9, 2007).
48. Ibid., 1.

49. Quoted in *Sputnik Resource 4: The Kitchen Debate* <http://www.turnerlearning. com/cnn/coldwar/sputnik/sput_re4.html> (July 9, 2007).
50. Hixon, *Parting the Curtain*, 204.
51. Davis, "Afterword," 429.
52. Ibid. Davis's comments at the end of Robinson's book also included a description of Davis's work with the computer. Davis mentioned the computer as one of the many "normal" items available to the U.S. public. However, many items at the American National Exhibit were, in fact, prototypes and not yet available for consumer use in the United States.
53. Quoted in Hixon, *Parting the Curtain*, 196.
54. Ibid., 171, 195. The United States had experienced a rude awakening on this point. In a major international exhibit mounted in Brussels two years earlier, the U.S. exhibit on "the American Negro" had provoked a rabid response from U.S. southern conservatives. Not only was this response a serious embarrassment, but the organizers were accused of being Communist sympathizers and unpatriotic. See Hixon, *Parting the Curtain*, 146.
55. Ibid., 196.
56. Davis, "How Negroes Live in Russia," 67–68.
57. Office of the Historian, U.S. Department of State, "109. Telegram from the Embassy in the Soviet Union to the Department of State," *Foreign Relations of the United States 1964–1968*, vol. 14: *Soviet Union* (National Archives and Records Administration, RG 59, Central Files 1964–66, POL 17 US-USSR. Confidential; Limdis) <http://www.state.gov/r/pa/ho/frus/johnsonlb/xiv/1376.htm> (July 9, 2007).
58. Ibid.
59. Ibid. In response to Garnett's expulsion, the U.S. government expelled a "relatively higher ranking member [of the] Soviet Embassy," and the Soviet first secretary, Stefan M. Kirsanov, was subsequently declared *persona non grata*.
60. Davis, "How Negroes Live in Russia," 71. Hulan Jack, the first black borough president, was elected in 1953.
61. Khanga, *Soul to Soul*, 91–92. Khanga noted that Juan lost his mother during the war and was raised in various foster families, not knowing his father was looking for him.
62. Hixon, *Parting the Curtain*, 193.
63. Richmond, *Cultural Exchange and the Cold War*, 49.
64. Davis, "How Negroes Live in Russia," 68, 69.
65. Ibid., 69.
66. Ibid.
67. Ibid.
68. Ibid.
69. Davis, "How Negroes Live in Russia," 66. Davis might have been comparing Ross's apartment with that of Robinson, who lived more modestly.
70. Ibid., 67.
71. Golden, *My Long Journey Home*, 44.
72. Davis, "How Negroes Live in Russia," 67, 72.
73. Golden, *My Long Journey Home*, 101. Lily Golden married Abdullah Hanga (Khanga) in 1961. In the transliteration of this last name into English, she chose to use the spelling Hanga (Golden, *My Long Journey Home*, 91), while her daughter, Yelena, chose Khanga.

74. Davis, "How Negroes Live in Russia," 71.
75. Golden, *My Long Journey Home*, 37.
76. Quoted in ibid.
77. Ibid., 37–38. Golden meant that in her Soviet passport her nationality was stated as Negro, which was an ethnic identification. There was no question that her citizenship was Soviet. In the physical descriptions of early U.S. passports, blacks were also described as Negro to distinguish their racial/ethnic identity within the U.S. context. Golden knew only about passports in the Soviet Union and, thus, may be correct in stating that she was the first in that country to be identified as a Negro on her passport. No doubt Robeson's and Du Bois's passports, issued by the U.S. government, identified them as Negroes because the use of racial designations in official U.S. documents was common in the 1950s and 1960s.
78. Goode interviews, 1994–1995.
79. At the time Lily was planning to travel not to the United States but to other Eastern European countries for her tennis competitions.
80. Goode interviews, 1994–1995.
81. Davis, "Afterword," 429.
82. Ibid., 430.
83. Ibid.
84. Margaret Scott is also referred to as Marjorie and Ulamei (Blakely, *Russia and the Negro*, 155). Her father, Henry Scott, died suddenly of suspicious causes just after delivering a talk on the Soviet experiment; Robinson, *Black on Red*, 304.
85. Davis, "How Negroes Live in Russia," 68.
86. Ibid., 69.
87. Goode interviews, 1994.
88. Davis, "How Negroes Live in Russia," 73.
89. Ibid. Tynes paid a visit alone in 1934 and then again in the 1980s.
90. Ibid., 65.
91. Ibid., 73.
92. Robert Robinson, Eslanda Goode, Lily Golden wrote to Davis from the Soviet Union; Amelia Tynes Mensah wrote Davis from Liberia. Davis interviews, Washington, D.C., 2005.
93. Golden, *My Long Journey Home*, 174.
94. Hixon, *Parting the Curtain*, 107.
95. Suny, *The Soviet Experiment*, 413.
96. Aptheker, ed., *Writings by W.E.B. Du Bois in Periodicals Edited by Others*, 4:300.

CHAPTER 12 *The Cold War, Solidarity Building, and the Recruitment of New Sojourners*

1. Golden, *My Long Journey Home*, 77.
2. Ibid., 76.
3. Ibid., 57
4. Ibid., 61–63.
5. "World Festival of Youth and Students," *Wikipedia* <http://en.wikipedia.org/wiki/World_Festival_of_Youth_and_Students.htm.> (July 4, 2007).
6. Golden, *My Long Journey Home*, 77.
7. Foner, ed., *Paul Robeson Speaks*, 464.

8. Aptheker, ed., *Writings by W.E.B. Du Bois in Periodicals Edited by Others*, 4:299–300.

9. The General Assembly meetings were held in October 1960.

10. Foner, ed., *Paul Robeson Speaks*, 465.

11. For background, see "Prime Minister Nehru: Speech to Bandung Conference Political Committee, 1955," *Modern History Sourcebook* <http://www.fordham.edu/halsall/mod/1955nehru-bandung2.html> (July 4, 2007).

12. Libya (1951), Egypt (1953), Morocco (1956), Sudan (1956), Tunisia (1956), Ghana (1957), Guinea (1958).

13. Duberman, *Paul Robeson*, 437.

14. Du Bois joined the party in 1963, on the eve of his departure for Ghana.

15. Duberman, *Paul Robeson*, 437.

16. Ibid., 460.

17. Lewis, *The Fight for Equality*, 557.

18. Aptheker, ed., *Writings by W.E.B. Du Bois in Periodicals Edited by Others* 4:275–276.

19. Paul Gorden Lauren, *Power and Prejudice: The Politics and Diplomacy of Racial Discrimination* (Boulder, Colo.: Westview Press, 1988), 222–223.

20. Foner, ed., *Paul Robeson Speaks*, 398–399.

21. Aptheker, ed., *Writings by W.E.B. Du Bois in Periodicals Edited by Others*, 4:236.

22. Aptheker, ed., *Writings by W.E.B. Du Bois in Periodicals Edited by Others*, 4:276.

23. M. Nakayama, "Causes behind the Cancellation, by U.S.A., U.K. and World Bank, of Once Pledged Financial Assistance to Egypt for the High Aswan Dam. Abstract," *Journal of Japan Society for Hydrological & Water Resources* 9, no. 4 (1996): 340–350.

24. Nikita Khrushchev, *Khrushchev Remembers* (New York: Little, Brown, 1970), 440.

25. *Summary Background Information for the Aswan High Dam* <http://www.Teacher link.ed.usu.edu/tlresources/units/byrnes-africa/KAYMUR/LINK.htm.> (July 4, 2007).

26. K. S. Kremen, "The Soviet Union and Africa, a Conference of Scholars in Moscow," in *Africa in Soviet Studies, 1969* (annual journal of the U.S.S.R. Academy of Sciences, Africa Institute) (Moscow: Nauka, 1971).

27. Blakely, *Russia and the Negro*, 128.

28. P. Ya. Koshelev, "Soviet-African Economic Co-operation: Record and Prospects," in *Africa in Soviet Studies, 1983* (U.S.S.R. Academy of Sciences, Africa Institute) (Moscow: Nauka,1983), 34.

29. Davis, "How Negroes Live in Russia," 68.

30. Ibid.

31. Quoted in Jan Carew, *Green Winter* (London: Martin Secker and Warburg, 1964), 111–112, 130.

32. Blakely, *Russia and the Negro*, 139.

33. Eslanda Goode graduated from Patrice Lumumba People's Friendship University in 1973. After graduate work in Lithuania, she taught at Lumumba University, as it came to be known, from 1976 to 1990. Goode interviews, 1994.

34. Because of the increasing numbers of students coming to the Soviet Union, the Soviets and their Eastern Bloc allies opened other, similar study programs. However, Lumumba University has remained the most famous.

35. Goode interviews, 1994.

36. Golden, *My Long Journey Home*, 53. Golden was taking dramatic liberties when she described her skin color. Although her complexion was darker than that of most Russians, she certainly did not have the color of the African students or of her dark-skinned father, Oliver Golden.
37. Ibid., 76.
38. Ibid., 84.
39. Ibid., 76–77.
40. Ibid., 84.
41. Ibid., 45.
42. Goode interviews, 1995. Tynes interviews, 2002.
43. Golden, *My Long Journey Home*, 110–111.
44. Ibid., 109.
45. Goode interviews, 1994, and Tynes interviews, 2002.
46. Valentina Soboleva interviews (Lincoln University, Lincoln University, Pennsylvania, 1998). Soboleva taught in the Sudan for twenty years before returning to the Soviet Union with her children. Also, Goode interviews, 1994–1996.
47. Goode interviews, 1995. Tynes interviews, 2002. Also, see Golden, *My Long Journey Home*, 63.
48. Such excuses are an age-old rationale. They first surfaced in the earliest days of the black student presence at KUTVA, in the 1920s and 1930s. They continue to be used frequently in "explaining" racist behavior in post-Soviet Russia.
49. Rachel L. Swarns, "Anticolonial U., Not a Hotbed of Business Majors," *New York Times*, October 22, 1996.
50. See the Appendix for additional details about the sojourner/expatriate families discussed here.
51. Khanga, *Soul to Soul*, 22. Khanga's estimates reflect information on a much larger cohort of 1920s–1930s sojourners than those written about here. This immediate group was estimated as of 2002 to be one hundred.
52. See Appendix.
53. Khanga, *Soul to Soul*, 22.
54. James Patterson, "Russia and Africa," quoted in Blakely, *Russia and the Negro*, 160.

BIBLIOGRAPHICAL ESSAY: A SURVEY OF SELECTED SOURCES

*A*n as yet little-explored body of litera-
ture provides background for the detailed and synthetic explorations of this
work. Most of the black sojourners who went to the Soviet Union in the 1920s
and 1930s did not publish their accounts, but information on them surfaces in
the works of others. Primary sources on the black sojourners consist of a small
number of autobiographical works and letters. Claude McKay's *A Long Way
Home* (1937) looks at his 1922 experiences as the first black man to be officially
celebrated by the Soviets and at his role as a symbol of Soviet solidarity with
people of African descent. W.E.B. Du Bois's *In Battle for Peace* (1952), written
on the occasion of his eighty-third birthday, looks at his initial 1926 journey
and his continued admiration for the Soviet experiment. Langston Hughes's *I
Wonder as I Wander* (1956) explores a range of Hughes's international experiences in the 1930s, including an intriguing focus on his year-long sampling of
the Soviet experiment in 1932–1933. Hughes also provides insight into two of
the larger groups that went in the 1930s: the *Black and White* film group, with
which he traveled, and the black agricultural specialist group, which was posted
to Soviet Asia. Paul Robeson's *Here I Stand* (1958), both autobiographical text
and political manifesto, looks back at his experiences in the Soviet Union and
clearly locates an alliance with the Soviets as vital for the future of peoples of
African descent. Homer Smith's *Black Man in Red Russia* (1964) explores his
fourteen-year experience, from 1932 to 1946, during which time he moved from
being an actor to postal-services innovator to foreign correspondent. William L.
Patterson's *The Man Who Cried Genocide* (1971) offers insight into his initial
political training in 1927 and the personal and political relationships that developed between Soviets and blacks. Harry Haywood's *Black Bolshevik* (1978)
provides detailed information on the political training done at the University of
the Toilers of the East and the role of the Lenin School in the 1920s. Through
Haywood one learns the names of many other black sojourners, although he
provides little detail on many of them. Haywood was also intimately involved

in the debates around the "Negro Question," and he provides an intriguing insider's view of the Comintern's relationship with the Communist Party of the United States of America. Robert Robinson's *Black on Red* (1988) uniquely describes the experiences of a black technical specialist over the forty-four-year period from 1930 to 1974. Complementing these books are many articles in newspapers, magazines, and journals written by Du Bois, McKay, Hughes, and others; these articles describe other aspects of the black experience in the Soviet Union.

The majority of these works were written by men who saw communism as the route to social change and looked forward to experiencing the Soviet experiment in particular. Patterson and Haywood were members of the Communist Party in the United States prior to their studies abroad. Theirs were political objectives. McKay, Du Bois, Hughes, Smith, while not formally aligned with the party, were close to progressive communities in the United States. None went for the purpose of overt political training, but they welcomed the opportunity to test out the Soviet promise of freedom from racism and of having fresh opportunities. For the most part, they accepted problems as they arose with a nod to the fact that this was a society in the building. Robinson was the sole person who had neither a political objective nor progressive leanings. His interests were clearly economics and professional opportunity. He repeatedly stressed his suspicions of communism and his concerns about ulterior motives, yet he was intrigued by the multiple examples of the Soviets' confrontation with racism and welcomed the constant recognition he received for his skills—hence, his frequently contradictory descriptions of events.

Although useful in providing firsthand accounts of life in the Soviet Union in the early years, these works have their limitations. Because many of them were published decades after their authors left the Soviet Union, the authors' ability to recall everything in detail and with accuracy was affected. Robinson's book came out fourteen years after he left the country, McKay's work came out fifteen years later, Smith's nineteen years, Hughes's twenty years, Haywood's thirty-three years, and Patterson's nearly thirty-five years. Furthermore, these authors were looking back on their experiences from the perspective of having had to adjust to life back in the anticommunist West. They may have started their memoirs years earlier, but the lack of publishers and self-censorship brought on by the Cold War affected the tenor of the works as well as the time when their works were finally published.

No less important, these are personal accounts, which, by their very nature, are often not evenhanded and dispassionate versions of events and persons. The purposeful slanting of facts for various effects was not uncommon. For whatever reasons, some works locate their authors at the epicenter of events; conversely, others remove them. For example, some of Hughes's accounts suggest an individual experience. His journey to Soviet Asia, for one, is presented as though no other blacks were present, although several other members of the film group were with him on the first journey. Smith's autobiographical account suggests that he was not part of the *Black and White* film group, while many other records indicate he was. Some, disenchanted with their experiences with communism and the Soviet experiment, not only critiqued their personal experiences there but applied their pessimistic perspectives to their retelling of the accounts of other black sojourners. Robinson, for example, repeatedly applied a skeptical eye to Soviet actions, even when people were awarded for jobs well done. There were, in fact, some intriguing internecine disagreements within the black community, both when they were sojourners and after they left the Soviet Union, about the interpretation and retelling of their experiences there.

A certain immediacy comes through the personal letters that discuss various connections to the Soviet experiment. One can learn about the lines of contact and networks through which information was shared and then gain some insight into the choices the sojourners made. Charles Nichols's *Arna Bontemps—Langston Hughes Letters, 1925–1967* (1980) offers correspondence between Hughes and Bontemps in which Bontemps, like Hughes, laments the frustrations of the black intellectual and weighs the prospects of going to the Soviet Union. Herbert Aptheker's *The Correspondence of W.E.B. Du Bois*, vol. 1, *Selections, 1877–1934* (1973), *The Correspondence of W.E.B. Du Bois*, vol. 2, *Selections, 1934–1944* (1976), and *The Correspondence of W.E.B. Du Bois*, vol. 3, *Selections, 1944–1963* (1978), along with the multivolume Aptheker production *Writings by W.E.B. Du Bois in Periodicals Edited by Others* (vols. 2–4, 1910 through 1961) (1982), demonstrate Du Bois's keen interest in socialism and his desire to see it in action. And the correspondence of George Washington Carver, found in the George Washington Carver Papers at Tuskegee Institute, provides a poignant window into the challenges faced by this highly trained chemist and his students to find outlets for their many talents. These letters include a fascinating series of documents in which he and Oliver Golden, serving as Stalin's intermediary, negotiate a response to the calls for specialists to come to the Soviet Union.

Yelena Khanga's *Soul to Soul* (1992) and Lily Golden's *My Long Journey Home* (2002) provide the most comprehensive multigenerational perspective of the black expatriate experience. The authors are mother (Lily) and daughter (Yelena), descendants of the fellow traveler and agricultural specialist Golden and his wife Bertha Bialek Golden. Both biographical and autobiographical, the works recount the story of the Goldens' political evolution and then their role in assembling and leading the 1930s agricultural specialist group to the Soviet Union. These are the only books that also offer a comparison of the family's experiences of black–white relations in the Soviet Union with their experiences in the United States. Their story stretches from the lives of Oliver's and Bertha's grandparents on through the authors' lives as Afro-Russians growing up in the Soviet Union. As their perspective reaches into the final years of the Soviet Union, they also observe the effects of the growing African student presence on the black expatriate community and on Soviet society in general.

In addition to the primary documents, a number of other works have been helpful. Among these are the many biographical works and collections on or by Paul Robeson, which offer useful information about his personal experiences and his role as an interpreter of the Soviet experiment. Robeson's memoir and manifesto, *Here I Stand*, published just as he and Du Bois won the court case to recoup their passports, stands as a challenge to the powers that be. Written in the late 1950s, it reiterates his unflinching support of the Soviet experiment. Martin Duberman's *Paul Robeson* (1989), one of the most comprehensive biographies of Robeson, takes painstaking effort to detail the Robesons' ties to the Soviet Union. It also offers some information on Robeson's brothers-in-law, John and Frank Goode, who also went to the Soviet Union in the early 1930s. These were the brothers of Robeson's wife, Eslanda. Philip Foner's *Paul Robeson Speaks* (1978) is a collection of Robeson's speeches, broadcasts, and newspaper interviews, all of which detail his growing interest in and support of the Soviet experiment. Freedomways journal's special publication *Paul Robeson* (1985; originally published, 1965) offers perspectives from both the United States and the Soviet Union on Robeson's role as a interpreter of the Soviet experiment for audiences in the global community. Paul Robeson Jr.'s *The Undiscovered Paul Robeson* (2001) focuses on Robeson's pre-World War II experiences in the United States, Europe, and the Soviet Union. It also offers autobiographical details on Robeson Jr., who went to school in Moscow in the mid-1930s, and on Robeson's extended family's attempts to settle there in the 1930s.

Along with these texts, a number of other sources can be tapped to construct the sociocultural contexts in which these early black-Soviet ties developed and to gain some insight into the long-term relationships that developed. George Padmore's *Pan-Africanism or Communism?* (1971) briefly describes his 1920s–1930s experiences in the Soviet Union and weighs the relative benefits of communism to his conception of Pan-Africanism. William "Bill" Davis's 1960 *Ebony* article, "How Negroes Live in Russia," reintroduces the blacks who went to the Soviet Union in the 1920s and 1930s in a unique way. Through Davis's own sojourn as a guide at the 1959 American National Exhibit in Moscow, readers are not only reconnected to this group but can see something of their and their families' lives over the many years since. Jan Carew's *Moscow Is Not My Mecca* (1964; U.S. edition, *Green Winter*) is a documentary novel based on interviews of African, Guyanese, and other Third World students who were studying in the Soviet Union in the 1960s. This work introduces the postwar desires of many new nations to build up their human capital and their willingness to take Soviet scholarships to do so. Faith Berry's *Good Morning Revolution* (1973) considers little-known work that Hughes had either suppressed in the McCarthy period or that was published in the Soviet Union.

Biographies of Hughes, McKay, and Du Bois not only provide useful information about their specific subjects but contain valuable details about others with whom they traveled and worked in the Soviet Union. These are works such as Arnold Rampersad's *The Life of Langston Hughes*, vol. 1, *1902–1941, I,*

Too, Sing America (1986); Faith Berry's *Before and Beyond Harlem: Langston Hughes, a Biography* (1992); Wayne Cooper's *Claude McKay* (1987); Tyrone Tillery's *Claude McKay* (1992); David Levering Lewis's *W.E.B. Du Bois: Biography of a Race, 1968–1919* (1994), and *W.E.B. Du Bois: The Fight for Equality and the American Century, 1919–1963* (2000). These texts provide information on the *Black and White* film group members, who went with Hughes; fellow traveler Otto Huiswood, who was in Moscow at the same time as McKay in the early 1920s and as Haywood in the later 1920s; and the Robesons, who were often in the Soviet Union at the same time as Du Bois in the 1930s to early 1960s. Like Robeson, Du Bois came to know some of the Afro-Russian descendants of other black sojourners. In addition to these direct accounts, contemporaneous newspaper and magazine articles, along with other published records, provide supplementary details on the black sojourner movements to the Soviet Union and back to the United States.

Other autobiographical and biographical works provide comparable discussions of the attraction of communism for blacks and their willingness to move elsewhere to be a part of new kinds of societies. Nelson Peery's *Black Fire* (1994) describes the socioeconomic conditions between World War I and World War II in the United States that encouraged Peery's move toward communism. Ollie Harrington's *Why I Left America and Other Essays* (1993) looks at Harrington's experiences growing up as a black communist in Harlem in the 1930s and the reasons for his escape to Europe. Michael Fabre's *The World of Richard Wright* (1985) describes Wright's rising interest in communism in the United States and his experiences in the United States and Europe after he left the Communist Party.

A number of helpful sources explore the links among blacks, communism, and other progressive movements. Wilson Record's *The Negro and the Communist Party* (1951) is an early discussion of the connections between the black community and the communist movement. A more recent discussion can be found in Earl Ofari Hutchinson's *Blacks and Reds* (1995). John Hope Franklin and Isidore Starr's *The Negro in the Twentieth Century* (1967) offers a selection of primary documents relating to the struggle around civil rights in the United States. Allison Blakely's seminal work, *Russia and the Negro* (1986), provides the first historical panorama of contacts between blacks and Russians, stretching from the seventeenth century to the latter years of the Soviet era. Kate Baldwin's *Beyond the Color Line and the Iron Curtain* (2002) is a more recent exploration of the special relationships formed by McKay, Hughes, Du Bois, and Robeson with the Soviets up to 1963. Thomas Borstelmann's *The Cold War and the Color Line* (2001), Mary Dudziak's *Cold War Civil Rights* (2000), Penny Von Eschen's *Race against Empire* (1997) and *Satchmo Blows Up the World* (2004), and Walter Hixon's *Parting the Curtain* (1997) look at the interplay of relations between blacks and whites with the added pressure of the Cold War. Many of these works clearly benefit from the post-Soviet-era release of information as many of the supporting documents would have never been released by the United States or the Soviet Union during the Cold War. Thus, they offer not only surface features but also behind-the-scene details that reveal the dynamics of international and national race relations.

For further insights into the formal ties between the Soviets, the U.S. Communist Party, and selected blacks, two extremely useful books focus on previously classified documents: *The Secret World of American Communism* (1995), by Harvey Klehr, John Earl Haynes, and Fridrikh Igorevich Firsov, and the subsequent *The Soviet World of American Communism* (1998), by Klehr, Haynes, and Kyrill M. Anderson. A companion work published some years earlier, Philip Foner's *American Communism and Black Americans* (1991), looks specifically at political writing issued by the Communist Party of the United States of America or those associated with that organization between 1930 and 1934, the period when the greatest number of sojourners were attracted to the Soviet experiment. Cedric Robinson's *Black Marxism* (1983) offers a broader, temporal and global perspective of the attraction of Marxism for U.S. blacks and others of African descent in other parts of the world.

Soviet-Russian historical and sociopolitical perspectives appear in a number of works. Roy Medvedev's *Let History Judge* (1989) provides a comprehensive analysis of the Stalinist era. Ronald Grigor Suny's *The Soviet Experiment* (1998) analyzes the evolution from tsarist Russia through the collapse of the Soviet Union and into the rise of the new Russia and the surrounding independent states. Robert Service's *A History of Twentieth-Century Russia* (1998) explores the grand sweep of Russia through the century.

I have incorporated data from a number of other corroborating sources, including contemporaneous U.S. and U.S.S.R. newspaper articles, particularly those of and about Du Bois, McKay, Robeson, Hughes and by other members of the *Black and White* film group, as well as press articles from around the time that larger groups went to the Soviet Union in the 1930s. George Hutchinson's *The Harlem Renaissance in Black and White* (1997) has been useful for setting the intellectual and literary context for the attraction of communism or other progressive thought to many of the 1920s and 1930s black artists and intellectuals. Documents about these and other sojourners to the Soviet Union in labor studies and other archives, such as the Mark Solomon & Robert Kaufman Research Files on Blacks & Communism in the New York University Tamiment Library, further flesh out key relationships. These archives contain useful Federal Bureau of Investigations (FBI) and Komitet gosudarstvennoi bezopasnosti (KGB) documents as well, as both the U.S. and the Soviet governments kept tabs on the movements of black sojourners.

Finally, in addition to reading the published works and archival documents, I have had the opportunity to interview a number of people as well as to review as-yet-unpublished materials by individuals and groups. Importantly, I have had access to some of the descendants who are still living in Russia or who have moved to the United States, including Lily Golden and her daughter, Yelena; Amelia Tynes-Mensah, daughter of George Tynes, an agricultural specialist in the same group as Golden, and her daughter Anastasia; James Patterson, son of *Black and White* film group member Lloyd Patterson; and Eslanda Goode, daughter of Frank Goode, Paul Robeson's brother-in-law, who settled in the Soviet Union in 1934. Their accounts have filled some of the gaps in the published work because they bring to the fore not only stories of their fathers or grandfathers but also accounts of the little-known personal experiences of growing up and living as Afro-Russians in both the Soviet Union and post-Soviet Russia.

INDEX

Abdelrahim-Soboleva (Soboleva), Valentina, 208, 256n46
Acheson, Dean, 57
Adamov, Joe, 178
Adams, Mary. *See* Burroughs, Williana
Africa: Soviet relations during Cold War, 12, 204–205. *See also* African students, in USSR
African Blood Brotherhood (ABB), 17, 22, 25, 28, 31, 36, 220n19
Africa Institute of the Academy of Sciences, 59, 60, 206
African students, in USSR, 192–193, 205–206; marriage with Afro-Russians, 206, 207–208; problems with, 208–209; Soviet mass media views of, 206; success of, 209
agricultural specialists, 3, 7, 9–10, 86–87, 92, 234n39–235n39; arrival in USSR, 103–105; children born in USSR, 107–108; formation of group, 97–98, 99–102; group heads to USSR, 102–103; legacy of collaborations, 112; life in Uzbekistan, 105–106; other projects, 109–110; racism by white Americans in USSR, 103; racism in Germany, 102–103; special contributions by J. Sutton, 110–111; special contributions by G. Tynes, 111–112; spouses accompanying group, 101, 102, 106–109; in

Soviet Central Asia, 103–112, 134; in Yangiyul, 105–107, 109, 112
Alberga, Lawrence O., 116, 128, 130
Aldridge, Ira, 7, 119, 126, 168, 245n76
Alexandrovna, Maria. *See* Tynes, Maria Alexandrovna
American National Exhibit, 185–186, 187–188; black expatriate community at, 193–198; black fashion models in, 190–191, 252n44; computers at, 191–192, 253n52; international students at, 192–193; legacy of, 199; and Nixon/Khrushchev "kitchen" debate, 191; race relations issues, 191–192
American Negro Labor Congress (ANLC), 32–33
anti-Semitism, 161, 162, 163, 180
Arle-Titz, Boris, 137
Arle- [Arli]Titz, Coretta, 34, 126, 135, 137–138, 182
Aswan High Dam project, 204
Atlanta Six, 36–37

Baker, Rudy, 33
Baker, Vincent, 69
Bandung Conference of Asian and African Nations, 202, 203–204
Bankole, Kweku (Bankole Awoonor-Renner), 34, 35, 179
Bialek, Bertha. *See* Golden, Bertha Bialek

ABOUT THE AUTHOR

JOY GLEASON CAREW is a sociolinguist and Russian specialist. Currently she is the resident linguist in the Department of Pan-African Studies at the University of Louisville. From 1993 to 2000, she was the director of the Center for the Study of Critical Languages at Lincoln University in Lincoln University, Pennsylvania.